MUSCLEMAG
INTERNATIONAL'S

Muscle Quest

Training Secrets of the Superstars

By Gerard Thorne & Phil Embleton

Copyright © 2000 by Robert Kennedy

Published by MuscleMag International
5775 McLaughlin Road
Mississauga, ON
Canada L5R 3P7

Designed by Jackie Kydyk
Edited by Matt Lamperd

Canadian Cataloguing in Publication Data

Thorne, Gerard, 1963-
    Muscle quest: training secrets of the superstars

ISBN 1-55210-024-3

    1. Bodybuilders--Biography. 2. Bodybuilding--Training.
I. Embleton, Phil, 1963- II. Title.

GV545.5.T46 2001   646.7'5'0922   C2001-900256-4

Distributed in Canada by
CANBOOK Distribution Services
1220 Nicholson Road
Newmarket, ON
L3Y 7V1
800-399-6858

Distributed in the States by
BookWorld Services
1933 Whitfield Park Loop
Sarasota, FL 34243

Printed in Canada

Acknowledgments

The authors would like to take the time to thank the following individuals for their contributions to this book:

Once again thanks to Annette Powell for "running wild" with the red ink in proof reading the manuscript. All the best in your future endeavors, Annette.

To Jackie Thibeault and her staff at MuscleMag International's book publishing division, thanks for another job well done.

Finally to Robert Kennedy, who despite his personal problems over the last couple of years still found time to offer encouragement.

Our sincere thanks to you all.

Table of Contents

Table of Contents

Paul Dillett, Sonny Schmidt and Dorian Yates

Preface

Has it been 60 years since the seemingly immortal John Grimek won the first of his two Mr. America titles? Has it been nearly 50 years since the Iron Guru, Vince Gironda, was told he was too muscular? Even better, has it been 25 years since Arnold, Lou Ferrigno, and Serge Nubret battled it out in South Africa for the 1975 Mr. Olympia title? Even within our own relatively short writing careers we've seen the torch pass from Lee Haney to Dorian Yates to Ronnie Coleman.

Bodybuilding like most sports is continuously evolving. The superstars of today give way to the next generation, and great debates are generated. Would Arnold at his best have been able to beat Lee Haney? Could Ronnie Coleman trade shots with Dorian Yates? How about Sergio Oliva matching muscle mass with Markus Ruhl and Nasser El Sonbaty? The comparisons are endless.

This book was written in response to the hundreds of requests we've had from people who bought our comprehensive *Encyclopedia of Bodybuilding*. Although we included dozens of routines from the stars in that book, readers wanted more. Surprisingly it wasn't just advice from the current crop of bodybuilders that they wanted. They expressed an interest in the champs from years gone by. It seems the nostalgia bug has crept into the sport of bodybuilding. Just as baseball fans love talking and reading about Babe Ruth, Hank Aaron, and Ted Williams, so too are bodybuilding fans becoming interested in what many call the "glory days" of Muscle Beach, and the "Arnold days" of the old Gold's Gym.

Unfortunately there's just too many stars in bodybuilding to be able to include them all in one book. So we decided it would be best to provide readers with a comprehensive sample of bodybuilding history. For every star there is a biography and a list of the major contests that the star won or competed in (found at the excellent online site *www.musclememory.com*). Each section then concludes with one or more of the star's training routines.

We are sure most readers have heard the old saying "the more things change, the more they stay the same." Well, this book is no exception. As you read through and compare the routines through the decades, you'll see that with the exception of some fancy new equipment, things haven't really changed all that much. The barbell and dumbell exercises followed by Pearl and Park are exactly the same as those used by Ferrigno and Arnold in the '70s, and Yates and Coleman in the '90s.

This book is inspired by the journalistic style that prevailed from the 1940s until the early 1980s. During that period, people bought bodybuilding books and magazines based solely on the bodybuilding star that appeared on the cover. Bodybuilders bought magazines specifically to see pictures of stars like Bill Pearl or Sergio Oliva, and read about the training routine that thousands attempted to emulate. It can be best classified as the star-focused era of bodybuilding journals.

The journalistic style underwent a complete change with the release of the revolutionary work, *The Underground Steroid Handbook*, by the late Dan Duchaine. Readers suddenly discovered that many pros were enhancing their genetic potential with more than just their training, drinking protein shakes and consuming skinless chicken. The days of a star's opinions being taken as gospel, were over as bodybuilders demanded hard facts, based on scientific research. The former "fanzines" became more information-based, while magazines began to feature writers' names on the covers. Biochemical terms became commonplace, and involved intellectual debates on hormonal feedback loops and receptor stimulation are now regular features. Today an article that is not referenced is an article that won't be published. In short, bodybuilding changed from being a personality cult to being a science.

This book is many things at once: First, it is a salute to the earlier era of bodybuilding magazines; second, it is a historical anthology of the greats of our sport; third, and most important for us, it illustrates something we have chosen to call "The Kovacs Effect."

Early champions like Grimek and Reeves now look like extras on Baywatch. And they are skinny guys when compared to Lee Haney or Dorian Yates. What we have found, and many others have reported (we are not claiming to be the first to observe this), is that since 1945, competitive bodybuilders are increasing in size by 50 lbs every 25 years. How can this be possible? We're going to go out on a limb and state a revolutionary concept (the Kovacs Effect); that human growth is not fixed, but only limited by available technology.

In the Middle Ages, the dashing knights who wore heavy suits of armor and took part in bloody jousts barely stood four feet tall! Poor diet and inadequate health care prevented the body from reaching it's true potential. Yet today in modern Europe, men are close to an average of six feet. That's an increase of two feet of vertical growth within eight hundred years! Sure, it's a long time span but it shows that human growth, within a specific population is not fixed throughout time. We are not talking about giants with overactive pituitary glands, which cause excessive growth that the body cannot properly support. The Kovacs Effect describes overall balanced growth in members of a group over time.

In a new millennium that offers drugs, supplements, dietary abundance, and now the beginnings of applied genetic technology, shortcuts to even more rapid growth are becoming available to the average bodybuilder. Thus the Kovacs Effect will still be observed, but in ever decreasing time periods.

This book is a collection of the stars from different periods in modern bodybuilding. Some of them, like Sergio and Greg Kovacs himself, represent the Kovacs Effect for their generations. Perhaps you, the reader, will become the next physical embodiment of the Kovacs Effect for your generation. Rest assured that when you do, we'd be honored to record your story.

Gerard Thorne
St. John's, Newfoundland, Canada

Phil Embleton
Elk Grove, California, USA

Foreword – By Robert Kennedy

"I love you." – My late wife, every day we were married.

This book is the first of it's kind from *MuscleMag*. Those who aren't familiar with bodybuilding (believe it or not, they do exist!), will pick up this book and dismiss it as some text interspersed with pictures of muscle men in skimpy trunks. They'll probably snicker, say it's all steroids to their girlfriends (who'll suddenly realize what's missing from the relationship), and put the book back on the shelf. And that's sad because this book isn't really about bodybuilding, its about time.

Competitive bodybuilding is about a moment in time. Bodybuilders train for months, sometimes years, just to grace a stage for a few hours. And during those few hours, they occupy the full attention of the crowd for mere minutes. But in that short time span something magical happens that makes it all worthwhile. Alone, onstage, you the competitor, are the center of the universe! Except for a pair of posing trunks you are totally naked and vulnerable, and yet at the same time you are in total control of that room. Thousands of pairs of eyes are glued to your aching muscles as you strike poses, voices scream encouragement in unison, and like a bloodied Roman general urging his troops back into battle, their hearts belong to you! That incredible emotional high, that moment when you alone rule the earth, that moment in time turns all those years of back-breaking work into chump change. Bodybuilding isn't about bigger calves and biceps, it's about seizing a moment in time and making it your own, forever!

No one really loses a bodybuilding contest. The Olympia is like the Oscars; they're all winners when their names are called. No one goes into bodybuilding for the money. There are easier, and far more certain ways to make a living. Competing is just like skydiving. Incredibly terrifying and exciting at the same time. It's when you find out what the Gods of chance have chosen for you. You're rolling the dice every time you go out there. Lose the audience and you're dead; thrill them and they're yours.

Competitive bodybuilders are adrenaline junkies. Why do rock stars continue to perform long after they've become the punch line on a TV sitcom? In a word, mortality. You can't escape it. We live, we die. And that life is a series of moments in time. You don't remember things equally. The first time you held a puppy does not equate to doing math homework that night in grade two. Certain moments loom like mountains, or dark valleys, and guide us in the choice of future moments.

Until recently I didn't really dwell on the concept of time, after all, I had it all. I had money, a dream job, and the perfect family. And then in only a few months I found myself in a hospital, my ear stitched to the side of my head, my son fighting for his life and my wife dead. The moment was gone, forever.

I have always been a photographer, and have the family photos to prove it. I had no idea how much comfort they would be to me. I can look at them and remember the moment when my wife agreed to share her life with me. The day my son first spoke, and my daughter was born. Those are my moments. And I remember. It was a period was I was blissfully happy. I just didn't know it.

Those pictures keep me going. I live for the moment when my son recovers. I know I will never be that happy again. But I have known moments of happiness and contentment that I would not part with for the riches of the world! They are the source of my strength now. They're all I really have to make my life meaningful. For me and for my children.

The photos you see in this book are moments in time. The champions are captured in black and white, in a way that they were and will never be again. Preserved so that even across an ocean of time, young bodybuilders can see these men, read about their lives, and for a moment, experience what it was actually like to be in the presence of the greats of our sport.

That's why I am dedicating this book to the memory of my wife. A finer woman I could never have found, and honestly her death was the only annoyance she ever caused me.

As you read this book, I passionately urge you, the reader to stop, reflect, and recognize those around you and what they mean to you now. This moment in time is all any of us really have. And it will end.

Robert Kennedy
Editor and publisher
MuscleMag International

Through the Ages

The death of John Grimek in November of 1998 signaled the end of an era. John was more than just one of history's first Mr. Americas, he epitomized a time of innocence in the sport, before the wonders of modern pharmacology took hold. To this day many believe that John represented the ideal male form. Certainly more representative of the classical physique immortalized by Greek and Roman sculptures. Of course each successive generation tends to consider the current stars the best in history. They counter that a 180-pound John Grimek has no place standing onstage next to a 250-pound Ronnie Coleman or 300-plus-pound Greg Kovacs.

Although John Grimek was probably the first of what we could call a modern bodybuilder, he was by no means the first individual to use weights or some other form of resistance training to improve his physique.

Legend has it that the ancient Greek strongman, Milos, used resistance training in the form of a growing bull! In the story Milos started lifting the animal while it was still a calf, and as the animal grew, so did Milo's strength. Then to the amazement of spectators and competitors alike, Milos walked into the sport's arena carrying the full-grown bull on his shoulders. Whether the story is true or not, what is important is that Milos (or the writer who made up the story) had a firm grasp on the basic principles of resistance training. Muscles will adapt and get bigger and stronger in response to an ever-increasing demand placed upon them.

The next group of individuals who knew a thing or two about physical conditioning were those hardy characters known as Roman Gladiators. For those who think fighting for parking space at suppertime is a challenge, consider for a moment what the typical gladiator endured 2000 years ago. Their physical development literally meant the difference between life and death. You see your typical Roman elitist had a unique view on the nature of entertainment. The main act at most public outings consisted of pitting slaves and gladiators against one another in mortal combat. To add some spice to the mix, the occasional lion or tiger was thrown in for good measure. The only thing common between the Roman and Los Angeles Coliseums is the name.

Given the importance of such spectacles, the owners of gladiators tended to treat their possessions well. A great deal of money could be riding on a given fight, so the gladiators were put through a rigorous training routine. They were taught the latest fighting techniques of the time along with an intense exercise program. In addition, the ancient Romans recognized that sound nutrition played a big role in recovery and physical health, so the gladiators were given the best of foods.

Although most gladiators were killed in combat or died as slaves, a lucky few made their owners enough money to earn their freedom. Then there was Sparticus who organized a revolt and took back their freedom. With the conquest of the Roman Empire by hordes of barbarians, the days of the gladiators came to an end. It would be nearly 2000 years before the next great movement in physical conditioning took place.

If warfare could be considered the dominant theme of the 20th century, then the 19th century will be remembered as the dawn of technology. Rapid developments in manufacturing techniques created a revolution in society that is with us to this day. This period of unprecedented growth became known as the industrial revolution. It was a time of Empire building and prosperity, but it carried with it a heavy price. The thousands of factories that sprang up needed to be run by workers. This resulted in a mass migration to the larger population centers. In no time at all small cities grew into thriving metropolises. Since there was no one to speak for them, factory workers were forced to work 12- to 16-hour days. Kids as young as eight were not left out because many times they were the only breadwinners in the family. Together with this abuse of employees came pollution on a scale never before witnessed. Most factories churned out tons of chemical byproducts, which started what is now known as global warming.

In response to what was seen as an assault on health, a group of enlightened individuals started a movement that focused on healthy eating and exercise. They went by different names but the most popular was physical culturists. In many respects physical culturists were the forerunners of today's strength coaches and personal trainers. They became experts on nutrition and exercise, setting out to combat the detrimental effects of the industrial revolution with steadfast conviction.

From this physical cultural movement emerged the one individual whose name became synonymous with physical perfection. In 1921, a young Italian immigrant who initially was called Angelo Siciliano, decided to Americanize his name to cash in on his growing popularity. The name he choose was Charles Atlas, and over 60 years later his comic book ad – the one about getting sand kicked in your face – has sold upwards of ten million copies of his "Dynamic Tension" courses. The fact that Atlas built his body primarily with weights has all but been forgotten. Yet modern bodybuilding owes Atlas a huge debt as he helped to foster the notion that if you are not happy with the way your physique looks there is something you can do about it.

By the 1930s strength and physique competitions were still intertwined, but it soon became apparent that contests focusing on just the physique were developing a clique all their own. Thus the stage was set for the emergence of the first generation of bodybuilding superstars.

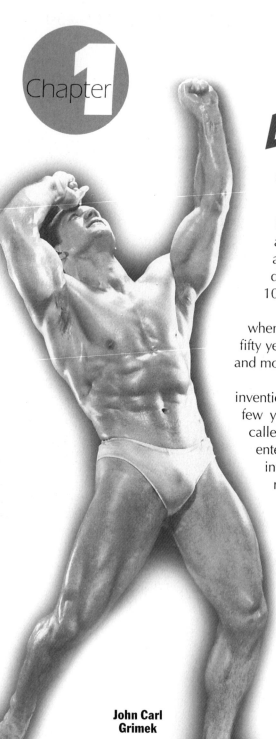

The 1940s

Hopefully we don't need to tell readers that the dominant news event of the 1940s was World War II. It took a combined effort of France, the US, the Soviet Union, and Great Britain, to stem Adolf Hitler's quest for world domination. Even then it was too late to save the six to 10 million who died in the Holocaust.

The embers from the war had barely gone out when a new war, the Cold War, had emerged. For the next fifty years the US and the Soviet Union played a game of cat and mouse, pitting democratic ideology against communism.

The other significant event of the '40s was the invention of television. Although slow to catch on, within a few years TV, as the new invention was popularly being called, had replaced radio as the number one form of home entertainment. Believe it or not, despite the carnage being inflicted by Hitler's armies in Europe, the US managed to maintain some sense of civility. Sport activities carried on as normal, including bodybuilding. In 1940 and 1941, John Carl Grimek won back-to-back Mr. America titles, and in doing so became the sport's first star.

The 1940s were the first decade that bodybuilding truly established itself as a distinct sport. Up until the late 1930s, physique display was seen as an after thought to athletic prowess. Contestants from such sports as wrestling, swimming, gymnastics, boxing, and Olympic lifting would be assembled to demonstrate their strength, muscularity, flexibility, and symmetry. It was not enough that you looked good, you also had to be able to do a handstand, series of chinups and pushups, and then maybe, show some muscle control. Yet as competitors became more and more muscular, the skill movements were dropped and contests began to focus exclusively on muscularity.

Early on it became obvious that the athletes who held the decisive edge in such contests were Olympic lifters. With their barbell-built physiques, they easily out-muscled the swimmers, boxers, and gymnasts. Of course word spread quickly, and before long the use of

John Carl Grimek

weights for the sole purpose of muscle enlargement became the rage. By the time of Grimek, bodybuilding contests were featuring a whole new generation of contestants who used barbells to build their physiques rather than those who relied on the muscle mass that just happened to be a side effect of some other form of physical activity.

The other major event in bodybuilding during the 1940s was the popularizing of a stretch of beach in Santa Monica, California, as a hang out for bodybuilders and other in-shape types. On any given day you could see such personalities as Vic Tanny, Jack Lalanne, and Vince Gironda, demonstrating their athleticism on the sands of what would be known as Muscle Beach. From pure weightlifting and gymnastics to physique and chinup contests, Muscle Beach seemed to have it all. The area retained its popularity until a couple of bodybuilders were accused of rape (they were later acquitted). This caused local politicians to bow to public pressure and do something about these people with too much time on their hands. It would be nearly 20 years before another area of beach located a few miles up the coast in Venice, would take on some of the atmosphere of the original.

If Grimek was the first true bodybuilder in terms of training with weights and muscle display, the honor of first true superstar goes to Steve Reeves. Reeves, like Frank Zane and Lee Labrada decades later, was considered to be as close to physical perfection as you could get. With 210 pounds spread perfectly over a 6'1 frame, and a face that Hollywood could only dream about, Reeves easily won the big three of bodybuilding, Mr. America, Mr. World and Mr. Universe. After conquering bodybuilding, Reeves set his sites on Hollywood, and thanks to such movies as *Hercules* and *Thief of Baghdad*, he became the number one box office draw in the world.

Vince Gironda was one of the many personalities demonstrating his athleticism on the beach known as Muscle Beach.

John Grimek will always be remembered as a man who played a major role in the history of bodybuilding.

John Grimek

John Grimek was the original pioneer of modern-day bodybuilding. His contemporary, Steve Reeves, had a more classical and symmetrical physique, but when it came to pure slabs of massive, thickly developed muscle, John was in a class of his own. The development that John sported set the mold for the kind of mass and size our current pros seek today.

He was born on June 17, 1910, in Perth Amboy, New Jersey. As a young man he became interested in weightlifting and by 1933, pictures of John were being used to illustrate images of strongmen. In 1936, John became a member of the United States Olympic Weightlifting team, routinely pressing more weight in competition than any other team member.

Up until this time few men knew anything about physique display. It was simply lift your chest and flex your arms! As John said, "It wasn't until I worked as a life model for art classes that I realized what posing was all about."

As a model John would walk around the class during break time and see how the different poses looked. He would then use these poses for his photo shoots. At dozens of lifting shows throughout the country, John was asked to pose and do his fantastic muscle routine. At first he was reluctant because he was there to lift weights. However, it soon became apparent that the audience preferred his muscle control and posing routine to his weightlifting. From that time on, he spent much less time lifting and more time doing bodybuilding exercises to add even more muscle to his already husky build. The result was an impressive list of achievements:

1939 York Perfect Man, Overall winner; York Perfect Man, Medium, 1st
1940 Mr. America AAU winner; Mr. America AAU most muscular, 1st
1941 Mr. America AAU winner
1948 Universe NABBA winner
1949 Mr. USA AAU winner

John could have bragged and promoted himself for personal gain or ego. Hollywood offered movie deals, but instead, John took a modest job as editor of *Muscular Development* magazine, which was owned by the York Barbell company and Bob Hoffman. John brought a simple, unpretentious philosophy to his readers, filling it with basic bodybuilding training principles. John was also a regular columnist with *MuscleMag*, and his ideas of hard work and sound diet mixed with an honest writing style made him a favorite with our readers.

John died on November 20, 1998. He will always be remembered as a wonderful man who played a major part in the history of our sport.

Steve Reeves

In his lifetime, Reeves was one of the most powerful athlete-actors of any of his predecessors or forerunners. Others came upon the screen only to be stereotyped whereas Reeves played practically ever role imaginable; a God, an Olympian, a pirate, a gladiator, a cowboy, and a thief. He eventually emerged to become one of the biggest stars to ever appear on the European screen and one of the worlds highest paid actors. In 1958, he was the number one box office draw in America putting John Wayne, Doris Day, and Rock Hudson in second, third and fourth positions respectively.

Steve was born January 21, 1926, in Glasgow, Montana. He moved to Oakland with his family as a child and began lifting weights when he was 16 years old.[1] He became interested in weight training at an early age, and soon met with success as the list shows:

1946 Mr. Pacific Coast AAU, winner
1947 Mr. America AAU, winner; Mr. California AAU, winner; Mr. Pacific Coast AAU, winner
1948 Mr. USA AAU; Mr. World, winner; Universe NABBA, 2nd
1949 Mr. USA AAU, 3rd
1950 Universe NABBA, overall winner; Universe NABBA, tall 1st

When Steve arrived in Europe in 1950 to make *Hercules*, the general consensus among most of the public was that musclemen were boring! People could not identify with them, understand them, nor care about them. An Italian producer, Frederico Teti, asked Reeves to assume the lead role in *Le Fatiche di Ercole (The Labors of Hercules)*. It was a shot-on-a-shoestring epic based loosely on the tales of Jason and the Argonauts, although it put Hercules' character into the lead role. When independent producer, Joseph E. Levine decided to release the film in the United States with a soundtrack dubbed in English, it became one of the surprise hits of 1959.[2] After *Hercules* exploded on the big screen, public opinion changed overnight. Steve was every director's dream. He had the perfect face on the perfect body. The "Reeves Look" became so popular that all the New York City and all of the European Ballet companies were instructed to begin weight training following Steve's well-known routines.

Steve Reeves had the perfect face on the perfect body.

Chapter One – The 1940s

Reeves starred in numerous films:
Jail Bait (1954)
Athena (1954)
La Fatiche di Ercole (*The Labors of Hercules*) (1957)
Agi Murad il diavolo bianco (*The White Warrior*) (1959)
La Battaglia di Maratona (*Giant of Marathon*) (1959) (USA)
Ercole e la regina di Lidia (*Hercules and the Queen of Lydia*) (1959)
Il Terrore dei barbari (*The Barbarian Terror*) (1959)
Il Ladro di Bagdad (*The Thief of Baghdad*) (1960)
Gli Ultimi giorni di Pompeii (*The Last Days of Pompeii*) (1960)
Romolo e Remo (*Romulus and Remus*) (1961)
Morgan il pirata (*Morgan the Pirate*) (1961)
Il Giorno più corto (*The Shortest Day*) (1962)
La Leggenda di Enea (*The Last Glory of Troy*) (1962)
La Guerra di Troia (*The Trojan War*) (1962)
Figlio di Spartacus (*Son of Sparticus*) (1963)
Sandokan, la tigre di Mompracem (*Sandokan the Great*) (1963)
Pirati della Malesia (*Pirates of Malaysia*) (1964)
Vivo per la tua morte (*Long Ride From Hell*) (1967)
Hercules Recycled (1994)[1]

In 1960, while filming *The Last Days of Pompeii,* Steve suffered a shoulder injury when his chariot crashed. The injury steadily grew worse and ultimately forced him to retire from film-making. He became a rancher and fitness guru and a leading proponent of drug-free bodybuilding. He wrote, *Building the Classical Physique – The Natural Way*, and promoted supplements and natural bodybuilding through his Steve Reeves International Society Web site.[1] The bodybuilding world was saddened when Steve died of lymphoma on May 1, 2000. He will always be fondly remembered.

Steve Reeves on the set of
The Labors of Hercules.

"Remember that I was fortunate enough to have always been an easy gainer. And in my workouts I always pursued maximum proportion and symmetry, never solely muscle size."

– Steve Reeves, Mr. America and the movie screen's greatest Hercules commenting on his goal in training, symmetry and proportion, rather than just size.

References:
1. http://us.imdb.com/M/person-exact?Reeves%2C+Steve
2. http://us.imdb.com/Bio?Reeves.+Steve

Training Routines

In some respects, Steve was 40 years ahead of his time. In an age where 20 and 30 sets per bodypart was the norm, Steve did just 3 sets per exercise and no more than three exercises per muscle group. Most modern bodybuilders follow these 9 sets in their routines. Steve would never be accused of being a gym rat either, since spending half a day hoisting weights never did appeal to him. During his heyday, Steve hit the gym three times a week for an average of 90 minutes. The result was what many consider the most perfectly proportioned physique of all time.

The following is a breakdown of Steve Reeves' training program during his Hercules years.

Shoulders
1. Upright rows – 3 sets of 7-11 reps
2. Behind-the-head presses – 3 sets of 7-11 reps
3. Incline lateral raises – 3 sets of 7-11 reps

Chest
1. Wide grip bench presses – 3 sets of 7-11 reps
2. Incline flyes – 3 sets of 7-11 reps
3. Decline flyes – 3 sets of 7-11 reps

Back
1. Wide grip chins – 3 sets of 7-11 reps
2. Seated cable rows – 3 sets of 7-11 reps
3. One-arm dumbell rows – 3 sets of 7-11 reps

Biceps
1. Preacher curls – 3 sets of 7-11 reps
2. Incline supination curls – 3 sets of 7-11 reps
3. One-arm dumbell concentration curls – 3 sets of 7-11 reps

Triceps
1. Triceps pushdowns – 3 sets of 7-11 reps
2. Behind-the-head cable extensions – 3 sets of 7-11 reps
3. One-arm dumbell extensions – 3 sets of 7-11 reps

Legs
1. Front squats – 3 sets of 7-11 reps
2. Leg curls – 3 sets of 7-11 reps
3. Leg extensions – 3 sets of 7-11 reps

Calves
1. Standing calf raises – 3 sets of 17-23 reps
2. Seated calf raises – 3 sets of 17-23 reps

Abdominals
1. Bent knee situps – 3 sets of 17-23 reps
2. Roman chair knee raises – 3 sets of 17-23 reps
3. Alternate knee raises – 3 sets of 17-23 reps

The 1950s

The 1950s were a time of extremes. On one hand the US economy was booming and life in the suburbs couldn't be better. Dwight Eisenhower had carried his military victory in Europe into the White House in 1952, and television forever changed what we did at home in the evenings. From Memphis, Tennessee, came Elvis Arron Presley, whose gyrating hips and hound-dog lyrics had teenage girls swooning all across America. Rock and Roll was born, and popular music has never been the same.

Yet it's hard to believe how a time period represented by the humorous antics of Milton Berle and Lucille Ball will also be remembered as a time when humans almost exterminated themselves. The US and Soviet union were locked in the middle of the Cold War. The partnership that had defeated Hitler's Nazi Germany soon dissolved into a game of world chess, but instead of two-inch chess pieces, the two superpowers faced one another with intercontinental ballistic missiles.

The top bodybuilders of the 1950s covered the full spectrum of physiques At one end the great Steve Reeves still epitomized refinement and symmetry. At the other end, South Africa's Reg Park, with his 220-pounds spread over a 6'2" frame, showed what could happen to large men who engaged in weightlifting. Besides heralding in the arrival of the next generation of bodybuilders, Park also served as a role model for one Austrian kid named Arnold Schwarzenegger. Native American Bill Pearl lay between Park and Reeves with 220-plus pounds on a 5'9" frame. Despite their differences, all three men won Mr. Universe titles, and were the sport's first true superstars in many respects.

Little did Reg Park realize that when he was training in the 1950s his workouts would play a big role in influencing a young Austrian kid named Arnold Schwarzenegger.

Reg Park

Reg Park was born on June 7, 1928, in Leeds, Yorkshire England. Reg was naturally athletic as a child, and excelled in track and soccer. Reg discovered weightlifting at the age of 16 and never looked back. "All the guys and girls used to go to the open-air swimming pool in my hometown. It was like a rendezvous. One day, when I was 16, I met a guy there about 24 who had a great physique. I asked him, 'What do you do?,' and he said, 'I work out with weights.' I said, 'What's that all about?' and he replied, 'Well, come down and I'll show you.' He and his mates had a tiny room with wooden floors and no wallpaper – just an old bar on the floor and two dumbells. They didn't have benches or anything like that … no, I didn't actually enjoy it. Back then I was into soccer. But the guy's mother used to make cookies for us, so after our workouts we'd go into the kitchen for tea and cookies. That was the only reason I went back. This was about a year and a half before I joined the army … I arrived off a boat from Singapore a few weeks before the Mr. Universe in London … My mother and father had arranged a great seat for me. Grimek and Reeves were competing that year, and I was completely mesmerized. I told everybody I was going to win that competition myself one day. People thought I was crazy…" He wasn't, and his record speaks for itself:

1946 Mr. Britain – NABBA, 4th
1949 Mr. Britain – NABBA, overall winner
1950 Universe – NABBA, tall, 2nd
1951 Universe – NABBA, overall winner
     Universe – NABBA, tall, 1st
1958 Universe, Pro – NABBA, overall winner
     Universe, Pro – NABBA, tall 1st
1965 Universe, Pro – NABBA, overall winner
     Universe, Pro – NABBA, tall 1st
1970 Universe, Pro – NABBA, tall, 2nd
1971 Universe, Pro – NABBA, tall, 3rd
1973 Universe, Pro – NABBA, tall, 2nd

Reg went on to make some movies in Italy:
Maciste in King Solomons Mines (1964)
Hercules, Prisoner of Evil (1964)
Hercules and the Captive Women (1963)
Hercules in the Center of the Earth (1961)[1]

Reg Park as Hercules.

Reg is an amazing man. He's one of those few people who've always had both oars in the water. Reg has never been involved in any scandals, and remains hopelessly devoted to his wife and children. If there was ever a bodybuilder role model to emulate, Reg Park is the man.

Reference:
1. http://us.imdb.com/M/person-exact?Park%2C+Reg

Routines

Back

It's refreshing to hear one of the top bodybuilders of all time admitting that they could have done more for a particular bodypart. Reg Park is one of the more humble members of the bodybuilding fraternity. Even though he was one of the more dominant bodybuilders in the 1950s, and could even hold his own right up until the early '70s, Reg freely admitted that he gave back training a short shift compared to other muscle groups.

Reg Park found that by strengthening his lower back, it not only gave him better posture, but also assisted him with many upper back exercises especially rowing movements.

"I wish I'd spent more time on back development."
– Reg Park, Multi-Mr. Universe winner, commenting on how even the top pros sometimes neglect to train muscles they can't see.

It was in an article in *MuscleMag International* in 1975 that Reg revealed his new approach to back training. This was based on more than 28 years of accumulated knowledge at the time. The first major change Reg made was to pay more attention to his lower back. He found that by strengthening his lower back, it not only gave him better posture, but also assisted him with many upper back exercises especially rowing movements.

Reg's first exercise in his revamped back program was stiff-legged deadlifts on a block. This not only gave him a greater range of motion, but also helped strengthen the hamstrings; a muscle which has been connected to lower back problems due to its weakening and tightening. As was the norm for someone of his generation, Reg suggests 5 to 6 sets of stiff-legs, alternating between heavy 5 to 6 rep days, and lighter, 10 to 15 rep days. He points out that those who are at a genetic disadvantage for stiff-legs (long body, short arms) can substitute such other lower back exercises such as hyperextensions or good mornings.

To hit his upper back, Reg usually started with barbell rows. He performed this exercise by keeping the knees slightly bent, upper body just slightly higher than parallel with the floor, and the bar pulled in to the stomach.

The second back exercise was usually seated rows. Once again, he kept the knees slightly bent and the torso never went back past vertical with the floor.

Reg's third lat exercise was often one-arm dumbell or cable rows. Reg typically did 5 sets of 10 reps for the previous three exercises, but occasionally he used slightly heavier weight for sets of 8.

To finish off his back, Reg performed either lat pulldowns or chins. For variety he did both the front and behind the head version of each exercise. Even though Reg preferred to conclude his back workout with chins, he advises beginners and those who have trouble lifting their bodyweight to start their back workouts with chins. Chins are one of the best exercises for lat width, something bodybuilders can never have too much of.

Besides the previous strength exercises, Reg would spend a great deal of time practicing back poses. This not only helped in development, but also gave him the muscle control he needed when on stage.

Reg Park – idol to millions, role model to Arnold, and one of bodybuilding's all-time greats!

Shoulders

Given the era he grew up in, it's not surprising that the bulk of Reg Park's training was done using barbells and dumbells. Such names as Atlantis, Nautilus, and Cybex, were far in the future.

Reg honed and refined his shoulder training while making a series of Hercules' films in Italy in 1960. Without the basics at hand, Reg formulated a routine based entirely on dumbells and barbells.

For his first delt exercise, Reg did either standing or seated barbell presses behind the head. After a couple of warmup sets he would do 5 sets of 5 to 10 reps. Although the standing press was at one time an Olympic event and very popular in gyms, we strongly advise you to do barbell presses while seated in a shoulder press chair. While it is true standing presses will help strengthen the spinal erector muscles, the exercise also puts tremendous stress on the lower back ligaments.

With behind the head presses out of the way, Reg switched to the front version. He found the front version better for isolating his front delts, while behind the head presses bring in the side delts, as well as such upper back muscles as the teres, traps, and rhomboids.

After barbell presses, Reg moved on to seated dumbell presses. Again he performed 5 sets of 5 to 10 reps.

To finish off his delts, Reg alternated between standing side laterals and bent-over dumbell laterals. On the bent-over laterals he would brace his torso on some sort of bench or high stool. This takes much of the stress off the lower back, and allows for total concentration on the rear delts. Reg usually performed 2 to 3 sets of 5 to 10 reps on his lateral exercises.

Biceps

Reg was one of the first bodybuilders to experiment with a wide variety of exercises for each muscle group. Up until the late forties/early '50s, most bodybuilders had a couple of "must do" exercises for each muscle group. Trying something

"I would say the area that improved more than any other was without doubt, my deltoids, and from actually hating pressing movements, I grew to like them. I suppose it's not surprising that as my deltoids improved I worked them more and more."

– Reg Park, Multi-Mr. Universe winner, commenting on his shoulder training and development.

Reg was one of the first bodybuilders to experiment with a wide variety of exercises for each muscle group.

different just wasn't the thing to do. Yet, Reg realized early on that if a given exercise didn't produce the results you wanted, it should be discarded in favor of something else. He also realized that sometimes it wasn't the exercise at fault but the set and rep ranges. In his case he discovered that 5 sets of 8 to 10 reps worked best.

> ## "Irrespective of which biceps exercises you choose to perform, particular attention must be paid to the performance of each exercise to ensure that you work the muscle over the full range and to do this, avoid swinging the weight or bending your body backwards and forwards."
>
> – Reg Park, offering advice on training the biceps.

Reg did four primary movements for 5 sets for his biceps. By today's standards, 20 sets for a small muscle group would be considered grossly overtraining. But through trial and error he found that such high volume training worked best for him. Such is the individual variation within the sport.

Reg's first exercise was usually seated concentration curls. As a tip for beginners, he suggests starting with the weaker arm. Let's face it, even though you rest between sets, you will be a bit tired when you start the second set. It only makes sense to put most of your energy into the weaker arm. During a typical workout, Reg did 5 sets of 8 reps of alternate concentration curls.

Reg Park

Exercise two was preacher cable curls. Reg would attach a straight bar to a low pulley and curl upwards until his forearm was perpendicular with the floor. He recommends using a bar with a revolving center as it puts less stress on the wrist. Again he did 5 sets of 8 reps.

After cable preacher curls, Reg moved on to barbell preacher curls. For many the two movements are the same, but not for Reg. He found that the barbell allowed a wider grip and gave his biceps a slightly different feel. He did 5 sets of 8 reps.

To finish off his biceps, Reg performed incline dumbell curls on a 45-degree bench. Unlike concentration curls, Reg preferred to do incline curls in an alternate style. That is as one dumbell rises the other lowers. As expected he did 5 sets of 8 reps. For variety Reg did dumbell incline curls in two styles. Sometimes he kept the palms facing upwards for the entire set, while on others he supinated or rotated the palms from facing the body to facing upwards.

Calves

Little did Reg Park realize that when he was training in the 1950s his workouts would play a big role in influencing a young Austrian kid named Arnold Schwarzenegger. But as Arnold later recounted in his best-selling book *Arnold: The Education of a Bodybuilder*, Reg's rugged physique and similar bone structure was the biggest influence in his early years.

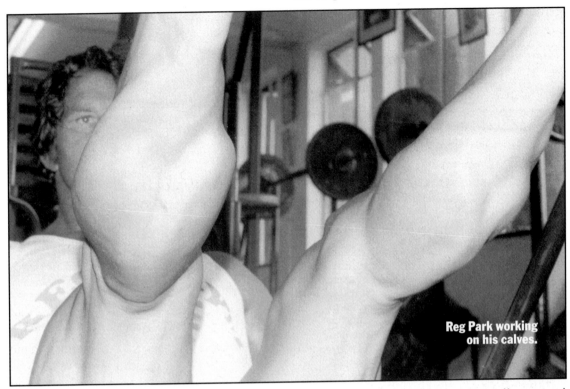

Reg Park working on his calves.

One of the muscle groups that Reg later became famous for, his calves, initially seemed destined for mediocrity. He later said that he thought all the years of soccer leaned out his calves and gave them that stringy, sinewy-look often seen in long-distance runners.

Just as he would later serve as Arnold's guide, Reg was heavily influenced by another famous bodybuilder of a few years earlier, named Clancy Ross. Clancy's calves were nothing to write home about when he won the 1945 Mr. America title. But three years later when he won the 1948 Mr. USA (over such greats as Steve Reeves) Clancy's calves had become full-grown cows. One of the first things Reg did when he visited the Weider Warehouse in New Jersey in 1949 was to have Joe Weider set up some training sessions with Clancy out in California. Their workouts at the time consisted of full body routines. For calves they did 3 sets of standing calf raises using weight, followed by free standing calf stretches using just bodyweight. Reg found that while his calves responded a little, there was nothing dramatic to talk about. Upon returning to New Jersey he revealed his predicament to Weider, and Joe suggested something radical, try training his calves three times a day. The results as they say are history: A couple of Mr. Universes, a lead in a Hollywood movie, inspiration to Schwarzenegger, you get the picture.

Over the following decades Reg came to rely on four basic exercises to hit his calves; standing machine raise; seated calf raise; Donkey calf raise and toe press on the leg press. Reg wold typically pick one of the previous four exercises and do 3 sets of 15 to 20 reps. Then the next day he would repeat but with a different exercise. For Reg the key was training his calves every day, not once or twice as some genetically gifted types can. You know who we are talking about, those guys who stroll into the gym with 18-inch protrusions below their knees and in all honesty ask, "Is that what you call a calf machine?"

Reg refused to accept defeat on calf development, and made it his number one goal. If your calves are lagging behind shouldn't you do the same?

Bill Pearl

Bill Pearl was born on October 31, 1930, in Prineville, Oregon. As a Nez Perce Indian, living on a reservation, he did all the things that normal kids did, but without much money to finance his boyhood dreams. Unlike many of bodybuilding's greats – past or present – he never entertained visions of becoming one of the greatest bodybuilders in the world. Rather than spending the little money he had on the purchase of muscle magazines, he saved his pennies and sent away for a mail order weight set instead. His intentions at that time had little to do with being seen on a stage. All he wanted was to grow big and strong and become physically adept at combating the bullying he took every day from his older brother. Bill became serious about bodybuilding at an early age:

Bill Pearl became serious about bodybuilding at an early age.

"When I was 11 years old, I sent away for a York Big Ten Special with money I'd saved from working all year long. I had a total of $22, and they'd ship it to your house for an extra $5. This was at the end of 1941. I got delivery of the York barbell set in 1945. It took me four years to get that weight set because of World War II."

But he found substitutes, and in 1950 Bill enlisted in the US Navy. He actually began serious weight training while doing sea duty on destroyers! He didn't leave the navy until 1954, but he had already started to compete:

1953 Mr. America – AAU, winner
     Mr. California – AAU, overall winner
     Universe – NABBA, overall winner
     Universe – NABBA, tall, 1st
1956 Mr. USA – AAU, winner
     Universe – Pro, NABBA, tall 1st
1961 Universe – Pro, NABBA, overall winner
     Universe – Pro, NABBA, tall, 1st
1967 Universe – Pro, NABBA, overall winner
     Universe – Pro, NABBA, tall, 1st
1971 Universe – Pro, NABBA, overall winner
     Universe – Pro, NABBA, tall, 1st

How does Bill feel about the public's perception of bodybuilding over the years?

"You can take this for what it's worth, but I believe I may have gotten more respect than the bodybuilders get today. Modern bodybuilders are putting themselves through a lot of abuse to get where they are. Back when Reg Park, Larry Scott, a host of others and I were competing, you got where you were with hard work, consistency and stability. That's how you got to be a Mr. America. I'm not saying, by any means, that bodybuilders today don't train as hard as I or the other champions did in those days, but the stigma attached to the drug scene of today's sport is much greater. People say, 'Well, if I did that, I could be Mr. Universe or Mr. Olympia.' Of course, that's not true, but now bodybuilding has such a negative connotation. The public believes more and more that these athletes are chemically engineered and that anyone could do it."

Vince Gironda – The Iron Guru

On October 18th, 1997, Vince Gironda passed away in Los Angeles, three weeks shy of his 80th birthday. Vince was considered the Iron Guru, the man whose unique training methods dominated the bodybuilding world in the '50s, '60s and '70s. In 1946, he opened Vince's Gym in Studio City, California (10 miles north of Los Angeles), which stayed open until 1995. In his own private iron dungeon, Vince trained many champion bodybuilders and Hollywood stars including: William Holden, George Hamilton, James Garner, Lou Ferrigno, Erik Estrada, Clint Eastwood, Tommy Chong, Cher, Johnny Carson, Keith and David Carradine, Joe Campanella, Maud Adams, Brian Keith, Michael Landon, Roddy Piper, Burt Reynolds, David Lee Roth, Richard Roundtree, Kurt Russell, John Schneider, O.J. Simpson, Randy Quaid, Clint Walker, Carl Weathers, Denzel Washington, Marty Feldman, Dudley Moore, Sean Penn and Arnold Schwarzenegger.

Most who knew him will admit Vince never had any diplomatic skills. For example, upon first meeting Arnold, Vince told him that he was a "fat Austrian boy." Since Arnold had an ego to match Vince's, he was suitably offended. Two weeks later, after Frank Zane beat Arnold at the Mr. Universe contest, Arnold returned to Vince's Gym and said, "I see what you mean."

Where did this guy get off telling Arnold that he was fat? Vince could do it because Vince was an expert and had the credentials to back up his reputation:

1950 Mr. USA – AAU
1956 Mr. USA – AAU
1957 Mr. USA – AAU, 3rd
1962 Universe – Pro, NABBA, short, 2nd

Vince was perhaps the first bodybuilder to study food intake. And his views on supplementation were decades ahead of their time. As he often said, "Bodybuilding is 85 percent nutrition." Yet he wasn't able to win any major bodybuilding contests. By his own admission, he was too defined for his time. Modern competitive bodybuilding is about both mass and definition, and Vince held to the belief that the extra mass was not necessary. To him, bodybuilding was about being ripped, both on and off-season. Although bodybuilding was his life, he didn't like the direction in which professional bodybuilding had gone: "Whatever happened to it? It's a drug cult. You don't have to know how to work out any more. I laugh at the exercises I see them doing in the magazines. They don't know beans."

Vince Gironda was perhaps the first bodybuilder to study food intake. And his views on supplementation were decades ahead of their time.

Chapter Two – The 1950s

Vince wrote many articles over the years, and co-authored one book with MuscleMag International's Robert Kennedy called *The Wild Physique*. His *Blue Print for the Bodybuilder* series is now considered a classic. Yet for a man who made his living communicating his ideas to others, he was probably the most difficult man to interview. In his mind there were two types of opinion; his and the wrong one. Vince was dogmatic in his beliefs, and volatile when he didn't like a question:

"First of all, I don't deal in bullshit! You're asking me questions and I'm giving you answers and you're drawing some kind of conclusions that only you have! I'm considered a success! I've been here 49 years! I've seen gyms come and go but I'm still here … You want me to be truthful, don't you? Aren't you used to people being truthful to you? Why should I try to bullshit you? You don't mean that much to me. I don't have to b.s. anyone. If you want to find out how successful I am, you should be interviewing people I know. Why don't you find out what my friends think of me, since you don't like my answers!"

Despite his badass attitude, he got results and the studios routinely sent the stars to train with him. He wouldn't answer questions about whether he was in WWII, causing more than one person to comment, "Probably because he feels guilty about causing it!" Yet everyone who knew him or has read his articles agrees that he was an intellectual who made a valuable contribution to the sport of bodybuilding.

Vince will always have a special place in the hearts of Bob Kennedy and the staff of *MuscleMag* as he was a columnist with *MuscleMag* since the first issue. We figure that if Vince makes it to heaven he'll have something to say about the way the place is run and how Saint Peter could improve his bench press. *MuscleMag* is grateful for your help and advice, Vince.

Despite his badass attitude, Vince got results and the studios routinely sent the stars to train with him. Here he is with Mohammed Makkawy.

Training Views

Rather than list off some exercises and routines Vince followed in his 60-odd years of training, we thought it more appropriate to discuss some of Vince's views on training the various muscle groups. As any regular follower of the sport is aware, Vince had some unique opinions when it came to training. To some he was stuck in a time warp, to others he was 50 years ahead of his time!

Shoulders

The first big-name bodybuilder that Vince helped with shoulder training was Larry Scott. History's first Mr. Olympia was not blessed with wide clavicles, the two collarbones that play the biggest role in determining the width of your shoulders. Yet under Vince's tutelage, Larry went on to build two of the largest deltoids in the sport's history. Only the presence of those wondrous arms kept Larry's delts from receiving more accolades.

Vince had some unique opinions when it came to training. To some he was stuck in a time warp, to others he was 50 years ahead of his time!

Vince was a firm believer in free weights despite the advances in machines over the years. He also advocated doing exercises for all three delt heads. Nothing radical so far, but where Vince starts to deviate from the norm is in his views that most modern day bodybuilders place too much emphasis on the traps. That sloped-shouldered look that most bodybuilders strive for was in Vince's view unnatural looking.

Vince also believed that many bodybuilders rely too much on racks for support, and having the weight already in position to start the exercise. For him, getting the weight into position was often part of the exercise. For example when doing shoulder presses, Vince suggested to stand up, hold the bar at thigh-level, clean it to shoulder height, and then press it over head. Vince considered the cleaning to the shoulders half the exercise.

A typical shoulder routine suggested by Vince would look something like this:

1. Clean and presses – 3 sets of 8 reps
2. Front lateral raises – 3 sets of 8 reps
3. Side lateral raises – 3 sets of 8 reps
4. Bench lateral raises – 3 sets of 8 reps

Chest

To say Vince was opinionated on chest training is to say the captain of the Titanic knew how to find ice! Until his dying days Vince could never understand how anyone would want to build huge, bulbous pecs. The male physique was never meant to, in any way, "resemble women's breasts." To Vince a huge thick chest only made someone look narrow. It also made them look fat in clothes. His opinion was to create the illusion of width by putting chest muscle in the "right" places.

Vince's most radical view on chest training was the bench press – he hated it! He believed it was one of the greatest front delt builders of all time. The fact that Nubret, Schwarzenegger, and Ferrigno, possessors of three of the greatest chests of all time, built their enormous pecs primarily with flat bench presses (in Nubret's case almost exclusively), meant diddly squat to Vince. He would admit that lying flat on a bench and lowering a barbell had a role to play, but only if it was done "his" way. For Vince this meant what he called "neck presses." Holding a bar with a wide grip and lowering it to the collar bone, not the mid or lower chest.

Vince's condemnation of the bench press was only matched by his praise of the parallel bar dip. He felt this was the true "king" of chest builders. It put muscle where he felt it should go, on the lower and outer pecs. This put a clean line under the pecs and helped create the illusion of width.

Vince Gironda

Another Vince idiosyncrasy was his views on chest expansion. He was adamant that unless you have an abnormally small rib cage, you should leave it alone. Stretching it out with pullovers and breathing squats will only create a deeper chest box and in his views, make you look fat!

A typical Gironda chest workout looked like this:
1. Wide parallel bar dips – 3 sets of 8 reps
2. Incline dumbell presses – 3 sets of 8 reps
3. Decline floor cables – 3 sets of 8 reps
4. Cable crossovers – 3 sets of 8 reps

Abdominals

This was the one muscle group where Vince's famous "bodybuilding is 85 percent nutrition" really struck home. He was one of the first to realize that no amount of abdominal training will spot reduce the fat off the midsection. You have to get your eating habits under control before any improvement in the waist region will be seen.

Using a combination of observation and physiology, Vince came to realize that the abs are like any other muscle group; you don't need hundreds of sets and reps to build them. In fact Vince theorized that overtraining the abs could lead to "hormonal imbalances" which could terminate growth in other muscle groups.

Vince also realized that the standard abdominal exercise of the day, the situp, was more of a hip flexor movement than an ab builder. He suggested that a half situp, where you shorted the distance between the pelvis and sternum, was a much more effective ab exercise. He was decades ahead of the pack with this one, as the exercise, which we now call the crunch, is the primary ab exercise performed by most bodybuilders.

Another Gironda view was that the obliques should not be built. Period! For a steroid-bloated bodybuilder with a 55- to 60-inch chest, adding size to the obliques is fine, but for anyone sporting a chest 50 inches or less, he stressed that they should leave such oblique-builders as side bends alone.

If you sought advice from Vince on building a great midsection, here's a routine he might suggest:

1. Crunches – 3 sets of 15 to 20 reps
2. Reverse crunches – 3 sets of 15 to 20 reps
3. Bent-leg, leg raises – 3 sets of 15 to 20 reps

Back

For Vince, nothing made the male physique like a wide, wide, back. Given all those years spent on Muscle Beach, it's not surprising that Vince's favorite back exercise was the chinup. It must have been something to watch Vince and others chinning outdoors as the California sun set into the Pacific Ocean.

Vince's views on back training are tame compared to his views on chest and leg training (next section). He recognized the size of the back, coupled with its two primary functions, necessitated doing a lot of work. This was probably the only muscle group where he advocated doing more than 15 total sets in a workout.

For those who experience trouble feeling the back muscles when training, try the following Gironda tip. As soon as you reach the contracted position on a back exercise, hold the position for a count of six, and squeeze the various back muscles as hard as possible. Vince believed that those who had difficulty feeling the lats during training had a poor nerve connection to the region. He believed that holding the contraction would stimulate the body to increase nerve impulses to the area. Whether that's true or not, most that try Vince's technique swear by its effects.

A typical Vince Gironda back workout looked like this:

1. Front chins – 3 to 5 sets of 8 reps
2. Narrow pulldowns – 3 sets of 8 reps
3. Front pulldown – 3 sets of 8 reps
4. Seated pulley rows – 3 sets of 8 reps
5. Back extensions – 3 sets of 10 reps

Legs

Vince's views on leg training, especially the thighs, never made him any friends. Like bench presses, he was totally against heavy back squats. He felt that they spread the hips and built huge butts. Vince tolerated Smith Machine squats with the feet kept forward, and regular squats if done light, or by women, who he felt couldn't overdevelop the thighs and glutes because of their lower testosterone levels. As for good old-fashioned ass-to-the-floor squats, they weren't allowed at Vince's gym!

For Vince, the ideal thigh exercise was the hack squat or "hack slide" as he called it. He felt the hack machine

Vince Gironda was one of the first to realize that no amount of abdominal training will spot reduce the fat off the midsection.

allowed you to shift the feet around to target different parts of the thigh. According to him he felt most bodybuilders overdevelop the upper thighs, while neglecting the lower and inner thighs.

He was also one of the first trainers and bodybuilders to recognize the importance the hamstrings made to a great physique. He also suggested bodybuilders do leg curls in two ways, flat on the machine to hit the lower hamstrings, and in a push-up position (torso braced on locked-out arms) to hit the upper leg biceps.

Here's a standard Vince Gironda leg workout:

1. Knees-in hack squats – 3 sets of 8 reps
2. Knees-out hack squats – 3 sets of 8 reps
3. Sissy squats – 3 sets of 10 reps
4. Flat lying leg curls – 3 sets of 10 reps
5. Push-up position leg curls – 3 sets of 10 reps

Vince Gironda works his biceps.

Arms

Given Vince's obsession with proportions, it's not surprising that in the last decade of his life he felt that most bodybuilders were carrying arm training too far. He cringed every time he saw a set of 20-inch arms on a pair of stilt-sized legs.

Another Gironda arm training philosophy was that medium-weight isolation exercises were superior to heavy weight compound movements. It wasn't that he was against basic exercise, but he felt bodybuilders stuck with them too long. To fully develop the three heads of the triceps, bodybuilders should be doing isolation movements for all three regions. There are two typical biceps and triceps routines:

Biceps

1. Preacher curls – 3 sets of 8 reps
2. Spyder curls – 3 sets of 8 reps
3. Narrow chins – 3 sets of 8 reps

Triceps

1. Rope kickbacks – 3 sets of 8 reps
2. Triceps pushdowns – 3 sets of 8 reps
3. Lying barbell extensions – 3 sets of 8 reps

The infamous Vince Gironda.

Chapter 3

The 1960s

Not counting World War II, the 1960s were by far the most turbulent decade of the 20th century, and there's an argument to be made that in many respects the '60s were more chaotic than the '40s. World War II was by far the defining event of the century, but the '60s had a greater variety of major issues. From the assassinations of Martin Luther King Jr. and the Kennedys, to the civil rights movement and the Cuban Missile Crisis. From the coulter culture revolution to the Vietnam War, the sixties seemed to have it all.

Larry Scott has two main claims to fame; his right and left biceps.

The biggest cultural event of the decade was of course Woodstock. This three-day rock festival, held at Max Yasgur's farm in New York State in August of 1969, became the defining event of the counterculture revoltion. Despite the mud and less-than-adequate sound system, half a million people celebrated free love and condemned the Vietnam War. By the time it was all over, most in attendance realized that they had participated in something so unique that it could never be recreated, and they were right. Despite other concerts at the time, and anniversary shows decades later, there was no way to capture the distinct atmosphere of the original.

In the bodybuilding arena, things weren't quite so tumultuous. The most significant event was the establishing of the Mr. Olympia contest by Joe Weider to determine who was the best bodybuilder alive. First held in 1965, bodybuilding's first winner was Larry Scott who proved it was no fluke by winning the title again the following year.

Another major event of the decade was the establishment of Venice Beach, California as bodybuilding's Mecca. California beaches had always been famous for musclemen to display their great physiques, but the '60s cemented Venice Beach as the place to be. In many respects we have Hollywood to thank for this. A series of

Beach movies staring Frankie Avalon and Annette Funinchello, regularly featured such greats as Dave Draper and Larry Scott, doing their thing. Before long, most of the greats in the sport headed west and took up residence in the Venice Beach area.

It was one of these "greats" whose arrival in 1968, laid the foundation for bodybuilding's dramatic increase in popularity a decade later. After conquering Europe, Austrian-born Arnold Schwarzenegger, decided to combat America's best at the 1968 Mr. Universe, held in Miami, Florida. Although he won the heavyweight class, he lost the overall to a much smaller, but more refined Frank Zane. Arnold, however, began to refine his physique using the same drive and determination that would one day make him the top box office draw in Hollywood. With the exception of a second-place finish to Sergio Oliva at the 1969 Mr. Olympia, Arnold made good on his boast of never losing another contest.

Let's take a look at the training routines of some of the top bodybuilders who made headlines during the flower power decade.

Larry Scott was smaller than the other kids in school and had to work at being good at sports.

Larry Scott

Larry Scott has two main claims to fame; his right and left biceps. The man who won the first and second Mr. Olympia contests in New York City is today a devout Mormon who lets his faith guide him through life.

Larry was born on October 12, 1938, in Blackfoot, Idaho. His family is descended from Scottish homesteaders. Larry had six brothers and sisters, who were all supported by his machinist father. Larry describes his father as being distant, but he was close to his mother. It was their influence that led Larry into bodybuilding. Larry's father was a physically powerful man and his mother admired strong men. Larry was smaller than the other kids and had to work at being good at sports. At first he tried gymnastics, but after seeing some old Weider magazines Larry decided to try building his biceps. In high school he got them to 12-1/2 inches! He then joined the YMCA and started training his whole body. Two years later, in 1958, Larry won the Mr. Idaho contest. It was only to be the beginning of an amazing career:

    1960 Mr. California – AAU, overall winner
    1962 Mr. America – IFBB, overall winner
    1964 Universe – IFBB, overall winner
    1965 Olympia – IFBB, winner
    1966 Olympia – IFBB, winner
    1979 Canada Diamond Pro Cup – IFBB, 9th
    Grand Prix Vancouver – IFBB

Larry had already started acting lessons before he won the first Mr. Olympia. While he wasn't able to launch a full-time career, he did get to meet the film stars of the time, Annette

Funicello and Frankie Avalon: "They were quite refreshing. Ironically, the regular surfers, who were not leads in that film, were a pain in the neck. They had egos six times the size of ours. I never met such an egotistical group. But Annette, Frankie, Don Rickles and Buddy Hackett were regular people. They were just great! I even went on a double date with Annette Funicello after the film wrapped. I took out a former Ms. USA, who was on the set of the movie, and she was great."

Larry appeared in the following:

Muscle Beach Party (1964)
Project Power (196?)
Thieves (1977)
Wilma (1977)
Siege (1978)

     Larry retired from competitive body-building in 1966. Though shaken by the loss of two of his five children, Larry's successes run much deeper than the muscle he built in the '50s and '60s. He maintains a strong marriage, is a prosperous businessman, and takes pride in the nucleus of a family that has been besieged by tragedy and sorrow. Once he was nothing more than a beach blond seeking nothing more than a shine on his Porsche, the ultimate pump, and the promise of a flourishing career in both Hollywood and Muscle Beach. Then he realigned his priorities and is now as strong in constitution as he once was on the Scott (preacher) bench that bears his name.

Although famous for his arms, particularly his biceps, Larry Scott also had one of the largest sets of deltoids of any competitor during the 1960s.

Shoulders

Although famous for his arms, particularly his biceps, Larry Scott also had one of the largest sets of deltoids of any competitor during the 1960s. The reason his delts never received the same recognition as his biceps was genetics. Larry, you see, wasn't blessed with the greatest shoulder width in the world. He has what's referred to in the sport as narrow shoulders. In other words his bone structure is a tad on the narrow side. Now Larry could have listened to the genetic gods and accepted defeat, but that wasn't his style. Larry reasoned (and quite correctly we might add) that while there was nothing he could do for his bone structure. He could create the illusion of width by adding inches to his deltoids. He did just that, to the point that many consider his delts to be on a par with his legendary biceps. Not bad for someone with so-called narrow shoulders.

"The Larry Scott exercise program is severe; always has been. Watching him pumping iron today one gets the same impression one had when observing his workouts of the '60s. His training is different; ahead of his time, even now."

– Editors of *MuscleMag International*, commenting on Larry Scott after watching him at a series of seminars in the late 1970s.

Larry usually started his shoulder training with dumbell presses, but not the conventional style. He starts with the bells held in the same position as if he just finished a two-arm dumbell curl. That is his palms are facing upwards. Larry would then start pressing upwards and slowly rotate the hands until his palms are facing forward. On some days Larry performed straight sets, while on others he did down the rack sets.

After dumbell presses, Larry moved on to standing dumbell lateral raises. Again Larry had his own variation on this exercise. Instead of the traditional elbows slightly bent, lift straight up version, Larry slowly moved his arms forward as he lifted the dumbells up to shoulder height.

To finish his shoulder training, Larry performed one-arm bent-over laterals. Again notice the Scott interpretation. How many bodybuilders these days do bent-over laterals one arm at a time? Not many we tell you, but Larry found he could concentrate and get a better feel in his posterior delts by training them this way. For support Larry rested his body on a bench.

With regards to sets and reps, Larry comes from the old school of high volume training. This means he did a minimum of 5 sets for each exercise, and sometimes went up to 10 sets per exercise. Larry was more consistent on rep ranges, and usually did 8 per set. The only change being his calves and forearms, which were trained for 15 to 20 reps per set.

Arms

Biceps

As history's first Mr. Olympia winner, it's not surprising that Larry Scott had a great pair of guns. In fact to this day, Larry's arms, particularly his biceps, rank among the greatest of all time. Larry was blessed with having both fullness and peak in his biceps. Many bodybuilders, like Sergio Oliva had larger biceps, but lacked the peak of the great Scott. Conversely such bodybuilders as Albert Beckles and Boyer Coe had slightly higher peaks, but didn't quite have the fullness of Larry's biceps. You could say Scott had the best of both worlds.

To this day, Larry's arms, particularly his biceps, rank among the greatest of all time.

To build those "inspirations" to millions, Larry relied heavily on the preacher bench. In fact Larry became so famous in bodybuilding circles for his outstanding arm development that when word got around about how many preacher curls he did, the little old bench started being called the Scott Bench. It's now to the point that you can go into any gym and just as many bodybuilders call it the Scott bench as the Preacher bench. Amazing what one set of 20-inch arms can do!

Larry began his biceps training with – surprise, surprise – two-arm dumbell preacher curls. He used a heavily stuffed pad to protect his elbows. He held his arms fairly close so that the ends of the two dumbells were almost touching. Larry would then lower the dumbells until his arms were straight, pause for a split second and then return to the starting position with his forearms vertical with the floor. At the end of 10 to 12 reps, Larry would then perform the technique for which he would become famous – burns. Although he could no longer do full reps, he would lower the weight part way, and then curl back up. Larry would do 4 to 6 of these partial reps or burns per set.

After dumbell curls, Larry switched equipment and did four to six sets of barbell preacher curls. Again he would do 10 to 12 reps per set, adding in four to six burns at the end of the set.

For his third exercise, Larry would do reverse curls using an EZ-Curl bar. As expected he did them on the preacher bench and threw in four to six burns at the end of each set.

Larry Scott found that by watching a muscle contract and relax on each rep, it allowed him to stimulate the muscle just a bit more.

Larry would sometimes do the previous exercises in triset fashion, doing four trisets for a total of 12 sets.

To finish off his biceps, Larry turned around on the preacher bench so his arms were hanging straight down. Larry called these barbell concentration curls, but the term most used these days is spyder curls. In any case Larry found them great for his upper biceps, and did 4 sets of 10 to 12 reps. A typical set would include 6 to 8 full reps and 4 to 6 burns at the end.

Triceps

After a short break, Larry moved on and attacked his triceps. He never quite received the attention for his triceps that he garnered for his biceps. This is too bad as the backs of Larry's upper arms weren't that far behind his biceps. Larry had a great pair of triceps and here's how he built them.

Larry would start with narrow presses using the EZ-curl. He'd put 200 to 225 pounds on the bar and do six reps to positive failure and then add on his customary four to six burns. With little or no rest he'd go over to the cable machine and do a set of 8 reps (plus four burns) of triceps pushdowns. Larry would alternate these two exercises for 6 sets each, or 12 sets total.

Over the years Larry tried a number of different hand positions and bars on the triceps pushdown, and discovered that a six-inch grip, using a V-shaped bar seemed to hit his triceps the most effectively. But he is first to admit that everyone is different and it may take sme experimenting to see what works best for you.

To finish off his triceps, Larry would stay at the cable machine and do four straight sets of 6 to 8 reps (plus 4 to 6 burns at the end of each set). Between each set Larry would walk around a 20-foot circle and take about ten deep breaths to get as much oxygen as possible. Those in non-airconditioned, over-crowded gyms may want to adopt Larry's practice.

As a final comment on Larry's arm training, he tried to set up his exercises so that he could see himself in the mirror. This may seem vain to some but Larry wasn't just admiring his handiwork. No, he found that the mirror allowed him to check his technique. It also helped him with the mind-muscle link. Years before Arnold was visualizing his biceps as mountains, Larry Scott was watching his pump up and down with regularity. Larry found that by watching a muscle contract and relax on each rep, allowed him to stimulate the muscle just a tad bit more. The end result was a physique that won the first two Mr. Olympia titles and earned Larry a prominent place in bodybuilding history.

Dave Draper – The Blond Bomber

Like the legendary Phoenix, a bird that could arise from it's own ashes, Dave Draper has returned to soar in the world of bodybuilding. He was a casting agent's dream come true; Dave was tall and muscular, with a full head of thick, blond hair. Before Arnold was able to make his first movie, Dave was starring with the ill-fated Sharon Tate in the movie *Don't Make Waves*. But the turbulence of the '60s left few in that era untouched, and Dave became one of its casualties. His biography, while impressive, can't help but leave the reader to wonder about what could have been.

Dave epitomized the California look with his bleach-blond good looks and 6'1", 230-pound physique.

Dave Draper was born April 16, 1942, in Secaucus, New Jersey. His family were hard-working people of German, Slavic and Jewish ancestry. There was never a lot of money around, yet he still grew up in a loving and well-supervised environment. When he was four, Dave found himself surrounded by the biggest students in his grade one class, so he turned to weightlifting to compensate for the size difference. By the time he was 15, Dave was getting good comments from his coach about how well developed his arms were. Dave continued his weightlifting in prep school, but he was always into bodybuilding for the joy of working out. He couldn't afford the magazines while growing up, and didn't really have any icons to emulate. Yet his bodybuilding career was changed forever by his shopping habits.

The story is best told in Dave's own words; "Joe's first offices were in Jersey City. That wasn't far from Secaucus, and I used to go there to buy things when I needed them. I'd take the bus and walk about five blocks. Leroy Colbert, who was a famous bodybuilder in those days, used to work in the store. He was a black guy – still is – with very large arms, and was a big star in Joe's magazines. He was a great guy, and I'd go to talk to him while I was there. See, when you were actually buying something, Leroy would come to the front counter and then go get what you wanted. I'd just stare at this guy. I think he was the first idol I had. I got to know Leroy well enough that he invited me to come up and to work one day. When I had a two-week vacation, Joe asked me to come and work for him. I quit my other job and moved to California."

Having competed in New Jersey, Dave soon began competing in California. He trained with, and grew up with, the giants of the sport. And as the results listed indicate, he held his own:

1965 Mr. America – IFBB, overall winner
        Mr. America – IFBB, tall, 1st
1966 Universe – IFBB, overall winner
        Universe – IFBB, tall, 1st
1967 Olympia – IFBB, 4th
1970 Mr. World – IFBB, overall winner
        Mr. World – IFBB, tall, 1st
        Universe – Pro, NABBA, tall, 3rd

But in those days big money was not part of the sport, and Dave admits that it was basically a minimum wage job. He heard that he could earn some money as an extra, so he went to audition with the rest of the gym rats. He had taken the next step, acting. Dave appeared as an extra in a number of films, with feature parts in the following:

Lord Love a Duck (1966)
Don't Make Waves (1967) (1)

Besides film roles, he appeared as David the Gladiator, a TV personality who introduced movies that had beefcake. That gig lasted for almost a year, but despite high ratings, he was unable to capitalize on his proven success. He continued his television work, and appeared on such American cultural icons as the *Monkeys*, the *Beverly Hillbillies*, the *Merv Griffin Show*, and the *Tonight Show* with host Johnny Carson.

Dave was always into bodybuilding for the joy of working out.

Dave chose to become a recluse, despite his impressive body of work. By 1971, he had fully withdrawn from competitive bodybuilding, and was making furniture. He was also using recreational drugs and alcohol.

At this point, the typical Hollywood story would end in a police morgue or a trailer park, but Dave came back. He struggled with his own demons, and won. A devout Christian, Dave runs gyms in Santa Clara and is involved with the Internet. He's also writing articles, while providing leadership and guidance to the next generation of bodybuilders. Dave is back, and bodybuilding is a better sport because of him.

To contact Dave, write him at http://davedraper.com/draper-bomber-talk.html.

Reference:
1. http://www.weightsnet.com/Links/Bodybuilding/screencredits.html

Back

Dave epitomized the California look with his beach blond good looks and 6'1", 230-pound physique. When he wasn't on a movie set with Frankie Avalon and Annette Funichello, Dave was in the gym building his physique. One of his most impressive features was his wide back. Let's take a closer look at how he developed it.

One of Dave's most impressive features was his wide back.

Given the lack of fancy chrome-plated equipment at the old Gold's Gym, it's not surprising that the bulk of Dave's back training consisted of free-weight exercises. He usually started with everyone's favorite width exercise, front chins. Dave took a wide grip on this exercise and pulled his body up until his chest touched the chinning bar. On a typical day Dave did five sets of 10 to 15 reps.

Dave's second exercise was often barbell rows. He would stand on a low block to get a good stretch, and always keep his knees slightly bent to reduce lower-back stress. Five sets of 10 to 15 reps was the norm.

For his third exercise Dave performed narrow-grip chins. Unlike the wide version, which primarily hit the upper and outer lats, narrow-grip chins target more of the lower and center lats. Dave leaned back slightly as he pulled up and normally did 5 sets of 10 to 15 reps.

To finish off his back, Dave did wide-grip pulldowns behind the head. Again it was 5 sets of 10 to 15 reps.

Shoulders and Chest

Shoulders
1. Presses behind head – 5 sets of 8 to 10 reps
2. Bent-over laterals – 5 sets of 8 to 10 reps
3. Dumbell presses – 5 sets of 8 to 10 reps
Note: Dave usually supersetted the first two exercises.

Chest
1. Flat barbell presses – 5 sets of 8 to 10 reps
2. Flat dumbell flyes – 5 sets of 8 to 10 reps
3. Incline dumbell flyes – 5 sets of 8 to 10 reps
4. Dumbell pullovers – 5 sets of 8 to 10 reps
5. Cable crossovers – 5 sets of 8 to 10 reps
Note: Dave often supersetted the first two exercises.

Rick Wayne

Rick Wayne was born on the island of St. Lucia. He began lifting weights at the age of 14 and in short order he won Mr. America, Mr. World, and Mr. Universe titles. His arms are considered to be two of the best in history.

Bodybuilding was not his only love, as it soon became apparent that Rick had great talent as a writer. Rick rose up through the writing hierarchy just like a bodybuilder rising through the ranks until he was editor of Joe Weider's *Muscle Builder Power*. He also wrote a number of significant bodybuilding books including *Muscle Wars* and *Three More Reps*.

A brilliant intellectual, Rick's scathing articles and controversial novels (*It'll be Alright in the Morning*, *The Bodymen*, and *Arms & Shoulders Above the Rest*) have given him a reputation for being confrontational. Rick explains himself:

"I know I'm often seen as racist and Communist; I am neither. But I am outspoken. I get people to face their prejudices and they don't like that. Let's admit it, the face of prejudice is not the most beautiful work of art imaginable ... Politics is life. Every decision that ultimately affects us is political ... Whether Americans continue to be free is a political question. I am amused when my critics suggest that my writing in *Muscle & Fitness* is too political. These are the same people who will tell you bodybuilding is today more politics than sport. It's like telling a boxing reporter that there's too much about boxing in his writing."

Love him or hate him, but you simply can't ignore him. We know the judges couldn't:

Bodybuilding was not his only love, as it soon became apparent that Rick Wayne had great talent as a writer.

1965 Universe – IFBB, short, 1st
1966 Universe – Pro, NABBA, short 2nd
1967 Mr. World, IFBB, overal winner
         Mr. World, IFBB, short 1st
1969 Universe, IFBB, medium, 1st
1970 Mr. World, IFBB, medium, 1st
         Pro Mr. America, WBBG, winner
1974 Mr. World, WBBG, 2nd
1981 Grand Prix California, IFBB
1982 World Pro Championships, IFBB, 8th

After leaving Weider Enterprises, Rick returned to his native St. Lucia to run a local newspaper but he still writes articles for various bodybuilding magazines (most notably *Muscle & Fitness* in the early '80s and *Muscular Development* in the mid '90s).

And the last word goes to Rick. When asked what he thought of Joe Weider, the bodybuilding business tycoon who arouses strong opinions among many bodybuilders, Rick said:

"I have very much respect for the man. He is a very talented man. He is also underestimated by many people. He is patient beyond belief. And his tolerance of fools seems to be boundless. Those who say bodybuilding would be better without Weider obviously speak without wisdom. Without Weider, bodybuilding as we know it would not exist ..."

Arms

There was no shortage of large muscular arms at the original Gold's Gym on Pacific Avenue, Venice Beach, in the late '60s and early '70s. On any day you could see Franco Columbu, Danny Padilla, Arnold you-know-who, and Robby Robinson. One of the most respected patrons of the gym was a St. Lucia native, Rick Wayne. Besides the name he was making for himself as a writer, Rick also sported two of the most complete arms around. In fact at the same Mr. World contest, which he won, he also took the trophy for best arms.

In his heyday, Rick had that perfect blend of size, shape, and symmetry. Like Robby Robinson a few years later, Rick's arms were mirror images of one another. His biceps and triceps were perfectly matched.

To build those great arms of his, Rick relied on straight sets of such basic exercises as dumbell and barbell curls, as well as pushdowns and lying extensions. Then close to a competition he'd start using such advanced techniques as trisets and giant sets. He also spent considerable time posing between sets and after his workout. This not only added an extra degree of hardness to his physique, but also gave him the muscle control that was essential while onstage. Here's a precontest Rick Wayne workout from the early'70s.[1]

1. Barbell curls – 3-4 sets of 8 to 10 reps
2. Cable pushdowns – 3-4 sets of 8 to 10 reps
3. Seated dumbell curls – 3-4 sets of 8 to 10 reps
4. Concentration curls – 3 sets of 8 to 10 reps
5. Close grip barbell curls – 3 sets of 10 to 10 reps
6. Seated behind the head barbell extensions – 3 sets of 10 to 12 reps
7. Seated dumbell curls – 3 sets of 8 to 10 reps

Note: 1. Exercises 1 to 4 were done as a giant set. 2. Exercises 5 to 7 were done as a triset.

Reference:
1. Sprague, Ken, Reynolds, Bill; Contemporary Books, Inc., Chicago, 1983.

In his heyday, Rick Wayne had that perfect blend of size, shape, and symmetry.

Chapter 4

The 1970s

It's ironic that a decade remembered for violence ended with a landmark peaceful event (Woodstock), while a decade that had a more casual approach started wth a mass shooting. Yet this is exactly what happened in May of 1970 when National Guardsmen opened fire on students at Kent State University in Ohio. The students were protesting President Nixon's continuance of the Vietnam War, and the shooting left four students dead and another nine wounded. There was a measure of satisfaction a few years later as President Nixon was forced to resign over the Watergate Affair.

Speaking of which, the presidential scene went from the resignation of Nixon to the stumbling of Ford; and from the southern charm of Jimmy Carter to the anti-communism of Ronald Regan. Four more distinct personalities couldn't be found for the oval office even if you tried.

But who cares! There was still bodybuilding to focus on. Just as the '40s are called the golden years of Hollywood, so too have the '70s been referred to as bodybuilding's good old days. The central character in all of this was of course, Arnold Schwarzenegger. After setting up shop at a relatively unknown Gold's Gym in Venice Beach, California, Arnold started to change the sport forever. It started with his first Mr. Olympia win in 1970, and continued right up to 1975. With six straight Mr. Olympia titles to his credit, Arnold was the undisputed king of the sport. Bodybuilders from all over the world flocked to southern California to bask in his presence. For many the annual trek to Gold's Gym became the highlight of their bodybuilding careers.

In 1975, Arnold took center stage in a documentary that focused on the rather obscure sport of the time – bodybuilding. *Pumping Iron* was the work of Charles Gaines and George Butler. A few years earlier they had released a book by the same name, and its success led to the capturing of these Herculean mortals on film. What made the film so popular was both the behind-the-scenes approach, and Arnold's personality. Where most athletes tend to come up short on film, it was obvious that Arnold couldn't get enough of the camera.

Bodybuilders from all over the world flocked to southern California to bask in Arnold's presence.

Pumping Iron was also significant in that it was the first time the general public got a glimpse of a 275-pound kid from New York. Lou Ferrigno was the largest bodybuilder on the scene. Although he placed third to Arnold and Serge Nubret at the 1975 Mr. Olympia, there were bigger things in store for him. In 1977 as Lou was getting in shape for that year's Mr. Olympia, Hollywood started advertising for a bodybuilder/actor to play the part of the comic book character, The Incredible Hulk. After taking one look at the 6'5", 275-pound Ferrigno, the producers easily made their choice, and before long Lou was center stage in a big Hollywood movie, and later primetime TV series.

The other significant publishing event of the decade was the creation of *MuscleMag International* by British immigrant Robert Kennedy. In 1974 Bob took the plunge and dove right into the madness that was the bodybuilding magazine publishing arena. From slow beginnings (Bob didn't even have a distrbutor lined up for the first issue) *MuscleMag International* has now grown to a monthly readership of over 250,000. This is in addition to *MuscleMag's* book division, Formula One line of supplements and clothing, and their new magazines *Oxygen* and *American Health and Fitness.*

With Arnold retired and Lou Ferrigno hulking out, the Mr. Olympia was up for grabs. The first post-Schwarzenegger winner was his good friend, Franco Columbu. Despite his 5'5" height, Franco packed 180 pounds on his physique, and took the title in 1976. With his dream realized Franco retired and put his energy into his chiropractic business. The Mr. Olympia was once again open to the masses, and Frank Zane emerged. Unlike the massive Schwarzenegger, or the very muscularily dense Columbu, Zane had only 190 pounds on his 5'10" frame, but what a 190 pounds. Frank brought refinement to an art form, and to many he represented the ideal male physique. Frank's Greek-god look reigned for three years, from 1977 to 1979.

Let's now take a look at some of the superstars from bodybuilding's *Pumping Iron* years.

Serge Nubret

In bodybuilding, age equals experience equates to knowledge. Unfortunately, a lot of body-builders, by the time they really know what they're doing, are ready to retire, but not Serge: "The only thing that will stop me from training is my death. I stopped training once for a period of three years. I lost mass and I gained fat. Of course, I was still training other people, so my mind was with them. I shaped them as I would have shaped myself. During that time I never once looked in the mirror. I started again, and I won't quit this time. The older you get, the harder it is to start again."

Many people consider Serge Nubret to be the embodiment of perfection.

Born in Guadeloupe, in the French West Indies, Serge has devoted most of his life to perfecting his body and the results are impressive:

1964 Universe, Pro – NABBA, tall, 2nd
1969 Mr. World – IFBB, tall, 2nd
1970 Mr. Europe _ IFBB, tall, 1st
1972 Olympia – IFBB, 3rd
1973 Olympia – IFBB, 2nd
1974 Olympia – IFBB, heavyweight, 3rd
1975 Olympia – IFBB heavyweight, 2nd
1976 Olympus – WBBG, 2nd
Universe, Pro – NABBA, winner
Universe, Pro – NABBA, tall, 1st
1977 Olympus – WBBG, winner
Universe, Pro – NABBA, 2nd
World Championships – WBBG, winner
1978 Universe, Pro – NABBA, 2nd
1981 Pro World Cup – WABBA, 2nd
1983 World Championships – WABBA, 2nd

Serge was probably just as famous for his training style as his physique.

Together with Arnold, Sergio Oliva, and Lou Ferrigno, Serge was one of the dominant personalities of the 1970s. His brief but memorable appearance in *Pumping Iron*, cemented his place in bodybuilding history. Many people consider Serge to be the embodiment of perfection. While his lower body was never a strong point, his upper still ranks as one of the greatest of all time. Serge had one of the greatest waist/chest differentials ever seen on the Olympia stage, and few bodybuilders looked as good as Serge did just standing there.

"Do not go gentle into that good night. Old age should burn and rave at close of day; rage, rage against the dying of the light."
– Quotation from the poem *Do Not Go Gentle Into That Good Night* by Dylan Thomas

Serge was probably just as famous for his training style as his physique. Take his chest as an example. For most of his competitive career, Serge did just one exercise, the flat barbell press, for 15 to 20 sets. He also liked to be different with regard to diet. While other bodybuilders were eating chicken, fish, and beef, Serge was chowing down on horsemeat!

With the exception of the Mr. Olympia, Serge won every major bodybuilding title. It was only Arnold that kept him from adding that title to his trophy shelf. After his split from the IFBB, Serge went on to compete in numerous rival federations and proved that he could hold his own against the best from any continent.

But the world of bodybuilding wasn't enough for Serge. He became an actor on both sides of the Atlantic:

Film

Le Professional (1981) with Jean-Paul Belmondo
Pumping Iron (1977) with Lou Ferrigno and Arnold Schwarzenegger
Seven Red Berets (a.k.a. Congo Hell and Seven Dirty Devils) (1968) with Ivan Rassimov, Kirk Morris, and Priscilla Drake; a war film directed by Mario Siciliano
Adventures in Bangkok (1965)
Curse of the Black Ruby (a.k.a. Der Fluch des Schwarzen Rubins) (1965) with Thomas Alder and Horst Frank; a spy film directed by Manfred Kohler
Goliath and the Rebel Slave (a.k.a. The Tyrant of Lydia vs. the Son of Hercules) (1963), with Gordon Scott and Ombretta Colli; directed by Mario Caiano
My Son, the Hero (a.k.a. The Titans) (1961)

Television

Salle N°8 (Room Number 8), a 1967-1968 French television series of which 65 episodes were made.
Petit Déjeuner Compris (Breakfast Included), a 1980 French mini-series[1]

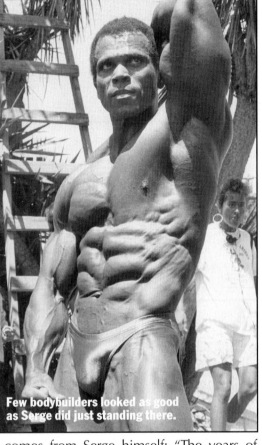

Few bodybuilders looked as good as Serge did just standing there.

Perhaps the best explanation of Serge's success comes from Serge himself: "The years of bodybuilding made me very strong in my mind. It taught me concentration. It taught me that if I believe in myself, I can do anything I want to do."

Truer words were never spoken.

Reference:
1. http://members.tripod.com/~BrianJ1/sergenubret.html

Calves

There's no way you could confuse Serge Nubret with Mike Mentzer after watching Serge train. To quote former *MuscleMag International* writer and photographer, Chris Lund, "Serge Nubret broke every heavy duty rule in the book."

To say Serge Nubret is a product of the high volume style of training is a gross understatement. A typical Nubret routine will see him perform 20, 30, even 40 sets per muscle group. And in this day of bodybuilders becoming famous for their strength, Nubret typically picked a weight that most modern bodybuilders would consider warm-up weight, but developing an ego was not his style. Instead he concentrated on building one of the most proportioned physiques of all time. When one talks of the all-time greats, Serge's name must rank near the top.

Let's look at Serge's training in a bit more detail. We'll start with the one muscle group that was his only true weakness, calves. Like many bodybuilders of African decent, Serge's weak calves were the result of genetics not an unwillingness to train them.

Serge's first calf exercise was the seated calf raise. Serge preferred volume and concentration over intensity. A light to moderate weight was chosen, and then 10 to 12 ultra strict sets were performed. At the top of each rep, Serge made a habit of pausing and squeezing the muscle.

His second calf exercise was the standng calf raise. Once again a moderately heavy weight was selected for 8 to 10 sets of 12 to 15 reps. Watching Serge perform calf raises was a lesson on poetry in motion. No bouncing, jerking, or lobbing the weight up. Every rep, and we mean every rep, was slow and deliberate.

Shoulders

A typical Nubret shoulder workout consisted of three exercises; lying one-arm lateral raise; barbell press behind the head; and upright rows. Unlike most bodybuilders who prefer standing dumbell laterals, Serge performed laterals one arm at a time while lying on his side. He would usually do 15 reps on the first set, and then try to add an additional rep with each set. Serge averaged 8 to 10 sets of lying laterals.

Serge Nubret is one of the enduring legends in the sport.

With his side delts now pre-exhausted, Serge moved on to a compound movement, usually barbell presses behind the head. If there was one exercise that separated Serge from most other bodybuilders it was behind the head presses. Instead of the 200-plus pounds routinely used by today's champs, Serge used, are you ready for it, 70 to 80 pounds max! Today's bodybuilders wouldn't be caught dead using such weight for shoulder presses. For a warmup, sure, but not as the main poundage for most of their sets, yet Serge used such weight, and in the process built one of the greatest sets of delts of all time.

Serge's presses were performed in a non-lockout piston type motion. As was the custom, he banged out 10 to 12 sets with as little rest in between as possible.

Serge performed narrow-grip upright rows to finish his delts. To force the delts to do most of the work and not the traps, Serge grabbed the bar with his hands touching each other. He pulled the bar right up to his chin, and then lowered it down to his thighs. Like side laterals and presses, Serge usually performed 8 to 10 sets of more of upright rows.

Biceps

Along with Sergio Oliva, France's Serge Nubret is one of the enduring legends in the sport. It's not just his physique either as his training routines have garnered their share of attention over the past couple of decades.

Take biceps training for example. Despite trying just about every exercise in the book, Serge eventually settled on one exercise to hit his upper arms – seated dumbell curls. No fancy machines, cables, or advanced training techniques, just 10 to 15 sets of 12 to 18 reps of good old fashioned dumbells.

Many have countered that if your wrist measurement is less than 8 to 10 inches, then building large muscular arms is darn near impossible. They also argue that you need more than one exercise to adequately train a muscle group. Well it seems that Serge broke two fundamental principles as his wrists are no more than seven inches, and he did just one exercise for his biceps. Yet those guns of his not only measured a solid 20 inches in their prime, but still hover around the same mark today. Remarkable when you consider that Serge is over 60 years of age.

> **"And here's the scoop, although Serge has tried a variety of biceps exercises in his long career, he currently only performs a single exercise for each biceps workout ... and that one exercise is the seated dumbell concentration curl."**
>
> – Robert Kennedy, *MuscleMag International* founder and executive editor commenting on Serge Nubret's biceps training.

Mike Katz

Chest

For those who've seen the 1977 documentary, *Pumping Iron,* one of the subplots was the rivalry between Ken Waller and Mike Katz. To psyche big Mike out, Ken stole Mike's favorite T-shirt. Whether such a little act of thievery would have changed the outcome of the contest (Ken Waller won the 1975 Mr. Universe), we'll never know, but there's no denying that Ken knew he'd need to pull every trick in the book if he hoped to defeat the 240-pound Katz.

When you list off the largest muscular chests of all time, Mike Katz is at the top. While he never quite had Arnold's degree of chest muscle development, his much larger rib cage gave Mike a slightly larger chest measurement. Mike was probably the first bodybuilder to reach the 60-inch barrier. But there's a downside to everything and Mike's oversized chest was it. Despite busting his ass at the squat rack and leg press while performing curl after curl, Mike never did get his limbs up to the same level as his chest.

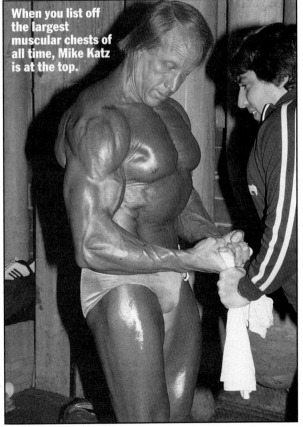

When you list off the largest muscular chests of all time, Mike Katz is at the top.

The Mr. Universe title forever remained just out of his reach.

As you might expect, Mike started his chest workout with that king of pec builders, flat barbell bench presses. As with most bodybuilders of his generation, Mike went to town on this exercise, doing 8 to 10 sets in total. He averaged 6 to 8 reps per set, but he occasionally did doubles and triples. He felt that this exercise more than any other made his chest what it was. He says they are an absolute must for beginners.

Mikes second exercise was an incline movement, usually incline dumbell presses. He would do one or two warm-up sets and then bang out five quality sets of 6 to 8 reps.

To finish off, the big fella did 5 supersets of flat bench flyes and parallel bar dips. As these were his finishing movements, Mike used slightly less weight and increased the rep range to 8 to 10.

Dennis Tinerino

Dennis Tinerino

Dennis Tinerino was born in Brooklyn, New York, in 1945. He is another one of the sports all-time greats, and with the exception of the Mr. Olympia, has won every major bodybuilding title (he won the Mr. Universe title an incredible four times). During his long career, Dennis established a reputation for his outstanding muscularity, incredible abdominals, and ultra-wide shoulders.

1965	Junior Mr. America – AAU, 3rd
	Junior Mr. USA – AAU, winner
	Mr. America – AAU, 9th
	Mr. North America – AAU, winner
	Mr. USA – AAU, 2nd
	Mr. USA – AAU, most muscular, 3rd
	Teen Mr. America – AAU, overall winner
1966	Junior Mr. America – AAU, 6th
	Mr. America – AAU, 6th
	Mr. America – AAU, most muscular, 3rd
	Mr. USA – AAU, winner
	Mr. USA – AAU, most muscular, 1st
1967	Junior Mr. America – AAU, winner
	Junior Mr. America – AAU, most muscular, 1st
	Mr. America – AAU, winner
	Mr. America – AAU, most muscular, 1st
	Universe – NABBA, tall, 2nd
1968	Universe – NABBA, overall winner
	Universe – NABBA, tall, 1st
1969	Universe – Pro NABBA, tall, 2nd
1970	Pro Mr. America – WBBG, 2nd
1971	World Championships – WBBG, 3rd
1972	Universe – Pro NABBA, tall, 1st
1973	Universe – Pro NABBA, tall, 1st

1975   World Pro Championships – IFBB, overall winner
        World Pro Championships – IFBB, heavyweight, 1st
1977   Olympia – IFBB, 6th
        Olympia – IFBB, tall, 3rd
1978   Natural America, Professional, 1st
        Night of Champions – IFBB, 6th
        Olympia – IFBB, 9th
        Olympia – IFBB, heavyweight, 4th
1979   Best in the World – IFBB, Professional, 4th
        Canada Diamond Pro Cup – IFBB, 4th
        Canada Pro Cup – IFBB, 6th
        Grand Prix Pennsylvania – IFBB, 4th
        Grand Prix Vancouver – IFBB, 4th
        Olympia – IFBB, heavyweight, 2nd
1980   Canada Pro Cup – IFBB, 3rd
        Olympia, – IFBB, 8th
1981   Grand Prix World Cup – IFBB, 5th
        Olympia – IFBB, 7th
        Professional World Cup – IFBB, 5th
        Universe – Pro, IFBB, overall winner
        World Pro Championships – IFBB, winner
1982   Olympia – IFBB, 14th

Legs

Dennis established a reputation for his outstanding muscularity, incredible abdominals, and ultra-wide shoulders.

It's not surprising that like most hardcore body-builders, Dennis started his leg workouts with squats. With a six-inch belt around his waist, he started with 135 pounds on the bar and worked up to 350 pounds. Dennis did 5 sets in this pyramid fashion, and then reduced the weight for an additional 2 sets. The reps on all his sets were between 6 and 8 and he squatted down until his thighs were parallel with the floor.

Next up it was leg extensions on the Nautilus machine. Dennis typically did 4 sets of 8 to 10 reps. He did leg extensions in a very slow fashion, trying to squeeze his thighs on each rep.

After leg extensions, Dennis hit his hamstrings with lying leg curls on the Nautilus machine. As with leg extensions, style and concentration was much more important than weight. He typically did 4 to 5 sets of 8 to 10 reps of lying leg curls.

We should add that Dennis performed straight sets for most of his training, terminating each set just short of positive failure.

"As we entered the gym floor area, Dennis stood out like a 'sore thumb' amongst the rest of the body-builders working out. Wearing a Vic Tanny training T-shirt, Dennis looked literally as big as a house."

– Chris Lund, former *MuscleMag International* writer and photographer describing his first impressions of Dennis Tinerino.

Roy Callender

A native of Barbados, Roy immigrated to Canada, and spent most of his competitive career operating out of Montreal. During the '70s and early '80s, he was one of the most massive bodybuilders on the pro circuit. Roy was famous for his high volume training, and routinely did 40 sets or more for each muscle group. After retiring, he moved to the province of Newfoundland, where he operated a gym for a number of years. Roy is currently living in the Barbados. Here's Roy's impressive competitive record:

1967   Universe – NABBA, medium, 2nd
1968   Universe – IFBB, 5th
1969   Universe – NABBA, medium, 2nd
1970   Mr. World – IFBB, medium, 2nd
1971   Universe – NABBA, medium, 2nd
1977   Canadian Championships – IFBB, overall winner
       Canadian Championships – IFBB, medium, 1st
       Mr. International – IFBB, heavyweight, 1st
       Universe – IFBB, middleweight, 1st
1978   Night of Champions – IFBB, 2nd
       Olympia – IFBB, 3rd
       Olympia – IFBB, heavyweight, 2nd
       Professional World Cup – IFBB, 3rd
       Universe – Pro IFBB, overall winner
1979   Best in the World – IFBB, Professional, 2nd
       Canada Diamond Pro Cup – IFBB, winner
       Canada Pro Cup – IFBB
       Grand Prix Pennsylvania – IFBB, 2nd
       Grand Prix Vancouver – IFBB, winner
       Olympia – IFBB, heavyweight, 4th
       Pittsburgh Pro Invitational   – IFBB, 4th
       Southern Pro Cup – IFBB, 6th
       Universe – Pro IFBB, overall winner
       World Pro Championships – IFBB, winner
1980   Night of Champions – IFBB, 3rd
       Olympia – IFBB, 7th
       Pittsburgh Pro Invitational – IFBB, 3rd
1981   Grand Prix California – IFBB, 2nd
       Grand Prix Louisiana – IFBB, 3rd
       Grand Prix Washington – IFBB, 2nd
       Olympia – IFBB, 4th
1982   World Pro Championships – IFBB, 5th
1984   Olympia – IFBB, 5th
1987   Grand Prix Germany[2] – IFBB, 7th
       Night of Champions – IFBB
       World Pro Championships – IFBB, 12th

"Some days I need to train longer before my muscles tell me they've gotten what they need, while on other days they can be optimally worked in less time."

– Roy Callender, Pro Mr. Universe, commenting on how he listens to his body with regards to training time in the gym.

Roy Callender wasn't blessed with the greatest genetics for building calves. But that didn't stop him from winning both the amateur and professional Mr. Universe titles.

Calves

Like many bodybuilders of African-American heritage, Roy Callender wasn't blessed with the greatest genetics for building calves. But that didn't stop him from winning both the amateur and professional Mr. Universe titles. Roy inherited what is commonly called "high calves." This means he found it difficult to build mass in the lower calf region. The result was that his calves were consistently being over-shadowed by his massive thighs.

Recognizing that his future in bodybuilding depended on trying to balance out his legs, Roy started using the priority principle. This meant training his calves first in his workouts when he was fresh, and beginning his calf training with seated calf raises to hit the weaker soleus region. After seated calves, Roy moved on to standing calf raises and then finished with toe presses on a 45-degree leg press machine.

Roy typically did sets in the 8 to 10 rep range for his calves. As for the total number of sets, who knows! Roy was famous for spending hour after hour in the gym during his workouts. A typical calf workout lasted one to two hours depending on how he felt. He would perform set after set for his calves until he felt they had enough. This easily worked out to 40 sets or more. Not for the faint of heart we assure you, but it worked for Roy.

Lou was athletic as a child and a natural bodybuilder.

Lou Ferrigno – The Incredible Hulk

Lou Ferrigno is one of the true legends in the sport of bodybuilding, and next to Arnold Schwarzenegger, its greatest spokesman. Lou was born in Brooklyn, New York in 1951. He was athletic as a child and a natural bodybuilder. In a time when Dave Draper and Arnold were the giants of the sport at 6'1" and 230 to 240 pounds, Lou's 6'5", 270 pounds literally dwarfed everyone else on the stage. Lou first came to prominence by winning the 1973 Mr. America, and just a few months later he was Mr. Universe.

Lou first got to compete against his idol, Arnold, at the 1974 Mr. Olympia. Arnold won the show but the stage was set for the 1975 showdown in South Africa. That show became immortalized in the 1977 documentary, *Pumping Iron*, which was based on the best-selling book of the same name. Together with Arnold, Franco, Mike Katz, Ken Waller, Robby Robinson, and Serge Nubret, Lou helped put bodybuilding on the map and intro-duce the sport to the mainstream public. Here's Lou's impressive competitive record:

1971 New Jersey Open Hercules – 22nd place [3]
Teen Mr. America – AAU, 4th
Teen Mr. America – AAU, most muscular, 5th
Teen Mr. America – WBBG, winner
1972 WBBG Mr. America – 2nd place [3]
Universe – NABBA, tall, 2nd
1973 Mr. America – IFBB, overall winner
Universe – IFBB, overall winner
Universe – IFBB, tall, 1st
1974 Mr. International – IFBB, overall winner
Mr. International – IFBB, tall, 1st
Olympia – IFBB, heavyweight, 2nd
Universe – IFBB, overall winner
Universe – IFBB, tall, 1st
1975 Olympia – IFBB, heavyweight, 3rd
1976 ABC Superstars Competition – 4th place
Tried out and played for the Toronto Argonauts (Canadian Football League) [3]
1977 World's Strongest Man Competition – 4th place [3]

Lou helped put bodybuilding on the map and introduce the sport to the mainstream public.

One should be aware of just how strong Lou really is: "My max for bench press was 560 lbs. and dead-lift was 850 lbs. and squat was 675 lbs. In the World's Strongest Man competition back in 1977, I lifted a car two feet off of the ground that totaled 2,600 lbs, which was a record for a professional bodybuilder."[4]

Lou returned to competitive bodybuilding in 1992 (at 40 years of age!) after a 17-year absence.

1992 Olympia – IFBB, 12th
1993 Olympia – IFBB, 10th
1994 Olympia – Masters, IFBB, 2nd[1]

When Lou hasn't been on stage, he's busy in front of the camera. His most famous role was of course the *Incredible Hulk* TV series. A role that was challenging just getting made up! When asked how long it took, Lou answered: "About 3 hours. They first had to apply appliances to the forehead along with a special grease green makeup which takes about one and a half hours. Then, they apply several coats of pancake makeup on the body, which takes about one hour. Then the wig was applied with the clothes as well. The eye contacts were applied on the set prior to shooting since I was only able to wear them for 15 minutes at a time."[4]

Images of the green-eyed Hulk throwing his trademark hissy fits are even now shooting out across our galaxy. One can only imagine the look on some poor alien's face the first time he sees the Hulk snarling back from the alien's monitor! We won't have any trouble with those guys! Unless it's a female alien. Women make up the vast majority of Hulk fans. Perhaps first contact might happen at a Lou Ferrigno book signing.

What a career this actor has had:
Pumping Iron (1977) … himself
The Return of the Incredible Hulk (1977) (TV) … the Hulk
The Incredible Hulk (1977) (TV) … the Hulk
The Incredible Hulk (1978) TV series … the Incredible Hulk
(1978) playing Carl Molino in episode *King of the Beach* (episode #4.9) 2/6/1981
Bride of the Incredible Hulk [a]1979) (TV) … the Hulk
Mister Rogers' Neighborhood playing himself 1979
Saturn Awards (1981) (TV)
(1981) playing himself in episode *The Winner* (episode #4.11) 12/19/1984
Matt Houston
(1981) playing Six in episode *Trauma* (episode #3.2) 9/28/1983
The Fall Guy
(1981) playing himself in episode *License to Kill* (episode #1.6) 1/13/1982
The Incredible Hulk
(1982) playing Steve Ott in episode *Blood Ties* (episode #2.19) 3/2/1984
The Fall Guy
Hercules (1983) … Hercules
The Seven Magnificent Gladiators (1983)
Trauma Center (1983) TV series … John Six
Night Court (1984) playing The Klondike Butcher in episode Battling Bailiff (episode 2.17)
The Adventures of Hercules (1985)
The Fall Guy (1985)
Desert Warrior (1988) … Zerak
The Incredible Hulk Returns (1988) (TV) … the Hulk
All's Fair (1989) … Klaus
Cage (1989/I) … Billy Thomas
Sinbad of the Seven Seas (1989)
The Trial of the Incredible Hulk (1989) (TV) – the Hulk
Liberty & Bash (1990) … Bash
The Death of the Incredible Hulk (1990) (TV) … the Hulk
Extralarge: Jo-Jo (1991) (TV) … Goodwin
Hangfire (1991) … Smitty
The Naked Truth (1992)
Hell Comes to Frogtown II (1993)
And God Spoke (1993)
Frogtown II (1993) … Ranger John Jones
Cage II (1994) … Billy
The Misery Brothers (1995) … Butler
The Incredible Hulk (1996) TV series (voice) … Hulk
Black Scorpion (1998) TV series … Slave Master

The Godson (1998) … Bugsy/Alice
Conan (1998) in episode The Three Virgins (episode #1.8)
G vs E (1999) playing himself in episode Sunday Night Evil (episode #1.9) 10/10/1999
Ping! (2000) … Dog Catcher[2]
You can visit his Web site at www.louferrigno.com, or reach by mail at: Lou Ferrigno, P.O. Box 1671, Santa Monica, CA 90406 or 621 17th St., Santa Monica, CA 90402. (3)

References:

1. http://musclememory.com/cgi-bin/serch?name=Lou+Ferrigno&gender=M
2. http://us.imdb.com/Name?Ferrigno,+Lou
3. http://members.tripod.com/~bugaev/faq.html
4. http://www.louferrigno.com/faq.html
5. http://members.tripod.com/~bugaev/criticssay.html

Lou Ferrigno as Hercules.

"Training was very basic because of the lack of equipment but usually I did about 20 to 25 sets per bodypart, three times per week. My workouts included a lot of supersets and trisets."

– Lou Ferrigno, star of *Hercules* and *The Incredible Hulk*, describing his workouts while filming in Italy.

Back

It's not surprising that big Lou favored doing supersets and trisets in his workouts. After all two of his heroes were Arnold and Sergio Oliva, both of whom made exercise combinations a major part of their workouts.

During a typical back workout, Lou would start with a superset of bent-over barbell rows on the Smith machine and parallel bar pulldowns.

Lou would start the rows by positioning a flat bench underneath the barbell. With a very wide grip he would then pull the bar up to his lower rib cage, and then lower. Lou did the reps very fast and completed 12 to 15 in nonstop fashion. Resting only as long as it took to reach the pulldown machine, Lou would grab the parallel grip bar and bring it down to his upper chest. Once again it was about 15 fast reps.

Returning to the Smith machine Lou added some more weight to the bar and did another set of bent-over rows. Then it was back to the pulldown machine. Lou would continue alternating this way for 5 supersets of both exercises. The poundages were increased on every set until he was forced to do the last few reps on the last set in a loose, heaving style.

To finish off his lats, Lou performed wide-grip behind-the-head pulldowns. Given his size, Lou needed to grab the bar almost on the ends to have what he would call a wide grip. Lou performed the reps from an arms-locked position to having the bar touch the base of his neck. Lou would normally do 5 sets of pulldowns, adding weight with each set.

Biceps

Lou trained biceps immediately after back, and his first exercise was that old stand-by, standing barbell curls. Lou would typically do 5 sets of barbell curls, starting with 90 pounds and working up to 130 pounds. This may not seem like a lot of weight for a guy weighing 280-plus, but Lou rested less than 30 seconds between each set. On other days he might throw 200 or more pounds on the bar and rest a couple of minutes between sets. The strength was there if he needed it, but it all depended on his goals.

Lou's second and third biceps exercises were a superset of seated alternate dumbell curls with standing preacher curls. Again weight was sacrificed for speed, and he typically did 5 sets of such supersets, averaging 12 to 15 reps on each set.

During the 1970s Lou tipped the scales at 260 pounds at a height of 6' 5.

Triceps

Lou typically started his triceps training with 5 sets of lying barbell extensions super-setted wth triceps pushdowns on the lat pulldown machine. Lou's third triceps exercise was a rather unique movement where he lies down on the gym floor and grabs a straight bar connected to a low pulley machine located behind his head. From here he pushed the bar downward towards his legs until he reaches the full arms locked out position.

Chest

By just about any standard you use, Lou Ferrigno is one of bodybuilding's biggest stars. And we mean big! During the 1970s he tipped the scales at 260 pounds at a height of 6' 5. At his best, the 1992 and 1993 Mr. Olympias, big Lou showed up on stage weighing over 300 pounds.

With the possible exception of Arnold Schwarzenegger, no other bodybuilder was as famous for his chest development as Lou Ferrigno was. Television's Incredible Hulk stretched the tape measure to nearly 60 inches with a full pump (56 inches cold). This measurement was not based on rumor either. It was done in front of about 50 million people on an episode of the

Mike Douglas show during the late 1970s. Mike brought out a tape measure to check Lou's frame out and came up with a relaxed chest measurement of 56 inches (his arms were over 22 inches as well). With an extra 40 pounds for the two Mr. Olympias in the early '90s, Lou's chest must have gone over the 60-inch mark.

Lou Ferrigno is one of the true legends in the sport of bodybuilding,

Lou is first to admit that he was not born with a big chest. He had to work very hard to bring it up to the level of the rest of his physique with his long torso and arms.

Lou was lucky in that early on he received some good advice on rib cage expansion. While you are in your teen years the ligaments and cartilage connecting the ribs to the sternum are soft and pliable. With proper training it is possible to stretch them slightly and expand the rib cage. And the bigger the rib cage the bigger the foundation on which to build the pectoral muscles.

Armed with this knowledge Lou embarked on a program of cross bench dumbell pullovers supersetted with breathing squats. The pullovers provided direct stress on the rib cage ligaments, while the deep squats inflated the lungs and expanded things from the inside out so to speak. Lou typically did five such supersets for 12 to 20 reps.

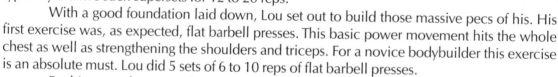

With a good foundation laid down, Lou set out to build those massive pecs of his. His first exercise was, as expected, flat barbell presses. This basic power movement hits the whole chest as well as strengthening the shoulders and triceps. For a novice bodybuilder this exercise is an absolute must. Lou did 5 sets of 6 to 10 reps of flat barbell presses.

For his second exercise the big guy moved on to the incline barbell press. Occasionally he substituted dumbells, but for pure mass he found he got more out of the barbell version. Incline presses pack slabs of meat on the upper chest as well as build the all-important pec delt tie-ins, the region where the front delts meet the upper chest muscles. Again Lou did 5 sets of 6 to 10 reps.

To target the lower and outer chest, Lou did 5 sets of decline presses. Again he sometimes used dumbells, but the barbell version was his preference. As with all his barbell chest exercises, Lou used a slightly wider than shoulder-width grip.

With these three basic mass builders completed, Lou moved on to his shaping movements. He usually started with flat dumbell flyes. As this was more for refinement than pure size, Lou kept the reps slightly higher, 10 to 12 per set. The key to flyes, says Lou, is to do the exercise in a hugging type motion. As soon as you start pushing vertically, the front shoulders come into play. But if you keep a constant angle at the elbows and hug up and inwards, it's nearly all chest. Lou did 5 sets of flat dumbell flyes.

To finish off his chest training, especially during the precontest season, Lou would superset 3 sets of dumbell pullovers with cable crossovers. Lou kept the reps high, 15 per set, and did them in a very slow and controlled manner.

As a final comment, Lou frequently employed forced reps in his chest training, but his partner only provided enough upward force to help Lou complete two or three reps. He witnessed too many young bodybuilders abusing forced reps over his many years of training. You should only need help on the last couple of reps. If your training partner has to start helping you from the very beginning you are using way too much weight.

Tony Pearson

Persistance paid off for Tony Pearson.

Tony is probably the only bodybuilder who has done shows in virtually every major bodybuilding organization, including the AAU, NABBA, WABBA, IFBB and WBF. And yet for all the accomplishments in his long and successful career, he is often the forgotten man in bodybuilding. He's kind of like the Rodney Dangerfield of bodybuilding in that he doesn't get the respect he deserves.

Tony is a truly cosmopolitan man. He lived in France for months training with Serge Nubret, then Germany for a year, then another year in Spain.

This world traveler was born in Memphis, Tennessee, in 1957. He grew up in Memphis, and then at the age of 14 he went to live with an aunt in St. Louis. It was in high school that Tony was introduced to bodybuilding. "I was wrestling on my school's wrestling team, and one of my coaches asked me if I wanted to go with him to a gym, so I said sure. He took me to Turner's gym for the first time and I was in seventh heaven. I worked out for about three hours, and then George Snyder came over to me and said, 'Hey, you're doin' everything wrong. Come into my office. I'm gonna train you.' He trained me for about six months. Then I got out of high school and went to LA right after that." The year was 1976, and Tony was 18. He was soon competing with the best, and kicking ass!

1977   Junior Mr. USA – AAU, short, 3rd
1978   Junior Mr. America – AAU, overall winner
          Junior Mr. America – AAU, medium, 1st
          Junior Mr. USA – AAU, overall winner
          Junior Mr. USA – AAU, medium, 1st
          Mr. America – AAU, overall winner
          Mr. America – AAU, medium, 1st
          World Championships – WBBG, winner
1979   Olympus – WBBG, winner
          Universe – NABBA, medium, 2nd
          World Championships – WABBA, overall winner
          World Championships – WABBA, medium, 1st
          World Championships – WBBG, winner

1980   Universe – Pro, NABBA, winner
        World Championships – WABBA, Professional, 3rd
1981   Canada Pro Cup – IFBB, 4th
        Grand Prix Belgium – IFBB, 6th
        Grand Prix Wales – IFBB, 5th
        Pro World Cup – WABBA, 7th
        World Pro Championships – IFBB, 3rd
1982   Night of Champions – IFBB, 6th
        World Pro Championships – IFBB, 4th
1983   Grand Prix Denver – IFBB, winner
        Grand Prix England – IFBB, 4th
        Grand Prix Las Vegas – IFBB, 6th
        Grand Prix Portland – IFBB, 2nd
        Grand Prix Sweden – IFBB, 6th
        Grand Prix Switzerland – IFBB, 6th
        World Pro Championships – IFBB, 8th
1984   Canada Pro Cup – IFBB, 3rd
        Olympia – IFBB, 12th
        World Grand Prix – 3rd
1985   Night of Champions – IFBB, 9th
        Olympia – IFBB, 12th
1986   Los Angeles Pro Championships – IFBB, 5th
        Night of Champions – IFBB, 4th
        World Pro Championships – IFBB, 9th
1987   Night of Champions – IFBB
        World Pro Championships – IFBB, 8th
1988   Grand Prix US Pro – IFBB, 6th
        Niagara Falls Pro Invitational – IFBB, 5th
        Night of Champions – IFBB, 8th
        World Pro Championships – IFBB, 8th
1989   Grand Prix France – IFBB, 11th
        Grand Prix Germany – IFBB, 9th
        Grand Prix Spain[2] – IFBB, 9th
        Grand Prix Spain – IFBB, 9th
        Grand Prix Sweden – IFBB, 11th
1990   Arnold Classic – IFBB, 6th
        Houston Pro Invitational – IFBB, 6th
        Ironman Pro Invitational – IFBB, 8th
1991   WBF Grand Prix – WBF, 11th
1993   Chicago Pro Invitational – IFBB, 13th
        Night of Champions – IFBB
        Pittsburgh Pro Invitational – IFBB, 16th
1994   Ironman Pro Invitational – IFBB, 14th
        Ironman Pro Invitational – IFBB, 15th
        San Jose Pro Invitational – IFBB, 16th

What words of wisdom does Tony have for his fans?

Focus on your dreams and work hard.
— Tony Pearson

"I would like to say thank you for all the support. Whatever part of the world I'm in, people recognize me, and its been really nice. It's what keeps me going because, like everyone, I have hard weeks and months, and when someone comes up to me and says, 'Hey man, you've been my favorite bodybuilder your whole career,' or 'I started bodybuilding because of you,' that really motivates me. It's very gratifying to hear that kind of stuff."

"For all the young guys coming into the sport I'll say this: Set your goals and don't let anything or anybody stop you. Don't let anything get in your way. Just focus on your dreams and work hard. Things come to those who are patient."

Arms

Tony trained triceps and biceps during the same session with triceps receiving more work because of their larger size. A typical triceps workout started with 6 sets of triceps pushdowns. For his first warm-up set, Tony used about 50 percent of the weight he would use on his heaviest set. After doing 15 to 20 reps on the first set, he would up the weight and thrash out 5 sets of 10 rep, with as little cheating as possible.

> **"I constantly push myself in the gym, forcing the reps out, but it's me that stays in command physically and mentally throughout the set."**
>
> – Tony Pearson,
> 1978 Mr. America

For his second exercise, Tony replaced the straight bar with a rope and did 4 sets of 15 reps of rope pulley pushdowns. He found that by flaring the hands out at the bottom of the movement he could throw a little extra tension on the outer head of his triceps.

To finish his triceps, Tony usually did a one-arm isolation movement like cable pushdowns. Again he averaged 4 sets of 12 to 15 reps per set.

Even with all the accomplishments in Tony's long and successful career, he is often the forgotten man in bodybuildng. He does not get the respect he deserves.

"There have always been bodybuilders with freaky bodyparts that amaze and bedazzle the onlooker. Arnold Schwarzenegger's biceps, Tom Platz's thighs, and Mike Matarazzo's calves are good examples. The development of those muscles on these particular men in their prime defies belief. And then there are Tony Pearson's lats. In bodybuilding where big lats are commonplace, Tony's lat development stands out among the rest. You might say there are lats ... and big lats ... and then there are Pearson's lats. Wide as condor wings, thick as uncut lumber."

– Greg Zulak, *MuscleMag International* contributor commenting on the super-sized wings of Mr. America Tony Pearson.

To start his biceps training, Tony usually did 6 sets of dumbell curls. For variety he alternated between curling the dumbells together, and curling them in an alternate fashion.

After dumbells Tony moved on to barbell preacher curls. During a typical workout Tony would do 4 sets of 12 reps.

To complete his arm session, Tony did 3 sets of 10 to 15 reps of reverse barbell curls. This exercise not only hits the biceps, but also develops the brachialis muscle that joins the forearm to the upper arm. Bodybuilders have been relying on this exercise for years to fill the gap between the forearms and biceps. To lessen the stress on his wrist, Tony did reverse curls using an EZ-curl bar.

Tony found the secret to great back development was using moderate poundages and totally isolating the muscle with proper form.

Back

Tony Pearson is another example of a bodybuilder who stayed true to his sport. While others went into the gym and become slaves of the weight, Tony became its master. This is surprising, as you'd think from looking at his back thickness that he used a ton of weight during his workouts. But you'd be wrong. Although he did train heavy at one time, he eventually found that the secret to great back development was using moderate poundages and totally isolating the muscle with proper form.

One person Tony learned a great deal from was Robby Robinson. During the early 1980s the two could be seen working out together at Gold's Gym in California. Even though by this time he had won both the Mr. America and Mr. Universe titles, Tony was humble enough to listen to Robby explain how to do T-bar and barbell rows correctly. Instead of pulling with the arms, shoulders, and lower back, Robby showed Tony how to isolate his lats more effectively.

Despite having retired from competitive bodybuilding, Tony continues to train as if the Mr. Universe was a couple of weeks away. He usually starts his back workout with chins. This was his sole back exercise for the first year of his training. He'd do 10 sets three times per week, alternating between front and rear. Nowadays he does 3 or 4 sets of each using a thumbless grip to reduce the amount of biceps involvement.

After chins, Tony moves on to barbell rows, doing them the way Robby Robinson taught him nearly twenty years ago, lower back slightly arched, knees bent, torso just short of parallel with the floor.

After barbell rows Tony moves on to the other primary thickening movement, T-bar rows. Again he keeps the knees bent, back arched, and torso nearly parallel. He also concentrates on pulling with his lats and not his arms.

As his final rowing movement Tony will do 4 sets of one-arm dumbell rows. To finish off his back workout, Tony moves onto deadlifts. He'll pyramid up in weight doing 4 sets of 10 reps.

From the previous you'll notice that Tony does proportionally more rowing movements than chns or pulldown. This is because he has all the width he needs in his lats and therefore does the rows to add thickness.

For variety Tony sometimes drops the chins in favor of pulldowns, and likewise replaces one-arm rows with seated cable rows, but the core of his back workout is the barbell and T-bar rows.

Bill Grant

Bill is another member of what has become known as the "original Gold's Gym gang." Bill never quite made it to superstar status, but with his near-perfect arms and abs, served as an inspiration to millions. Bill won both the Mr. America and Mr. World titles, and had a respectable career on the pro circuit during the '70s and '80s.

Bill Grant's near-perfect arms and abs served as an inspiration to millions.

Today Bill is the worldwide official spokesperson for the official Arnold Schwarzenegger Web site (www.schwarzenegger.com) and works directly with Schwarzenegger/Lorimer Productions as host, announcer and interviewer for the site. He also works with VKT and Virtual Martial Arts bringing fitness training to the martial arts community through sponsorship of the Martial Arts Festival at the Arnold Fitness Weekend.

Here's Bill's record:

1967	Mr. USA – AAU, 10th
1968	Mr. America – AAU, 17th
	Mr. USA – AAU
1970	Junior Mr. America – AAU, 7th
	Junior Mr. America – AAU, most muscular, 3rd
	Mr. America – AAU, 12th
	Mr. America – AAU, most muscular, 7th
1971	Pro Mr. America – WBBG, 2nd
1972	Pro Mr. America – WBBG, winner
	Universe – NABBA, medium, 3rd
1973	Mr. International – IFBB, medium, 2nd
1974	Mr. International – IFBB, medium, 1st
	Mr. World – IFBB, overall winner

1976   Olympia – IFBB, lightweight, 4th
1977   Olympia – IFBB, 8th
        Olympia – IFBB, short, 5th
        World Championships – WABBA, Professional, 3rd
1978   Night of Champions – IFBB, 3rd
        Olympia – IFBB, lightweight, 7th
        Professional World Cup – IFBB, 6th
1979   Canada Diamond Pro Cup – IFBB, 6th
        Canada Pro Cup – IFBB
        Grand Prix Pennsylvania – IFBB
        Grand Prix Vancouver – IFBB
        Night of Champions – IFBB, 5th
        Pittsburgh Pro Invitational – IFBB, 7th
        Southern Pro Cup – IFBB, 8th
1980   Canada Pro Cup – IFBB, 5th
        Night of Champions – IFBB, 7th
1981   Grand Prix Belgium – IFBB, 7th
        Grand Prix California – IFBB
        Grand Prix Wales – IFBB, 6th
        Grand Prix World Cup – IFBB
        Professional World Cup – IFBB
1982   Grand Prix Belgium – IFBB, 7th
        Grand Prix Sweden – IFBB, 8th
1983   Grand Prix Las Vegas – IFBB, 7th
1984   Canada Pro Cup – IFBB, 7th
        Olympia – IFBB, 15th
        World Grand Prix – 7th
        World Pro Championships – IFBB, 3rd
1985   Night of Champions – IFBB, 10th
1986   Night of Champions – IFBB, 9th
1988   Chicago Pro Invitational – IFBB, 13th
        Night of Champions – IFBB, 13th
1994   Olympia – Masters, IFBB, 8th

Bill Grant

Chest and Shoulders

Chest
1. Flat barbell bench presses – 4 sets of 12 to 15 reps
2. Incline barbell presses – 4 sets of 12 to 15 reps
3. Flat dumbell flyes – 4 sets of 12 to 15 reps
4. Dumbell pullovers – 4 sets of 12 to 15 reps

Shoulders
1. Universal shoulder presses – 4 sets of 12 to 15 reps
2. Side dumbell laterals – 4 sets of 12 to 15 reps
3. Bent-over dumbell laterals – 4 sets of 12 to 15 reps
4. Shoulder shrugs – 4 sets of 12 to 15 reps

Kal Szkalak

Kalman Szkalak was born in Budapest, Hungary, in 1953. Following the Hungarian Revolution, Kal, his parents, a younger sister and older brother, slipped over the border in Austria and hopped on a cargo plane bound for New Jersey. With little money to their name, life was tough for the Szkalak's, but Kal's father was very resourceful, and by the time Kal graduated from high school, his father was an engineer.

Kal first started bodybuilding to increase leg and arm strength for his swimming, but his physique was soon drawing attention from both sexes. With friends urging him on, Kal entered his first bodybuilding contest, and promptly won the 1973 Mr. Delaware contest. He followed this up with the 1976 Mr. California, and 1976 Mr. America. By 1977 he was Mr. Universe. Only the Mr. Olympia remained out of his grasp. Kal placed fifth at the 1978 Mr. Olympia, and soon left the IFBB for the rival WABBA and NABBA federations. Kal retired in 1982, but in many respects his massive physique gave audiences a preview of what the future of competitive bodybuilding would look like. Let's look at his competitive career:

Kal Szkalak had shoulders that intimidated most other competitors.

1976	Mr. America – AAU, winner
	Mr. America – AAU, most muscular, 2nd
	Mr. America – AAU, tall, 1st
	Mr. California – AAU, winner
1977	Mr. USA – IFBB, overall winner
	Mr. USA – IFBB, heavyweight, 1st
	Universe – IFBB, heavyweight, 1st
1978	Olympia – IFBB, 5th
	Olympia – IFBB, heavyweight, 3rd
1981	Pro World Cup – WABBA, 6th
1982	Universe – Pro, NABBA, 2nd

Shoulders

When he competed regularly back in the late '70s and early '80s, Kal Szkalak was the Paul Dillett and Kevin Levrone of his day. That is, a set of shoulders that reduced most other competitors to little bundles of quivering terror. It wasn't just their size that intimidated other competitors, but also their separation and detail. Each shoulder head was clearly separated from the other two, and criss-crossed with striations and veins.

Kal usually started his shoulder workouts with his favorite mass builder, standing barbell presses. Kal came from the old school where heavy barbell work was king, and dumbells were considered only for finishing movements.

Kal would stand with his feet shoulder width apart and hold the bar at neck level. He'd then press the bar up to just short of lockout. He found this not only put less stress on his elbows but also kept his delts under tension throughout the full set. Kal would start with 135 pounds for one or two warm up sets, and then work up to 230 pounds for 4 sets of 8 reps. If it was one of those days, Kal would have a training partner help him complete the last few reps in forced rep fashion.

Kal's second shoulder exercise was often EZ-bar upright rows. Kal would grab the bar on the inner bend and do 4 sets of 12 to 15 reps. Unlike heavy presses, Kal preferred to use moderate weight on uprights for slightly higher reps.

Next up were heavy side laterals. By heavy we mean 60-pound dumbells for 4 sets of 8 reps. Kal would keep a slight bend in his elbow and raise the dumbells to just past the parallel position.

To finish those amazing delts of his, Kal did 4 sets of seated, bent-over lateral raises. Kal found that to really isolate the rear delt heads, he had to pause and squeeze at the top of the movement before lowering the dumbells back down.

Kal's massive physique gave audiences a preview of what the future of competitive bodybuilding would look like.

Arms

There must be something to supersetting biceps and triceps, as four of the largest arms in bodybuilding history (Arnold, Sergio Oliva, Albert Beckles, and Kal) all belonged to men who did just that.

Kal trained his arms using 4 sets of four exercises each for biceps and triceps. This means 16 sets each for biceps and triceps, or put another way, 32 sets in total.

The first thing Kal did was one light warmup set of each exercise. Then he got down to business. Kal's first superset was standing barbell curls and pulley pushdowns. Kal did barbell curls the same way Arnold did them, arms tucked to his sides but with a wider than shoulder-width grip. To give you an idea of Kal's strength, he often worked up to 190 to 220 pounds for 8 reps on barbell curls.

Kal did his pushdowns using a short slightly bent bar. Unlike many who do pushdowns in a pressing type manner (elbows flared out to the sides) Kal preferred the traditional elbows tucked in to his sides.

After a short rest, Kal began his second combination, Scott curls and lying EZ-bar extensions. Kal's version of the Scott curl was the way Vince Gironda taught Larry Scott, a shoulder width grip and elbows fairly narrow. Kal did not do complete reps on Scott curls. He preferred to keep the tension on the biceps by stopping just short of a lockout at the bottom, and his forearms just short of perpendicular at the top. Kal was no slouch on this exercise either as he worked up to 170 pounds for 4 sets of 8 reps.

For his lying EZ-bar extensions, Kal lowered the bar to the bench above his head. Then using only his triceps he pressed the bar back up to just short of a lock out.

Superset three was incline dumbell curls and one-arm dumbell extensions. Once again Kal preferred to stop the exercise before locking out at the bottom, and he didn't curl right up either, stopping just short of shoulder level. Four sets of 8 reps using 80 pounders was the norm.

Even in this day and age it's hard to believe anyone could use 85-pound dumbells for one-arm dumbell extensions, but Kal did. With his free hand holding on to something for support, Kal would lower the dumbell down as far as possible behind his head, and then extend back up to just short of a lockout.

To finish his arms, Kal would do one final combination consisting of cable curls and triceps kickbacks. For cables, Kal preferred the two-arm version, but would alternate between a straight and bent bar.

Triceps kickbacks were done in the one-arm dumbell row position, with one arm braced on a bench, and the other locked into his side. Kal would extend back using as little upper arm movement as possible.

Arnold dominated the sport for most of the late 1960s and early 1970s. Even to this day he is regarded as the sport's greatest bodybuilder.

Arnold Schwarzenegger – The Austrian Oak

The most famous man in bodybuilding, Arnold's name is synonymous with the sport. He is also the embodiment of the American dream. Arnold's story is America's story, a folk-lore of immigrants arriving with the clothes on their backs and no knowledge of the English language. And years later, those same immigrants have become vital parts of the national fabric. Yet Arnold has gone one better, he is a living American Icon, his charming German accent as fondly accepted as that of Henry Kissinger.

Arnold was born in Graz, Austria on July 30, 1947. He had a happy family situation, and life was comfortable. While much of Arnold's life is well known, few are familiar with how Arnold became involved in weight training.

"I was always interested in proportion and perfection. When I was fifteen, I took off my clothes and looked in the mirror. When I stared at myself naked, I realized that to be perfectly proportioned I would need twenty-inch arms to match the rest of me."

"Hasta la Vista, baby!"
– One of Arnold's famous movie lines.

One day in the late fall of 1962, during one of the last warm days of the season, on the banks of Thaler Lake near Graz, Arnold struck up an acquaintance which was destined to have perhaps the most important consequences for him. For a long time he had been watching a young man whose outstanding physique literally commanded attention. Arnold tried to approach this young man, but Arnold didn't have enough confidence to even strike up a conversation. Kurt Marnul, who was at the time the ideal of all Austrian bodybuilders, had naturally noticed the admiring glances of the youngster, and spoke to him directly. The conversation ended with an invitation to Arnold to come along to a training session. The very next day Arnold appeared in the training rooms of the weightlifting club, Athletic Union, and met Kurt, who was employed there as a trainer. Under the guidance of this experienced bodybuilder and weightlifter, Arnold made rapid progress, and in a comparatively short time it became clear to all that here was an extraordinary talent. At the beginning of his training, Arnold's measurements were: weight 154 lbs., height 5'11 1/2", upper arm 13", chest 41 1/4", waist 27 1/2 ", thigh 21", and calf 14 3/4". By the following summer, Arnold's measurements had improved markedly: weight 176 lbs., height 6', upper arm 16", chest 45 3/4", waist 28", thigh 23", and calf 16".

As early as January of 1964, Arnold was able to reap the first benefits of his intensive training in curling (a popular sport in Europe and Canada in which teams send heavy stones into a target area by sliding the stones across an ice rink). He went with his father, Gustav, to curling meets. His considerable strength allowed him to become state and provincial champion (junior class), and Arnold took second place in the general European Curling meet held in Yugoslavia. Arnold had achieved his first ambition while barely 17 years of age, and his father was justly proud of him.

Arnold had achieved his first ambition while barely 17 years of age, and his father was justly proud of him.

Arnold and his friend and training partner Franco Columbu were brought to America by bodybuilding business tycoon, Joe Weider. Joe is a smart man, and he knew talent when he saw it. It would be superfluous to go into Arnold's competitive career in detail. Suffice to say he dominated the sport for most of the late 1960s and early 1970s. Even to this day he is regarded as the sport's greatest bodybuilder. Here's what we mean:

1966   Universe – NABBA, tall, 2nd
1967   Universe – NABBA, Overall winner
        Universe – NABBA, tall, 1st
1968   Universe – IFBB, 2nd
        Universe – IFBB, tall, 1st
        Universe – Pro, NABBA, overall winner
        Universe – Pro, NABBA, tall, 1st
1969   Mr. Europe – IFBB, overall winner
        Mr. Europe – IFBB, tall, 1st
        Mr. International – IFBB, overall winner
        Mr. International – IFBB, tall, 1st
        Olympia – IFBB, 2nd
        Universe – IFBB, overall winner
        Universe – IFBB, tall, 1st
        Universe – Pro, NABBA, overall winner
        Universe – Pro, NABBA, tall, 1st
1970   Mr. World – AAU, overall winner
        Mr. World – AAU, Pro tall, 1st
        Olympia – IFBB, winner
        Universe – Pro, NABBA, overall winner
        Universe – Pro, NABBA, tall, 1st
1971   Olympia – IFBB, winner
1972   Olympia – IFBB, winner
1973   Olympia – IFBB, winner
1974   Olympia – IFBB, overall winner
        Olympia – IFBB, heavyweight, 1st
1975   Olympia – IFBB, overall winner
        Olympia – IFBB, heavyweight, 1st

In 1979 Arnold Graduated from the University of Wisconsin-Superior with a major in international marketing in fitness and business administration.[2] He then came out of retirement and won the 1980 Mr. Olympia in Sydney, Australia. The win was not popular given Arnold's less than perfect shape, but it didn't seem to hurt his image.

After conquering the world of body-building, Arnold decided to make his name in motion pictures. Hampered by his impossible name and thick accent, success eluded him for many years. One of his first American films, *Hercules Goes Bananas*, was dubbed! It wasn't until he found the tailor-made role of Conan that he truly came into his own as a performer.[2] Of course, Arnold almost blew that role when he

Arnold shaking hands with Dennis Tinerino.

Arnold is flanked by Dave Draper and Reg Park.

first met Dino DeLaurentis. Dino is a short man, and he had a huge desk. In the gym, Arnold was known as the "Great Intimidator." He would establish his own dominance by telling someone that he looked bad or should work on a weak bodypart that wasn't really weak. Competitive bodybuilding was and still is a dog-eat-dog world, and Arnold couldn't afford to be nice. This survival skill that had worked so well in the gym did not carry over well into regular life. When Arnold was first introduced to Dino, Arnold infuriated the man by saying, "Why does such a small man need such a huge desk?" Initially, Dino didn't want to give the part to Arnold. No one likes working with prima donnas, especially muscular ones. It was only after a subsequent meeting with a much better behaved Arnold, that the part of Conan was given to him. The movie made Arnold a box-office sensation and a succession of action films made him an international box office star. By alternating violent action films with lighter, comedic fare, he has solidified his position as one of the most popular – if not the most popular – movie stars in the world. Here's a list of his films:

Collateral Damage (2001) … Ben Stride

Terminator 3 (2001)

The Sixth Day (2000)

Intimate Portrait: Kelly Preston (1999) (TV)

Intimate Portrait: Loni Anderson (1999) (TV)

End of Days (1999) … Jericho Cane

Batman & Robin (1997) … Mr. Freeze/ Dr. Victor Fries

Terminator 2 3D: Battle Across Time (1996) … The Terminator

Jingle All the Way (1996) … Howard Langston

Eraser (1996) … U.S. Marshal John Kruger (the Eraser)

Sinatra: 80 Years My Way (1995) (TV) … himself
Beretta's Island (1994)
A Century of Cinema (1994) … himself
Junior (1994) … Dr. Alex Hesse
True Lies (1994) … Harry Tasker
The Last Party (1993) … himself
Last Action Hero (1993) … Jack Slater/ himself
Dave (1993) … himself
Lincoln (1992) (TV) (voice) … John G. Nicolay
Feed (1992) … himself
Terminator 2: Judgment Day (1991) … The Terminator
Kindergarten Cop (1990) … John Kimble
Total Recall (1990) … Douglas Quaid
Twins (1988) … Julius Benedict
Red Heat (1988) … Ivan Danko
The Running Man (1987) … Ben Richards
Predator (1987) … Major Dutch Schaeffer
Raw Deal (1986) … Kaminski
Triple Identity (1986)

Arnold with training partner and life-long friend Franco Columbu.

Commando (1985) … Col. John Matrix
Red Sonja (1985) … Kalidor
The Terminator (1984) … The Terminator
Conan the Destroyer (1984) … Conan
Carnival in Rio (1983) (TV)… himself, as host
Conan the Barbarian (1982) … Conan
The Jayne Mansfield Story (1980) (TV) … Mickey Hargitay
The Villian (1979) … Handsome stranger
Scavenger Hunt (1979) … Lars
Pumping Iron (1977) … himself
Stay Hungry (1976) … Joe Santo
The Long Goodbye (1973) (uncredited) … One of Augustine's Hoods
Hercules Goes Bananas (1970) (as Arnold Strong)[2]

And just in case you're wondering what kind of salary Arnold commands, here's what he was paid for two of his movies:

Batman & Robin (1997) $25,000,000
End of Days (1999) $25,000,000[1]

In 1983 Arnold became a US citizen. What does the future hold for this media superstar? We're going to make a prediction here. Within the next 20 years Arnold Schwarzenegger will be the first foreign-born President of the United States. Think about it. He's married to Maria Schriver, a member of the Kennedy clan. So, Arnold is now related to American royalty. For many years, Arnold has been a dedicated member of the Republican Party. Politics is about reciprocal relationships. You help me, I help you. And the Republicans owe Arnold big time! Then there's his incredible personal popularity. Everyone loves the guy. He even looks presidential! He has a degree in business, and has shown that he knows how the economy works. He had a wild youth (who didn't?), but since his marriage he is one of the few public figures who actually believes in family values. There are no sex scandals or harassment suits lurking. And of course, all it takes is an amendment to the Constitution, and Arnold becomes a viable candidate. It wouldn't matter who the Democrats ran against him, Arnold would win by a landslide.

Let us close this bio with Arnold's most famous movie line: "I'll be back."

References:

1. http://us.imdb.com/Bio?Schwarzenegger,+Arnold
2. http://us.imdb.com/M/person-exact?Schwarzenegger%2C+Arnold

Shoulders

Given his incredible drive to be the absolute best bodybuilder alive, it's not surprising to learn that Arnold experimented with every deltoid exercise in the book. Arnold found that like most people, some exercises worked and some were useless. He recommends that beginners and intermediates do the same. Don't get hung up on one particular exercise just because "it's the one you are supposed to do."

Over the years Arnold reduced his shoulder exercises to nine movements:

1. Arnold presses
2. Standing dumbell lateral raises
3. One-arm cable raises
4. Lying one-arm dumbell raiseses
5. Seated behind-the-neck presses
6. Seated dumbell presses
7. Seated front presses
8. Standing alternate front raises
9. Bent-over dumbell raises

Arnold backstage with Franco Columbu.

For traps he found that the following were most effective:

1. High pulls
2. Upright rows
3. Shrugs

The number of total exercises Arnold did during a workout depended on the time of season. If it was in the off-season, and adding size was his priority, he would pick five deltoid exercises and one trap movement. Conversely, when he switched to his precontest mode, he upped the total to nine exercises.

Compared to today's bodybuilders who employ such advanced training techniques as drop sets, rest-pause, trisets, pre-exhaustion, etc., Arnold primarily stuck to straight sets for 5 sets of 8 to 12 reps each. Occasionally he would run the rack on dumbell exercises.

He normally selected two pressing movements each time he trained delts. He nearly always did "Arnold presses" and rotated the other three. One day he'd add seated behind-the-neck presses, while the next it might be front military presses. No matter which exercise, however, Arnold always took a wide grip. He found this prevented him from locking the arms out straight, thus helping put more stress on the side shoulders. It also reduces the amount of triceps involvement.

Laterals were exercises that Arnold always performed in strict style. Arnold's tip for doing side raises is no doubt familiar to most readers, but for those new to the sport it deserves repeating. Arnold always lifted his arms as if holding a jug of water in each hand. As he lifted, he would "pour the water" out of the jug. This forced him to keep the elbows higher than his wrists for most of the exercise. This may not seem like a big deal, but it is. If you let the hands and wrists rotate higher than the elbows, the front delts start doing most of the work. But by keeping the elbows high, the side delt is the primary mover.

A few other tips that Arnold emphasizes for beginners include keeping the elbows slightly bent to reduce the stress on the joints; raising and lowering the dumbells in a slow and controlled manner to reduce body momentum; and concentrating on the deltoid head you are working.

One final pumpup before going on stage.

"The deltoids are visible from every angle – front, back, and sides. They are impossible to hide. If you are a competitive bodybuilder they are involved in every pose."
– Arnold Schwarzenegger commenting on the importance of great deltoid development for competitive bodybuilders.

To hit the traps Arnold picked one or two exercises and did 4 sets of each for 6 to 12 reps. Even though Arnold agrees that heavy weight is best for stimulating the traps, it should not at the expense of technique. During his heydays at Gold's he frequently saw bodybuilders load up the bar with hundreds of pounds, only to bounce it up and down for a few inches of motion. In fact it was because of this that Arnold preferred dumbell shrugs over barbell shrugs. He found this way he raised his traps a tad further. He was a firm believer in the old training tip of trying to touch the traps off the ears.

After shrugs Arnold did either high pulls or upright rows. Even though he did these exercises in a slightly faster tempo than most exercises, he was careful to only use enough body momentum to keep the weight moving. He points out that if you have to yank or jerk the weight up and down, it probably makes sense to lower the poundage.

Arms

When drawing up a list of the greatest arms in bodybuilding history, Arnold is usually at or near the top. During his dominance of the sport from the late '60s and early to mid '70s, few competitors would dare go head to head with Arnold in arm poses. They were that good.

What made Arnold's arms stand out wasn't just their size. Sergio Oliva had the same size arms as Arnold. In fact proportionally they may have been a tad larger. But where Sergio's

"When I first became involved in bodybuilding as a skinny 15-year-old kid in Austria, I was already six feet tall, but weighed only 150 pounds. My arms were like pipe cleaners. I was determined that they would not stay that way for long, however, especially after I saw pictures in the American muscle magazines of great champions like Jack Delinger, Larry Scott, Ray Routledge, Steve Reeves, and of course, my idol, Reg Park."

– Arnold Schwarzenegger, telling how he first got interested in bodybuilding.

One can't imagine Arnold Schwarzenegger with arms the size of pipe cleaners.

arms looked like two large blocks, Arnold's were neatly divided into sections. All three heads of the triceps stood out. His forearms looked like steel chords. And those biceps rose like the proverbial mountains they were. Until Arnold came on the scene, the term baseball-sized was used to describe bodybuilders with large biceps. But when the Austrian Oak arrived, writers had to grab the dictionary and conjure up new terms. The results were the phrases grapefruit-sized and cannon-ball sized.

When he first started training in Austria and Germany before coming to America, Arnold's biceps' routine consisted of primarily four exercises – cheating barbell curls, Zottman curls, incline dumbell curls (Reg Park's favorite biceps exercise) and one-arm concentration curls. Arnold relied on these four exercises to develop huge, thick, full, peaked biceps. Later, when he came to America he started training at Vince Gironda's gym and because everyone there was doing preacher curls, he added them to his routine. But he quickly found that preacher curls didn't work for him like they worked for other greats like Larry Scott. Even though he continued to include preachers in his training from time to time, he never got the same effect as from other exercises like incline curls or standing barbell curls.

Arnold uses this last point as advice to beginners and intermediate bodybuilders. Find the exercises that you best respond to and stick with them.

Let's take a closer look at the exercises that Arnold used to build perhaps the most photographed biceps in bodybuilding history.

Arnold divided his biceps movements into free and restricted exercises. In restricted exercises the arm is making contact with something like a bench in preacher curls and the thighs or knees in concentration curls. Free movements are just that, the arms are free from any contact with any surface or part of the body. Although he did the former, Arnold favored free exercises in his routine.

Arnold also divided his biceps training into mass and shaping exercises. For mass he performed standing barbell curls and seated incline curls. For shape he performed standing alternate dumbell curls and standing free, concentration curls. During his heavy phase of training, Arnold did 5 sets of each exercise for 6 to 10 reps. Here's a detailed description of how Arnold performed each exercise.

1. Standing cheat barbell curls – This was Arnold's primary mass building exercise. At one time (the 1966 NABBA Mr. Universe) Arnold came out on stage and cheat curled 275 pounds for 3 reps. Arnold is quick to add that you cheat to use extra weight and overload the biceps, not cheat just to flatter the ego. Anyone can heave or jerk a loaded barbell up using the legs, shoulders, and lower back. Arnold grabbed the bar with a slightly wider than shoulder width grip, and locked his wrists. When he curled the bar up, he never let it fall into the shoulders. This is only giving the biceps a rest. He also tried to keep his elbows as close to the body as possible. Once again by letting them flare out too much, other muscles tend to take over. Once he reached the bottom, arms straight position, he would gently rock the body to start the barbell on its upward journey. Notice we said nudge not heave. The movement is still a curl not a power clean. If you have to imitate an Olympic lifter, then the weight is too heavy. Arnold also kept his chest arched and delts low to prevent the traps from doing much of the work. Arnold pyramided the weight on cheat curls doing sets of 10, 8, 6, and 6, respectively.

2. Incline dumbell curls – Arnold started doing these in his biceps routine after reading that they were favorites of Steve Reeves and Reg Park. Arnold did this exercise while lying back on a 45-degree angle incline bench. The rationale behind leaning back on an angle is that it gives the biceps a greater degree of stretch. This in turn leads to a greater degree of motion. As with

Boyer Coe, Arnold Schwarzenegger and Chris Dickerson.

barbell curls, Arnold locked his wrists and tried to keep his palms parallel with the floor throughout the exercise. To keep the shoulder from doing too much of the exercise, Arnold kept his elbows slightly forward. He found that when he let the shoulders creep forward, they took much of the strain off the biceps.

For variety Arnold did a modified version of incline curls called a three-part curl. At the bottom of the exercise with the arms held straight down, he would rotate the wrists until his palms are facing backward as if doing a reverse curl. Then when he started raising he would slowly rotate or supinate the hands until they were facing inward at the mid point and completely upwards at the finishing point.

3. Standing alternate dumbell curls – As with seated curls, Arnold performed this exercise in two styles; strict and supinated. Unlike barbell curls where he employed a slight cheat to keep the weight moving, Arnold always performed standing dumbell curls in a strict manner. This meant little or no body movement. The only thing that moved was his forearms.

4. Freestanding concentration curls – Arnold attributes this exercise for adding the most peak to his biceps. Unlike the majority of bodybuilders who prefer to sit on a bench and brace the elbows against the knees, Arnold stood up, bent over and with one arm braced on his knee, let the free arm hang straight down. He then rotated his wrist until his palm was facing backward. As he lifted he slowly rotated his palm from the down position to the up position. Once again Arnold never let his upper arm move. For those who have trouble with the exercise, Arnold recommends lowering the weight and practicing the technique until you have it down perfect. Then and only then should you start worrying about weight.

Triceps

Arnold was the first one to admit that his triceps never quite got him the attention as his enormous biceps. Even after revamping his training and bringing his triceps in balance with his biceps, they never seemed to evoke the same degree of awe.

Arnold, Franco Columbu and Serge Nubret

Like many bodybuilders early in their careers, Arnold devoted far more time to the more showy biceps than the less glamorous but potentially more useful triceps. Even up until he won the 1968 NABBA Mr. Universe, his triceps still lagged behind. It was only after coming to California and losing the 1968 IFBB Mr. Universe to Frank Zane, that he decided to get serious about balancing out his arms.

Early on Arnold learned that he had to do slightly higher reps for his triceps as compared to biceps. Instead of the standard 6 to 10 on most biceps exercises, he had to increase the reps for

"My triceps took a long time to catch up to my biceps out of sheer ignorance. I neglected my triceps totally for the first couple of years of training. I did not realize that two-thirds of upper-arm mass comes from full triceps development."

– Arnold Schwarzenegger, commenting on how he made the same mistake as many novice bodybuilders, neglecting the triceps in favor of biceps.

Possibly, the most photographed biceps in bodybuilding history.

triceps training from 10 to 20. He also discovered that given the triceps' more complex make-up, three heads instead of two, he had to employ a wider assortment of exercises.

During a typical triceps workout, Arnold would select five exercises from his list, and do 5 to 6 sets of each. By today's standards, 25 to 30 sets for triceps would be considered grossly overtraining. But Arnold found that the medium intensity, high volume training paid the biggest dividends. He is first to admit nowadays that most bodybuilders can get by on less total sets.

Arnold's first triceps exercise was nearly always triceps pushdowns on the lat machine. He'd start with 2 to 3 sets of about 20 reps to warm up the elbows. Then he'd put more weight on the stack until he could just force out 3 or 4 sets of 10 to 12 reps. For variety he sometimes alternated between a wide and narrow grip.

After pushdowns Arnold next moved on to seated French presses using an EZ-curl bar. To add back support he used a preacher bench and placed his back against the pad. Arnold did 5 sets of 12 reps with his elbows pointed towards the ceiling at all times. He would lower the bar down behind his head until he felt a good stretch in his triceps, and then push or extend upwards until his arms were about one inch short of locking out.

For his third exercise Arnold often did one-arm triceps extensions. Once again he kept his elbow pointing at the ceiling and close to his head at all times. Again he did about 5 sets of 12 reps.

To finish off his triceps Arnold did bench dips. Depending on how he felt, and more important, how much his triceps had left in them, Arnold would either use just his bodyweight, or have a training partner place a barbell across his thighs. This was one exercise that Arnold preferred to do higher reps, usually in the 20 to 30 range.

The previous is just one triceps routine that Arnold followed in his career. Other exercises he included in his training included lying triceps extensions, weighted dips, kickbacks, and one-arm pushdowns.

Forearms

As with triceps, Arnold totally neglected his forearms early in his career. But all that changed when he first came to America and saw the amazing forearms on such superstars as Sergio Oliva, Larry Scott, Chuck Sipes, Dave Draper, and Bill Pearl. All it took was a couple of quick glances and he realized that specialized forearm training was a must.

Arnold based his forearm training on two exercises, wrist curls and reverse curls. And to show how serious Arnold took forearm training, he didn't just do them on arm days, no he trained them six days a week. That's ten sets a workout or 60 sets a week. He'd either do straight sets or supersets depending on how he felt. A typical training cycle would see him doing barbell reverse curls followed by preacher reverse curls on Tuesdays, Thursdays, and Saturdays. Then on Mondays, Wednesdays, and Fridays he would do barbell wrist curls followed by one-arm dumbell wrist curls.

> **"Don't forget that half of a 50-inch chest is back development. You can have fully developed pecs but if your back is thin or your lats lack width, you'll never stretch the tape past 50 inches."**
>
> – Arnold offering good advice to bodybuilders who get hung up on chest training.

Some advice Arnold would give beginners is to work hard on developing the mind-to-muscle link when training back.

We are going to leave the last word on arm training to Arnold: "Picture your arms as you want them to be. Set a goal for developing an impressive pair of arms. Then train like hell to get them."

Back

Just as Arnold neglected triceps in favor of biceps early in his career, so too did his back take second billing to his chest training. In fact it was because of the size and strength of his biceps that Arnold found back training so difficult. It seemed no matter what back exercise he did, his biceps kept taking over. It took him years to learn how to keep his biceps from dominating especially when he did chins, rows, and pulldowns.

The first piece of advice Arnold would give beginners is to work hard on developing the mind-to-muscle link when training back. Too often he says, bodybuilders use too much weight and end up bringing in other muscles to help with the exercise. They train like Olympic weightlifters and powerlifters rather than bodybuilders.

Another tip Arnold passes on is variety. He's firmly convinced that most bodybuilders undertrain their lats. They bomb the chest with 15, 20, even 30 sets, and then throw in 8 to 10 sets for back and seem satisfied. To Arnold this doesn't seem logical given that the back is made of so many different muscles. You have the lats, traps, teres, rhomboids, and the often-neglected spinal erectors. All of these muscles must be developed to the max if you want to make an impression on stage. And let's not forget the safety aspect. A strong upper back helps prevent lower back injuries.

As Arnold trained traps on a different day, we'll focus our attention here on the exercises he used to build the other major back muscles. During a typical back workout, Arnold would pick four to six of the following exercises, and perform 5 sets of between 6 to 12 reps. He made it a point to select exercises that added width and thickness to his upper back, as well as strengthening his lower back. Here are some of is favorites:

1. Wide-grip chins to the front – Arnold usually made this the first exercise in his back workout. He found that they not only added width to his lats, but also helped widen the shoulder girdle. Arnold often set a certain number of chins as his goal on this exercise. On some days he'd do fewer sets for higher reps, while on others he'd strap some weight around his waist and perform more sets for lower reps. As a guide he suggests that as soon as you can do 30 reps in two sets, increase your goal to 40 or 50 reps. As you pull yourself up to the bar, Arnold recommends that you arch the chest and keep your shoulders down on back. This is the best way to maximize lat tension and minimize biceps involvement.

Arnold based his forearm training on two exercises, wrist curls and reverse curls.

2. Wide-grip chins behind-the-head – For variety Arnold often did chins behind the head. As this is a more difficult exercise, most bodybuilders won't need to add extra weight around their waists. As before he would do 5 sets to failure.

3. Triangle-bar chins – To hit his lower lats and serratus, Arnold performed chins using a small v-bar, usually the same or similar to the one used on the seated row machine. Unlike the wide front and back chins where remaining vertical was the goal, Arnold performed narrow chins by leaning back and trying to touch the bar off his lower chest. Again he did 5 sets of as many reps as possible.

4. Bent-over barbell rowing – With his widening exercises out of the way, Arnold moved on to the heavy rowing movements for thickness. On most days the first exercise was usually barbell rows. Standing on a low bench or block, Arnold would grab a standard Olympic bar with a shoulder width grip. With his knees slightly bent and lower back slightly arched, he would pull the bar up to his abdominal region. Even though you can go heavy on barbell rows, Arnold is quick to add that technique is far more important than weight on this exercise. Too many bodybuilders load up the bar and pull and yank with the lower back to keep it moving. If you can't lift with just the lats and arms, and keep the torso stationary, lower the weight.

5. T-bar rows – Instead of barbell rows, Arnold often substituted T-bar rows. As with barbell rows, the legs should be kept bent and the lower back slightly arched. Arnold would pick a weight that allowed for 5 or 6 reps in perfect style, and then he'd use a slight swing to keep the weight moving for another 5 or 6 reps. In many respects Arnold performed T-bars like light barbell chest curls for his biceps. The goal being to use just enough body movement to assist the lats not take over from them. As you probably guessed, Arnold did 5 sets of 10 to 12 reps of this exercise.

6. Seated cable rows – Arnold did seated rows for mid back thickness. Using a narrow v-bar, he would sit on the machine's pad and keep his knees slightly bent. He would stretch forward until the plates were within an inch or two of touching, and then pull the handle into his midsection as his torso reached the vertical. As with most back exercises, Arnold recommends squeezing the shoulder blades together and arching the chest slightly as you pull the handle to the midsection. Arnold did 5 sets of 8 to 12 reps of seated rows.

7. Behind-the-head lat pulldowns – After a couple of rowing movements Arnold switched back to another width exercise. Although he occasionally varied his grip, Arnold preferred doing pulldowns with a wide, overhand grip. As with barbell rows, Arnold liked to use a little body momentum to keep the weight moving on the last couple of reps. But he's first to admit that when the biceps take over and you can no longer feel the lats, it's time to terminate the set.

8. Cross-bench dumbell pullovers – This was one of Arnold's favorite finishing movements as it not only gives the lats a good stretch, but also brings in the serratus, and warms up the chest muscles which he often trained with or after back. Arnold preferred to do pullovers lying across a bench rather than lengthwise. Lie so that your shoulders are on the back edge of the bench and with the arms just short of locked out, drop the hips so that they are below bench level.

Arnold, Chris Dickerson and Frank Zane

During his competitive days, Arnold's chest was one of his best bodyparts.

Stretch the arms back over the head and lower the dumbells as far as comfortably possible. For younger bodybuilders, Arnold urges you to concentrate on filling the lungs with as much air as possible. This helps stretch the ligaments and connective tissues of the rib cage and can add a couple of inches to your chest measurement. As this was as much of a stretching as strength and size exercise, Arnold did slightly higher reps, usually 12 to 15, for 4 to 5 sets.

9. Stiff-leg deadlifts – Arnold found stiff-leg deadlifts by far the best exercise to directly attack his lower back. The fact that they also work the hamstrings, traps, and forearms, doesn't hurt either. The most common mistake Arnold observes when many people deadlift is rounding of the lower back, and pulling the weight with too much arm strength. The back must be kept slightly arched at all times. This not only puts more stimulation on the spinal erectors, but also places less unwanted stress on the lower back ligaments. To get a good stretch at the bottom, Arnold usually stood on a low bench or block. For those with uneven arm strength, Arnold suggests grabbing the bar with the strong arm facing back, and the weaker arm facing up. With the arms held straight, slightly straighten up until the torso is in line with the lower body. At the top pull your shoulders back and arch your chest slightly. As deadlifts are such a taxing exercise, Arnold recommends that many bodybuilders may only need to do them once a week. Unlike his other back exercises, Arnold preferred lower reps on deadlifts, usually 4 sets of 4 to 8 reps.

Despite the preachings of many modern trainers, Arnold is convinced that a minimum of three exercises is needed to adequately train the back. You need one for width, one for thickness, and one for the lower back. With time you can prioritize depending on whether you need more width or thickness. For variety, Arnold suggests supersetting chest with back. This was a popular technique of both Arnold and Sergio Oliva, both of whom became famous for their incredible upper bodies.

Chest

Even by today's growth hormone-insulin-steroid-induced standards, Arnold's chest has few equals. For those in doubt, check out page 620 of the soft-

"During my competitive days my chest was one of my best bodyparts. People always told me how impressed they were with the size, thickness and fullness of my pectorals. They probably thought I always had a huge chest. It wasn't so."

– Arnold commenting on one of bodybuildings great misconceptions, that he was born with a great chest.

cover edition of *Arnold's Bodybuilding Encyclopedia*. Even Franco Columbu, seen in the background, is taken aback by those two enormous slabs of beef. Arnold was one of the first bodybuilders who could raise his arms above his head and still display his chest. Most bodybuilders temporarily lose their pecs on overhead poses as they don't have the necessary thickness. But Arnold had depth to spare.

As unbelievable as it sounds, Arnold's chest never gave any hints early in his career that it would soon develop into one of bodybuildings greatest bodyparts. Given his height, Arnold's rib cage looked rather small, and his pecs rather thin, when he first started training.

The inspiration for Arnold to build an enormous chest was South African great, Reg Park. With three Mr. Universe titles to his credit, and a similar frame (about 6' 2), Arnold used Reg's physique and training as a template. As Arnold later said, "When I saw magazine photographs of him doing a side chest pose, I knew I had to one day have a chest like his. Notice I did not say I wanted to have a chest like Reg's. No, I had to have a chest like his. I lusted for it."

When Arnold first started training in Austria, and later Germany, he used basic exercises like flat barbell bench presses, incline presses, and pullovers. Later he realized that for complete chest development, he would need to start incorporating exercises that hit the upper, lower, middle, inner, and outer areas of the pecs. He also realized that with his tall frame, expanding his rib cage was a must. For this reason he started dumbell pullovers pretty much from day one. Despite the objections of some, which say pullovers do nothing to expand the rib cage, Arnold feels they added inches to his chest measurement.

The inspiration for Arnold to build an enormous chest was South African great, Reg Park.

The first chest routine Arnold followed looked like this:
1. Bench presses – 5 sets of 6 to 10 reps
2. Incline barbell presses – 5 sets of 6 to 10 reps
3. Flat dumbell flyes – 5 sets of 6 to 10 reps
4. Weighted dips – 5 sets of 6 to 10 reps
5. Barbell pullovers – 5 sets of 6 to 10 reps or
6. Dumbell pullovers – 5 sets of 6 to 10 reps

On all exercises Arnold strove to use as much weight as possible. When he met up with Franco Columbu in Germany, he started following Franco's pyramiding style of training. This meant adding weight with each set up to a couple of maximum lifts, and then decreasing the weight and increasing the reps.

As expected Arnold's favorite exercise was the flat barbell bench press. In fact he often did 8 to 10 sets of bench presses during a workout. He's firmly convinced that flat bench presses will do more for chest development than any other chest exercise. For beginners they are an absolute must. Even for intermediates and advanced bodybuilders, they should be performed on a regular basis. Despite being a bodybuilder, Arnold occasionally did singles, doubles, and triples on the bench press. He found the extra strength allowed him to use heavier poundages on his bodybuilding rep sets.

Arnold used Reg Park's physique and training as a template.

Arnold stuck to the previous routine right up until he had won his second Mr. Universe title in 1968. Every now and then he switched dumbells in place of the barbell on inclines, but for the most part his routine was consistent. All that was to change, however, after the 1968 Mr. Universe in Miami, Florida, when Arnold, at 235 pounds, was beaten by a much smaller, 185-pound, Frank Zane. Despite his awesome size, Arnold lacked the refinement of Zane, who had the shape, cuts, and completeness that was becoming vogue at the time. Arnold convinced Joe Weider to move him to California, and the rest as they say is history. As soon as he started training at the original Gold's in Venice, he began to see that there was more to chest training than bench presses and inclines. Guys like Dave Draper, Frank Zane, and Rick Wayne, were doing such exercises as cable crossovers, and prioritizing their training. Arnold dropped many of his lower pec exercises like weighted dips, and began to specialize on the areas of his chest which were weak. He did more incline work for his upper chest, and changed the sequence of his exercises so that his inclines came at the beginning of his workout when he was fresh. He also started supersetting chest and back together. This not only gave him a more balanced physique, but also shortened his workouts. Two sample chest routines Arnold followed for most of his Mr. Olympia years were as follows:

1. Incline barbell presses – 6 to 8 sets of 8 to 12 reps
2. Flat barbell presses – 6 sets of 8 to 10 reps
3. Flat dumbell flyes – 6 sets of 8 to 10 reps
4. Cross-bench pullovers – 5 sets of 10 to 12 reps
5. Cable crossovers (precontest) – 5 sets of 12 to 15 reps

1. Bench presses – 5 sets of 6 to 20 reps supersetted with
2. Wide-grip chins – 5 sets of 8 to 15 reps
3. Incline barbell presses – 5 sets of 10 to 15 reps supersetted with
4. T-bar rows – 5 sets of 10 to 15 reps
5. Dumbell flyes – 5 sets of 10 to 15 reps supersetted with
6. Wide-grip barbell rows – 5 sets of 10 to 15 reps
7. Parallel-bar dips – 5 sets of 15 reps supersetted with
8. Close-grip chins – 5 sets of 12 reps

Legs

While Arnold never quite brought his legs up to the standard of his upper body, nevertheless he displayed one of the most balanced sets of legs during the early '70s. In fact many argue that today's bodybuilders have brought things way out of proportion with their 30-plus inch thighs.

The first thing Arnold changed about his leg training when he came to America was his

"It's no big secret that I neglected my legs early in my career. Like most beginners I made the mistake of not training my legs at all my first year. When I began bodybuilding, all I cared about was big biceps and big pecs."

– Arnold, admitting that he fell victim to the "upper body only" syndrome early in his career.

Lou Ferrigno and Arnold

attitude. Arnold is a firm believer that in order to improve a weak muscle group, you first must change your mindset so you actually love training that muscle. As Arnold much preferred training chest or biceps to legs, it's not surprising that his legs lagged way behind during his competitive days in Europe. As soon as he immigrated to America, one of the first things he did was divide his training so that he trained legs by themselves twice a week. No more throwing in a few sets of squats after training some other upper body muscle. His thighs, hamstrings, and calves would now get equal billing. In fact his calves, which to this day are regarded as among the best ever, were bombed five or six days a week.

Probably the biggest boost to Arnold's leg training came from witnessing Chet Yorton, at the 1966 NABBA Mr. Universe, in London. Chet had just won "best legs" at the 1966 Mr. America, and onstage at the Mr. Universe Arnold saw why. He had diamond shaped calves and fantastic thigh separation. As Arnold later remarked, "Second place at the Universe was no disgrace, but I hadn't trained for four years to be runner-up. I knew I had to work on my legs if I hoped to have a chance of winning the Mr. Universe title in 1967."

Arnold's next boost came from Reg Park. A series of correspondence letters led to an invitation by Reg to travel with him throughout England and Ireland. With three Mr. Universe titles to his credit, Reg had one of the best sets of legs around. After witnessing Reg train calves with 800 pounds, as compared to his own 400, Arnold decided right then and there that leg training would have to become a priority.

After Arnold set up shop at Gold's Gym in 1968, he immediately went to work to

Arnold, Mike Mentzer, Frank Zane and Dennis Tinerino.

bring up his legs. As he still needed more mass, his routine consisted of basic exercises for a high number of sets:

1. Squats – 10 to 12 sets of 12 reps
2. Leg extensions – 10 sets of 12 reps
3. Leg curls – 10 sets of 12 reps
4. Standing calf raises – 10 sets of 12 reps
5. Donkey calf raises – 10 to 15 sets of 10 to 15 reps

The pictures of Arnold doing donkey calf raises with two men on his back (the usual riders being Franco Columbu, Denny Gable, and Bill Grant) are now legendary. As soon as he couldn't get another rep, he'd have one rider hop off and continue the set. When even this was too heavy he'd have the second man jump off and he'd rep out with just his bodyweight.

> **"Whether you are a competitive bodybuilder, or just someone who wants to look good at the beach or walking down the street, sharply defined, fat-free abdominals are an absolute must for optimal appearance."**
>
> – Arnold commenting on the importance of a great midsection, no matter who you are.

When it came to thigh training, Arnold paid his dues at the squat rack. He's a firm believer that the key to large, powerful quads, lies with squats. Sure leg presses are a close second, but it's a fact that endless sets at the squat rack have built more thighs than any other movement. Another benefit of squats is that they also strengthen the lower back, something leg extensions and leg presses don't really do.

Even among those who regularly squat, Arnold sees mistakes. It makes no sense to put on a weight that you can lift for 12 reps, and stop at 6. To quote Arnold, "You have to put on a weight you can barely get 6 to 8 reps with – and somehow get 12. That's how to make your legs grow."

On leg curls and leg extensions Arnold would use the heaviest weight possible for 12 reps. He'd only rest about a minute.

After a couple of years of such training, Arnold's overall leg development improved considerably. With most of the mass he needed, it was now time to refine it. For this he used the following leg program:

1. Squats – 5 sets of 4 to 10 reps (pyramiding up)
2. Front squats – 5 sets of 10 reps
3. Vertical leg presses – 5 sets of 8 to 10 reps
4. Leg extensions – 5 sets of 12 reps
5. Leg curls – 8 sets of 8 to 12 reps

In conclusion Arnold is first to admit that some people are blessed with great genetics for building legs. But most bodybuilders who suffer from poor leg development are not genetically deficient, but simply unwilling to invest the time and energy needed to build championship legs. Bodybuilding is one sport where the old saying "a house is as only good as its foundation" definitely applies. And the foundation to a great physique is a powerful set of legs.

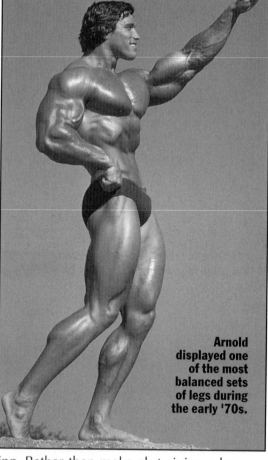

Arnold displayed one of the most balanced sets of legs during the early '70s.

Abs

It doesn't matter how big your chest, thighs, or arms, show up onstage with a 40-inch waistline and you can kiss the winner's trophy goodbye. Far too many bodybuilders treat abs like calves; they throw in a few half-hearted sets toward the end of a workout and call it quits.

One of the first things Arnold noticed about Frank Zane at the 1968 Mr. Universe was Frank's fantastic midsection. From abs and intercostals to serratus and spinal erectors, Frank had it all.

This one contest more than any other convinced Arnold to get serious about his ab training. Rather than make ab training a long, drawn out affair, Arnold trained them hard and fast. He would normally take five or six exercises and do 3 to 4 sets of each for 25 to 50 reps. Here's a description of Arnold's favorite ab and lower back exercises:

1. Roman-chair situps – Like most bodybuilders Arnold started doing this exercise after watching the legendary Zabo Koszewski perform tens of thousands of them on a weekly basis. For those not familiar with the exercise, you'll need a proper chair (actually a sort of decline bench with leg rollers on it). With the legs locked in under the rollers and arms crossed in front of the chest, lower yourself down until the torso is at about a 70-degree angle to the floor. Going all the way down not only shifts most of the stress to the hip flexors, but also puts extra stress on the lower back. After pausing for a split second at the bottom, rise back up until the torso is just short of vertical to the floor. Although Arnold usually lists sets and reps on this exercise (4 sets of 25 to 50), he often did Roman chairs for time. He'd go nonstop for about 10 minutes and do as many as possible.

2. Hanging knee raises – To work his lower abs, Arnold would grab a chinning bar and raise his knees until his thighs were parallel with the floor. Although bending at the knees brings more hip flexor into the exercise, it puts less stress on the lower back ligaments than if the legs were kept straight. For those who have trouble holding onto the bar, Arnold recommends using a set of wrist straps, the same ones you'd use for shrugs or barbell rows.

3. Lying leg raises – Another favorite lower ab exercise, Arnold did many different versions of lying leg raises. On some days he'd lie flat on the floor. On others he'd use a flat bench. And if he was feeling particularly energetic, he'd lie back on an incline bench. No matter which version you perform always keep a slight bend at the knee to reduce lower back stress. Don't let your feet touch the ground or board either as it gives the abs a momentary rest. Arnold preferred to do the middle three fifths of leg raises. This means he didn't raise his legs to a 90-degree angle, and he didn't let them come all the way back down.

4. Sitting leg-ups – Arnold did this exercise to hit both his upper and lower abs. Sit on the edge of a flat bench and lean slightly backward. Extend your legs in front but keep a slight bend at the knee. Draw the legs toward the upper body until your knees touch the rib cage. Extend the legs back stopping just short of locking out.

5. Hyperextensions – As Arnold frequently points out in his publications and lectures, the lower back is

Arnold would go nonstop for about 10 minutes and do as many roman chair situps as possible.

half the midsection. Even bodybuilders who are serious about reducing and tightening their midsections often fail to take this into account. In addition a strong set of spinal erectors are essential for good posture, and reducing lower back problems later in life. Position your body facedown on the hyperextension bench with the feet locked under the rollers or bars, depending on the design. Lower the upper body down until it's just short of vertical with the floor. Rise back up until the torso is in line with the legs, or just slightly past. Even though the name is hyperextensions, you shouldn't hyperextend (excessively arch the lower back). This can cause injury to the spinal disks and ligaments.

The previous are the main exercises Arnold employed in his abdominal training. But like most muscle groups, he would occasionally do others such as crunches, reverse crunches, and hanging leg raises in a chair. Arnold also points out that you can do all the abdominal exercises you like and still not have a great midsection if your diet is slack. Only by eating healthily (low fat, medium to high protein, and medium to high carbohydrate) can you ever hope to develop the much coveted washboard abs.

Danny Padilla – The Giant Killer

Danny Padilla was born in Rochester, New York, on April 3, 1951 to a large Hispanic family of seven sisters and two brothers. He took up bodybuilding at the age of seven! He won his first show at the age of 16. In 1975 he won the USA Championships and was sent to South Africa to represent USA at the IFBB Mr. Universe contest. To his shock and dismay, he was pulled from his class at the last minute to allow Mike Katz to compete in the heavyweights along with Ken Waller. Katz ended up fourth in his class, while Danny, who was a shoo-in for the short class (Danny stood 5'2", at a weight of 174 lbs.), sat in the audience watching. This disappointment started a string of bad luck that would plague Padilla throughout his up-and-down career.

During the 1970s he was one of the top bodybuilders in the world. He often lived in California and trained at the old Gold's Gym with the greats of the time.

In 1981, he entered the Mr. Olympia in the best shape of his life and cruelly was given only fifth place. Everyone but the judges felt that he should have been in the top three. That heart-breaking moment caused Danny to drop out of bodybuilding.

In 1989, Danny planned a comeback at the Night of Champions contest in New York. Because he arrived late, he was not allowed to compete!

Despite the ups and downs Danny had a great career:

During the 1970s Danny Padilla was one of the top bodybuilders in the world.

1973	Junior Mr. America – AAU, 15th
	Mr. America – AAU, 15th
1974	Junior Mr. America – AAU
	Mr. America – AAU, 18th
	Mr. World – AAU, short
1975	Mr. USA – ABBA, overall winner
	Mr. USA – ABBA, short, 1st
1976	Mr. America – IFBB, short, 1st
	Universe – IFBB, lightweight, 2nd
1977	Mr. America – IFBB, overall winner
	Mr. America – IFBB, lightweight, 1st
	Universe – IFBB, lightweight, 1st
1978	Olympia – IFBB, 6th
	Olympia – IFBB, lightweight, 3rd
	Professional World Cup – IFBB, 2nd
	USA vs. the World – IFBB, lightweight, 1st
1979	Best in the World – IFBB, professional, 5th
	Grand Prix Pennsylvania – IFBB, 5th
	Night of Champions – IFBB, 2nd
	Olympia – IFBB, lightweight, 5th
	Southern Pro Cup – IFBB, 3rd
1980	Grand Prix Miami – IFBB, 3rd
	Olympia – IFBB, 10th
1981	Olympia – IFBB, 5th
1982	Night of Champions – IFBB, 5th
	Olympia – IFBB, 12th
1983	Night of Champions – IFBB, 9th
1984	World Pro Championships – IFBB, 7th
1985	Olympia – IFBB, 16th
1986	World Pro Championships – IFBB, 13th

1990   Grand Prix England – IFBB, 5th
        Grand Prix Finland – IFBB, 4th
        Grand Prix France – IFBB, 5th
        Grand Prix Germany – IFBB, 7th
        Grand Prix Holland – IFBB, 7th
        Grand Prix Italy – IFBB, 4th
        Niagara Falls Pro Invitational – IFBB, 2nd
        Night of Champions – IFBB, 3rd
1991   WBF Grand Prix – WBF, 10th
1994   Olympia – masters, IFBB, 7th

The last word goes to Danny, who summarizes his bodybuilding career: "… Sure, I never made a million dollars from bodybuilding, but I was lucky. I got to travel, to see the world and I was Mr. Universe. For that one minute of my life I was the best. That's something most people will never have."

Biceps

With all the talk nowadays of overtraining, it's refreshing to hear that many bodybuilders back in the '70s also recognized that smaller muscle groups like the arms didn't need the same training volume as the larger muscles. Danny Padilla made the same mistake. When he found his arms responding to 10 to 15 sets, he concluded that 20 to 25 must be even better. But after a couple of weeks his growth came to a halt. In fact he could've sworn they actually started shrinking!

Danny had a string of bad luck that plagued him throughout his up-and-down career.

When he started getting serious about his Mr. Olympia training in the late '70s and early '80s, Danny reduced his arm training volume by about 30 percent, and made the best gains of his life. Here's what he did.

Danny's first exercise was usually alternate dumbell curls for 5 sets of 6 to 8 reps. He did one or two warm-up sets but didn't count them in his set totals. As expected of someone who trained at the original Gold's Gym, and watched Arnold training his gargantuan arms on a regular basis, Danny supinated his hands as he curled the dumbells upward.

Danny's second exercise was concentration curls. Although he saw Arnold's version close up, with his elbow held away from his leg, Danny found this too hard to master, so he did the traditional elbow-against-the-knee version. He did 4 sets of 8 to 10 reps.

Danny's third exercise was incline dumbell curls. He liked the way this exercise gave the biceps a good stretch. Through trial an error he found the 45-degree incline worked best. He did 4 sets of 8 to 10 reps.

The giant killer finished off his biceps routine with barbell curls. He used a medium grip as the wide and narrow versions didn't seem to target the biceps the way he wanted. He also rarely cheated on this movement even though many of those surrounding him, including Arnold, regularly did so. He found strict style for the entire set worked best. He did 4 sets of 8 to 10 reps.

You'll notice that Danny's entire biceps routine was 17 sets in total. By today's standards still high, but for the '70s generation, below the 20-plus norm. But the end result was two of the largest arms proportionally on the pro scene.

Sergio Oliva - The Myth

This Cuban colossus is perhaps one of the least known great bodybuilders with the general public. But anyone who has studied this sport will agree that Sergio's physique reflected the

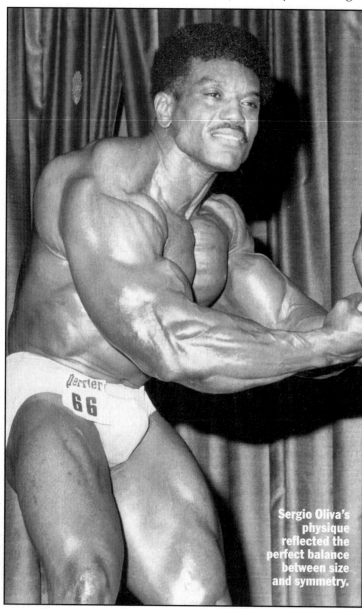

Sergio Oliva's physique reflected the perfect balance between size and symmetry.

perfect balance between size and symmetry. So massive and unbelievably proportioned that he was nicknamed "the Myth." He's one of the few men to have beaten Arnold in competition. Yet Arnold's name is synonymous with bodybuilding, and Sergio's name remains relatively unknown among the public, and one simple, and ugly explanation may explain this, racism. At the time he became involved in bodybuilding, segregation was still legal in the US. The civil rights movement was still fighting its greatest battles. The majority of consumers were white, and they bought supplements and magazines that featured white bodybuilders. If Sergio had been white, we might remember Arnold as an obscure Austrian bodybuilder that competed against Sergio.

Sergio Oliva was born in Havana, Cuba on July 4, 1941. He was born into a large family of 10 brothers and seven sisters. There was never a lot of money around, but he grew up loved, excelling in sports. Interestingly, he wasn't interested in bodybuilding because he didn't believe it was real. He thought the few pictures he had seen were faked. It was when he actually met two bodybuilders that he saw what was possible, and decided to try. Shortly after the Cuban revolution, Sergio was drafted into Castro's army to fight the remaining members of the defeated Batiste army. It was during this combat tour that his entire bodybuilding career was almost consigned to the ashcan of history.

One day, after months of being without the comforts of female company, a rather horny Sergio surprised what he thought was a fair young maiden. She stood with her back to him, long blond hair blowing tantalizingly in the cool mountain air. Slim hips silhouetted in the

Even after being shattered by gunfire, Sergio built his arms up to almost 23 inches of very strong and impressive muscle.

morning sun. The sexy young thing turned around, and Sergio was confronted with an armed, Batiste soldier, complete with a full face of whiskers. In the resulting firefight, Sergio's right arm was shattered by gunfire. "That arm," said the doctors at the army hospital, "will never be the same." It wasn't. It went on to become almost 23 inches of very strong, very big and very impressive muscle!

Not happy living in Castro's communist utopia, Sergio planned his escape. Many tried by sea, but while Sergio would risk his life in combat, he would not tempt fate with sharks. Training hard, he secured a position on the Cuban National weightlifting team, and took part in the Pan Am Games in Jamaica, in 1962. It was there that he defected.

Sergio quickly took his rightful place in the bodybuilding world. In quick succession, he became the first black athlete to win the IFBB Mr. America, Mr. World, Mr. Universe and Mr. Olympia titles. In fact, he won the Olympia three times, and many bodybuilding experts feel he should have won in Essen, Germany in 1972, when Arnold Schwarzenegger scored a controversial victory.[1] Just when it seemed the Myth had faded into history, Sergio stepped onstage at the 1984 and 1985 Mr. Olympias and placed a respectable eighth at both shows. Even in his '40s he carried more muscle mass than most of the younger competitors in their '20. Sergio's competitive record is truly impressive:

1964   Mr. America – AAU, 7th
       Mr. America – AAU, most muscular, 3rd
1965   Junior Mr. America – AAU, 2nd
       Junior Mr. America – AAU, most muscular, 1st
       Mr. America – AAU, 4th
       Mr. America – AAU, most muscular, 1st
1966   Junior Mr. America – AAU, winner
       Junior Mr. America – AAU, most muscular, 1st
       Mr. America – AAU, 2nd
       Mr. America – AAU, most muscular, 1st
       Mr. World – IFBB, overall winner
       Mr. World – IFBB, tall, 1st

Even in his forties Sergio carried more muscle mass than most of the younger competitors in their twenties.

Sergio was one of those genetic marvels that seem to come along only once a generation.

<table>

	Olympia – IFBB, 4th
1967	Olympia – IFBB, winner
	Universe – IFBB, overall winner
1968	Olympia – IFBB, winner
1969	Olympia – IFBB, winner
1970	Mr. World – AAU, pro tall, 2nd
	Olympia – IFBB, 2nd
1971	Universe – Pro, NABBA, tall, 2nd
1972	Olympia – IFBB, 2nd
1973	Mr. International – IFBB, professional, 1st
1974	Mr. International – professional, 1st
1975	Olympus – WBBG, winner
1976	Olympus – WBBG, winner
1977	World Championships – WABBA, professional, 1st
1978	Olympus – WBBG, winner
1980	World Championships – WABBA, professional, 1st
1981	Pro World Cup – WABBA, winner
1984	Olympia – IFBB, 8th
1985	Olympia – IFBB, 8th

</table>

After immigrating to the United States, Sergio lived in Miami briefly, then settled in Chicago. He still trains seriously, gives seminars and looks only slightly less mythical than in his glory days.[1]

Reference:

1. http://www.sergiooliva.com/history.html

Chest, Back and Shoulders

Even by today's pharmaceutically enhanced standards, Sergio Oliva is in a class by himself. We may see 55-inch chest at every turn, but how many of these guys have a 28-30-inch waist to go with it? Sergio was one of those genetic marvels that seem to come along only once a generation. From his three Mr. Olympia wins in the late '60s, to his eighth place finishes at the 1984 and 1985 Mr. Olympias, Sergio has been an inspiration to millions.

In this day of double-split routines, one bodypart per session, Sergio's training was a refreshing change. He regularly combined muscle groups in an alternating fashion. One of his favorite groupings being chest and back.

Being the old weightlifter he was, Sergio usually started his training with flat bench presses. For his first 2 sets he would put 135 pounds on the bar and do 10 to 12 reps as a sort of warmup. Sergio used a short range of motion, fast-paced tempo on his warmups, with no pausing at the top or bottom.

On his third set the weight would be increased to 185 and again Sergio would pump out a set of fast-paced, non-lockout reps, this time for 20.

> **"Somatically speaking he's a near perfect mesomorph; some have big legs and arms but small torsos or a big torso and small arms and/or legs. Sergio is big all over."**
>
> – Greg Zulak, former *MuscleMag International* editor describing the incredible genetic make-up of The Myth, Sergio Oliva.

With these three light, warm-up sets out of the way, Sergio would start putting some weight on the bar. During a typical workout, Sergio would go from 225 up to 315 for sets of 15. Even though he could go much heavier (he was after all the Cuban weightlifting champion), he found the lighter weight for higher reps better for working his chest.

After these 6 straight sets of bench presses, Sergio would then go over to the lat pulldown machine and bang out 14 reps with about 185 pounds. Then it was back to the flat bench press for another 15 reps with 315. Back to the lat machine for 10 reps with 230 pounds and so on. Sergio would do 5 to 6 alternate sets in this fashion, never at any time going less than 10 reps on either.

Next Sergio alternated wide-grip chins to the front using his bodyweight with reverse pulldowns on the lat machine, for 2 sets of 10 reps each.

For his second set of back combinations Sergio alternated seated cable rows with one-arm dumbell rows. On the cables he normally went up to about 250 pounds for sets of 10, while 80- to 120-pound dumbells sufficed on the one-arm rows for sets of 10.

A note on the seated rows, Sergio preferred to do this in what could be called a loose fashion. That is, using just enough body momentum to keep the weight moving, without taking the tension off his lats. A sort of rowing equivalent of cheat curls if you like.

Next up Sergio alternated two sets of front pulldowns with two sets of behind-the-head pulldowns. On a typical day Sergio would use 250 to 275 pounds for sets of 10.

It was at this point that Sergio really went off on a tangent. Most bodybuilders would be taxed just to combine two muscle groups together, but Sergio often added a third! After his seated rows, Sergio alternated bent-over cable laterals and standing side laterals for his delts. He did these in normal superset fashion, resting as little as possible between each set. Two supersets of 10 reps each was the norm.

By now most bodybuilders would be ready to leave the gym or passed out on the floor. But Sergio is only half done! After a short rest he began to train his upper chest.

With an adjustable bench set at 45 degrees, Sergio would do 3 sets of Smith machine incline presses for 10 to 12 reps each. Typically weights ranged from 135 to 225.

With 3 sets of straight inclines completed, Sergio went back to his all too familiar alternating style, this time combining cable upright rows with additional sets of Smith machine inclines. Depending on the day, Sergio would perform 2 to 4 such alternate sets of each, averaging 12 to 15 reps per set.

Sergio has been an inspiration to millions.

If you thought it was all over, think again. The incline bench would be removed and a decline bench substituted. From here Sergio would alternate 3 sets of decline Smith presses with 3 sets of Pec Deck flyes, averaging 12 reps per set.

To finish off his chest, Sergio did one last two-exercise combo, standing cable laterals and dips. For the cables he used about 50 pounds for 2 to 3 sets of 10 reps. For dips he used his bodyweight for 12 to 14 reps. On some days he'd do the 14 reps straight, while on others he'd do 6 to 8, rest for a few seconds, and then try to force out 6 to 8 more.

From looking at the previous routine, the first thing that comes to mind is haphazard. Alternating muscle groups like that sort of goes against the norm. But Arnold frequently did the same thing. And Albert Beckles would frequently alternate arm exercises. All three men are among the sport's true greats. If you feel that your training is becoming too regimental give Sergio's approach a try and see what happens!

Arms

Sergio Oliva is another of those bodybuilders who came to epitomize perfect proportions. Every muscle was in perfect balance with the others and he had few if any weaknesses. But what separates Sergio from other characteristically proportioned bodybuilders is his muscle mass. Not only was Sergio one of the most aesthetically pleasing bodybuilders onstage, he was usually the largest!

Many of today's bodybuilders carry as much muscle mass as Sergio at his best, but how many of them would like to compare waist sizes? A typical growth-hormone inflated midsection

Bertil Fox, Sergio Oliva and Tony Pearson

Sergio still trains seriously, gives seminars and looks only slightly less mythical than in his glory days.

today pushes the 36- to 38-inch mark, while Sergio's probably never measured more than 30 inches in his entire life. Combine that miniscule waist with that great upper body of his and you end up with proportions that most bodybuilders drool over.

Sergio was probably the first bodybuilder to easily break the 20-inch arm barrier. Such other champs as Bill Pearl, Larry Scott, and Leroy Colbert had arms that measured 20 inches, but Sergio's went over 21 inches in contest shape. To this day Sergio is probably the only body-builder whose arms appear larger than his head in a front or rear double biceps pose.

As with chest and back, Sergio was a big fan of supersets when it came to building those monstrous hams. He usually started with a superset of standing barbell and reverse barbell curls. He did the barbell curl first as he felt it was the best overall biceps builder there was. The reverse curls were included to beef up the brachialis, the muscle that connects the forearms to the upper arm. Sergio did 5 supersets of each, doing 8 reps for the barbell curls and 15 reps for the reverse barbell curls.

Sergio's second combination was a biceps and triceps superset, involving the machine preacher curl and standing barbell extension. Even though Sergio was more partial to free weights than machines, he found the preacher machine at the gym he trained in seemed to hit his biceps even more direct than the free barbell version. Sergio did the standing barbell extension (French presses) as his first triceps exercise. He would do 5 or 6 reps in strict style and then use a little body momentum to keep the weight moving. Again it was 5 sets of 8 to 10 reps.

For his third superset, Sergio did two triceps movements. First he would do a set of lying triceps extensions, and then a set of one-arm dumbell extensions. He averaged 5 such supersets for 8 reps per set.

Superset four was a combo of seated dumbell curls and concentration curls. As these were his last biceps exercises he used slightly lower weight and higher reps, usually in the 10 to 12 range.

To finish off his triceps, Sergio did 5 supersets of cable pushdowns and reverse pushdowns. Again it was ultra-strict style and reps in the 10 to 12 range.

Mike Mentzer

Few bodybuilders have generated as much controversy as Mike Mentzer. It wasn't Mike's physique that did it as he deservedly won the Mr. America and Mr. Universe titles. Mike has been claiming for nearly 30 years now that all it takes is one set per muscle group to build a great physique. He discovered early on that his physique responded just as well to brief, intense workouts, just as well if not better than the traditional high volume form of training.

Mike was heavily influenced by the writings of Dr. Arthur Jones, inventor of the Nautilus line of training machines. Mike took Jones' work, built on it, and called it Heavy Duty. Mike made a tidy sum from his *Heavy Duty* books and seminars, and in he process made a great many friends, and a truckload of critics!

Mike made good on his vow to never compete again after Arnold's controversial 1980 Mr. Olympia win in Sydney, Australia. He spent the best part of a decade in a sort of bodybuilding limbo, but made a great comeback as a writer and lecturer in the early '90s. He wrote for a number of years for *Muscular Development* magazine, and is still in big demand as a guest speaker.

Most bodybuilding experts disagree with Mike's "one set to failure" philosophy. But most agree his general views on overtraining are correct. Most bodybuilders in the world today are doing far fewer sets in their workouts than 20 years ago. No less an authority than Dorian Yates has said that Mentzer's ideas played a major role in shaping his training style. Mike Mentzer, love him or hate him, he's one of the most influential figures in bodybuilding history. Here's his competitive record:

1971 Mr. America – AAU, 10th
        Teen Mr. America – AAU, 2nd
        Teen Mr. America – AAU, most muscular, 2nd
1975 Mr. America – IFBB, medium, 3rd
        Mr. USA – ABBA, medium, 2nd
1976 Mr. America – IFBB, overall winner
        Mr. America – IFBB, medium, 1st
        Universe – IFBB, middleweight, 2nd
1977 North American Championships – IFBB, overall winner
        North American Championships – IFBB, middleweight, 1st
        Universe – IFBB, heavyweight, 2nd

Mike Mentzer is one of the most influential figures in bodybuilding history.

1978   USA vs. the World – IFBB, heavyweight, 1st
        World Amateur Championships – IFBB, heavyweight, 1st
1979   Canada Pro Cup – IFBB, 2nd
        Florida Pro Invitational – IFBB, winner
        Night of Champions – IFBB, 3rd
        Olympia – IFBB, heavyweight, 1st
        Pittsburgh Pro Invitational – IFBB, 2nd
        Southern Pro Cup – IFBB, winner
1980   Olympia – IFBB, 5th

Back

Mike's first back exercise was often seated cable rows. With his feet planted firmly against the footpad in front of him, Mike released the tension on the pulley so he was forced to bend right over toward his thighs. From this outstretched position Mike smoothly pulled the cable handle right into his waist and lower rib cage area. At this point Mike would squeeze and tense his back muscles and force his chest out as far as possible. After a brief pause at the contracted position, Mike slowly returned to the outstretched position.

Mike kept this style up for 6 to 8 reps per set, with each one going to absolute muscular failure.

With little rest Mike moved on to his second lat exercise, reverse-grip pulldowns on the lat machine. Mike used a false, thumbs free grip about 12 inches wide and pulled the bar right down to his chest where it was held for a second or two before returning to the overhead position. Mike normally did 10 slow, steady reps, and as with seated rows, squeezed and tensed his back muscles at the bottom position.

For his second set of pulldowns, Mike would up the weight to the point he could only do 3 or 4 on his own. He'd then have a training partner assist him with 3 or 4 forced reps. By this point most lesser mortals would quit, but Mike had something else up his sleeve. He would have his training partner push the bar down to his chest, and then Mike would slowly raise it back to the starting overhead position. Mike would typically do 3 negative reps in this fashion.

To finish his back training Mike did regular or conventional (knees bent) deadlifts. Given the weight used, Mike would wear wrist straps to help him hold on. The deadlifts were performed in perfect style with his back slightly arched, knees bending, and head up. Mike would usually do 4 sets working up to a weight that limited him to only 4 reps.

Mike's triceps were among the largest on the pro scene in the late '70s and early '80s.

If you do the math you see that Mike's entire back routine consists of just 9 sets. And this we should add is his long workout. In true Heavy Duty fashion, Mike often performed just one set of two or three exercises for his entire back workout. Of course each set included forced, negative, and sometimes rest-pause reps, but nevertheless Mike's back routine took all of ten minutes.

Triceps

Like many bodybuilders, Mike did pushdowns as his first triceps exercise, both as a good overall movement and an excellent warm-up exercise. Mike preferred a very short, slightly bent bar for his pushdowns, and started the exercise with the bar at nose level. He'd then push down to an arms locked out position. On a typical workout, Mike would pick a weight that allowed just 6 reps in good style, he'd then have a training partner help him squeeze out approximately 2 forced and 2 negative reps.

After just one set of such madness, Mike concluded his triceps training by doing 2 sets of parallel bar dips to failure. Mike chose these two exercises and performed them in this order to take advantage of the pre-exhaust principle of training. First proposed in the late '60s by *MuscleMag International* founder, Robert Kennedy, it involves performing an isolation movement first to tire out the desired muscle, and then performing a compound exercise to use secondary muscles to assist in training the desired muscle to total failure. In Mike's case, pushdowns almost totally isolate the triceps, while dips bring in the chest and shoulders.

Once again doing the math reveals that Mike performed just 3 sets total for his triceps. Compare this to the 9 to 12 averaged by most bodybuilders. Yet his triceps were among the largest on the pro scene in the late '70s and early '80s.

Legs

It's not surprising that Mr. Heavy Duty trained his legs in that same style as his other muscle groups – short but intense!

Being a big believer in pre-exhaust, Mike's first leg exercise was usually leg extensions on the Nautilus machine. Mike would do one all out set of leg extensions for 6 to 8 reps, and then without any rest switch pads and bang out a set of leg extensions. A typical leg workout would see Mike do two such supersets, using as much weight as possible on both exercises. After he regained his breath, he'd then head over to the squat rack and do 4 sets of squats, working up to over 550 pounds.

To finish his legs, and we mean finish, Mike did 3 sets of lying leg curls. After first getting his 6 reps to positive failure, Mike would have a training partner give him a few forced reps, and then a couple of negative reps.

Mr. Heavy Duty trained his legs in that same style as his other muscle groups – short but intense!

Frank Zane

Frank Zane's bodybuilding career witnessed the explosive growth of modern competitive bodybuilding.

Frank Zane was born on July 14, 1941. Studious by nature, Zane holds two bachelors' degrees and a master's degree in Experimental Psychology. While living in Los Angeles, he taught middle-school math for 13 years. An intellectual, he met with an amazing amount of ignorance when he first took up bodybuilding in high school: "With bodybuilding you can create exactly the kind of body you want. Bodybuilding is the fastest way to change your appearance. When I started training in the 1950s, I was asked: 'Why are you lifting weights? You're just going to get slow, and you won't be good in sports.' My typing teacher even told me: 'Zane, you're never going to learn how to type, Your fingers are muscle-bound.' Bodybuilding should be a positive experience, a growth experience. It permits you to reshape yourself inside and out – mentally, physically and spiritually."

Never one to listen to bad advice, Frank pursued his dream. He was the right man at the right time. His bodybuilding career witnessed the explosive growth of modern competitive bodybuilding: "I think the '70s were really the golden era of bodybuilding. Arnold had a lot to do with it, being the strong personality he was the fact that he got involved in organizing contests. He brought the prize money way up from what it was. If it weren't for him, they'd still be giving a thousand bucks to the winner of the Mr. Olympia. As late as 1975 the winner of the Olympia got $1,000. Then for the longest time, the prize money stayed at around $20,000. Now the winner gets $110,000. The Arnold Classic first prize is the same amount."

Here's Frank's competitive record:

1965	Universe – IFBB, medium, 1st
1966	Mr. America – IFBB, medium, 1st
1967	Mr. America – IFBB, medium, 1st
1968	Mr. America – IFBB, overall winner
	Mr. America – IFBB, medium, 1st
	Mr. International – IFBB, overall winner
	Mr. International – IFBB, medium, 1st

	Universe – IFBB, winner
	Universe – IFBB, short, 1st
1969	Mr. World – IFBB, overall winner
	Mr. World – IFBB, medium, 1st
1970	Universe – NABBA, overall winner
	Universe – NABBA, medium, 1st
1971	Universe – Pro, NABBA, short, 1st
1972	Olympia – IFBB, 4th
	Universe – Pro, NABBA, overall winner
	Universe – Pro, NABBA, short, 1st
1974	Olympia – IFBB, lightweight, 2nd
1975	Olympia – IFBB, lightweight, 4th
1976	Olympia – IFBB, lightweight, 2nd
1977	Olympia – IFBB, winner
1978	Olympia – IFBB, winner
1979	Olympia – IFBB, overall winner
1980	Olympia – IFBB, 3rd
1982	Olympia – IFBB, 2nd
1983	Olympia – IFBB, 4th

Frank has mentored numerous bodybuilders over the years, and is refreshingly honest on the most controversial subjects: "People often ask me if they have to take steroids to succeed in bodybuilding, and I tell them 'No, you don't have to. You can enter a competition without taking steroids. The question is, Will you win?' Nobody talks about physique quality anymore. People just talk about size. They've lost track of what bodybuilding is all about. The winner of the Mr. Olympia has to possess the entire package. He has to be well developed everywhere. People call it symmetry, but it's really not symmetry. It's proportion. That's where every bodypart on your physique fits and is balanced."

His three-straight Mr. Olympia wins in the late '70s helped establish Frank as one of the sport's all-time greats.

Frank retired from competitive bodybuilding in 1983. With Christine, his wife of 31 years, they established Zane Haven, a plush Palm Springs-based live-in bodybuilding and fitness resort. He expanded the business, renaming it Zane Experience, and moved the thriving enterprise to La Mesa, California. At his new facility he trains clients in every aspect of bodybuilding and fitness.

The author of numerous books including, *Zane Nutrition, Fabulously Fit Forever*, and *Frank Zane: Mind, Body and Spirit*, he has also written numerous physique training manuals. He publishes an informative newsletter, which disseminates his legendary training advice, and markets 40 training-related audiocassettes, many of which take listeners through a workout as if he were their personal trainer.

Chest

The words perfection, symmetrical, and proportioned get tossed around loosely these days, but few would argue that Frank Zane was the embodiment of all these terms. His three-straight Mr. Olympia wins in the late '70s helped establish Frank as one of the sport's all-time greats. To many, Frank's physique is what the male form should look like, good muscle tone and size, excellent muscularity, and near-perfect symmetry. Oh what symmetry. Look in a bodybuilding dictionary and you are bound to see a picture of Frank next to that word.

Frank was nicknamed the chemist during his competitive years. Today the term refers to something all together different. In Frank's case it meant someone who, despite having limited genetic potential, used his great intelligence to overcome the physical barriers and succeed. To this day, bodybuilders and trainers seek out Frank's advice on nutrition, training, and posing.

It's not surprising that someone who started training in the '60s relied mainly on barbells and dumbells to build his physique. Frank's chest training was a perfect example and with the exception of cable crossovers at contest time, consisted primarily of barbell and dumbell presses, flyes, and pullovers.

Frank started his chest routine with the flat barbell press. Frank followed a sort of half pyramid on this exercise. He'd do a couple of light warm-up sets and then start adding weight and decreasing the reps. Like most bodybuilders past and present, Frank considered this exercise the best for overall size and strength. As such, he did 6 to 8 sets of 6 to 10 reps. Even though he was never a 500-pound bench presser, Frank could easily rep with over 315 pounds in his day. And keep in mind this is a guy who rarely exceeded 200 pounds in bodyweight.

After flat presses, Frank moved on to inclines to hit his upper chest. After much trial and error, Frank discovered that the standard 30-degree angle was still too steep for him. It was putting too much stress on his front shoulders. Frank found 20 to 25 degrees worked best for him. He also preferred to do his inclines with dumbells to get an extra few degrees of stretch at the bottom. Frank typically did 6 sets of 10 reps of this important upper chest builder.

After inclines, Frank usually moved on to flat flyes to give his chest a good stretch. Again Frank deviated from the norm and did the exercise on a low decline bench. He found that by declining slightly he could take the shoulders out of the exercise and put maximum stress on his pecs, particularly the lower and outer pecs. Frank did 6 sets of 10 reps.

> **"I should have pointed out that I work out six days a week, each session lasting about two hours. There is no rushing the sets; I work comfortably with about 15 sets per bodypart."**
>
> – Frank Zane, three-time Mr. Olympia, commenting on his style of training during the late '70s and early '80s.

To this day, bodybuilders and trainers seek out Frank's advice on nutrition, training and posing.

Frank was famous for his great serratus development and he built those finger-like projections by finishing off his chest routine with 6 sets of 15 reps of dumbell pullovers. He did the exercise across a bench as it allowed him to drop the hips and obtain a greater stretch in his torso.

Ken Waller

Ken Waller has won most of bodybuildings top contests including the Mr. America, Mr. World, and Mr. Universe. There's even an argument to call him Mr. Olympia as he won the heavyweight class at the Mr. Olympia in 1976. At the time the Mr. Olympia was divided into above and below 200 pounds, and Franco Columbu won the under 200 and overall.

Despite being one of the sport's all-time greats, Ken will go down in history as the "thief" in *Pumping Iron*. To try and throw big Mike Katz off his game plan, Ken stole Mike's T-shirt. This act of thievery was one of the subplots to the documentary and forever immortalized Ken as someone to watch backstage at contests!

Here is Ken's incredible competitive record:

Despite being one of the sport's all-time greats, Ken Waller will go down in history as the "thief" in *Pumping Iron*.

1968	Mr. America – AAU, 4th
	Mr. USA – AAU, 4th
1969	Junior Mr. USA – AAU, winner
	Junior Mr. USA – AAU, most muscular, 1st
	Mr. America – AAU, 3rd
	Mr. USA – AAU, winner
	Mr. USA – AAU, most muscular, 1st
1970	Junior Mr. America – AAU, 2nd
	Junior Mr. America – AAU, most muscular, 2nd
	Mr. America – AAU, 2nd
	Mr. America – AAU, most muscular, 2nd
	Mr. World – AAU, overall winner
	Mr. World – AAU, tall, 1st
1971	Mr. America – IFBB, overall winner
	Mr. International – IFBB, tall, 1st
	Universe – NABBA, overall winner
	Universe – NABBA, tall, 1st
	World Championships – WBBG, 2nd
1972	Mr. International – IFBB, overall winner
	Mr. International – IFBB, tall, 1st
1973	Mr. World – IFBB, overall winner
	Universe – IFBB, tall, 2nd
	World Championships – NABBA, overall winner
1974	Universe – IFBB, tall, 2nd
1975	Universe – IFBB, overall winner
	Universe – IFBB, tall, 1st
1976	Olympia – IFBB, heavyweight, 1st
1977	Olympia – IFBB, 5th
	Olympia – IFBB, tall, 2nd
1979	Night of Champions – IFBB, 6th
1980	Olympia – IFBB, 16th
	Pittsburgh Pro Invitational – IFBB
1981	Olympia – IFBB, 16th

Chest

As one of the old Gold's Gym members during the '70s, Ken primarily used barbells and dumbells. He usually started his chest training with either flat or incline barbell presses. He alternated the two, starting with flats first on one day and inclines first the next. The other exercise would then be his second exercise. Ken would then do a decline movement as his third exercise, usually decline dumbell presses. To finish off, Ken would do standing cable crossovers.

A typical Ken Waller chest workout would look something like this:

1. Flat barbell presses 5 sets of 8 to 12 reps
2. Incline barbell presses 5 sets of 8 to 12 reps
3. Decline dumbell presses 5 sets of 8 to 12 reps
4. Cable crossovers 5 sets of 12 reps

Robby Robinson – The Black Prince

If there was ever a pro bodybuilder to whom the term enigma could be ascribed, Robby Robinson is that man. Throughout his long, illustrious career he has drifted in and out of the spotlight, often with many years between contest appearances. Yet as casual as his approach has seemed to what after all has been his life's work – competitive bodybuilding – whenever the Black Prince has deigned to strip off before his public, without exception he has been in superb condition.

Mike Mentzer, Danny Padilla, Robby Robinson and Boyer Coe.

Robert Lee Robinson was born on the island of St. Lucia on May 24, 1946. His family later moved to Damascas, Georgia, and then Tallahassee, Florida where Robby grew up. In school Robby was an all-round athlete who played baseball, basketball, football and ran track. After high school Robby played football for Florida A&M and was elected to the All-Southern Conference, but it was in high school that Robby became serious about bodybuilding:

"I guess my interest began when I started reading bodybuilding magazines around 1965. I was about 13 years old and had never seen anything like that before. When I first saw pictures of Sergio Oliva at the 1967 Mr. Olympia, I was amazed! I didn't think that there was any way possible for a man to look like that – to build his body to that extreme – just from lifting weights. Immediately I fell in love with bodybuilding and wanted to go for it from that point on. Also, I was kind of vain. Still am, I suppose. I remember I would look at myself in my bedroom mirror and think that I might have a chance of making it as a bodybuilder. I found bodybuilding to be such a challenge and went at it full force."

In school Robby was an all-round athlete who played baseball, basketball, football and ran track.

He certainly did.

1974   Mr. USA – AAU, medium, 2nd
1975   Mr. America – AAU, 5th
        Mr. America – AAU, medium, 2nd
        Mr. America – AAU, most muscular, 1st
        Mr. America – IFBB, overall winner
        Mr. America – IFBB, medium, 1st
        Mr. World – IFBB, overall winner
        Mr. World – IFBB, medium, 1st
        Mr. World – IFBB, most muscular, 1st
        Universe – IFBB, medium, 1st
1976   Mr. International – IFBB, overall winner
        Mr. International – IFBB, medium, 1st
        Universe – IFBB, overall winner
        Universe – IFBB, middleweight, 1st
1977   Olympia – IFBB, 2nd
        Olympia – IFBB, tall, 1st
1978   Night of Champions – IFBB, winner
        Olympia – IFBB, 2nd
        Olympia – IFBB, heavyweight, 1st
        Professional World Cup – IFBB, winner
1979   Best in the World – IFBB, professional, 1st
        Canada Pro Cup – IFBB, 4th
        Grand Prix New York – IFBB, winner
        Night of Champions – IFBB, winner
        Olympia – IFBB, lightweight, 3rd
        Pittsburgh Pro Invitational – IFBB, winner
        Southern Pro Cup – IFBB, 2nd
1980   Grand Prix California – IFBB, 2nd
        Night of Champions – IFBB, 2nd
        Pittsburgh Pro Invitational – IFBB, 4th
1981   Pro World Cup – WABBA, 3rd
        Universe – pro, NABBA, winner
        World Championships – WABBA, professional, 2nd

1982	Night of Champions – IFBB
1983	World Pro Championships – IFBB, 4th
1984	Olympia – IFBB, 17th
1985	Night of Champions – IFBB, 8th
1986	Los Angeles Pro Championships – IFBB
	Night of Champions – IFBB, 7th
1987	Grand Prix France – IFBB, 2nd
	Grand Prix Germany (2) – IFBB, 5th
	Grand Prix Germany – IFBB, 2nd
	Night of Champions – IFBB, 5th
	Olympia – IFBB, 5th
1988	Grand Prix England – IFBB, 8th
	Grand Prix Germany – IFBB, 10th
	Grand Prix Greece – IFBB, 7th
	Grand Prix Spain – IFBB, 9th
	Grand Prix US Pro – IFBB, 3rd
	Niagara Falls Pro Invitational – IFBB, winner
	Night of Champions – IFBB, 2nd
	Olympia – IFBB, 17th
	World Pro Championships – IFBB, 3rd
1989	Arnold Classic – IFBB, 2nd
	Grand Prix Melbourne – IFBB, 2nd
	World Pro Championships – IFBB, winner
1990	Arnold Classic – IFBB, 4th
	Night of Champions – IFBB, 5th
1991	Arnold Classic – IFBB, 8th
	Musclefest Grand Prix – IFBB, winner
	Olympia – IFBB, 13th
1992	Ironman Pro Invitational – IFBB, 2nd
	Night of Champions – IFBB, 3rd
1993	Ironman Pro Invitational – IFBB, 8th
1994	Olympia, Masters – IFBB, winner
1995	Olympia, Masters – IFBB, 2nd
1996	Olympia, Masters – IFBB, 4th
1997	Olympia, Masters – IFBB, Masters 50+, 1st
1998	Arnold Classic – IFBB, Masters, 3rd
	Masters Arnod – IFBB, 3rd
1999	Olympia, Masters – IFBB, 6th

Robby is one of the sport's most enduring champions.

How would Robby improve bodybuilding?

"More money. If a guy wins $100,000 at a contest, more than half of that is going into contest preparation, so after all is said and done, he's not walking out with much … and that's if he wins! Compare bodybuilding with any other professional sport and you'll find that we're lightyears behind when it comes to financial compensation. In my opinion the sport is being held back. It's been held back for years and its still not going forward. I don't know if it ever will. I'm always amazed at how some bodybuilders have lost their lives trying to get on covers or in the magazines.

"Back in the '70s the competitors were much friendlier and more supportive of one another. Now everyone seems so distant – as if they dare not even speak to other competitors. The money has made them all more concerned for their individual success. It has destroyed unity."

Biceps

Robby Robinson is another bodybuilder who has straddled so many decades; we could have easily put his routines in the 1980s or 1990s. From the Mr. America title in the early '70s, to his Master's Mr. Olympia title in the '90s, Robby is one of the sport's most enduring champions.

Drawing up a list of the "greatest arms" of all time, you are sure to find Robby's name near the top. Robby was (and still is) one of those bodybuilders that had perfect balance and size in both arms. Most bodybuilders have arms that fall into three categories. There are those with medium size but great peak; those with huge arms but little peak; and those who have one arm high and peaked and the other long and full. But then there are a few genetic freaks like Robby Robinson who have size and peak in both arms. In fact Robby's arms were like mirror images of one another. The triceps hung down and cleanly separated into three heads, while his biceps resembled two perfectly round baseballs.

Being a product of the 1970s and what many bodybuilding historians call the "Gold's Gym" years, it's not surprising to hear that Robby's biceps' routine consisted primarily of free weight exercises. The old Gold's Gym in Venice Beach, California, didn't have the collection of

Robby divided his back training into exercises for width, and exercises for thickness.

chrome-plated machines that most modern gyms are famous for. Instead most patrons relied on barbells and dumbells to hone and chisel their physiques. Were they deprived? Do the names Schwarzenegger, Columbu, Waller, and Padilla, ring any bells?

Robby usually began his biceps routine with basic, old-fashioned, standing barbell curls. Despite their simplicity, barbell curls have probably built more great arms than any other exercise. After a couple of light warm-up sets, Robby did 4 heavy sets, averaging 6 to 8 reps per set.

After barbell curls Robby moved on and targeted his lower biceps with preacher curls. For variety he sometimes did dumbell preachers, but more often than not the barbell formed the nucleus of his training. Robby typically did 4 sets of 6 to 8 reps of this exercise.

With two basic mass builders out of the way, Robby finished off his biceps training with one-arm dumbell concentration curls. Robby used medium weight on this exercise, and every rep was performed in a slow and deliberate manner. None of that yanking the dumbell up with body momentum like many bodybuilders. Again it was 4 sets of between 8 and 12 reps.

Back

The best way to sum up Robby's back training is variety. He found the more exercises he did the better his back got. Robby had over 20 exercises in his back repertoire, and during a typical workout would select four or five. Robby divided his back training into exercises for width, and exercises for thickness. No matter what set or rep range he employed, Robby always did at least one exercise for width and one for thickness in his back training.

Robby started with bent-over barbell rows in a typical back workout. To get a good stretch he'd stand on a high block or bench. He also used a thumbless grip as the standard grip tended to bring in too much biceps. Robby would do the first set with a light weight for about 20 reps, and then proceed to do 5 sets of 12 to 15 reps, pyramiding the weight up with each set. Although a stickler for full range of motion, Robby occasionally added in a few partial reps at the end of a set.

After rows Robby moved on to a basic width exercise like narrow-grip chins. For variety Robby alternated between doing them upright, and leaning back. With either style he stretched all the way up and brought the bar right down to his chest. No half reps. A typical back workout would see Robby do 5 sets of 10 to 15 reps of chins.

For his third exercise, Robby went over to the seated pulley row, one of his favorites for upper back development. Robby would pull the narrow attachment into his lower rib cage, arch his chest, and then stretch forward until the plates were just short of touching the stack. Again Robby did 5 sets of 12 to 15 reps.

To finish off his lats, Robby moved on to wide-grip pulldowns. Leaning back slightly, Robby would pull the bar to his upper chest, and squeeze his shoulder blades and arch his chest as he brought the bar down. You guessed it, 5 sets of 10 to 12 reps.

Despite doing 20 sets, Robby would complete the previous routine in 25 to 30 minutes. Any chitchat was saved for after his workout.

A combination of great genetics and heavy lifting turned Franco into one of the thickest bodybuilders around.

Franco Columbu

To many he will be remembered as Arnold's good buddy and "Sardinian sidekick." But there's much more to Franco Columbu. He holds advanced degrees in chiropractic and nutrition, won the Mr. Olympia title twice, and competed in the World's Strongest Man contest.

Franco was born on Sardinia, an island off the coast of Italy. His first love was boxing, but he switched to powerlifting after nearly killing a competitor in the ring. While attending a powerlifting meet in Germany he witnessed the first bodybuilding contest, won by a young Austrian kid named Arnold Schwarzenegger. The two struck up a friendship, with Arnold introducing Franco to bodybuilding, while Franco pushed Arnold to lift heavier. It wasn't long after Arnold's immigration to America that Franco followed.

Despite his 5'5" height, a combination of great genetics and heavy lifting turned Franco into one of the thickest bodybuilders around. In fact Franco was probably the first short, under-200-pound bodybuilder that could trade shots with much taller bodybuilders and get away with it. Certainly very few bodybuilders of any height or weight wanted to compare lat spreads.

Within a few short years Franco won all the major contests, and only Arnold's presence kept him from winning the Olympia.

Franco had a small part in the landmark documentary *Pumping Iron* (his role being reduced because of his chiropractic studies), and held his own in The World's Strongest Man contest until he fractured a leg while running with a refrigerator strapped to his back. His controversial 1981 Mr. Olympia win didn't seem to reduce his popularity, and he's still one of the most sought-after lecturers.

At full spread, Franco's lats looked like two wings capable of flight.

1968	Universe – NABBA, most muscular, 1st
	Universe – NABBA, short, 2nd
1969	Mr. Europe – IFBB, medium, 1st
	Mr. World – IFBB, short, 2nd
	Universe – IFBB, short, 1st
	Universe – NABBA, most muscular, 1st
	Universe – NABBA, short, 1st
1970	Mr. Europe – IFBB, overall winner
	Mr. Europe – IFBB, short, 1st
	Mr. World – AAU, pro short, 1st
	Mr. World – IFBB, short, 1st
	Universe – IFBB, overall winner
	Universe – IFBB, short, 1st
	Universe – NABBA, short, 2nd
1971	Mr. World – IFBB, overall winner
1972	Olympia – IFBB, 5th
1973	Olympia – IFBB, 2nd
1974	Olympia – IFBB, lightweight, 1st
1975	Olympia – IFBB, lightweight, 1st
1976	Olympia – IFBB, overall winner
	Olympia – IFBB, lightweight, 1st
1981	Olympia – IFBB, winner

Back

More than any other bodybuilder, Franco Columbu defined the "manta ray look" when doing a rear lat pose. At full spread, Franco's lats looked like two wings capable of flight. Many modern bodybuilders have overtaken Franco in overall back development and detail, but none have Franco's lat density. Let's see how he did it.

Franco was probably the first short, under-200 pound bodybuilder that could trade shots with much taller bodybuilders and get away with it.

Very few body-builders of any height or weight wanted to compare lat spreads with Franco.

Franco started his back workout with what he considered the bast lat width exercise there is, chinups. He would start with chins to the rear and take a wide grip. With his body held vertical, he'd pull himself up until he touched the bar to his neck. He'd then lower back down to a full stretched position. Franco would normally do 5 sets of 10 reps of this exercise.

Franco's second exercise was chins to the front. Because of the biomechanical strength advantage of this exercise, Franco would strap extra weight around his waist. he'd also lean back slightly as he pulled up. Again it was 5 sets of 8 to 10 reps.

With two primary width movements completed, Franco moved on to his thickness exercises. He started with one of his favorite movements, T-bar rows. It must have been a treat to watch Franco at the old Gold's Gym rowing with 6, 7, even eight plates on the machine. Normal sets and reps were 5 sets of 8 to 10 reps.

To finish off the greatest lats in history, Franco did either seated cable rows or one-arm dumbell rows, going for a complete stretch at the end. He was never one for half reps. As expected he did 5 sets of 8 to 10 reps.

Ed Corney – Beach Bum Turned Master Poser

The magazines gave Ed the name Master Poser because of his unique, fluid and highly emotional posing routines. Equal responsibility for the moniker must go to Arnold for his proclamation in the movie, "Dat's what I call posing," as Ed executed with precision his classic pivot transition from a back double biceps to a front double biceps shot. For those too young to remember, prior to Ed most posing was done without music or transition moves.

"I've been responsible for bringing posing to a certain point … Before me Frank Zane was the innovator in posing. After it was Chris Dickerson, then Mohamed Makkawy. Today there's a whole new set of standards. I was just responsible for one phase."

In 1960 Ed was your basic 27-year-old Hawaiian beach bum when he decided to start lifting weights. He was 30 when he entered his first contest, and quite a few of his peers looked at him questioningly, wondering what an old guy like Ed was doing onstage in his briefs. He obviously wasn't wasting his time, as his record clearly shows:

1968   Mr. California – AAU, 5th
1970   Mr. America – AAU, 11th
         Mr. California – AAU
         Mr. California – AAU, most muscular, 2nd
         Mr. Iron Man – winner
1971   Mr. America – AAU, 4th
         Mr. California – AAU, winner
         Mr. California – AAU, most muscular, 1st
         Mr. USA – IFBB, winner
         Universe – IFBB, medium, 3rd

1972 Mr. America – IFBB, winner
      Mr. International – IFBB, short, 1st
      Universe – IFBB, overall winner
      Universe – IFBB, medium, 1st
1973 Mr. World – IFBB, Class one, 1st
1974 Mr. International – IFBB, short, 1st
      Mr. World – IFBB, Class one, 1st
1975 Olympia – IFBB, lightweight, 2nd
      World Pro Championships
      – IFBB, lightweight, 2nd
1976 Olympia – IFBB, lightweight, 3rd
1977 Olympia – IFBB, 3rd
      Olympia – IFBB, short, 2nd
1978 Night of Champions – IFBB, 4th
      Olympia – IFBB, 7th
      Olympia – IFBB, lightweight, 4th
1979 Canada Pro Cup – IFBB
      Grand Prix Pennsylvania – IFBB
      Night of Champions – IFBB, 8th
      Olympia – IFBB, lightweight, 9th
      Pittsburgh Pro Invitational – IFBB, 8th
      Southern Pro Cup – IFBB, 7th
      World Pro Championships – IFBB, 5th
1980 Grand Prix Miami – IFBB, 6th
      Night of Champions – IFBB, 4th
      Olympia – IFBB, 11th
      Pittsburgh Pro Invitational – IFBB, 6th
      Universe – Pro IFBB
      World Pro Championships – IFBB
1981 Olympia – IFBB, 13th
1983 Olympia – IFBB, 14th
1994 Olympia Masters– IFBB, 10th
      Olympia Masters – IFBB, Masters 60+, 1st
1995 Olympia Masters – IFBB, 11th
      Olympia Masters – IFBB, Masters 60+, 1st
1996 Olympia Masters – IFBB, 11th
      Olympia Masters – IFBB, Masters 60+, 1st
1997 Olympia Masters – IFBB, Masters 60+, 2nd
1998 Arnold Classic – IFBB, Masters, 10th
      Masters Arnold – IFBB, 10th

"Now dats what I call posing!"

– Arnold Schwarzenegger commenting on Ed Corney's posing in the groundbreaking documentary *Pumping Iron.*

Ed Corney was known for his unique, fluid and highly emotional posing routines.

"I never think about my age. When people start to think of age they begin to use it as an excuse. They think they're too old to do this or that. They think it's okay to get fat, to get lazy … People ask me all the time whether it's tougher to stay in shape now than 20 years ago. Of course it is! You have to work harder. What makes you think it's supposed to get easier? You train a little harder, a little smarter, and there's no reason why anyone has to get out of shape. Getting older doesn't get you out of shape. Getting lazy is why people get fat and old."

Ed is perhaps best known for his appearance in the classic movie, *Pumping Iron*. No single event in the history of bodybuilding has shaped the public's perception of the sport so profoundly as that 1977 film. It propelled both Arnold Schwarzenegger and Lou Ferrigno into the Hollywood spotlight. The year was 1975, and Ed will always remember it as one the best.

"I was living in Oregon when Arnold called. Franco Columbu had always been his partner, but there was a scheduling problem and Arnold needed someone else to train with. He picked me. It didn't take long for me to make up my mind – I packed my bags and moved to LA … The scene where I'm squatting is one that people always think was staged. There was no acting back then – we trained like animals, and Arnold was the biggest animal of all. His intensity was unforgettable. It's shaped my training all these years … For four months it was fantastic. The changes in my physique were dramatic. Everything became organized, regimented, focused. Filming had begun, and they filmed everywhere – at Arnold's home, in the gym, on the beach. We were celebrities, and it was a crazy time of women and parties. Most of all it was the training that made it special."

Today Ed sponsors contests and on October 28, held the first annual NPC 2000 Ed Corney Muscle Classic. If you're interested in entering, contact Ed. You're never too old to start. To contact Ed you can E-mail him at classic@edcorney.com or write him by mail at Ed Corney, 4438 Cahill Street, Fremont, CA 94538.

Biceps

Being another of Arnold Schwarzenegger's Gold's Gym buddies, it's not surprising to hear most of Ed's training routines were based on free weight exercises, with the occasional cable movement thrown in for good measure. On any given day in the old Gold's Gym you'd see Robby Robinson in one corner doing chinups, Danny Padilla repping out on the leg press, and the king himself, Arnold, inflating those enormous pecs of his with flat bench presses.

If it happened to be Ed's biceps' day, the first exercise he'd probably start with was the standing barbell curl. This one exercise has built more biceps than any other has. Ed would take a medium-width grip and do 3 to 4 sets of 8 to 10 reps. A typical set would consist of 6 to 8 strict reps, and then 2 to 4 cheat reps at the end.

Ed's second exercise was another Gold's Gym staple, preacher curls. Although Ed occasionally did the barbell version, he preferred doing them one arm at a time with dumbells. Again it was 3 to 4 sets of 8 to 10 reps.

To finish off those well-proportioned biceps, Ed did 3 to 4 sets of two-arm cable curls. As this was a finishing exercise, Ed kept the weight medium and did slightly higher reps, usually in the 10 to 12 range.

Ed's ageless physique is the result of living the bodybuilding lifestyle.

Chapter 5

The 1980s

The 1980s started with the election of former actor and California Governor, Ronald Regan, as President. Besides bringing a touch of Hollywood to the Oval office, his stern anti-Communist stance was a major contributor to the collapse of the Soviet Union in 1988.

If one word could summarize the 1980s it was commercialism. It seemed every manner of making a buck was tried. Of course the '80s will also be remembered for the number of bankruptcies.

On the bodybuilding scene the decade started with controversy as six-time Mr. Olympia, Arnold Schwarzenegger, came out of retirement and won a record seventh title in Sydney, Australia in 1980. But unlike his victories in the early '70s, for the first time in his career he was booed at his acceptance speech. A combination of Arnold not quite being up to his '70s condition, and the remarkable shape of some of the other competitors, left many in the audience disillusioned with the decision.

If Arnold's victory in 1980 raised a few eyebrows, it was Franco Columbu's winning in 1981 that shook the sport. While a strong argument could be made that Arnold was top five material in 1980, Franco was clearly not the best bodybuilder onstage in Columbus, Ohio. Further, Franco's mediocre legs and gynocomastia, were highlighted by the incredible shape of Chris Dickerson, Tom Platz, Roy Callender, and Danny Padilla. Many in the audience compared the result to the 1919 Chicago White Sox baseball scandal. The question was, could bodybuilding recover?

It took just one year for the previous question to be answered as Chris Dickerson won the 1982 Mr. Olympia held in London, England. After placing second to both Arnold and Franco, Chris decided to give it one more try, and despite challenges from Frank Zane, Tom Platz, and Casey Viator, emerged victorious.

Tom Platz

1983 Mr. Olympia
Samir Bannout

The 1983 Mr. Olympia was significant as not only did it feature a relative unknown as the winner, but also it signaled the beginning of the next dynasty in the sport. Samir Bannout, a Lebanese immigrant to the US, was a popular winner with his great symmetry and muscularity. But it was the third place finisher that made the audience sit up and take notice. Atlanta native Lee Haney weighed 245 pounds in contest shape, and not since Arnold had spectators witnessed such incredible muscle mass. Starting with the 1984 Mr. Olympia, and continuing up until 1991, Haney won eight straight Mr. Olympia titles, smashing Arnold's consecutive victories record (six) and overall record (seven).

Another major development of the 1980s was the abolishing of most of the "Mr." titles and replacing them with "Championships." Most bodybuilding federations realized that if bodybuilding was to become more popular, it would have to reorganize in the same manner as most other sports. As such the old Mr. America title became known as the US Nationals. Likewise the amateur Mr. Universe became the World Championships. Even such titles as Mr. California and Mr. New York, were renamed the California and New York Championships.

Closely related to the previous, was the renaming of the professional Mr. Universe the Arnold Classic. Arnold and his business partner, Jim Lorimer, had been promoting contests for years, but in 1989, they gave the Mr. Universe a permanent home in Columbus, Ohio. The contest became a huge hit and to this day almost rivals the Olympia in prestige and popularity.

The final major event of the decade was the establishing of a series of smaller professional contests known as Grand Prix events. Initially they were held in the US, but over the last decade they have moved to Europe, and give professional bodybuilders a chance to increase their income.

Here are some of the stars of the 1980s and the routines they used to reach the pinnacle of the sport.

Casey Viator became one of the dominant bodybuilders on the Grand Prix circuit in the early 1980s.

Casey Viator

Casey Viator was history's youngest Mr. America winner. At just 19 years of age he stepped onstage and literally blew everyone else away. Never had anyone that young, and at that height, displayed such muscle density. Most assumed the young Louisiana native would displace Arnold from the throne. But such was not to be. Casey tired of the sport and disappeared for nearly eight years.

Casey was an early follower of Dr. Arthur Jones' high intensity form of training, but soon found his physique responded best to the more traditional high sets style of training. When he made his comeback in the late '70s, Casey immediately picked up where he left off and in short order had won a couple of Grand Prix events and a third at the 1982 Mr. Olympia. Casey retired in 1982, and with the exception of a 12th place finish at the 1995 Masters Mr. Olympia, is no longer active in the sport. Here's his impressive contest record:

1969	Teen Mr. America – AAU, 6th
1970	Mr. America – AAU, 3rd
	Mr. America – AAU, Most muscular, 3rd
	Mr. USA – AAU, winner
	Mr. USA – AAU, most muscular, 1st
	Teen Mr. America – AAU, winner
	Teen Mr. America – AAU, most muscular, 1st
1971	Junior Mr. America – AAU, winner
	Junior Mr. America – AAU, most muscular, 1st
	Mr. America – AAU, winner
	Mr. America – AAU, most muscular, 1st
1978	Universe – NABBA, medium, 2nd
1979	Canada Pro Cup – IFBB, 5th
1980	Grand Prix California – IFBB, 3rd
	Grand Prix Louisiana – IFBB, winner
	Grand Prix Miami – IFBB, 2nd
	Night of Champions – IFBB, 5th
	Olympia – IFBB, 13th
	Olympia – IFBB, 14th
	Pittsburgh Pro Invitational – IFBB, winner

1981   Grand Prix California – IFBB
1982   Grand Prix Belgium – IFBB, 4th
        Grand Prix Sweden – IFBB, 3rd
        Olympia – IFBB, 3rd
        Olympia, Masters – IFBB, 12th

Roy Callender and Casey Viator

Chest

You'd think that any guy who won the Mr. America title at 19 would grow merely by looking at a barbell. But such was not the case for casey Viator. True, his arms and legs seemed to grow from whatever he did, but the same could not be said for his torso muscles. Even when he won the Mr. America title, his side chest poses were mainly rib cage. When he came out of retirement in the late 1970s, the first thing Casey did was start prioritizing his training to bring up his lagging muscle groups.

For those not aware, Casey was a follower of Dr. Arthur Jones' (and later Mike Mentzer's) high intensity style of training. Although he never subscribed to it in its purest sense – 1 set per body-part to failure – you rarely saw Casey doing more than 4 to 6 sets in total for any one muscle. Such training seemed to work wonders for his limbs, but his torso muscles, especially his chest, lagged far behind. Starting around 1979 Casey sought the advice of the Master Blaster himself, Joe Weider. Joe suggested Casey give the high volume style of training a try. The results were worth it, as Casey became one of the dominant body-builders on the Grand Prix circuit in the early 1980s. Only a near perfect Chris Dickerson prevented him from winning the coveted Mr. Olympia in 1982.

Here's the chest routine Casey credits with helping him become one of the star players in the early eighties:

1. Incline barbell presses – 3 sets of 5 to 6 reps
2. One-arm pec flyes – 2 sets of 5 to 6 reps
3. Parallel bar dips – 2 sets of 6 to 8 reps
4. Incline dumbell presses – 2 sets of 5 to 6 reps
5. Flat dumbell flyes – 2 sets of 6 to 8 reps
6. Cable crossovers – 2 sets of 10 to 12 reps

Andreas Cahling

Andreas Cahling was born in 1953, in Sweden. His own father admits that Andreas was an uncontrollable child. Once, when his father saw a headline about a firebomb being used in Poland, he asked Andreas, who had just been there, "Why did you do it?" Not "if he did it." Andreas hadn't done it, but given his behavior, it's easy to understand why his father wasn't so easily convinced.

At the age of 17, Andreas hid on a train and rode through Siberia. That adventure ended in Japan, where he trained in Judo and worked as a bartender. Andreas was always a bit of a con-artist and that's how he landed the job as a bartender.

"I got the job after I fooled the bartender. I said I could open beer bottles with only my fingers. He didn't believe me so I took two bottles from a case and popped them open with a faked show of exertion. He tried to do the same, but of course didn't succeed. What he didn't know was that I had prepared the bottle caps in an unguarded moment."

> **"You won't get that look from doing only conventional high repetition ab work. To get those washboard abs you must work them like any other muscle group – with weights."**
>
> – Andreas Cahling, 1980, Mr. International offering good advice on ab training.

Today Andreas has a successful online business selling clothing, supplements and bodybuilding paraphernalia.

Andreas competitive record is as follows:

1969	Jr. Mr. Sweden 3rd
	Jr. Mr. Scandinavia 3rd
	Mr. Sweden
1975	Mr. Sweden 5th
1976	Mr. Venice Beach 1st
	Mr. America's Bicentennial Man 2nd
	AAU Mr. Western States 2nd
	AAU Mr. Gold's Classic 1st
1977	Mr. America – AAU, short, 4th
	Mr. World – IFBB, middleweight, 2nd
	AAU Mr. California 6th
1978	Mr. International – IFBB, middleweight, 6th
	World Amateur Championships – IFBB, middleweight 5th
1979	Mr. International – IFBB, middleweight, 2nd
1980	Mr. International – IFBB, overall winner
	Mr. International – IFBB, light heavyweight, 1st
1981	Canada Pro Cup – IFBB, 6th
1984	World Pro Championships – IFBB, 6th
1990	Niagara Falls Pro Invitational – IFBB, 4th
1993	Chicago Pro Invitational – IFBB, 20th
	Niagara Falls Pro Invitational – IFBB, 18th
	Pittsburgh Pro Invitational – IFBB

Today Andreas doesn't have to con anyone. He has a successful online business, The Andreas Cahling Collection. There he sells clothing, supplements and bodybuilding paraphernalia.[1]

Reference:

1. www.andreascahling.com

Abdominals

Although he never quite made the impact on the pro scene that was forecast by his 1980 Mr. International win, nevertheless Andreas Cahling sported one of the greatest midsections on the bodybuilding scene in the early 1980s.

Andreas usually started his abdominal training with Roman-chair situps and stretch to warm up his midsection. To reduce the stress on his lower back, Andreas only leaned half-way back, instead of going all the way down to the bottom. Likewise he didn't come all the way up. This was not so much out of safety but to keep the tension on his abs at all times. Coming all the way up brings in the hip flexors to a great extent.

After Roman-chair situps, Andreas moved on to crunches. For those not familiar with the exercise, Andreas lay back on the floor with his

Andreas Cahling sported one of the greatest midsections on the bodybuilding scene in the early 1980s.

knees bent and feet flat on the floor. With his hands behind his head and elbows pointing outward, he would lift his torso about ten to 12 inches off the floor, pause for a second, and then lower back down. Andreas found crunches to be highly effective for his upper abs.

After crunches, Andreas moved on to bench leg raises to hit his lower abs. He would sit on the edge of a flat bench and with his knees bent slightly, raise his legs up and down. Andreas points out that the key to leg raises is to minimize body momentum. Swinging the legs up and down is not doing much in the way of stimulating the abs. Every rep must be slow and controlled.

To finish his ab training, Andreas moved on to hanging leg raises on a chinning bar. Again, the hardest part of this exercise is reducing the temptation to swing. For those who still have trouble mastering the exercise, Andreas recommends having a training partner help out by holding his hand on your back. For variety Andreas would do hanging leg raises to the sides. First he'd raise his legs to one side, and then to the other.

With the direct ab exercises out of the way, Andreas would go over to a mirror and practice a number of ab poses. This not only helped bring out separation in his ab muscles, but also gave him the control he needed when posing onstage.

Tim Belknap

Every once in a while a bodybuilder comes along that seems to raise the density bar to a new level. No sooner had fans got used to a 180-pound Franco Columbu on a 5'5" frame, when along comes 190-pound Tim Belknap at a couple of inches shorter.

Tim was born in Rockford, Illinois in 1958. At an early age he was athletic, and as a bodybuilder, numerous magazine articles raved about his muscle-packed torso and overall density, especially his ripped quads, vascular arms and thick neck. Especially noteworthy was the fact that Belknap made his great achievements despite having diabetes.

"I've been diabetic since I was 15. That makes my contest preparation 250 percent harder than normal. That's not a complaint, but rather a fact that I have to deal with. Diabetes is a disease in which sugar and starch aren't properly absorbed by the body. Statistics say it's the third largest killer disease in the world. It brought me close to death twice, so I've learned to deal with it with respect. I see a doctor and specialist regularly and have the necessary tests done. I'm full of finger-pricks now from all the blood testing. I take insulin, monitor my diet, and control my weight. I also pay a lot of attention to how my body feels, especially when I'm bulking up or cutting down, and use my body feedback in determining any increase or decrease in

Tim Belknap won his titles with perseverance, determination, and drive.

"The most densely muscular physique ever seen."

– Don Ross, describing Tim Belknap.

Numerous magazine articles raved about Tim's muscle-packed torso and overall density, especially his ripped quads, vascular arms and thick neck.

the amount of insulin. I do what I have to do, because I want to avoid the complications of diabetes: blindness, kidney and nerve damage, and high incidence of limb amputation. I think that the most important thing about all this is to realize that even if you have a handicap you get to the top. I won my titles by perseverance, determination, and drive to do my best."

And his record proves his point:

1981   Mr. America – AAU, overall winner
        Mr. America – AAU, light heavyweight, 1st
        World Amateur Championships – IFBB, light heavyweight, 2nd
1982   National – NPC, heavyweight, 3rd
1983   Grand Prix Las Vegas – IFBB, 10th
1984   Universe – NABBA, short, 1st
        World Championships – NABBA, overall winner
        World Championships – NABBA, short, 1st
1985   Universe – NABBA, overall winner
        Universe – NABBA, short, 1st
        World Championships – NABBA, overall winner
        World Championships – NABBA, short, 1st

Tim had the world by the tail. He was a champion bodybuilder, but on the minus side, Tim was taken to task for his lack of interpersonal skills and his uneven personality at the time; usually friendly and outgoing but unfortunately at times he was also abrasive, moody, volatile, and bad tempered. In 1985 Tim dropped out of bodybuilding.

"A series of things happened all at once, like everything in life was going wrong! My job folded, I was depressed about my father's death, my grandmother died, by brother was having health problems, my diabetes flared up, my ex moved in with another guy … Hey, I'm telling it to you straight. My ex even took my dog – that was the crowning unjustice! … So when I won the World I said, 'This is it. There's no money to be made. I'm outta here.' … I kept up my training and went into business. I worked for the Sports Club in Los Angeles. In no time I was one of their top-producing salespeople. I set records in sales and in working out clients. I would do as many as 12 a day, starting at 4:30 a.m. and going to 6 p.m.

Tim was an inspiration to millions of diabetics and shorter people everywhere.

Basically I was a workaholic, but I liked to work and I enjoyed the business world. I learned techniques of negotiation, different ways of working with people, and the process of making money. I like the money: I went from driving a Blazer to a 525 BMW to a 535 BMW. Now I'm looking into an 850… The stability and income were bound to change my outlook. I developed many friends and business associates, I learned how to get along with people better, and my personality improved. I'm not as arrogant or as cocky as I used to be – I've mellowed out. No more attitude, no more ego trips."

"I also learned more about physiology, kinesiology and training. I already knew some things from my study of health science at Northwestern Illinois University, where I intend to complete my BA work sometime. I needed certification to work at the Sports Club, so I became certified with the National Academy of Sports Medicine. I learned better biomechanics, better techniques, the importance of proper training, and what not to do. That put me in the shape I'm in today … Then when I was working out I heard a song with lyrics saying: 'You're the only one who can do it. You can change your life.' So I went home, went into my den, looked at my pictures on the wall, said a prayer, and decided to give it my best shot.

There's always a positive end to a negative road, I believe. I knew that, if I came back, I had to come back better than ever."

1991   Niagara Falls Pro Invitational – IFBB, 10th
        San Jose Pro Invitational – IFBB, 7th
1992   Ironman Pro Invitational – IFBB, 14th
        Ironman Pro Invitational – IFBB, 18th

Shoulders

At his prime, Tim Belknap had few weaknesses. Every muscle was built to the max and shoulders were no exception. As expected from someone who competed as a light heavyweight despite his lightweight height, Tim trained heavy and hard. Not a lot of fluff, just basic movements using ponderous poundages.

He usually started his shoulder training with barbell presses. If it was the off-season he'd do them to the front, but close to a contest he'd switch to the rear. Tim did 4 to 5 sets of presses, averaging 6 to 8 reps per set.

After presses, Tim usually moved on to front dumbell raises. Tim admitted he got a little loose on this exercise. But he only used enough body momentum to keep the weight moving. He cheated to put more stress on his delts (by using heavier weights) not less. Again he did 4 sets of 6 to 8 reps.

To finish off his delts, Tim did 4 sets of bent-over lateral raises. Once again he added variety to this exercise. In the off-season he stood up, got a little loose, and used heavy weight. But close to a contest he lay facedown on a flat bench and go ultra strict. We should add that close to a contest, Tim would add in side lateral raises to his routine.

Although Tim never made the impact on the pro level that many expected, nevertheless he was an inspiration to millions of diabetics and shorter people everywhere.

Lance Dreher

Lance was another of those bodybuilders who romped through the amateur ranks, winning both the Mr. America and Mr. Universe titles, but then had a poor pro career. With the exception of some success in the WABBA and NABBA, Lance never lived up to the promise he showed while an amateur.

Lance started training while in his teens and by the time he was 18 was benching 450 pounds. Despite a poor outing as a pro, Lance developed two of the greatest arms in history and they served as inspiration for millions of bodybuilders. Here's his record:

Lance developed two of the greatest arms in history and they served as inspiration for millions of bodybuilders.

1976   Collegiate Mr. America – AAU, overall winner
1977   Mr. America – AAU, medium, 9th
1980   Mr. America – AAU, heavyweight, 3rd
1981   Gold's Classic – NPC, heavyweight, 3rd
          Mr. America – AAU, heavyweight 1st
          World Amateur Championships – IFBB, overall winner
          World Amateur Championships – IFBB, heavyweight, 1st
1982   Olympia – IFBB, 15th
1983   Olympia – IFBB, 15th

1984   Universe – Pro NABBA, 3rd
        World Championships – WABBA, professional, 3rd
1985   Universe – Pro NABBA, 2nd
        Universe – Pro NABBA, 3rd
        World Championships – WABBA, professional, 5th
1986   Universe – Pro NABBA, winner
        World Championships – WABBA, professional, 5th
1988   Chicago Pro Invitational – IFBB, 6th
1989   Arnold Classic – IFBB, 9th
1991   Musclefest Grand Prix – IFBB, 15th
1992   Chicago Pro Invitational – IFBB, 19th

Chest

Lance Dreher was lucky early in life as he received good advice from his father about training. His father came from the old school where strict style was king. It's fine to lift some meaningful weight, but not at the expense of technique. His father also instilled in Lance an appreciation for basic movements. As such Lance's first chest routine consisted of just two movements, flat bench presses and pullovers. Lance did 5 to 6 sets of each exercise for 6 to 8 sets of each, three times per week. Did it work? Well, by the time he was eighteen he was using 450 pounds! How many 18-year-olds are hoisting 450 pounds off their chest we ask? Not many.

"The man has got one hell of a chest, by the time he was 18 he was using 450 pounds ... strict bench with no collars on the bar."

– Marc James, former *MuscleMag International* contributor commenting on 1980 Mr. America winner Lance Dreher.

A piece of advice from Lance – don't get too impatient.

Lance is a firm believer that many beginners get caught up in the "more is better" philosophy, all too prevalent in life. He stresses that beginners can achieve great results on only 6 to 8 sets total for chest. As he used to tell members at his club, "Don't get too impatient."

Over the years, Lance's own chest routine changed. After trying just about every chest exercise in the book, he found that some movements gave great results, while others did little or nothing. The chest routine he eventually settled on was a combination of barbell and dumbell movements, alternating between flat and incline exercises.

The first thing Lance usually did was a warm-up set of flat dumbell presses using 35- to 40-pound dumbells for 15 to 20 reps. He then got serious by grabbing a set of 140-pounders and doing 4 to 5 sets of 6 to 8 reps. On days when he couldn't get at least 6 reps on the last set or two, he would lower the weight.

With his basic flat exercise out of the way, Lance usually moved on to incline dumbell flyes. Through trial and error, Lance found an angle of 30 degrees worked his upper chest best, while minimizing front shoulder involvement. With his chest warmed up from the heavy flats, Lance would go right into his heavy weight on incline flyes. On most days this meant 90-pound dumbells or more. Lance did 5 sets of 6 to 8 reps on dumbell incline flyes. Sometimes he'd throw in a forced rep or two at the end with the help of a spotter.

Lance's third exercise was flat flyes. He did these using the same technique as incline flyes. He started with a 110-pound dumbell and banged out his customary 6 to 8 reps. If the strength was there he'd use heavier dumbells, but sometimes he'd need to drop the weight on the last couple of sets to get the six rep minimum.

Lance's last chest exercise was incline dumbell or barbell presses. If he used a bar he'd start with 225 pounds for 6 to 8 reps and then increase to 285 pounds for the next 3 sets. As with incline flyes, Lance preferred an angle no higher than 30 degrees.

Although the previous exercises made up the core of Lance's chest routine, the order was not fixed in stone. He regularly "shuffled" things around. And close to a contest he added pec flyes and cable crossovers to bring out the extra detail in his chest, particularly the inner chest region.

Albert has been competing for 39 years. He has won more titles than just about any man alive today.

Albert Beckles – The Ageless Wonder

When Albert first began training many years ago, there weren't many real professional contests with huge cash prizes. A bodybuilder actually making a living from the sport alone was unheard of.

But if the money was meager, the man was not. Albert could always be counted on to thrill the audience with the sight of his incredible split-peaked biceps muscles and razor sharp development of his rear deltoids and back.

Albert was born in the Barbados. He was a late bloomer in the sport, and didn't begin bodybuilding until he was 27 years old. Albert has been competing for 39 years. He has won more titles than just about any man alive today, his favorite being the Mr. Universe in Paris, France in 1971.[1]

Take a look at his incredible career:

1965 Universe – NABBA, medium, 3rd
1966 Universe – NABBA, medium, 6th
1967 Mr. Britain – NABBA, 3rd
       Universe – NABBA, medium, 1st
1968 Mr. Britain – NABBA, 2nd
1969 Mr. Britain – NABBA, 2nd
       Mr. World – IFBB, medium, 2nd
       Universe – NABBA, medium, 3rd
1970 Mr. Britain – NABBA, winner
       Mr. Europe – overall winner
       Mr. Europe – medium, 1st
       Universe – NABBA, medium, 2nd
1971 Mr. Britain – NABBA, winner
       Mr. World – AAU, winner
       Mr. World – AAU, most muscular, 1st
       Universe – IFBB, overall winner
       Universe – IFBB, medium, 1st
       Universe – NABBA, medium, 1st
1973 Mr. Europe – IFBB, overall winner
       Mr. Europe – IFBB, medium, 1st
       Universe – IFBB, medium, 1st
1975 Olympia – IFBB, lightweight, 3rd
       Universe – IFBB, medium, 2nd
1977 Olympia – IFBB, 7th
       Olympia – IFBB, short, 4th
1978 Olympia – IFBB, lightweight, 8th
1979 Best in the World – IFBB, professional, 3rd
       Grand Prix Pennsylvania – IFBB, 3rd
       Olympia – IFBB, lightweight, 7th
       World Pro Championships – IFBB, 2nd
1980 Universe – Pro, IFBB, 4th
       World Pro Championships – IFBB, 4th
1981 Canada Pro Cup – IFBB, 2nd
       Grand Prix Belgium – IFBB, 2nd
       Grand Prix California – IFBB, 4th
       Grand Prix Louisiana – IFBB, 2nd
       Grand Prix Massachusetts – IFBB, 2nd
       Grand Prix New England – IFBB, winner
       Grand Prix New York – IFBB, 2nd
       Grand Prix Wales – IFBB, 3rd
       Grand Prix World Cup – IFBB, 6th
       Night of Champions – IFBB, 2nd
       Professional World Cup – IFBB, 6th
1982 Grand Prix Belgium – IFBB, 2nd
       Grand Prix Sweden – IFBB, 4th
       Night of Champions – IFBB, winner

Albert was a late bloomer in the sport, and didn't begin bodybuilding until he was 27 years old.

Olympia – IFBB, 5th
World Pro Championships – IFBB, winner
1983 Grand Prix England – IFBB, 5th
Grand Prix Las Vegas – IFBB, 3rd
Grand Prix Portland – IFBB, 4th
Grand Prix Sweden – IFBB, 5th
Grand Prix Switzerland – IFBB, 5th
Night of Champions – IFBB, 3rd
Olympia – IFBB, 7th
1984 Canada Pro Cup – IFBB, winner
Olympia – IFBB, 4th
World Grand Prix – winner
World Pro Championships – IFBB, winner
1985 Night of Champions – IFBB, winner
Olympia – IFBB, 2nd
1986 Olympia – IFBB, 4th
1987 Grand Prix France – IFBB, 4th
Grand Prix Germany (2) – IFBB, 6th
Grand Prix Germany – IFBB, 4th
Olympia – IFBB, 7th
World Pro Championships – IFBB, 3rd
1988 Chicago Pro Invitational – IFBB, 4th
Grand Prix England – IFBB, 7th
Grand Prix France – IFBB, 11th
Grand Prix Germany – IFBB, 8th
Grand Prix Italy – IFBB, 8th
Grand Prix Spain (2) – IFBB, 8th
Grand Prix Spain – IFBB, 7th
Night of Champions – IFBB, 5th
Olympia – IFBB, 15th
World Pro Championships – IFBB, 10th
1989 Arnold Classic – IFBB, 7th
Grand Prix England – IFBB, 9th
Grand Prix Finland – IFBB, 9th
Grand Prix France – IFBB, 9th
Grand Prix Holland – IFBB, 11th
Grand Prix Melbourne – IFBB, 4th
Grand Prix Spain (2) – IFBB, 10th
Grand Prix Spain – IFBB, 10th
Grand Prix Sweden – IFBB, 9th
Grand Prix US Pro – IFBB, 4th
Night of Champions – IFBB, 8th
Olympia – IFBB, 15th
World Pro Championships – IFBB, 4th
1990 Arnold Classic – IFBB, 9th
Houston Pro Invitational – IFBB, 11th
Niagara Falls Pro Invitational – IFBB, 12th

Many feel that like a vintage wine, Albert got better as he got older.

Today, Albert still trains hard and keeps his body in top condition through proper eating. At a height of 5'7", he maintains an off-season weight of 220 to 230 pounds.

Albert works as a personal trainer, and enjoys a dedicated following. With his experience he is considered to be among the best. Albert trains each client to his or her own abilities and goals. With Albert's guidance, his clients are reaching their fitness goals and feeling better than ever thought possible.

Albert is an inspiration to all that are fortunate enough to meet him. He is a gentleman who truly deserves and lives up to his title "The Ageless Wonder" every day.[1]

Reference:
1. http://www.dreamtan.com/albert.html

Albert Beckles and Mohammed Makkawy.

Arms

Despite competing against competitors half his age, Albert Beckles was one of the most dominant bodybuilders of the 1980s. In fact many feel that like a vintage wine, Albert got better as he got older. And when it came to trading arm shots, few pros wanted to be standing next to Albert in the lineup.

Like Arnold and Sergio Oliva, Albert frequently supersetted exercises for opposing muscles, and one of his favorite routines was to alternate biceps and triceps exercises.

Albert's first exercise in his biceps/triceps routine was standing barbell curls. Albert's technique on this exercise was in a word, flawless. He always kept his upper arms close to his sides and allowed his elbows to move slightly forward as he curled the bar up. His upper body did not sway or in any way help him lift the weight. If he couldn't keep it moving using biceps strength alone, the weight was decreased. Using a medium speed tempo, Albert did 12 reps of barbell curls.

When it came to trading arm shots, few pros wanted to be standing next to Albert in the lineup.

"Look Chris, you've got to realize something about my arms. I didn't build the shape into it. Heredity did that for me."

"Yes I know, but you built the buggers to 21 inches!"

– Chris Lund, former *MuscleMag International* writer and photographer responding to the "ageless wonder," Albert Beckles, when Albert suggested he was blessed with great genetics for building huge arms.

After one set of barbell curls, Albert went over to the lat machine and did a set of triceps pushdowns. He did these at a slower pace than curls. He pushed the bar down until his arms were locked out straight at the bottom. As with curls, Albert tried to keep his upper arms and elbows in a fixed position, and did everything possible to keep his upper body from contributing to the exercise.

Albert did 4 supersets of barbell curls and triceps pushdowns, trying to rest as little as possible between sets.

Albert's next superset consisted of seated dumbell curls and lying triceps extensions. Albert began his dumbell curls with the palms facing his body. As he curled upward he rotated his palms upward.

As soon as the last rep was completed Albert lay back on the bench and grabbed a barbell and commenced to do lying triceps extensions. Unlike many bodybuilders who locked the elbows inward or pointing at the ceiling at all times, Albert let them flare outward as he lowered the bar to his forehead. Albert found this version much less stressful on the elbow joint than the standard more rigid version.

Albert could always be counted on to thrill the audience with the sight of his incredible split-peaked biceps muscles and razor sharp development of his rear deltoids and back.

Again Albert did 4 such supersets of both exercises resting as little as possible in between.

It's surprising given his generation that Albert rarely did more than 8 to 10 sets for his arms, but as he said "I've been doing this routine for years and it's always given me the results I want. So why change it?"

Chest

Albert is another bodybuilder who presents difficulties when trying to nail down a training routine. And while the sets and reps usually remain constant (4 sets of 12), the exercises changed on a regular basis. A typical Beckles chest workout would see him start with flat dumbell presses supersetted with cable crossovers or parallel bar dips. Albert would do one light set to warm up his chest, and then increase the weight with each set. He would hold the dumbells as if holding a barbell, and lower them so that the inner plates of the dumbell chest touched his chest. Resting only as long as it took him to reach the cable crossover machine, Albert would then do an ultra strict set of cable crossovers for 12 reps. At the bottom of the movement he would pause for a split second and squeeze his pecs.

With four supersets of dumbell presses and cable crossovers out of the way, Albert would finish his chest with 4 sets of flat dumbell flyes. This was one exercise where Albert never deviated the slightest from ultra strictness. Each rep was deliberate and controlled. Not a jerk or bounce to be seen.

Back

During his prime (the late '70s and early '80s) Albert Beckles sported a back that ranked right up there with such other greats of the time including Franco Columbu, Roy Callender, and Robby Robinson.

To build such width and thickness, Albert always started his back training with wide grip chins for 4 sets of 12 reps each. He would increase the weight with each set by tying a dumbell around his waist, and pull his body up until his chin was above the bar.

Albert's second exercise was usually bent-over barbell rows. Albert did these great back developers while standing on the end of a flat bench. He would take a wide grip on the bar and pull it up to his lower chest. As expected he did 4 sets of 12 reps.

To finish off his back, Albert did 4 sets of a seldom seen superset, wide grip pulldowns and bent-over dumbell laterals. He found the pulldowns hit the outer lats, while the bent-over dumbell raises hit the upper and center back.

Shoulders

Albert usually started his shoulder routine with a superset consisting of seated barbell presses and dumbell side raises. For presses Albert would sit on the end of a low bench and position an Olympic bar across his upper chest. With a medium-width grip he would lower the bar to his front delts and then extend to just short of a lockout. As soon as he completed the twelfth rep he would pick up a pair of light dumbells and go right into side lateral raises.

Albert is an inspiration to all that are fortunate enough to meet him. He is a gentleman who truly deserves and lives up to his title "The Ageless Wonder" every day.

Albert would do side laterals with his arms slightly bent and in perfect style. Even though the dumbells used were light by most standards, remember this exercise is done without rest after the barbell presses. Further, the huge poundages lifted by many bodybuilders are the result of excessive swinging and cheating. If they performed their reps in the same immaculate style as Albert, we are sure the dumbells wouldn't be so heavy.

Albert typically did 4 such supersets of presses and laterals, averaging 12 reps per set.

For his third exercise, Albert normally did barbell presses behind the head. Albert rarely supersetted behind the head presses with anything else as he found this movement was intense enough as it was. He typically did 4 sets of 12 reps, pyramiding the weight up with each successive set.

To finish those melon-sized delts of his, Albert moved on to one-arm cable laterals. He did these by holding the cable with his opposite hand and raising slightly forward and upward until his hand was just about head height. He always made it a point to hold the contracted position for a second or two, before lowering the handle back down.

Albert would do 4 sets of 12 reps for each side. Before leaving the gym, Albert liked to add a finishing touch to his shoulder workouts by hitting a few poses. For those lucky to be within viewing distance, the sight was nothing short of sensational. All three delt heads would leap to attention, with striations and cross-striations abounding.

Boyer Coe

Another of the sport's true greats Boyer Coe was born in Lake Charles, Louisiana on August 18, 1946. Boyer considers himself born to be a bodybuilder. "From the earliest I can remember, even as far back as five, I used to either buy or steal bodybuilding magazines from the local grocery store and gaze at the pictures … I remember in school we had to write an essay on what we wanted to be when we grew up. I wrote about how I wanted to be a bodybuilder and work out in California, etc. The teacher read my paper in front of the class and denounced it as being ridiculous. At that time professional bodybuilding didn't even exist … I started training when I was about 13. In high school I had a pretty good physique and actually won my first contest a few days before graduating."

Boyer considers himself born to be a bodybuilder.

And he kept winning contests:

1965	Mr. Texas – AAU, winner
	Mr. Texas – AAU, most muscular, 1st
1966	Junior Mr. America – AAU, 5th
	Junior Mr. America – AAU, most muscular, 5th
	Mr. USA – AAU, 2nd
	Mr. USA – AAU, most muscular, 3rd
	Teen Mr. America – AAU, winner
1967	Junior Mr. America – AAU, 2nd
	Junior Mr. America – AAU, most muscular, 2nd
	Mr. America – AAU, 5th
	Mr. America – AAU, most muscular, 5th
	Mr. Southern States – AAU, 2nd
1968	Junior Mr. America – AAU, 2nd
	Junior Mr. America – AAU, most muscular, 1st
	Junior Mr. USA – AAU, overall winner
	Mr. America – AAU, 2nd
	Mr. America – AAU, most muscular, 1st
	Mr. USA – AAU, 2nd
	Mr. USA – AAU, most muscular, 1st
1969	Junior Mr. America – AAU, overall winner
	Mr. America – AAU, winner
	Mr. America – AAU, most muscular, 1st
	Universe – NABBA, overall winner
	Universe – NABBA, medium, 1st
1970	Mr. World – AAU, pro short, 2nd
	Universe – Pro, NABBA, short, 1st
1971	Mr. International – IFBB, overall winner
	Mr. International – IFBB, medium, 1st
	World Championships – WBBG, winner
1972	Universe – Pro, NABBA, short, 2nd
	World Championships – WBBG, winner

1973	Universe – Pro, NABBA, overall winner
	Universe – Pro, NABBA, short, 1st
	World Championships – WBBG, winner
1974	Mr. World – WBBG, winner
	Universe – Pro, NABBA, short, 2nd
	World Championships – WBBG, winner
1975	Universe – Pro, NABBA, overall winner
	Universe – Pro, NABBA, short, 1st
	Universe – Pro, PBBA, winner
	World Championships – WBBG, winner
1976	Olympia – IFBB, lightweight
1977	Olympia – IFBB, 4th
	Olympia – IFBB, short, 3rd
1978	Night of Champions – IFBB, 4th
	Olympia – IFBB, 4th
	Olympia – IFBB, lightweight, 2nd
	Professional World Cup – IFBB, 5th
1979	Best in the World – IFBB, professional, 5th
	Canada Diamond Pro Cup – IFBB, 3rd
	Canada Pro Cup – IFBB, 3rd
	Grand Prix Pennsylvania – IFBB, 5th
	Grand Prix Vancouver – IFBB, 3rd
	Night of Champions – IFBB, 4th
	Olympia – IFBB, lightweight, 2nd
	Pittsburgh Pro Invitational – IFBB, 5th
	Southern Pro Cup – IFBB, 4th
1980	Canada Pro Cup – IFBB, 2nd
	Grand Prix California – IFBB, 5th
	Grand Prix Miami – IFBB, 5th
	Olympia – IFBB, 4th
	Pittsburgh Pro Invitational – IFBB, 5th
1981	Canada Pro Cup – IFBB, winner
	Grand Prix Belgium – IFBB, winner
	Grand Prix California – IFBB, 3rd
	Grand Prix Massachusetts – IFBB, winner
	Grand Prix New England – IFBB, 3rd
	Grand Prix New York – IFBB, 3rd
	Grand Prix Wales – IFBB, winner
	Grand Prix Washington – IFBB, 3rd
	Grand Prix World Cup – IFBB, winner
	Night of champions – IFBB, 3rd
	Professional World Cup – IFBB, winner
1982	Grand Prix Belgium – IFBB, 8th
	Grand Prix Sweden – IFBB, 9th
	Olympia – IFBB, 11th
	World Pro Championships – IFBB, 2nd
1984	Olympia – IFBB, 13th

"After only a few minutes I'm heartily greeted by the great man himself splendidly dressed in a navy track suit bottom, white socks, navy training shoes and a navy "Bodymasters" tank top which made Boyer look incredibly massive as the cloth stretched itself to the limit across that incredible back!"
– Chris Lund, former *MuscleMag International* contributor and photographer Chris Lund, commenting on the first appearance of Boyer Coe for a photo shoot at Ken Wheeler's Gym in Ontario, 1982.

Taking a lesson from Arnold's philosophy of training the weak areas first, Boyer usually started leg training with calves.

Boyer Coe was another bodybuilder whose great leg development was overshadowed by his outstanding upper body.

1994   Olympia – Masters, IFBB, 3rd
1995   Olympia – Masters, IFBB, 10th[1]

And does Boyer have a life outside of bodybuilding? "I was building a gym in New Orleans years ago called Boyer Coe's Body Masters. There were very limited funds, so we built – by hand – all the equipment. Other gym owners started coming around and wondering where they could buy the stuff! We decided to start building and selling it. That's how it started … the business has evolved from a two-man operation under a shed to where we now have a 90,000 square foot manufacturing facility, probably 200 people on the work floor, and 65 sales reps around the world."

Calves and Thighs

Boyer Coe was another bodybuilder whose great leg development was overshadowed by his outstanding upper body. It's a pity as despite having one of the greatest torsos in bodybuilding history, Boyer's legs were not too shabby either.

Taking a lesson from Arnold's philosophy of training the weak areas first, Boyer usually started leg training with calves. His first exercise was the seated toe press on the leg press. During a typical workout Boyer would put anywhere from 850 to 1000 pounds on the leg press and do 4 sets of 10 reps each. On the last couple of reps of each set, Boyer would bend his knees slightly and use his thighs just to get the weight into the starting position. He'd then emphasize the lowering or negative part of the movement.

After toe presses, Boyer usually moved on to seated calf raises and standing calf raises. Boyer liked to alternate these two movements together for 3 supersets. Again he tried to squeeze out at least 10 reps before calling it a set.

At this point most bodybuilders would figure their calves had had enough, but Boyer had one more surprise in store for them. Realizing that the key to great calf development is flexibility (the greater the flexibility of a muscle the greater the range of motion you can work it through), Boyer would conclude calf training by doing at least ten minutes of one-legged standing calf raises using just his bodyweight. When he could no longer do any meaningful reps this way, he'd use two legs. For those limited by poor calf flexibility, give Boyer's approach a try.

With calves out of the way, Boyer moved on to thighs. As both a warmup and a way to bring out extra separation in his thighs, Boyer did 3 supersets of leg extensions and leg curls. Boyer preferred to do leg extensions one leg at a time. He is a firm believer in the evidence that suggests you can engage more impulses by training one limb at a time, whereas the brain has to split impulses when training two limbs together. Whether true or not, Boyer employed it in his training.

The heart of Boyer's leg routine was heavy leg presses. During a typical workout he'd do 4 sets of 8 to 12 reps.

To finish off his thighs Boyer would hit the squat rack for one set of 20 all-out reps using as much weight as he could handle.

We should add that Boyer frequently switched things around and he might go heavy on the squats for 3 or 4 sets and then finish with one set of leg presses.

Triceps

Boyer Coe is another bodybuilder whose triceps development was overshadowed by two of the greatest biceps in bodybuilding history. Yet Boyer's triceps by no means took a backseat to his biceps. They were in perfect balance. But such is the price you pay for having a set of Matterhorn's protruding from the front of your upper arms.

Boyer learned early on that while the biceps are the most visible and glamorous arm muscle, its the triceps that makes up about two-thirds of the arms total size. The triceps are also the site of most of the arm's power, particularly on such pressing movements as flat barbell presses and military presses.

Boyer usually started his triceps training with the first exercise he ever learned for the muscle, cable pushdowns. Boyer found this exercise so effective that he has kept it in his triceps' routine to this very day. Through trial and error Boyer found that a slightly narrower than shoulder width grip worked best for him. He also discovered that he had to lock his arms completely out to fully activate his triceps.

One problem Boyer has repeatedly witnessed over the years is bodybuilders swaying their bodies back and forth to lift the weight. He's also seen his share of people leaning forward. Both forms of cheating only incorporate other muscle groups. For those lucky enough to have witnessed Boyer performing the exercise the only thing that would be moving was his forearm. Boyer typically did 4 to 5 sets of 8 to 12 reps.

Boyer's triceps were in perfect balance.

After pushdowns Boyer often moved on to lying extensions. For variety he alternated between an EZ-curl bar and two dumbells. He found the EZ-curl bar better than dumbells as the grip seemed to place more stress on his triceps. Two things Boyer always stressed to beginners about this exercise when giving seminars, always keep the elbows locked in close to the sides, and lower the barbell to the forehead. As soon as the elbows flare out, or you lower the bar behind the head, other muscles such as the chest and delts take over. Once again the only thing that should be moving is the forearms. Boyer did 4 to 5 sets of 8 to 12 reps of this basic mass builder.

To finish off his triceps Boyer moved on to a one-arm exercise like dumbell extensions. As with lying extensions, Boyer always kept his elbows pointing directly at the ceiling. He lowered the dumbell to a comfortable stretch and then extended his arm to a fully locked-out position. Four to five sets of 8 to 12 reps was the norm.

For variety Boyer sometimes gave the extensions a pass and did dumbell kickbacks instead. Boyer would place one hand on a flat bench and lock the upper arm of the working arm parallel to the floor. He'd then extend his forearm back until it was locked completely out. Again the only thing you'd see moving was his forearm. As soon as the upper arm starts swaying the rear delts and lats take over.

Scott Wilson

Scott Wilson was a fixture on the pro scene during the early '80s. Besides winning the Mr. International and Pro Mr. America titles, Scott was an excellent power-lifter, having done a 625-pound squat, 665-pound deadlift, and 470-pound bench press, all at a weight of around 230 pounds. During his career, Scott was known for having among the widest shoulders on the scene. Here's his competitive record:

Scott Wilson was known for having among the widest shoulders on the scene.

1974	Mr. California – AAU, overall winner
1975	Mr. America – AAU, 6th
	Mr. America – AAU, medium, 3rd
1976	Pro Mr. America – WBBG, winner
1978	Natural America, Professional, 5th
1979	Natural America, Professional, 3rd
1980	Mr. International – IFBB, heavyweight, 2nd
1981	Canada Pro Cup – IFBB, 7th
	Mr. International – IFBB, overall winner
	Mr. International – IFBB, heavyweight, 1st
1983	Grand Prix Denver – IFBB, 6th
	Grand Prix Portland – IFBB, winner
	World Pro Championships – IFBB, 5th
1984	Canada Pro Cup – IFBB, 6th
	World Grand Prix – 6th
	World Pro Championships – IFBB, 9th
1985	Night of Champions – IFBB, 14th
1986	Los Angeles Pro Championships – IFBB, 10th
	World Pro Championships – IFBB, 12th
1987	Night of Champions – IFBB
1988	Grand Prix USA Pro – IFBB, 4th
	Niagara Falls Pro Invitational – IFBB, 8th
	World Pro Championships – IFBB, 6th
1994	Olympia, Masters – IFBB, 11th
1998	North Carolina Super Natural – NABF, heavyweight, 2nd
1999	Olympia, Masters – IFBB, 10th

Shoulders

As with Pete Grymkowski in the '70s and Paul Dillett in the '90s, Scott Wilson was usually the widest bodybuilder onstage during his competitive days in the 1980s. Granted, Scott was blessed with wide bone structure. Still, he realized that judges don't reward points for bones – only large, fully developed muscles.

As expected from someone with his shoulder mass, Scott preferred to start his shoulder training with a basic pressing movement. Occasionally he used a barbell, but more often than not he opted for the Universal machine press. A typical workout would see Scott blast out 4 to 5 quality sets of machine presses. The number of reps usually depended on the time of the year. If it was off-season, he would go heavy, averaging 6 to 8 reps per set, while contest time saw the weight being decreased and the reps increased to 10 to 12.

> ## "Oh, I was blessed with wide shoulders and a wide back and these bodyparts did respond very quickly when I first started training."
>
> – Scott Wilson,
> Mr. International winner talking about something most bodybuilders would kill for; naturally wide shoulders.

Recognizing the importance of rear shoulder development, Scott would do 4 to 5 sets of bent-over laterals as his second shoulder movement. Once again Scott would use variety to keep the muscles guessing. On some days he'd sit down on the edge of a bench and do the exercise ultra strict, while on others he'd stand up and use a slightly loose style, using just enough body momentum to keep the dumbells moving.

With his rear delts out of the way, Scott would go back to front and side delts by doing 4 to 5 sets of seated dumbell presses. Again the rep range depended on the time of the season.

To finish off his cannonball-sized shoulders, Scott did 4 to 5 sets of standing lateral raises. Unlike some bodybuilders who keep a large bend in the elbow and lift the dumbbells forward as they lift up, Scott kept his arms nearly straight and lifted out to the side.

Although retired from competitive bodybuilding, Scott Wilson will go down in history as being one of the few bodybuilders who came close to obtaining that much coveted "yard-wide" shoulder look!

Steve Davis

Steve was always athletic and large, and like most American teens played both baseball and football in high school. It was then that he first began weight training. By the age of 19 Steve weighed 285 pounds! But after two years with the US Army in Europe as director of the Army Ski Team, he was an impressively chiseled 155 pounds. After leaving the forces Steve pursued bodybuilding full-time:

1974   Mr. International, tall 3rd
1975   Mr. America – IFBB, tall, 2nd
1977   Mr. America – IFBB, heavyweight, 4th
        Mr. World – IFBB, middleweight, 1st
        Universe – Pro, NABBA, 3rd
1979   Canada Pro Cup – IFBB
        Olympia – IFBB, lightweight, 10th
1980   Canada Pro Cup – IFBB, 5th
        Universe – Pro, IFBB
        World Pro Championships – IFBB
1981 – Canada Pro Cup – IFBB, 12th
        Grand Prix California – IFBB
        Grand Prix World Cup – IFBB
        Olympia – IFBB, 14th
        Professional World Cup – IFBB

He didn't have the largest arms on the pro scene, but few bodybuilders displayed the same degree of ripped muscle mass as Steve Davis.

Like most bodybuilders of his generation, Steve Davis used moderate weight and rep ranges.

What did Steve think of competitive bodybuilding?

"I define an athlete as an individual who trains for competition. But I don't care to be thought of as an athlete – I see myself as a performer. I train to prepare myself for a performance, to give entertainment to others. The fact that I am an athlete has no bearing on the audience reaction – performance does."

Triceps

It's true he didn't have the largest arms on the pro scene, but few bodybuilders displayed the same degree of ripped muscle mass as Steve Davis. And remember the guy tipped the scales at over 280 smooth pounds at one time.

Steve's triceps were particularly impressive and if one word could sum up his training approach it was variety. During a typical triceps workout, Steve would take four or five triceps exercises and do 3 to 4 sets of each. Like most bodybuilders of his generation, Steve used moderate weight and rep ranges (8 to 12). Here's a typical Steve Davis triceps workout from the early "80s:[1]

1. Cable pushdowns – 4 sets of 12 reps
2. Lying EZ-bar extensions – 3 sets of 10 reps
3. Behind-the-head rope extensions – 3 sets of 8 to 12 reps
4. Parallel bar dips – 3 sets of 8 to 12 reps
5. Bench dips – 3 sets of 15 to 20 reps

Reference:

1) Reynolds, Bill and Weider, Joe. *The Weider System of Bodybuilding*, Contemporary Books, Chicago, 1983.

Johnny Fuller

Johnny was born in Clarandon, Lionee Town, Jamaica. At the age of seven Johnny took up soccer, and he eventually entered the junior leagues and then made the Jamaican National Team by 18 years of age. After moving to Birmingham, England, he took up boxing, karate, and judo. Today Johnny holds four dans in three different styles, plus two dans in Jiu-jitsu! It was while Johnny was studying boxing that he first started lifting weights. Johnny took to bodybuilding like a fish to water and it wasn't long before he racked up this impressive record:

1978   Universe – NABBA, short, 4th
        World Amateur Championships – IFBB, middleweight, 8th
1979   Mr. International – IFBB, middleweight, 1st
        World Amateur Championships – IFBB, light heavyweight, 3rd
1980   European Amateur Championships – IFBB, light heavyweight, 1st
        World Amateur Championships – IFBB, light heavyweight, 1st
1981   Canada Pro Cup – IFBB, 3rd
        Grand Prix Belgium – IFBB, 4th
        Grand Prix California – IFBB, 5th
        Grand Prix New England – IFBB, 5th
        Grand Prix New York – IFBB, 4th
        Grand Prix Wales – IFBB, 4th
        Grand Prix Washington – IFBB, 4th
        Grand Prix World Cup – IFBB, 4th
        Night of Champions – IFBB, 4th
        Olympia – IFBB, 8th
        Professional World Cup – IFBB, 4th
1982   Grand Prix Belgium – IFBB, 5th
        Grand Prix Sweden – IFBB, 5th
        Night of Champions – IFBB, 3rd
        Olympia – IFBB, 9th
        World Pro Championships – IFBB, 3rd
1983   Grand Prix England – IFBB, 6th
        Grand Prix Las Vegas – IFBB, 9th
        Grand Prix Portland – IFBB, 3rd
        Grand Prix Sweden – IFBB, 7th
        Grand Prix Switzerland – IFBB, 7th
        Night of Champions – IFBB, 4th
        Olympia – IFBB, 8th
        World Pro Championships – IFBB, 6th
1985   Olympia – IFBB, 18th
1987   World Pro Championships – IFBB, 13th
1998   Musclemania, Masters, 5th

Pound for pound Johnny Fuller was one of the largest bodybuilders onstage during the early '80s.

Johnny has had to endure his share of injuries. Including a pec tear:
"I was training in Tucson Arizona for a contest in Las Vegas in '82. I had been on a very heavy diet for weeks and my bodyfat was 3.3 percent. It was only a week before the contest so I was drying out a little. I picked up a bar with 80 pounds on it and was warming up on a bench, then buff, the noise traveled to the other end of the gym! It was strange. It didn't hurt until days after. Anyway, the operation's been done. They pinned it in place … It took some time to grow back, but at least my symmetry was back when I did double biceps and other compulsories. This is where I was losing valuable points."

When asked why he returned to competition so soon after such a severe injury, Johnny answered: "… But a man's got to eat. No publicity, no work. No work, no money. It's a tough business and only the toughest survive…" – Johnny Fuller, the ultimate survivor!

Legs

The first thing you noticed about Johnny Fuller was his infectious smile. Where most other bodybuilders look like they can't wait to get off stage, Johnny appeared to be having the time of his life. He had this ear-to-ear grin that seemed to say "Man I've found my calling." The second thing you notice about Johnny was his incredible muscle density. Pound for pound Johnny was one of the largest bodybuilders onstage during the early '80s, and leading the way were those enormous legs of his. Dare we say it but Johnny was one of the few bodybuilders who could stand next to leg-king, Tom Platz and trade leg shots and not look stupid. Nobody had Tom's mass or cuts, but at least Johnny could make Tom stop and take notice.

Johnny never subscribed to Mike Mentzer's theories of high intensity training. Mike would be showered and headed out the door before Johnny was finished his first exercise! No, Johnny's idea of a good workout was to take four or five exercises, use a medium weight, and do lots of sets. Let's look at the routine that built those incredible legs.

During the off-season Johnny would take four or five exercises and do upward of 5 sets each. On a movement like leg presses he often did ten sets in total. Then during the precontest season he'd add on a couple of more exercises. Here's a typical Fuller routine from the early '80s:

1. Leg presses – 10 sets of 15 to 20 reps
2. Front squats – 5 sets of 10 to 15 reps
3. Squats – 5 sets of 10 to 15 reps
4. Leg extensions – 5 sets of 10 to 15 reps
5. Lunges – 5 sets of 15 to 20 reps
6. Leg curls – 10 sets of 10 to 15 reps

Detroit native Ron Love, was a fixture on the pro scene for a five year period.

Ron Love

"I was working narcotics. Me and my sergeant and two other officers were just exiting a building where we had been talking to an informant. We were undercover so nobody knew we were police officers. Just as we were approaching our vehicle, we saw two white guys dressed in black clothing – they were vigilantes from some motorcycle gang, only they were on bicycles, not motorcycles. They walked up behind our vehicle, and one of them said, "Hey man, we don't allow niggers in our neighborhood." We all burst out laughing. One of the officers was white, but he had a real deep tan, so maybe they thought he was black too. Anyhow, I laughed, and then they pulled out guns and started shooting. I just froze. I couldn't believe these guys were shooting at us. Finally, when I realized what was going on, I looked around, and seeing that the doors had already been opened on the vehicle, I dove inside. The other two cops were in the front. I didn't see my partner, so I thought he had been shot, but he was moving pretty fast getting out of the way. His door was open on the other side, so I slid over, pulled my gun, and returned fire. I shot one of the guys, and he fell off his bike. He tried to get up, and I shot him again. I tried to pursue the other guy, but I fell to the ground. I didn't know at first, but I had been shot in the leg. I pulled up my pant leg, and the blood started gushing, but I didn't feel it until the situation got under hand a little bit – and then I could really feel it! That's what happened. That's what led me into bodybuilding because I had to go through rehab."

Ron Love was born in Detroit on July 2, 1951. He led a wild youth, graduated high school and played two years of semi-pro baseball. Then by chance he encountered a police recruiter, and for the next 17 years was a member of Detroit's finest. But as he became more involved in bodybuilding, he realized that he couldn't serve two masters. Ron dedicated himself to bodybuilding. And what a rap sheet this ex-cop has!

Ron's chest was his most impressive muscle group.

1983   Nationals – NPC, heavyweight, 10th
1985   Junior USA – NPC, overall winner
        Junior USA – NPC, heavyweight, 1st
        Nationals – NPC, heavyweight, 1st
        World Amateur Championships – IFBB, heavyweight, 3rd
1986   Night of Champions – IFBB, 2nd
        Olympia – IFBB, 8th
1987   Detroit Pro Invitational – IFBB, 3rd
        Grand Prix France – IFBB, 9th
        Grand Prix Germany (2) – IFBB, 10th
        Grand Prix Germany – IFBB, 7th
        Night of Champions – IFBB, 3rd
        Olympia – IFBB, 9th
        World Pro Championships – IFBB, winner
1988   Grand Prix England – IFBB, 11th
        Grand Prix France – IFBB, 7th
        Grand Prix Germany – IFBB, 7th
        Grand Prix Greece – IFBB, 8th
        Grand Prix Italy – IFBB, 6th
        Grand Prix Spain (2) – IFBB, 6th
        Grand Prix Spain – IFBB, 10th
        Olympia – IFBB, 9th
1989   Arnold Classic – IFBB, 8th
        Grand Prix England – IFBB, 8th
        Grand Prix Finland – IFBB, 7th
        Grand Prix France – IFBB, 7th
        Grand Prix Germany – IFBB, 8th
        Grand Prix Holland – IFBB, 10th
        Grand Prix Melbourne – IFBB, 5th
        Grand Prix Spain (2) – IFBB, 8th
        Grand Prix Spain – IFBB, 6th
        Grand Prix Sweden – IFBB, 8th

Niagara Falls Pro Invitational – IFBB, winner
Night of Champions – IFBB, 5th
Olympia – IFBB, 10th
World Pro Championships – IFBB, 6th

1990   Grand Prix England – IFBB, 10th
Grand Prix Finland – IFBB, 12th
Grand Prix France – IFBB, 9th
Grand Prix Germany – IFBB, 11th
Grand Prix Holland – IFBB, 15th
Grand Prix Italy – IFBB, 13th
Olympia – IFBB, 12th

1991   Arnold Classic – IFBB, 14th
Grand Prix Denmark – IFBB, 3rd
Grand Prix England – IFBB, 4th
Grand Prix Finland – IFBB, 2nd
Grand Prix Italy – IFBB, 2nd
Grand Prix Spain – IFBB, 2nd
Grand Prix Switzerland – IFBB, 2nd
Musclefest Grand Prix – IFBB, 4th
Night of Champions – IFBB, 5th
Olympia – IFBB, 11th
Pittsburgh Pro Invitational – IFBB, 6th
San Jose Pro Invitational – IFBB, winner

1992   Arnold Classic – IFBB, 12th
Grand Prix England – IFBB, 7th
Grand Prix Germany – IFBB, 8th
Grand Prix Holland – IFBB, 6th
Grand Prix Italy – IFBB, 7th
Ironman Pro Invitational – IFBB, 8th
Olympia – IFBB, 9th
Pittsburgh Pro Invitational – IFBB, 5th

1993   Arnold Classic – IFBB, 11th
Grand Prix England – IFBB, 9th
Grand Prix Finland – IFBB, 6th
Grand Prix France (2) – IFBB, 9th
Grand Prix France – IFBB, 7th
Grand Prix Germany – IFBB, 9th
Grand Prix Spain – IFBB, 8th
Ironman Pro Invitational – IFBB, 11th
Olympia – IFBB, 14th

Ron Love

When asked whether he had ever experienced racism in bodybuilding, Ron had this to say: "Other than hearing that some of the magazines don't like to put blacks on the covers because it cuts down sales, no I haven't, really. I think we've broken those barriers, because I've done a lot of seminars down south. I remember one occasion when I was invited to a seminar in Mobile, Alabama. After the seminar a guy walked up to me and said, "Mr. Ron, when you first came in here, I had this idea about blacks, but you know, you changed all my feeling about blacks, because you're very intelligent and very articulate, very down-to-earth, a nice person,

Keep the muscles guessing was Ron Love's motto.

and a real humanitarian, and for that reason you'll always have a place in my heart." They invited me back again to do another seminar, and that guy was one of the first ones in the door. That's all it took. A lot of people see you in a different light, and they listen to their own peers telling them that blacks are dumb, that they stink, things like that, and until you actually get close to a person, you don't really know."

Chest

With all the attention focused on Ronnie Coleman's career as a police officer, many readers may be surprised to hear another "man in blue" competed regularly back in the late '80s and early '90s. Detroit native Ron Love, was a fixture on the pro scene for a five year period, and together with the likes of Mike Christian and Lee Labrada, made Lee Haney work for his eight Mr. Olympia titles.

Ron trained on a six-day schedule, hitting each muscle twice a week. As his chest was one of his more impressive muscle groups, let's take a closer look at what the big fella did to build it.

Ron usually started his chest training with a couple of shoulder exercises! Ron recognized early on that most chest exercises stress the shoulders, many in an unnatural manner. So he reasoned it only made sense to properly warm the shoulder up before hitting any heavy chest exercises.

Another Love principle was variety. Some workouts consisted entirely of dumbell movements, while others were centered around barbell exercises. Keep the muscles guessing was Ron's motto. Let's look at a dumbell chest workout.

A favorite starting dumbell exercise for Ron was flat dumbell presses. For variety he alternated between straight pressing, and rotating his wrists as he pushed the dumbells up. He typically did 4 sets of 8 to 12 reps.

To hit his upper chest Ronnie did incline dumbell presses. Through trial and error he found a 25- to 30-degree angle hit his upper chest the best without too much front shoulder involvement. Again it was 4 sets of 8 to 12 reps.

To finish off his all-dumbell chest workout, Ron dropped the weight and did 4 sets of incline dumbell flyes. Done properly flyes almost totally eliminate the shoulders and triceps.

We should conclude by saying that during the precontest season, Ron added dumbell pullovers to his chest routine. He also increased his rep range to 12 to 20.

Berry DeMey built his massive legs with basic exercises using extremely heavy weight.

Berry DeMey – The Flying Dutchman

Berry was born in Rotterdam, Holland, and was a natural athlete while growing up: "I always was involved in sports, and from the age of ten on I did swimming, boxing, tae-kwon-do, and running, so I was into sports on an everyday basis. I always knew I wanted to do something physical. I was even going to go in the army, but at the age of 16, just by coincidence, I picked up some weights in the gym where I was boxing. From the moment that I first started lifting weights that first day, I knew that was what I wanted to do. I always liked personal sports, and bodybuilding is the most personal sport – you can adapt it to any body, any age, all that. To be honest, I just wanted to have a muscular, athletic physique. I didn't even like bodybuilders who had taken it to that extreme. When I do seminars, I look back on that. People who never saw a bodybuilder before will sometimes say, "Oh, that's too much – all those veins and things," and I can really relate to that because I had the same attitude in the beginning. But it's like wine – you have to learn how to appreciate it."

The judges certainly appreciated Berry's efforts, as his record shows:

1980	Holland Hercules – NPBO, junior, 1st
	Holland Iron Man – NPBO, junior, 1st
	Mr. Holland – NPBO, junior, 2nd
1981	Mr. Europe – WABBA, junior, 3rd
	Mr. Holland – BBBN, junior, 1st
1982	European Amateur Championships – IFBB, heavyweight, 1st
	Holland Grand Prix – NBBF, heavyweight, 1st
1983	World Amateur Championships – IFBB, heavyweight, 2nd
1984	World Amateur Championships – IFBB, heavyweight, 2nd
1985	Olympia – IFBB, 6th
	World Games – IFBB, overall winner
	World Games – IFBB, heavyweight, 1st
1986	Night of Champions – IFBB, 6th
	Olympia – IFBB, 5th

1987   Grand Prix France – IFBB, 6th
       Grand Prix Germany – IFBB, 9th
       Grand Prix Germany – IFBB, 6th
       Olympia – IFBB, 6th
1988   Grand Prix England – IFBB, 3rd
       Grand Prix France – IFBB, 3rd
       Grand Prix Germany – IFBB, 2nd
       Grand Prix Greece – IFBB, 3rd
       Grand Prix Italy – IFBB, 4th
       Grand Prix Spain[2] – IFBB, 3rd
       Grand Prix Spain – IFBB, 3rd
       Olympia – IFBB, 3rd
1990   Grand Prix Holland – IFBB, 4th
1991   WBF Grand Prix – WBF, 3rd
1993   Night of Champions – IFBB, 10th
1994   Arnold Classic – IFBB, 15th

Berry usually started his leg training with very heavy squats.

So why did Berry relocate to the USA?

"The first time I came to the United States was in '83. I always liked the United States. There was always something that attracted me here and I always wanted to live here. On that first visit I stayed for two months. I trained at Gold's Gym and some Powerhouse Gyms, and I knew from that time that I really wanted to live here forever. One of the main reasons was for the weather in California, plus the opportunities in general, and bodybuilding, of course. This is where it all happens."

Legs

One of the memorable moments from many of the Mr. Olympia contests in the mid eighties was watching Berry DeMey flex his thighs. Most bodybuilders stick one leg forward and simply tense the muscles, but Berry first shook his leg so the muscles swayed back and forth. Then he brought the house down by making a downward swiping motion with his hand and flexing his quads. As soon as the electrical impulses hit his quads they separated into four distinct heads with each head crossed and crisscrossed with striations. Even Lee Haney who was in the middle of his record run of eight-straight Mr. Olympias knew better than to make direct leg comparisons with the "Flying Dutchman."

As you'd expect from someone with that kind of thigh development, Berry built his massive legs with basic exercises using extremely

From the moment that I first started lifting weights, I knew that was what I wanted to do. – Berry DeMey

heavy weight. Never one to shy away from torture on a regular basis, Berry usually started his leg training with squats, very heavy squats. At one point in his career he was up to 660 pounds for reps.

During a typical workout Berry would bang out 3 to 4 heavy sets of squats (after a couple of quality warm-up sets) alternating between 6 to 8 reps in the off-season and 15 to 20 reps in the precontest phase.

Berry's thighs responded so well to squats that he had to ease back on the weight and intensity to try and bring his upper body into proportion. He started adding more refining movements like leg extensions and hack squats to his routine. The end result was those incredible leg shots that highlighted many a Mr. Olympia contest during the mid to late eighties.

Here's a typical Berry DeMey leg workout from his Mr. Olympia years:

1. Squats – 3-4 sets of 15 to 20 reps
2. Leg Presses – 3-4 sets of 10 to 15 reps
3. Hack squats – 3-4 sets of 10 to 15 reps
4. Leg extensions – 3-4 sets of 10 to 15 reps
5. Leg curls – 3-4 sets of 10 to 15 reps
6. Standing leg curls – 3-4 sets of 10 to 15 reps

Bertil Fox

Bertil Fox has become the O.J. Simpson of the bodybuilding world. From the pinnacle of popularity to death row, Foxy's gone the full spectrum.

Bertil Fox was born in St. Kitts but immigrated to England. It wasn't long after picking up his first barbell that Foxy's genetic potential started coming through. He dominated the junior ranks, swept through the best the NABBA had to offer, and headed to California and the IFBB to seek greater fortune. Unfortunately Foxy had two strikes against him, Lee Haney and his physique. With Lee Haney on the scene for most of the 1980s, Foxy (like everyone else) had to sit back and observe the 245-pound Atlanta native dominate the pro ranks. It didn't help matters either that Bertil was about ten years ahead of his time. His 230 pounds on a 5'7" frame would have been more at home on a mass-dominated '90s stage than the symmetrically influenced '80s.

Bertil never realized his potential in the IFBB federation. After retiring from bodybuilding Bertil moved back to St. Kitts where his troubles only intensified. Without going into the details, suffice to say Bertil was found guilty of murdering his girlfriend and her mother, and sentenced to death. As of this writing he is still on death row.

It wasn't long after picking up his first barbell that Bertil Fox's genetic potential started coming through.

"Look, I ain't no bleedin' ballet dancer! I'm a bodybuilder!"

– Britain's Bertil Fox, after someone suggested he needed to "add more grace" to his posing routine.

Here's Bertil's impressive competitive record:

1969 Mr. Britain – NABBA, junior, 1st
1970 Mr. Britain – NABBA, junior, 1st
1971 Mr. Britain – NABBA, junior, 1st
       Mr. Europe – junior, 1st
1976 Mr. Britain – NABBA, overall winner
       Mr. World – AAU, overall winner
       Universe – NABBA, medium, 2nd
1977 Universe – NABBA, overall winner
       Universe – NABBA, medium, 1st
1978 Universe – Pro, NABBA, winner
1979 Universe – Pro, NABBA, winner
1980 World Championships – WABBA, professional, 2nd
1981 Grand Prix Belgium – IFBB, 5th
1982 Night of champions – IFBB, 2nd
       Olympia – IFBB, 8th
1983 Grand Prix Sweden – IFBB, 4th
       Grand Prix Switzerland – IFBB, 2nd
       Olympia – IFBB, 5th
1984 World Pro Championships – IFBB, 5th
1986 Olympia – IFBB, 7th
1987 Grand Prix Germany – IFBB, 9th
       Night of Champions – IFBB, 7th
       Olympia – IFBB, 12th
1989 Arnold Classic – IFBB, 6th
       Grand Prix melbourne – IFBB, 6th
       Olympia – IFBB, 11th
       World Pro Championships – IFBB, 5th
1992 Arnold Classic – IFBB, 16th
       Pittsburgh Pro Invitational – IFBB, 9th
1994 Ironman Pro Invitational – IFBB, 13th

Bertil's 230 pounds on a 5'7" frame would have been more at home on a mass-dominated '90s stage than the symmetrically influenced eighties.

Chest

When he competed regularly in the early '80s, Bertil Fox was in some respects preparing bodybuilding fans for the type of physique that would become the norm in the 1990s. Standing around 5'8" and weighing 225 to 230 pounds in contest shape, Bertil was easily the most massive bodybuilder competing in the early eighties. A couple of bodybuilders may have outweighed "Foxy," but for his height, Bertil was the densest, most muscular man onstage.

Despite his recent legal troubles, Bertil's chest still conjures up nightmares for many of his fellow competitors from the '80s.

Bertil usually started his chest routine with, surprise, surprise, flat barbell presses. For his first set he put 135 pounds on the bar and did 20, non lockout reps as a warm up. From there it was successive sets adding a set of 45's with each set. Eventually Foxy was up to 405 pounds for 8 clean reps. He then had a training partner spot him for a couple of forced reps. One final "burnout" set of 315 pounds was then performed for as many reps as possible.

After flat barbell presses, Bertil moved on to incline barbell presses. It was at this stage that Bertil's individuality came through. Most bodybuilders prefer 30 degrees or less on incline, but Bertil found such a shallow angle too similar to regular flat benches. To hit his upper chest, he preferred an angle of about 60 degrees. As with flat presses, Bertil usually did one light, high-rep set to warm up the upper chest, and then put 225 pounds on the bar and did 4 sets of as many reps as possible.

Bertil's third and fourth exercises were often done in a superset manner. With an adjustable bench set at 60 degrees, Bertil would do one set of incline dumbell flyes, and then head over to the parallel bars and bang out a set of weighted dips. Bertil usually did 5 such supersets, trying to rest as little as possible in between sets.

To finish off his massive chest, Bertil did 5 sets of kneeling cable crossovers. Like his previous exercises, Fox performed cables in a lose fashion using as much weight as possible.

Greg "Rocky" DeFerro

In his short pro career, Greg DeFerro established a reputation as one of the thickest competitors around. Standing 5'8" and weighing 220 pounds in contest shape, Greg sported 21-inch arms and a 53-inch chest. With his striking facial resemblance to actor Sylvester Stallone, it wasn't long before the bodybuilding press started calling him Rocky. Greg's biggest win was the 1979 Mr. International contest. He also placed 2nd at the 1983 New York Night of Champions.

Here's Greg's short, but impressive contest record:

1974 Mr. New Jersey – AAU, 6th
1977 Mr. USA – IFBB, heavyweight, 3rd
1979 Mr. America – AAU, medium, 2nd
      Mr. International – IFBB, overall winner
      Mr. International – IFBB, heavyweight, 1st
1980 Mr. America – AAU, heavyweight, 2nd
      Universe – Pro, IFBB, 5th
      World Pro Championships – IFBB, 6th
1981 Grand Prix California – IFBB, 6th
      Grand Prix New England – IFBB, 4th
      Grand Prix World Cup – IFBB
      Night of Champions – IFBB, 8th
      Professional World Cup – IFBB
1982 Night of Champions – IFBB, 9th
1983 Grand Prix Las Vegas – IFBB, 4th
      Night of Champions – IFBB, 2nd
      World Pro Championships – IFBB, 2nd
1984 World Pro Championships – IFBB, 2nd

Greg "Rocky" DeFerro

Triceps

About the only thing similar between Greg DeFerro and Sylvester Stallone, is the facial features. Sure the original Rocky got into decent shape for many of his movies, but let's be reasonable here. Sylvester Stallone never had the same size guns protruding from his shirt sleeves as Greg DeFerro. When he competed on the bodybuilding scene in the early to mid 1980s Greg's arms were among the largest around. From biceps to triceps to forearms, Rocky's guns were a sight to behold at close range.

From biceps to triceps to forearms, Greg's guns were a sight to behold

Although he found his biceps responded fairly easily to training, his triceps were a tad stubborn. He learned many years ago that he needed to trick or fool his triceps into doing nothing else but grow. Greg is convinced that many bodybuilders are following triceps routines that are not only ineffective, but also downright dangerous.

The first triceps exercise in his routine was usually triceps pushdowns on the lat machine using a straight bar. Greg used a narrow, eight- to nine-inch, false grip, and pushed down until his arms were completely locked out straight. Greg pyramided the weight on each set, going from 15 to 12 to 8 reps. Then on the fourth set he would do a strip set by removing 15 to 20 pounds from the bar. With his triceps pre-exhausted, Greg then moved on to a basic compound movement, usually narrow presses on a Smith machine.

With his legs elevated off the bench and crossed, Greg would hold the bar with a nine-inch grip and press upward to a locked out position. He'd then lower the bar down until it just touched his upper chest. With his triceps now begging for mercy, Greg immediately went over to an 80-degree incline bench and banged out a set of behind-the-head pulley extensions. Greg would normally do 3 supersets of these two exercises.

To finish his triceps Greg performed a variation of the one-arm extension. Instead of using a dumbell, however, he used a single-hand pulley attachment. Like Larry Scott before him, Greg found pulleys gave a better feel to his triceps.

"Oh, the delts for sure. I mean when your delts are in good shape the whole of the upper body appears just that much more impressive and dynamic to the eye. That's why Scott and Howorth looked so damned good. Arnold too, could never have gotten away with those unbelievable three-quarter back shots if he hadn't built such terrific delts!"

– Greg DeFerro, responding when asked what's the most impressive muscle group.

Greg DeFerro established a reputation as one of the thickest competitors around.

"Sure, I train very hard. In fact I train so damned hard at times that I often question my sanity! What a lot of bodybuilders don't realize is there exists a very fine line between hard training and overtraining."

– Greg DeFerro, Mr. International winner commenting on training.

Shoulders

The deltoids are definitely one muscle group that can never be too large. As soon as the competitors for a typical contest file out onstage, the first thing most audience member's notice is who has the widest shoulders. Granted bone structure has much to do with it, but deltoid size also plays a major role.

When Greg DeFerro was into his competitive training back in the early '80s, he sported two cannonball-sized deltoids that ensured he was always one of the widest competitors onstage.

Like most bodybuilders, Greg liked to start his shoulders with a heavy pressing movement. But surprisingly he preferred the Universal shoulder press machine to the more popular barbell version. He found the machine not only gave him a better stretch in his delts, but also gave him much better control.

Grabbing the bar with a false grip, Greg performed his reps for a full range of motion, all the way up to a locked out position, and down as far as he could possibly lower. Greg usually did 4 sets of shoulder presses, going from a medium weight for 12 reps, up to a heavy weight for 6 reps. On the last set he often threw in a strip set by reducing the weight by twenty pounds and struggled to get an additional 4 to 6 reps.

Greg's second delt exercise was usually standing side dumbell raises. In true Rocky style, he added his own twist to this exercise. Most bodybuilders only raise the dumbells to shoulder height, but Greg liked to raise the dumbells way above his shoulders, almost to the vertical. Altogether he did 3 sets of 12 to 6 reps.

Realizing that the side heads add the most to shoulder width, Greg made one-arm cable laterals as his third delt exercise. Greg would reach across and grab the handle with his opposite hand, and raised his arm until it was just slightly higher than shoulder height. On most days he did 2 sets of 10 to 12 reps per side.

Greg's fourth delt exercise was another seldom-seen movement, straight-bar front cable raises. Standing with his back to a low pulley, Greg would grab a low pulley and raise the bar so that the attached pulley was between his legs. Again he raised to just above shoulder height. For this one, Greg did 3 sets of 12 to 15 reps.

To finish off his delts, Greg liked to superset seated dumbell presses and upright rows. He did the presses in the Arnold fashion, that is start with the palms facing inward and rotating until his palms are facing forward at the top. Upright rows were performed using a small straight barbell. Again he added his own variation. Instead of bringing the bar up to his chin, he brought it right up to his forehead. And out of all the shoulder exercises, he did this one using a very quick tempo.

Mike Quinn

Mike Quinn was born in Brockton, Massachusetts, in 1961. Mike was what could be called a teenage prodigy in bodybuilding, winning the Teenage Mr. Bay State at 16, the Teenage Mr. Massachusetts at 19, and AAU Teenage Mr. America at 19. Unfortunately Mike's success on the pro circuit didn't mirror his accomplishments as a teenager. His only major pro win was the 1984 NABBA Mr. Universe.

Mike cites Robby Robinson as an early idol. Unlike the taller Arnold and Lou Ferrigno, Robby had the same height as Mike. He also sported two of the greatest arms in the sport, and a back to match. Mike would go on to build those muscles up to nearly the same standard as his idol.

Mike left the IFBB in the early '90s and joined Vince McMahon's short-lived WBF federation. After rejoining the IFBB in 1993 Mike had limited success on the pro tour, with his best finish being fifth at the 1994 New York Night of Champions. Mike is since retired from the sport. Here's his competitive career:

One of Mike Quinn's early idols was Robby Robinson.

1981	Mr. America – AAU, heavyweight, 10th
	Teen Mr. America – AAU, overall winner
	Teen Mr. America – AAU, heavyweight, 1st
1982	Junior Nationals – NPC, heavyweight, 2nd
1983	USA Championships – NPC, heavyweight, 4th
1984	Mr. America – AAU, medium, 3rd
	Universe – NABBA, medium, 1st
	World Championships – NABBA, medium, 2nd
1986	Nationals – NPC, heavyweight, 4th
1987	Detroit Pro Invitational – IFBB, 4th
	USA Championships – NPC, overall winner
	USA Championships – NPC, heavyweight, 1st
1988	Grand Prix England – IFBB, 5th
	Grand Prix France – IFBB, 5th
	Grand Prix Germany – IFBB, 4th
	Grand Prix Greece – IFBB, 4th
	Grand Prix Italy – IFBB, 7th
	Grand Prix Spain (2) – IFBB, 5th
	Grand Prix Spain – IFBB, 4th
	Grand Prix US Pro – IFBB, 5th
	Olympia – IFBB, 6th
	World Pro Championships – IFBB, 4th
1989	Grand Prix England – IFBB, 7th
	Grand Prix Finland – IFBB, 8th
	Grand Prix Holland – IFBB, 7th
	Olympia – IFBB, 7th

1990   Grand Prix Holland – IFBB, 12th
        Olympia – IFBB, 11th
1991   WBF Grand Prix – WBF, 12th
1993   Night of Champions – IFBB
1994   Night of Champions – IFBB, 5th
        Olympia – IFBB, 19th
        San Jose Pro Invitational – IFBB, 11th
1999   Night of Champions – IFBB
        Professional World Cup – IFBB, 17th

Mike had outstanding back development.

"To witness a Quinn back workout you need either a high security clearance, a radiation shield, or both. Talk about intensity!"

– Fairfax Hackley,
MuscleMag International
contributor commenting on
Teenage Mr. America winner,
Mike Quinn.

Back

One of the main reasons Mike Quinn won the 1980 Teenage Mr. America title was his outstanding back development. Many in the audience were wondering if in fact Franco Columbu had retired, or if the kid on stage was somehow Franco in disguise. Mike's lats were that thick and wide.

To build those monsters, Mike preferred to work his back in the descending sets fashion. Training this way allowed him to use his heaviest weights first, thus putting the most stimulation on the muscle. Mike also liked to alternate most of his chinup and pulldown exercises between front and rear. He usually kept his reps in the 10 to 12 range. A typical back workout for the former teenage phenomenon is as follows:

1. Front or rear chins – 3 sets of 10 to 12 reps
2. Front or rear pulldowns – 3 sets of 10 to 12 reps
3. T-bar rows – 3 sets of 10 to 12 reps
4. Reverse grip pulldowns – 3 sets of 10 to 12 reps
5. Dumbell or seated rows – 3 sets of 10 to 12 reps
6. Dumbell pullovers – 3 sets of 10 to 12 reps

Mike Christian – The Iron Warrior

Mike Christian was born on December 5, 1955. He spent his youth in the tough ghetto area of south central Los Angeles. Influenced by gangs, it would have been easy for Mike to turn out a victim or product of his environment. Instead, this influence turned Mike around and set him on a path that would lead to fame and fortune.

"There was one guy on our block who was very muscular. I was immediately impressed with his huge arms and rippling physique. I found out that he lifted weights. A friend of mine had some weights in his back yard. Every day I was there working out. I didn't know what I was

Mike Christian

doing but I was determined to be built in record time. I worked out every day doing the same exercises, mostly arm work."

Mike didn't stop at his arms, as his record clearly shows.

1979   Junior Mr. America – AAU, tall, 3rd
       Mr. Pacific Coast – AAU, 3rd
       Mr. USA – AAU, tall, 4th
1980   Junior Mr. America – AAU, heavyweight, 4th
1981   Mr. California – AAU, heavyweight, 1st
1982   Gold's Classic – NPC, heavyweight, 3rd
       Nationals – NPC, heavyweight, 5th
       North American Championships – IFBB, heavyweight, 4th
       USA Championships – NPC, heavyweight, 4th
1983   California Classic – NPC, overall winner
       California Classic – NPC, heavyweight, 1st
       Nationals – NPC, heavyweight, 3rd
1984   Nationals – NPC, overall winner
       Nationals – NPC, heavyweight, 1st
       World Amateur championships – IFBB, heavyweight, 1st
1985   Night of Champions – IFBB, 4th
       Olympia – IFBB, 5th
1986   Los Angeles Pro Championships – IFBB, 2nd
       Olympia – IFBB, 3rd
       World Pro Championships – IFBB, 2nd

1987   Grand Prix France – IFBB, 5th
           Grand Prix Germany (2) – IFBB, 4th
           Grand Prix Germany – IFBB, 3rd
           Olympia – IFBB, 4th
1988   Grand Prix US Pro – IFBB, winner
           World Pro Championships – IFBB, winner
1989   Grand Prix England – IFBB, 4th
           Grand Prix Finland – IFBB, 5th
           Grand Prix France – IFBB, 2nd
           Grand Prix Germany – IFBB, winner
           Grand Prix Holland – IFBB, 6th
           Grand Prix Spain (2) – IFBB, winner
           Grand Prix Spain – IFBB, winner
           Grand Prix Sweden – IFBB, 2nd
           Olympia – IFBB, 6th
1990   Arnold Classic – IFBB, 2nd
           Olympia – IFBB, 4th
1991   WBF Grand Prix – WBF, 2nd

The wide back of Mike Christian.

Mike left the IFBB federation, and joined the ill-fated WBF in 1990. As Gary Strydom was being groomed to be the king of the new federation, big Mike had to settle for second. It soon became obvious that Vince McMahon's lofty ambitions were a bust, so Mike hung up the posing trunks for good.

Mike always saw more to bodybuilding than just competition and he transferred his success in bodybuilding over to the business world. In demand as a trainer, Mike has also made training videos for aspiring bodybuilders. After teaching thousands of bodybuilders how to grow their muscles, Mike saw a need for tailored clothing to show off those fantastic physiques. Today he is the proud owner of the Platinum Everywear (Trademark Sports) clothing line.[1] Check it out on the Internet at http://www.getbig.com/almanac/body-mcd.htm.

Reference:
(1) http://www.getbig.com/almanac/body-mcd.htm

Back

Despite winning eight straight Mr. Olympia titles, Lee Haney never had a free ride. Guys like Lee Labrada, Berry DeMey, and Rich Gaspari, did their utmost to rest the title from the TotaLee Awesome one. And then there was Mike Christian. Mike was one of the few bodybuilders who had the overall size and shape to stand next to Lee and hold his own.

With his tall frame, Mike had to work hard to fill in his physique. This was especially true for his back. Recognizing that the only way to beat Haney was to match him bodypart for bodypart, Mike redesigned his back training to bring it to the level of his gargantuan shoulders.

Five exercises made up his back routine. The specific movements often varied, but not the format.

Mike liked to start his back training with a chinning exercise, usually narrow chins using the seated row attachment. He did the first two sets without any weight for reps of 12. He then attached a 45-pound plate around his waist and commenced to do 4 more sets of 10, 10, 8 and 7 reps respectively.

After narrow chins, Mike moved on and did 4 sets of 8 to 12 reps of wide chins. Mike found wide grip chins superior for his upper, outer back, while the narrows took care of the lower insertions.

Mike's third lat exercise was often the Nautilus Pullover machine. He performed this exercise for both the middle back region and the lower insertions of his lats, where they tie in to the serratus. Mike's goal on this exercise is 4 sets of 15 reps each. Mike is convinced that many bodybuilders abuse this exercise by piling on too much weight. Sure it's easy to load on the stack, but never at the expense of proper technique.

Exercises four and five are seated cable rows and wide-grip pulldowns. On the seated cable rows, Mike preferred the wide straight bar over the normal narrow, V-bar attachment. For extra support Mike would strap himself on with wrist straps and then pull the bar into his mid-abdominal region. Mike would do one warm-up set and then four heavier sets.

To finish his back, Mike performed wide-grip pulldowns. Again he did one warm-up set and then four sets of 12.

The late Mohammed Benaziza, Gary Strydom, Mike Christian and Ben Weider.

Samir Bannout – The Lion of Lebanon

Ask most people to name the most famous Arab actor, and they'll respond with Omar Shariff. Ask a bodybuilder to name the most famous Arab bodybuilder, and they'll all answer with the same name, Samir Bannout.

Perhaps one of the most generally well liked bodybuilders in the business, if there was an award for congeniality in bodybuilding contests, Samir would have taken every one.

Samir was born in the then very peaceful Paris-of-the-Middle-East, Beirut, Lebanon, on November 11, 1955. His family is a mixture of French and Lebanese. He studied French for 15 years, and combined his academic studies with sports: track and field, volleyball, soccer and prophetically, weightlifting. In fact it was weightlifting that would soon derail his academic career (for a short time), and change his life forever.

It did not begin well, and Samir's career almost ended with his first visit to the gym, and his first deadlift. Never one to take half measures, Samir attacked the iron like a pro and attempted 315 pounds. Unlike a pro, Samir was 16 and weighed only 120 pounds. He hurt his back so badly that he couldn't walk for a week after. But Lions are most dangerous when they're injured, and Samir returned to the gym with a vengeance. Less than two years later, an 18-year-old Samir represented Lebanon at the IFBB Mr. Universe contest in Verona, Italy. There Samir first met the Giants: Lou Ferrigno, Ken Waller, and Roger Walker.

Samir's father, like many parents, dreamed of his son becoming an engineer or a doctor. But after two and a half years of college, the headstrong Samir quit college to dedicate himself to bodybuilding full time. He also decided that to pursue his dreams, he would have to leave his native Lebanon and travel to America. He first settled in Detroit, but Michigan is not California, and for bodybuilding that's where the action is. Joe Weider made it possible by paying Samir for articles, with which Samir was able to support himself.

> **"At the Olympia, Samir was literally a standout in the lineup of competitors, and while he is universally famous for his amazing symmetry and proportion I think it was the fact that he had made so much improvement to his fantastic deltoids that made the standout occur."**
>
> – Chris Lund, former *MuscleMag International* writer and photographer commenting on Samir Bannout's shape at the 1982 Mr. Olympia.

Samir was known for both his size and proportions.

He soon became a force to be reckoned with, and chalked up a number of titles.

1976   Universe – IFBB, middleweight, 12th
1977   Mr. International – IFBB, middleweight, 2nd
1978   Mr. International – IFBB, middleweight, 2nd
1979   Best in the World – IFBB, amateur, 1st
        Canada Pro Cup – IFBB
        World Amateur Championships – IFBB, light heavyweight, 1st
1980   Grand Prix California – IFBB, 4th
        Night of Champions – IFBB, 10th
        Olympia – IFBB, 15th
        Pittsburgh Pro Invitational – IFBB
1981   Grand Prix California – IFBB, 7th
        Grand Prix New England – IFBB, 6th
        Night of Champions – IFBB, 10th
        Olympia – IFBB, 9th
1982   Grand Prix Sweden – IFBB, 2nd
        Olympia – IFBB, 4th
1983   Olympia – IFBB, winner
1984   Canada Pro Cup – IFBB, 5th
        Olympia – IFBB, 6th
        World Grand Prix – 5th
1985   World Championships – WABBA, professional, 1st
1986   World Championships – WABBA, professional, 1st
1988   Grand Prix England – IFBB, 10th
        Grand Prix Italy – IFBB, 9th
        Olympia – IFBB, 8th
1989   Arnold Classic – IFBB, 4th
        Grand Prix Finland – IFBB, 6th
        Grand Prix France – IFBB, 8th
        Grand Prix Germany – IFBB, 5th
        Grand Prix Holland – IFBB, 5th
        Grand Prix Spain[2] – IFBB, 5th
        Grand Prix Spain – IFBB, 5th
        Grand Prix Sweden – IFBB, 3rd
        Olympia – IFBB, 9th
1990   Arnold Classic – IFBB, disqualified
        Grand Prix England – IFBB, 6th
        Grand Prix Finland – IFBB, 5th
        Grand Prix Italy – IFBB, 6th
        Houston Pro Invitational – IFBB, 3rd
        Olympia – IFBB, 8th
        Pittsburgh Pro Invitational – IFBB, winner
        World Championships – NABBA, professional, 2nd
1991   Olympia – IFBB
1992   Arnold Classic – IFBB
        Grand Prix Germany – IFBB, 11th
        Olympia – IFBB, 16th

1993   Arnold Classic – IFBB, 13th
          Ironman Pro Invitational – IFBB, 13th
          Ironman Pro Invitational – IFBB, 15th
          San Jose Pro Invitational – IFBB, 10th
1994   Grand Prix England – IFBB, 14th
          Grand Prix Germany – IFBB, 13th
          Grand Prix Italy – IFBB, 12th
          Grand Prix Spain – IFBB, 12th
          Olympia – IFBB, 19th
1996   Olympia – Masters, IFBB, 6th

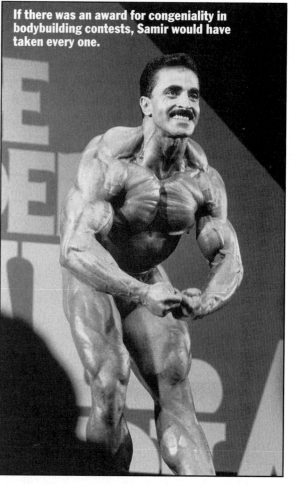

If there was an award for congeniality in bodybuilding contests, Samir would have taken every one.

Many bodybuilders have moved on to successful careers in the movies. Samir tried, but his first movie was a disaster with the critics (through no fault of his own). Even Arnold made *Hercules Goes Bananas*, though that movie ranks with *Gladiator* by comparison to Samir's film *The Babysitters*.[1]

Fortunately, Samir has his education to rely on. In 1982, Samir finished his degree in Civil Engineering.

Fans wanting to get into contact with Samir can reach him at samir.ctr.bannout@faa.gov If you want to contact Samir for guest posing or seminars, write him at P.O. Box 733, Santa Monica, CA 90406.

References:
1) http://us.imdb.com/Name?Bannout,+Samir
2) http://www.weightsnet.com/Links/Bodybuilding/screencredits.html

"I will weigh 210 pounds of rock hard, ripped-to-the-bone muscle! I tell you Chris, I will be ripped to shreds! I swear to God I will be Mr. Olympia!"

– Samir Bannout, The Lion of Lebanon vowing to former *MuscleMag International* writer and photographer, Chris Lund, that he will one day win bodybuilding's most coveted title. Samir made true on his promise in 1983.

Chest

During his heyday in the early 1980s, Samir was known for both his size and proportions. Next to his arms, his chest was one of his more outstanding features. Samir was a great believer in that old standby the flat barbell bench press. Even though the bench press has come under attack in recent years as an inferior chest exercise, Samir made it the primary exercise in his chest training.

Samir used a fairly wide, thumbs-free grip on the bar and did a couple of light, warmup sets before putting some serious weight on the bar. For light sets he kept his feet on the bench, but as soon as he went heavy he put his feet down for stability.

Samir would pyramid the weight up with each successive set, doing from 6 to 12 reps per set. Despite his medium, 200-210 pound size, he regularly went over 400 pounds on flat bench presses. During a typical chest workout, Samir would do 6 sets of bench presses.

Samir's next exercise was usually parallel bar dips. During the off-season he would tie a heavy dumbell around his waist, but in the months leading up to the Olympia he would just use his bodyweight. Samir rarely counted reps on dips, preferring instead to go to positive failure. On most days 4 sets sufficed.

To conclude his chest training, Samir did cable crossovers. Unlike most bodybuilders who perform cables two arms at a time, Samir preferred to do them one arm at a time. He felt that he could concentrate this way. During his Mr. Olympia preparations, Samir usually did 4 sets of 12 reps of cable crossovers.

To finish his chest routine, Samir would go over to a mirror and hit a number of chest shots. This not only brought out all those extra striations that the judges and fans craved, but also helped him gain better control over his pectoral muscles.

> **"I feel my biceps are in fairly good proportion with the rest of my body, and I have never really had a problem developing them."**
>
> – Samir Bannout, 1983 Mr. Olympia commenting on his near perfect biceps.

Samir Bannout and Dorian Yates.

Shoulders

Samir, like most top bodybuilders, preferred to start his shoulder training with a heavy, basic pressing movement. One of his favorites was the Smith machine, which enabled him to work his delts in safety and comfort. Samir did 5 sets of Smith presses using a false grip and leaning just slightly back.

For his second exercise Samir moved on to dumbell side laterals. Samir like to go heavy on this exercise, frequently using dumbells that many bodybuilders would consider respectable pressing weight! Samir commenced the exercise with both dumbells by his sides, palms facing his body. With only the slightest degree of body movement, Samir raised both dumbells in a bent-arm circular fashion until his elbows were roughly parallel to the ground and he continued until he could no longer reach that position. The reps were usually for between 8 and 10.

To finish his side delts and also hit the traps, Samir did upright rows. He grabbed the bar with a six-inch wide grip and pulled straight up until the bar was just below his chin. Again it was 4 sets of about 8 reps.

To hit the rear delts, Samir performed that old standby, bent-over dumbell laterals. Rather than sit on the edge of a bench, however, he preferred to stand and bend slightly forward with his knees slightly bent. Samir did 4 sets of this great rear delt builder.

As a finishing movement, Samir liked to do one-arm cable laterals. Standing about three to four feet from the pulley machine, he would reach across with his opposite hand and grab the handle. With a slight bend at the elbow he would raise out and upward until his arm was parallel with the floor. Throughout the exercise he kept his elbow held high.

Biceps

The Lion of Lebanon took a practical approach to biceps training. He only trained them twice a week, and hit them just after back training, which serves as a good warmup. Besides straight sets, Samir would throw in such advanced training techniques as cheat reps, negative reps, and forced reps. Given the almost perfect symmetry of his biceps, it's not surprising to learn that Samir selected his exercises to hit the biceps from different angles. The following are sample exercise from Samir's favorite biceps' routines.

1. Barbell preacher curls – Samir used a wide grip on this exercise, slightly wider than shoulders. On a typical day he would do 3 to 4 sets of 7 to 12 reps, using as heavy a weight as possible.

2. Alternate dumbell curls – With the dumbells positioned by his sides, Samir would raise his arms up until the dumbells were just in line with his shoulders. He experimented with supination, but found straight curls (palms facing up at all times) the most productive. Again it was 3 to 4 sets of 7 to 12 reps.

3. Cable concentration curls – To finish off his biceps, Samir would squat down in front of a cable machine and do one-arm cable curls. Unlike dumbell curls, Samir would supinate his hands on this exercise, rotating from a palms in to a palms-up position. Samir usually did 3 to 4 sets of 7 to 10 reps of this exercise.

The previous is just one routine The Lion used to prepare for the 1983 Mr. Olympia. Keep in mind he would also include such exercises as barbell curls, standing cable curls, and concentration curls.

Given the almost perfect symmetry of his biceps, it's not surprising to learn that Samir selected his exercises to hit the biceps from different angles.

Mohamed Makkawy

Mohamed Makkawy first came to prominence when he burst on the scene and snatched the 1976 Mr. Universe title from the favorite, Danny Padilla. A native of Egypt, Mohamed moved to Canada and joined the IFNN pro circuit. For a period in the early '80s he was the top bodybuilder in the world. Under the tutelage of the "Iron Guru" Vince Gironda, Mohamed had a reputation for coming into every contest in shredded condition. He also exhibited some of the best proportions in bodybuilding history.

1972   Universe – IFBB, short, 3rd
1974   Universe – IFBB, short, 2nd
1976   Universe – IFBB, lightweight, 1st
1977   Mr. International – IFBB, overall winner
        Mr. International – IFBB, lightweight, 1st
        Universe – IFBB, lightweight, 2nd
1978   Olympia – IFBB, lightweight, 6th
        Professional World Cup – IFBB, 7th
        USA vs. the World – IFBB, lightweight, 4th
1979   Canada Diamond Pro Cup – IFBB, 8th
        Grand Prix Pennsylvania – IFBB
        Grand Prix Vancouver – IFBB
1980   Canada Pro Cup – IFBB, 9th
        Night of Champions – IFBB, 8th
        Universe – Pro, IFBB, 6th
        World Pro Championships – IFBB, 5th
1981   Canada Pro Cup – IFBB, 10th
        Grand Prix Belgium – IFBB, 10th
        Grand Prix Belgium – IFBB, 9th
        Grand Prix Wales – IFBB, 8th
1982   Grand Prix Belgium – IFBB, winner
        Grand Prix Sweden – IFBB, winner
        Night of Champions – IFBB, 4th
        Olympia – IFBB, 7th
        World Pro Championships – IFBB, 6th
1983   Grand Prix England – IFBB, winner
        Grand Prix Las Vegas – IFBB, 8th
        Grand Prix Sweden – IFBB, winner
        Grand Prix Switzerland – IFBB, winner
        Olympia – IFBB, 2nd
        World Pro Championships – IFBB, winner
1984   Olympia – IFBB, 2nd
1985   Olympia – IFBB, 4th
1997   Canada Pro Cup – IFBB, 19th
        Ironman Pro Invitational – IFBB
        Night of Champions – IFBB, 16th
1998   Arnold Classic – IFBB, masters, 7th
        Ironman Pro Invitational – IFBB, 17th
        Masters Arnold – IFBB, 7th
1999   Night of Champions – IFBB

Mohamed Makkawy exhibited some of the best proportions in bodybuilding history. Here he is with Johnny Fuller.

Arms

As a student of the legendary Iron Guru, Vince Gironda, it's not surprising that Mohamed Makkawy developed such perfect proportions. Vince was decades ahead of his time in that regard. When Mohamed started training under Vince in the early '80s the first thing Vince did was redesign Mohamed's routine to focus on his weak points. The end results was a string of Grand Prix wins against guys outweighing him by 40 or 50 pounds.

Mohamed and Lee Haney

Vince's arm routine for Mohamed was planned around hitting the triceps and biceps from as many different angles as possible.

Mohamed's first triceps exercise was usually lying EZ-bar extensions. Holding a straight bar with a false (thumbless) grip, about 12 inches from the center, Mohamed lowered the bar right down to his forehead. The bar was then returned to just short of a locked out position. When Mohamed couldn't do another rep in strict fashion, he brought the bar to his lower rib cage and performed three quarter range, narrow presses. Both exercises were considered part of the same set.

Mohamed's second triceps exercise was usually two-arm triceps kickbacks. Where most bodybuilders prefer the one-arm version, Mohamed favored the two-arm style. With his elbows locked close to his sides, and upper arm parallel to the floor, Mohamed would extend or "kick" the dumbells back until his arms were straight. Again strict style was the order of the day. Jerking, yanking, or throwing the weight up was not allowed in Vince's Gym!

For his third triceps exercise, Mohamed did kneeling rope extensions.

> **"I do not believe in pushing beyond muscular failure because I feel you will create a state of hormone depletion which means you will actually lose muscle."**
>
> – Mohamed Makkawy, Mr. Universe and numerous Grand Prix contests winner, offering his views on all out training to failure workouts.

Vince's Gym has a special low cable that allowed bodybuilders to rest their elbows on it while doing the exercise. For those not familiar with the exercise, grab a rope (the triceps pushdown rope being the most common) and kneel down so you are facing away from the machine. With your elbows resting on a low bench, extend your hands forward until they are in a locked out position. Return to the starting position by bending at the elbow and stretching the forearms behind the head.

Vince Gironda's arm routine for Mohamed was planned around hitting the triceps and biceps from as many different angles as possible.

To finish his triceps, Mohamed performed triceps pushdowns on a special machine unique to Vince's Gym. Resembling a Nautilus triceps pushdown machine, Mohamed would hold a handle in each hand and pushed his arms down from chest height to a straight position. For those who don't have access to such a machine, parallel bench dips can be substituted.

For variety Mohamed often performed the previous exercises in a circuit fashion, doing three sets of each in the process. Although reps were not religiously counted. On average Mohamed did between 8 and 12 reps per set.

With triceps out of the way, Mohamed moved on to his biceps, again following a sequence of exercises.

The first exercise for biceps was usually incline dumbell curls. Using a 40-degree incline bench, Mohamed would sit down with his legs crossed in front of him. Once when an inquisitive reporter asked Vince the significance of crossing the legs, Vince grabbed a set of dumbells and yelled, "We cross the legs so the damned dumbells don't hit them, see!"

Like Reg Park and Arnold before him, Mohamed performed incline curls using the supination style. This means as he curls the dumbells upward he rotates his wrists from a palms-facing-in to a palms-facing-up position.

For his second exercise, Mohamed moved on to one of Larry Scott's favorites, dumbell preacher curls. With his elbows and forearms resting on an 85-degree preacher bench, palms facing the floor, Mohamed curled the dumbells upward, rotating his wrists as he lifted. By the time his forearms were vertical with the floor, his palms were facing the ceiling. He then lowered the dumbells to just short of a locked out position, rotating his palms back to the starting position.

Mohamed's third exercise was another Gironda Classic, spyder curls. The spyder bench is a small bench built and designed by Vince and consists of a flat bench attached to a perpendicular-like frame at one end. You simply lie face down on the bench so that the upper arms are handing over the end. In this position, Mohamed would hold the bar with a false grip about twelve inches apart. From a locked out position he curled the bar up as far as he could. He then lowered in a slow and controlled manner until his arms were back to the straight position.

To finish his biceps, Mohamed did one arm concentration curls while sitting on a low stool or bench.

Like triceps, Mohamed often did the previous exercises in a circuit fashion, doing one set of each, for three cycles or loops. The end result was 12 intense sets of biceps-blasting torture!

Legs

Even though he had won the Amateur World Championships and a number of Grand Prix events, Mohamed was the first to admit his thighs were not quite in balance with his upper body. After trying numerous exercises and techniques, he finally headed to Southern California and the wisdom of the Iron Guru, Vince Gironda.

Vince set Mohamed up on a triset routine, incorporating leg curls, leg extensions, and hack squats. He would start with leg curls and do one set to failure, usually with reps in the 18 to 20 range. Those who witnessed Mohamed at the time say that the only thing that moved was the Egyptian's lower legs. There was none of the usual rocking motion that most bodybuilders engage in.

What Mohamed may have lacked in lower body development was more than made up for by his almost perfectly balanced upper body.

With little or no rest, Mohamed hopped on the leg extension and did another 18 to 20 reps of perfect style extensions. At the top of the exercise, Mohamed would stop for a split second and give his thighs an extra squeeze.

When he reached failure on the leg extension, Mohamed positioned himself under the hack slide machine and banged out a set of parallel depth squats. As he descended he let his knees flare out to the sides.

Mohamed would do three such trisets for his thighs and hamstrings, all together performing nine quality sets.

For calves, Vince had Mohamed perform another series of trisets. He would start with regular standing calf raises on the machine, move on to seated raises with a barbell laid on top of his thighs, and then finish with standing calf raises facing inward on the hack slide machine.

As with his thighs, Mohamed would do three trisets for calves, averaging 30 reps per set.

Shoulders

What Mohamed may have lacked in lower body development was more than made up for by his almost perfectly balanced upper body. During his best years, the late '70s and early '80s, Mohamed displayed one of the most complete torsos ever to have graced a bodybuilding stage. He never had the overall mass of Haney or Coleman, or the ruggedness of Yates or Markus Ruhl, but for many, the magic Egyptian exhibited a physique that came as close to the ideals of Greek sculptures as humanly possible.

The center of Mohamed's great upper body was his fantastic shoulder development. They were full and balanced, with each head clearly separated from the other two.

To build those great delts, Mohamed usually started with standing side laterals. Early on Mohamed realized that while the front and rear delts were important, it was the side shoulders that added the most width to the deltoids, so he prioritized and trained them first. He would start the exercise with his knuckles facing in front, and then as he raised he'd rotate in a sort of semi circle. Mohamed always did this exercise while facing a mirror. This not only allowed him to check his style, but also gave him motivation as he could watch his side delts swelling with each rep.

With his side deltoids now pre-exhausted, Mohamed moved on to seated dumbell presses. This exercise not only hits the front delts, but also gives them more stimulation.

To finish off his shoulders, Mohamed did standing barbell presses from a rack, supersetted with bent-over dumbell laterals. The standing press is one of the best overall shoulder exercises, while the bent-over laterals take care of the rear delts. Even though most bodybuilders start with a barbell exercise, Mohamed preferred to do them toward the end. A shoulder injury incurred a few years before, necessitated going slightly lighter on his barbell exercises. He also found that to avoid re-injuring his shoulders he needed to have them fully warmed up. So it only made sense to do them after the other exercises.

We didn't mention sets and reps as Mohamed constantly changed things around. He was a firm believer in the instinctive style of training. On average he did 4 to 5 sets of an exercise for 8 to 12 reps.

Mohamed exhibited a physique that came as close to the ideals of Greek sculptures as humanly possible.

Jusup Wilkosz

Throughout his competitive career Jusup Wilkosz was known as the Stuttgart strongman. He had a solid background in Olympic lifting (three times German National Champion) and other sports (swimming, skiing and biking) as well as bodybuilding (Mr. Germany, Mr. Europe, amateur Mr. Universe and Professional Mr. Universe). Jusup impressed fans worldwide with his rugged looks and tremendous muscularity. At 6 feet tall he was usually the tallest man on stage, and with his 52" chest, 20" arms, and 245-plus pounds of mass, he was never overlooked.

Jusup Wilkosz was sometimes called the Renaissance Man of bodybuilding.

Sometimes called the Renaissance Man of Bodybuilding because of his intellectual interests in classical music, literature, philosophy, writing, painting, stamp collecting, and electronics (he builds his own TV and radio sets), Jusup has always had exceptional strength. In grammar school he could do pushups with a classmate sitting on his back, and at 13 he was stronger than most of his teachers.

This gentle giant, noted for his unusual combination of brains, brawn and sensitivity, was in the forefront of professional bodybuilding during the 1980s.

1978   World Amateur Championships – IFBB, heavyweight, 2nd
1979   German Championships – overall winner
        German Championships – tall, 1st
        World Amateur Championships – IFBB, heavyweight, 1st
1980   Universe – Pro, IFBB, winner
        World Pro Championships – IFBB, winner
1981   Canada Pro Cup – IFBB, 5th
        Grand Prix Belgium – IFBB, 3rd
        Grand Prix Wales – IFBB, 2nd
        Olympia – IFBB, 6th
1982   Grand Prix Belgium – IFBB, 3rd
        Grand Prix Sweden – IFBB, 6th
        Olympia – IFBB, 10th
1983   Grand Prix England – IFBB, 3rd
        Grand Prix Sweden – IFBB, 3rd
        Grand Prix Switzerland – IFBB, 4th
        Olympia – IFBB, 6th
1984   Canada Pro Cup – IFBB, 4th
        Olympia – IFBB, 3rd
        World Grand Prix – 4th
1986   Olympia – IFBB, 12th

The number of reps Jusup did depended on the time of the year it was.

Tragedy struck in 1990 as Jusup's beloved wife Ruth became seriously ill with cancer, and finally succumbed. Jusup seemed to disappear from sight, fueling a storm of rumors that have continued to the present.

"I never quit bodybuilding completely. I just laid my pro bodybuilding career to rest for some time. What happened was that my wife, Ruth, fell ill with cancer, which finally and slowly killed her in 1990. So I had more important matters to attend to …"

Jusup has a message for his fans: "… Thank you for being such dedicated fans. It is important for anyone – but even more so for a professional athlete – to know during a time of crisis and trouble that there are supportive people out there, like all of you. I'm very happy that you remember the German bodybuilding legend, Jusup Wilkosz!"

Shoulders

With his background as an Olympic lifter, it's not surprising that Jusup Wilkosz liked to start his shoulder training with barbell presses. He felt that behind-the-neck barbell presses did the most to beef up his shoulder mass, and beginners should do at least one pressing movement in their shoulder training. During a typical training session, Jusup would do 5 sets of shoulder presses, gradually adding weight with each set. The number of reps he did depended on the time of the year. If it was off-season and adding to his shoulder mass was the goal, he would use heavier weight and do sets of 8 to 10. Then close to a contest he would lighten the weight and shoot for 15 reps per set.

> **"In training the shoulders you must keep in mind that there are three heads of the deltoids, front, side, and rear. In our every-day training the front delts get plenty of work through your various chest exercises. Common sense would tell you to spend more time and energy on the side region."**
>
> – Jusup Wilkosz, heavyweight Mr. Universe winner, offering advice to beginners on what areas of the shoulders need the most work.

Jusup's second shoulder exercise was one-arm dumbell raises. Using between 50 and 60 pounds on this exercise, Jusup would pound out 5 sets of 12 reps for each side, resting as little as possible between sets.

To attack his rear delt heads, Jusup would sit on the end of a bench and with a 40- or 50-pound dumbell in each hand, perform 6 super-intense sets of bent-over lateral raises. As with standing laterals, Jusup did 12 reps per set.

With all three heads given a good going over, most bodybuilders would call it quits at this point, but not Jusup. To really blast the shoulders into submission, he would often grab a lighter set of dumbells and do what he liked to call "front seesaw raises." He would first raise one dumbell to the front and then as it hit shoulder level, bring it across the front of his face. As each arm was lowered he would immediately raise the other. Jusup did 6 sets of 12 reps of this exercise using a 30-pound dumbell.

For his fifth and final shoulder exercise, Jusup liked to go back to a basic power movement, this time barbell pullups. Using about 180 pounds on the bar he did 4 sets of 8 reps. After years of experimentation he found that a wide grip of about 20 inches worked best.

There you have the shoulder routine of the Stuttgart strongman, Jusup Wilkosz.

Forearms

Jusup credits his extensive background in Olympic lifting with playing the biggest role in developing his Popeye-like forearms. The constant cleaning and jerking gave him a very firm grip and plenty of foundation to build his forearms. In fact it was one of the main reasons why he could handle such powerlifting-type poundages in his workout. Besides the indirect stimulation from his Olympic lifting, Jusup also included direct forearm exercises in his workouts. During a typical workout Jusup would pick two or three of the following:

1. Zottman curls – These are similar to standard dumbell curls in that you start curling with the palms facing upward, but as soon as you reach the top, you rotate the hands so the palms are facing downward, and then lower back to the starting position.

Jusup Wilkosz, noted for his unusual combination of brains, brawn and sensitivity, was in the forefront of professional bodybuilding during the 1980s.

2. Reverse barbell curls Considered one of the best forearm extensor builders there is, reverse curls also stress the brachialis and biceps to a lesser degree. Grab a barbell with a shoulder-width grip, but with the palms facing downward. From here the exercise is identical to a regular barbell curl. For variety Jusup also did this exercise on a preacher bench.

3. Wrist curls – Another Wilkosz favorite, grab a barbell with a narrow, palms up grip, and rest your forearm on a flat bench. Curl the hands up and down. Resist the urge to lift your forearms off the bench. Wrist curls are great for the flexor muscles of the forearm.

4. Reverse wrist curls – These are identical to the previous except you grab the bar with a palms facing down grip. Most bodybuilders are not as strong on this exercise as regular wrist curls. This exercise primarily works the extensors of the forearm.

5. Behind-the-back wrist curls – This exercise is seldom seen in gyms, but Jusup did it on a regular basis. Grab a barbell with a palms facing up grip so that it is behind your body, around butt level. Flex up and down until you can't complete another rep.

Although it varied, Jusup usually did 3 sets of a couple of the previous exercises for 12 to 15 reps per set.

Lee Haney

Lee Haney was born in Spartanburg, South Carolina on November 11, 1959. Lee grew up in a happy Baptist family and his parents were always supportive: "My father was a wonderful man and I wanted to be like him. He worked hard and was an excellent provider. He never said anything hurtful to me. He always had a strong hand and was very caring. My mother had the same qualities. She was sort of like my dear, dear friend. We used to talk a lot because my father would be on the road so much…"

Lee developed an interest in body-building at an early age: "Even when I was a little guy, I used to pick things up. I'd look at TV shows such as Hercules, and I was always fascinated by the Biblical story of Samson. A lot of what I saw, I wanted to be and do. That started my curiosity for, and love of, weight training. My parents brought me a set of plastic weights when I was 12. I used to read anything I could get my hands on about weight training. By the age of 16 I was competing in some local bodybuilding contests."

And Lee's father did all he could to help his son: "I recall him taking me to compete in bodybuilding competitions when I was 16 years old. Sometimes I would place, and some-times I wouldn't. He knew how to weld real well, so he welded a T-bar row machine, one of the first machines he built for me. It must be the reason for these wide lats I have!"

Starting with his 1984 Mr. Olympia win, Lee dominated pro bodybuilding for the

Lee Haney had a good support system from early on.

next eight years, and in the process broke Arnold's record of seven Mr. Olympia wins. Here's his incredible competitive record:

1979   Teen Mr. America – AAU, overall winner
          Teen Mr. America – AAU, tall, 1st

1980   Mr. USA – heavyweight class, 4th

1981   Lee graduated from Livingstone College in Salisbury, North Carolina, with a degree in Juvenille Corrections.

1982   Junior Nationals – NPC, overall winner
          Junior Nationals – NPC, heavyweight, 1st
          Nationals – NPC, overall winner
          Nationals – NPC, heavyweight, 1st
          North American Championships – IFBB, heavyweight, 1st
          World Amateur Championships – IFBB, heavyweight, 1st

1983   Grand Prix England – IFBB, 2nd
          Grand Prix Las Vegas – IFBB, winner
          Grand Prix Sweden – IFBB, 2nd
          Grand Prix Switzerland – IFBB, 3rd
          Night of Champions – IFBB, winner
          Olympia – IFBB, 3rd
          World Pro Championships – IFBB, 3rd

1984   Olympia – IFBB, winner

1985   Olympia – IFBB, winner

1986   Olympia – IFBB, winner

1987   Grand Prix Germany (2) – IFBB, winner
          Olympia – IFBB, winner

1988   Olympia – IFBB, winner

1989   Olympia – IFBB, winner

1990   Olympia – IFBB, winner

1991   Olympia – IFBB, winner

Lee Haney literally dwarfed most other competitors during his reign in the 1980s.

    After his retirement in 1991 Lee started giving back to the community: "I have a 40-acre retreat center for kids called "Haney's Harvest House" located in College Park, Georgia … A lot of inner-city kids come out, groups of kids from churches that do sleep-overs. We have hayrides, horseback riding, cookouts, mentoring programs … It's a nice safe environment for kids. We also have petting zoos, basketball courts, baseball fields… I spend most of my time there. I love it so much. Sometimes I'm out there, and I'll say to myself, 'Now wait a minute – you've gotta tend to other stuff.' Being there is so rewarding and relaxing, and I have a lot of fun there. It's nice to get away from the city…"

    Lee haney, a champion in every sense of the word!

Lee Haney, a champion in every sense of the word!

Shoulders

Like Arnold and Sergio before him, Lee Haney literally dwarfed most other competitors during his reign in the 1980s. Not only was he one of the tallest competitors in the lineup, but he carried as much muscle mass as the next two competitors. Weighing nearly 250 pounds in contest shape, Lee set the stage for the behemoths we see onstage nowadays.

With perhaps Mike Christian as his only rival in the width department. Lee easily stood out in a lineup with his shoulder development – he was that wide.

Lee usually started his shoulder workouts with a seldom-used exercise, behind-the-head Smith machine presses. Lee found that the machine's plane of motion kept the reps ultra strict and hit his delts deeper than conventional barbell presses. Lee started with a couple of light warm up sets, and then worked up to 170 to 185 pounds for 5 sets of 8 to 10 reps. At this point most normal bodybuilders would head to the dumbell rack for various lateral movements, but not Lee. Instead he increased the weight and banged out another 5 sets of 8 to 10 reps! For those not keeping count, that's 10 sets of presses. Is it any wonder his delts got so large and full?

With his delts fully swollen with blood, Lee went over to the dumbell rack and ground out 5 sets of standing lateral raises for his side delts. With his delts more than warmed up from the presses, Lee jumped right into his first set of laterals using 35 pound dumbells. After a couple of sets with the 35's he went up to the 45's and performed a few additional sets.

To finish off his enormous shoulders, Lee did 5 sets of bent-over laterals. Most bodybuilders use less weight on this exercise than side or front raises, but not Lee. He kept the

"There is no question that if any part on Lee is more outstanding than another it is his round thick deltoids. The man naturally is very wide just through heredity, but add the extra thickness of his cantaloupe-sized delts and you have an exaggerated shoulder width so wide that the man blocks out the light."

– Garry Bartlett, *MuscleMag* contributor, commenting after watching 8-time Mr. Olympia Lee Haney, go through a shoulder workout in 1985.

45's and leaned over with his knees slightly bent, and raised and lowered the dumbells in a smooth piston-like manner for 12 reps per set.

After concluding his shoulder training, Lee would hit a few shoulder poses to both check his development and bring out the separation in his delts and upper back. As expected, such displays garnered a heap of spectators. But when you are Mr. Olympia, such admiration is to be expected. And during his 8-year dominance of the sport, no bodybuilder was more admired than Atlanta's "totaLee" awesome Lee Haney.

Steve Brisbois was proof that size is not everything.

Steve Brisbois

Most authorities will readily admit that Steve Brisbois is one of Canada's all-time great bodybuilders. He didn't have the mass of Nimrod King or Paul Dillett, but this French-Canadian from Timmins, Ontario, had one of the most complete physiques in the late '80s and early '90s.

Bodybuilding came naturally to Steve and with only nine months of training under his belt won the Novice Ontario Championships. By 1986 he was the Canadian overall champion. Despite his diminutive height (5'3"), Steve managed to hold his own against some of the mass monsters of the late '80s and early '90s. On a number of occasions Steve placed fourth or fifth in contests dominated by 220 and 230 pounders. Although since retired, Steve still serves as inspiration to thousands of shorter bodybuilders. Steve Brisbois was proof that size is not everything. Here's his record:

1986   World Amateur Championships – IFBB, bantam weight, 1st
1987   Night of Champions – IFBB, 9th
        Olympia – IFBB, 18th
1988   Niagara Falls Pro Invitational – IFBB, 11th
        Night of Champions – IFBB, 18th
1989   Niagara Falls Pro Invitational – IFBB, 4th
        Night of Champions – IFBB, 6th
1990   Arnold Classic – IFBB, 5th
        Houston Pro Invitational – IFBB, 7th
        Ironman Pro Invitational – IFBB, 7th
        Niagara Falls Pro Invitational – IFBB, 5th
        Night of Champions – IFBB, 13th
        Pittsburgh Pro Invitational – IFBB, 4th
1991   Arnold Classic – IFBB, 6th
        Ironman Pro Invitational – IFBB, 6th
        Pittsburgh Pro Invitational – IFBB, 5th
        San Jose Pro Invitational – IFBB, 6th
1992   Arnold Classic – IFBB, 5th
        Grand Prix England – IFBB, 11th
        Grand Prix Germany – IFBB, 9th
        Grand Prix Holland – IFBB, 5th
        Grand Prix Italy – IFBB, 4th
        Ironman Pro Invitational – IFBB, 7th
        Olympia – IFBB, 11th

Shoulders

Early in his career, Steve trained his delts with the customary heavy presses to the front and to the rear. In a typical workout it was as much weight as he could handle for 5 to 8 reps. Even when numerous minor shoulder injuries kept cropping up, Steve continued to do heavy presses. After all, you want a big chest you do heavy flat presses, right? You want huge thighs you squat heavy, right? You want thick lats, you perform heavy rows, right? Steve figured the key to cannonball-sized delts was all-out heavy presses.

"The guys who go really heavy on delts are always injuring themselves."

– Steve Brisbois,
1986 Mr. Universe, outlining the relationship between heavy weight and shoulder training.

Steve Brisbois had one of the most complete physiques in the late '80s and early '90s.

Steve was a firm believer in style and technique over weight.

Then he read about Englishman Roy Duval, who after severely injuring his wrist had to give up heavy presses and rely on dumbell and cable exercises. Not only did the new program increase the size of his delts, but also it played a major role in his winning the world championships.

Steve figured that if it could work for Roy, why not him? So he revamped his shoulder training and dropped the heavy barbell presses in favor of more quality dumbell and machine exercises. Instead of the all-out 5 to 8 reps with as much weight as he could handle, he opted for moderate weight of 12 to 15 ultra strict reps. The shoulder routine that Steve felt played the biggest role in his success consisted of four exercises, two for the side delts, and two for the rear. He gave up training the front delts almost entirely. Twice a month, usually on chest day, he would throw in 5 sets of seated dumbell presses. But that was it. He felt that his chest exercises did more than enough for his front shoulders.

The first exercise of Steve's revamped shoulder routine was one-arm side laterals. Steve usually performed this exercise one arm at a time as he found that he could concentrate better on his side delts. Although it varied, Steve usually performed 4 to 5 sets of 12 to 15 reps.

After machine side laterals Steve moved on to rear delts. Again he used a machine and banged out 4 to 5 quality sets of 12 to 15 reps.

Steve's third exercise was standing dumbell laterals. Where the machine version thoroughly warmed his side delts up, dumbell laterals totally finished them. Again he did 4 to 5 ultra strict sets of 12 to 15 reps.

To finish off his delts, it was back to another rear delt exercise, this time seated bent-over dumbell laterals for 4 to 5 sets of 12 to 15 reps.

For those who question a shoulder routine totally devoid of barbell exercises, we let Steve have the last word. "My delts have more separation and detail now. They've really improved. Why risk injury and possibly ending my career by going back to super-heavy pressing when I can get better results with lighter weights? I'm sticking with my new method."

> **"Although I have been training for almost nine years, and I've been a pro since 1987, I continue to learn and improve when it comes to triceps training and development."**
>
> – Steve Brisbois

Triceps

In some respects Steve Brisbois was the Lee Priest of the late 1980s and early 1990s. True he didn't have Lee's overall mass, but like Lee, Steve made up for his diminutive height by developing an almost flawless physique highlighted by two perfectly proportioned arms.

John Hnatyschak, Steve Brisbois and Shane DiMora.

Early on Steve recognized that "triceps" meant more than just a name. The prefix "tri" is indicative that the muscle is composed of three sub muscles or heads. Many bodybuilders treat their muscles as singular entities, but not Steve. He designed his triceps routine to hit all three heads.

He didn't play favorites when it came to triceps training. He had seven different exercises in his triceps workout and picked three on any given workout. He would then do 4 sets of 10 to 15 reps for each. The next workout he would choose three different movements. On the third triceps workout he might go back to the first three, but change the order. The bottom line was that he never did the exact same triceps workout two days in a row.

Steve was also a firm believer in style and technique over weight. He quickly realized that his small bone structure would not be able to endure repeated bombardment with heavy weight. Which is not to say Steve couldn't hoist some serious iron when he wanted too. It's just that he always considered himself a bodybuilder first, and given the number of people he's witnessed over the years with chronic joint problems, he decided to play it safe and use moderate weights in his workouts.

Steve's first exercise in a typical workout would be lying triceps extensions. On some days he would perform 12 to 15 reps, while on others he might add a few extra pounds to the bar and stop at 10 reps. Steve would also vary the style on this exercise. Some days he lowered the bar behind his head with the elbows kept in tight, while on others he let the elbows drift wide and lowered the bar to his throat.

Steve's second exercise was often triceps pressdowns. Notice we said pressdowns not pushdowns. Steve preferred to do cable pressdowns as it felt more like a lying triceps press with a barbell. After trial and error Steve found that pressdowns built more mass than regular, elbows to the side, pushdowns.

To finish off his triceps, Steve usually did a dumbell exercise, one of his favorites being dumbell kickbacks. Steve would place one hand on a bench, torso parallel to the floor, and kick the other arm back until fully extended. Unlike some bodybuilders who sway the upper arm just to lift more weight, Steve always locked the elbow tight to the body and held the upper arm parallel to the floor.

The previous is just one triceps routine Steve regularly employed to build his "horseshoes." On another day he might start with bench dips, move on to single arm behind-the-head extensions, and finish with rope extensions.

Legs

As expected, any bodybuilder who could win the 1986 Mr. Universe has great legs. As Greg Zulak once said, "He has the whole package, calves that are long, full and diamond shaped; hamstrings that look like steel chords beneath his skin; and quads that are large with plenty of sweep and separation."

During his heyday, the mid to late 1980s and early 1990s, Steve trained on a three days on, one day off routine. This meant that he hit legs all by themselves.

Early in his career Steve devoted a considerable amount of time to heavy squatting. At one time he was using over 500 pounds for 6 reps. The result was the leg size he needed at the world level, but not the quality and separation. A combination of intelligence and a knee injury forced Steve to give up squatting completely for over ten months. In that time he was also influenced by Canadian bodybuilding trainer extraordinaire, Gunnar Sikk, to give high rep leg training a try.

Steve Brisbois has the whole package.

With a considerable amount of skepticism, Steve embarked on a leg training program consisting of mostly hack squats and 45 degree leg presses, for sets of 30 to 40 reps. Steve was convinced that his legs would shrink from the lack of heavy weight and low reps. But low and behold his legs actually grew two full inches and his shape, separation, and muscularity improved dramatically. Steve was hooked and became a firm believer in high rep leg training.

After his knees improved, Steve went back to squatting, but the old 500-pound squats were given a pass in place of 20 to 30 rep sets using about 250 pounds.

Since Steve eventually reached the point where his thighs became his strong point, he changed the order of his leg exercises and began hitting hamstrings first in his leg workouts. After first warming up with some light stretching exercises, Steve would superset lying leg curls with stiff-leg deadlifts standing on blocks. For a typical workout he would perform about 8 sets of 15 to 20 reps. Steve rested less than a minute in between supersets. During his precontest preparations Steve added lunges to his hamstrings' routine. Although he tried using a barbell, he discovered that two dumbells held by his sides seemed to provide better stimulation. Steve typically did 5 sets of 12 reps for lunges.

After hamstrings Steve moved on to thigh training, starting first with two or three very light sets of high rep leg extensions. He did this to both warm up his thighs, particularly the knees, and to partially pre-exhaust his quads. After leg extensions it was over to the squat rack for 4 sets of high rep squats. A typical squat workout looked like this:

135 pounds x 20 reps
225 pounds x 20 reps
225 pounds x 20 reps
250 pounds x 25 to 30 reps

Steve Brisbois, one of Canada's all-time great bodybuilders.

These high rep sets of squats were real killers (if you don't believe us try them!) but Steve found them far superior for both size and separation, than conventional heavy weight, low rep sets. Because of the increased oxygen demands made by high rep squats, Steve would rest about two to three minutes between sets, versus the normal minute or so for most exercises.

With squats out of the way, Steve headed to the 45-degree leg press for his second primary thigh movement. Once again setting powerlifting records wasn't his goal. Instead about 400 pounds was placed on the machine for 6 to 8 sets of 30 to 40 reps. If that doesn't impress you, we should add that Steve performed leg presses in a non-lockout style. That is, constant tension with no rest in between.

To finish off his thighs, Steve went back to the leg extension machine and did 4 to 6 sets of 20 to 25 reps.

Even though Steve made the three previous exercises the mainstay of his thigh routine, for variety he occasionally included sissy squats.

All of which brings us to calf training. Many readers will not be happy to hear that Steve falls into the category of "genetically blessed" when it comes to calf training. Calves are the one muscle where the old saying "you either have them, or you don't" certainly holds true. Some guys blast the little suckers for 20 years and are lucky if they add an inch or two. Others walk into the gym on day one sporting 18 to 20 inch cows and never did a calf raise in their life! Steve didn't have 20-inch calves when he first started training, but he has low insertions and plenty of muscle cells in his calves. This meant that regular calf training brought him the results he wanted. In other words his time and energy investment were rewarded.

One thing that separated Steve from most of his bodybuilding contemporaries was that he only did one exercise during a typical calf training session. Instead of the usual two to three exercises for 3 to 4 sets each, Steve would pick just one exercise and do 6 to 8 sets of 20 to 25 reps. He found it better to do one exercise and keep his mind focused on his calves rather than constantly switching things around. Steve's favorite calf exercises were standing calf raises, seated raises, donkey calf raises and toe presses on the hack machine.

Mike Ashley

Mike was born in Portland, Jamaica, West Indies on August 1, 1959. In some ways he was a comet in the world of bodybuilding. He quickly won a couple of prestigious events including the 1988 Detroit Grand Prix and 1990 Arnold Classic, and then faded from the picture. During his career Mike was famous for his near flawless symmetry and proportions. He also vows to this day to be 100 percent natural. Here's his competitive record:

1978   Pro Mr. America – WBBG, teen, 3rd
1982   Natural America – overall winner
        Natural America – short, 1st
1984   Nationals – NPC, middleweight, 9th
1986   Nationals – NPC, light heavyweight, 2nd
        World Amateur championships – IFBB, light heavyweight, 1st
1987   Detroit Pro Invitational – IFBB, winner
        Grand Prix France – IFBB, 10th
        Night of Champions – IFBB, 2nd
        Olympia – IFBB, 10th
1988   Grand Prix England – IFBB, 9th
        Grand Prix France – IFBB, 12th
        Grand Prix Germany – IFBB, 9th
        Grand Prix Greece – IFBB, 9th
        Grand Prix Italy – IFBB, 11th
        Grand Prix Spain (2) – IFBB, 9th
        Grand Prix Spain – IFBB, 8th
        Niagara Falls Pro Invitational – IFBB, 4th
        Olympia – IFBB, 14th
1990   Arnold Classic – IFBB, winner
        Ironman Pro Invitational – IFBB, 2nd
        Pittsburgh Pro Invitational – IFBB, 2nd
1991   Musclefest Grand Prix – IFBB, 5th
        Night of Champions – IFBB, 8th
1992   Arnold Classic – IFBB, 14th
        Ironman Pro Invitational – IFBB, 9th
        Pittsburgh Pro Invitational – IFBB, 10th
1993   Arnold Classic – IFBB, 13th
        Ironman Pro Invitational – IFBB, 9th
        San Jose Pro Invitational – IFBB, 6th
1994   Chicago Pro Invitational – IFBB, 10th
        Niagara Falls Pro Invitational – IFBB, 6th

Mike Ashley vows to this day to be 100 percent natural.

Hamstrings

When Mike Ashley competed regularly in the late '80s and early '90s, he made a special effort to include his hamstrings in just about every pose possible. And why not? When you were blessed with two of the best hams in the business it only made sense to give the judges and audience a closer look. Mike was rewarded for his efforts with his close, but convincing win at the 1990 Arnold Classic.

Mike was a devoted follower of the periodization style of training, popularized by Fred Koch. This involved a heavy phase of six to eight weeks of 6 to 8-rep sets, followed by another couple of months of lighter, 12 to 15-rep sets. Mike found his body could only handle all-out training for a couple of months before the symptoms of overtraining took hold. The lighter phase allowed the body to catch its breath so to speak. In fact Mike often found that he actually grew while following the lighter routines.

Mike's approach to hamstring training was basically the same, whether during the heavy or light phase. The exercises stayed the same, it was just the reps that varied. Being a firm believer in the value of stretching for muscular development, Mike usually started his hamstring training with stiff-leg deadlifts. He did 4 sets of stiff-legs, starting with one lighter set for 12 to 15 reps, and then pyramiding up in weight until he was doing 365 pounds for 6 to 8 reps.

The second exercise after stiff-leg deadlifts was standing leg curls. Again he did 4 sets of 6 to 8 reps. As Mike considered this exercise the leg equivalent of concentration curls, he performed every rep in a slow and deliberate style.

The third and final hamstring exercise was the lying leg curl. As expected he did 4 sets of 6 to 8 reps. This was the only exercise where Mike would occasionally employ the cheating principle. After 4 to 6 reps in ultra strict style, Mike would cheat the weight up and then emphasize the lowering or negative part of the movement.

During his career Mike was famous for his near flawless symmetry and proportions.

The previous was the routine that Mike used to build one of the greatest sets of hamstrings ever to appear on a bodybuilding stage. For variety Mike replaced standing leg curls with seated leg curls. But no matter what the exercise he did 12 sets in total. This is something to keep in mind for those readers who throw 3 sets of lying leg curls at the end of a leg workout and call it hamstring training.

Triceps

When he was going head to head with Shawn Ray and others back in the late '80s and early '90s, Mike was known for having two of the best-developed triceps around. They had it all, size, shape, and separation.

To build his massive horseshoes, Mike employed three different routines. His heavy day usually started with reverse-grip bench presses, and typical reps and poundages looked like this: 95 x 10, 135 x 10, 185 x 8, 225 x 6, 315 x 6 (for 3 sets).

Mike would then move on to cable pushdowns: 80 x 12, 100 x 10, 130 x 8 (again for 3 sets).

"Mike alternates between three types of workouts. He utilizes heavy workouts that highlight three intense working sets with as much weight as he can handle for about 6 reps. He has a moderate weight workout, where the weights used allow him to complete 10 to 12 reps on his three working sets. The third type of workout that comes to Mike's rotation he calls light, meaning his repetition range is around 15."

– Gayle Hall, former *MuscleMag International* contributor, commenting on the diversity of training styles employed by Mike Ashley.

It was only when he did his light day that Mike would make substantial changes to his biceps routine.

To finish those massive suckers off, Mike would do 5 sets of Icarian machine pushdowns: 60 x 8, 80 x 8, 100 x 8 (3 sets).

Mike's main concern on this routine was going as heavy as possible. His 3 final sets of each exercise were the working sets and he used as much weight as possible to limit his reps to 6 to 8.

Mike's medium workout again started with reverse-grip bench presses, but this time he used a weight that allowed reps in the 10 to 12 range. He also did pushdowns for slightly higher reps as well. The main change was the replacing of the Icarian pushdowns with reverse-grip one-arm pushdowns. Mike would alternate back and forth for 5 sets (two light, three medium) on each arm.

Mike's third triceps routine consisted of isolation movements for 5 sets of 15 reps per set. Typical exercises included straight bar reverse-grip pushdowns, dumbell French presses, and dumbell kickbacks. Mike put such concentration into his reps on light day that he found it more difficult than either his heavy or medium days.

Biceps

As with most of his muscle groups, Mike Ashley alternated three different workouts for biceps, light, medium, and heavy. On heavy days Mike would start with alternate dumbell curls for 5 sets of 6 to 10 reps pyramiding up in weight from 50 pounds to 80 pounds.

For his second exercise Mike would do barbell preacher curls. With his biceps already warmed up from the dumbell curls, Mike would start heavy, going from 100 to 130 pounds for 3 sets of 6 to 10 reps.

Mike's third exercise on his heavy day was usually incline dumbell curls. Again he did an average of 6 to 10 reps pyramiding up with each set.

Mike's medium day consisted of the same exercises as his heavy day, but he would start with preacher curls and finish with alternate curls. And instead of a weight that limited him to 6 reps, he would select a weight that allowed for a good 12 reps per set.

It was only when he did his light day that Mike would make substantial changes to his routine. He would first start with straight bar cable curls, doing 4 sets of 15 reps. Next up it was preacher curls, but instead of straight sets he would do 21's. Finally he would finish off with seated incline curls for 4 sets of 15 reps.

Abdominals

If you draw up a list of the top abdominals of all time, Mike Ashley's name will be at or near the top. Everything that characterizes a great midsection could be seen on Mike. Each ab row was thick and well developed and clearly defined. And as for separation, well you could lose a quarter up there.

Mike's attributes much of his great ab development to all the situps he did when he was in track and field in his younger days. At one time he was doing 70 situps with a 45-pound plate behind his head. He even

Mike Ashley and Shane DiMora

managed 10 reps with two 45's behind his head. He was one of the guys in class who could bang out 65 situps in 60 seconds. Mike is first to admit that genetics played a big role in his outstanding ab development, but he's also had to work hard to bring them up to pro bodybuilding standards.

By the time he reached the pro ranks Mike had cut back on the situps (a movement that is hard on the back for many) and instead switched to various crunches.

Mike generally started his ab training with regular crunches for his upper abs. On some days he'll keep his legs across a bench, on others they are held about two feet off the floor. Next Mike would do reverse crunches to hit the lower abs. For those not familiar with the exercise, lie down flat on the floor with the legs elevated about two feet off the ground. With the torso held stationary, draw the legs toward the upper body by bending the knees. The key is to try and keep the lower legs parallel to the floor.

To finish his abs, Mike would throw in some cable crunches. Mike would do straight sets on the previous exercises on one day, and then do twisting versions of them the next. He averaged 3 sets of each exercise and aimed for 50 reps per set.

Before leaving abs we should emphasize something Mike is a firm believer in. "No matter how many situps, crunches, or reverse crunches you do, you must have your fat percentage under control to see your abs." This means good eating and regular sessions of aerobics. The greatest abs in the world are useless if covered by a layer of fat!

Lee Labrada

Like Rich Gaspari, only Lee Haney prevented Lee Labrada from winning the Mr. Olympia on more than one occasion. Many feel that during his heyday in the late '80s and early '90s Lee came as close to physical perfection as was humanly possible. At his best Lee carried 180 almost flawless pounds on his 5'6" frame. Bodybuilding writers nicknamed him "mass with class," and Lee came to represent the embodiment of bodybuilding perfection. Throughout his ten-year pro career, Lee won just about every contest there was. And on two occasions pushed Lee Haney to the wire. Only Haney's mass and reputation saved the day.

With the emphasis on overall mass starting to dominate the '90s Lee called it quits. But being the shrewd businessman he is, he started his own line of supplements. Today his company, Labrada Nutrition, is one of the largest supplement manufacturers in the world. Here's the "mass with class's" incredible competitive record:

1984 Nationals – NPC, middleweight, 5th
       USA Championships – NPC, light heavyweight, 2nd
1985 Nationals – NPC, middleweight, 1st
       World Amateur Championships – IFBB, middleweight, 1st
1986 Night of Champions – IFBB, winner
1987 Grand Prix France – IFBB, 3rd
       Grand Prix Germany (2) – IFBB, 3rd
       Olympia – IFBB, 3rd
       World Pro Championship – IFBB, 2nd
1988 Grand Prix England – IFBB, winner
       Grand Prix France – IFBB, 2nd
       Grand Prix Germany – IFBB, 3rd
       Grand Prix Greece – IFBB, winner
       Grand Prix Italy – IFBB, 2nd
       Grand Prix Spain (2) – IFBB, winner
       Grand Prix Spain – IFBB, 2nd
       Olympia – IFBB, 4th
1989 Grand Prix England – IFBB, winner
       Grand Prix Finland – IFBB, winner
       Grand Prix Holland – IFBB, winner
       Olympia – IFBB, 2nd
1990 Olympia – IFBB, 2nd
1991 Olympia – IFBB, 4th
1992 Olympia – IFBB, 3rd
1993 Arnold Classic – IFBB, 2nd
       Ironman Pro Invitational – IFBB, 2nd
       Olympia – IFBB, 4th
1995 Arnold Classic – IFBB, 5th

"Mass with Class"
Lee Labrada.

Chest

Early in his career, Lee was like most bodybuilders in that he did a lot of heavy barbell work. But he paid the price in the early 1990s when he strained a rotator cuff. The injury was a godsend, however, as it forced him to rely on dumbells. In time he began to prefer dumbells to barbells, even though his rotator injury had recovered.

The first exercise on chest day was usually a combination of flat presses and flyes. This does not mean he did the exercises separately. Instead he rotated his palms as if doing flyes (palms facing the body) but kept the movement more in a vertical plane of motion as if doing presses, as opposed to the wide hugging motion of typical flyes. Typically Lee worked up to 120-pound dumbells for sets of either 5 to 8 in the off-season. Close to competition he would drop the weight back and do 10 to 12 reps.

"My training has become more scientific. I've learned what works and what doesn't work. I'm more likely to plan my training now rather than playing by the seat of my pants as I used to."

– Lee Labrada, IFBB Mr. Universe revealing the mindset that helped make him one of the top bodybuilders in the late 1980s and early 1990s.

Next up was either flat or incline Hammer Strength presses. Again he did 3 to 4 sets of 8 to 10 reps.

To finish off his chest training, Lee did incline dumbell or cable flyes.

From the previous you'll see a typical Labrada chest workout involves no more than 10 to 12 total sets. Lee was heavily influenced by the writings of Mike Mentzer, in that fewer all-out sets are more productive than 20 or more low volume sets. Lee doesn't subscribe to Mentzer's theory in the pure sense (one set per bodypart) but admits most bodybuilders would get just as much, if not more, out of their workouts by cutting back on their volume.

Legs

Even though Lee considered his legs to be one of his fastest developing bodyparts, he still subjected them to regular bouts of brutality. He selected a couple of basic exercises, employed high intensity and always used full range of motion.

Lee modified his leg training over the years. Initially he would start with heavy leg extensions and then move onto leg presses. But then he started developing knee problems. Recognizing the biomechanical disad-

Many feel that during his heyday in the late '80s and early '90s Lee came as close to physical perfection as was humanly possible.

Lee Labrada with Vince Taylor and Alq Gurley.

"A lot of people can't believe I've developed the physique that I have when they see how quickly I'm in and out of the gym."

– Lee Labrada

vantage of leg extensions over such pure movements as squats and leg presses, Lee modified his training, leaving leg extensions 'til the end of his routine.

The leg routine Lee followed for most of his pro days was as follows:

1. Leg presses – Lee would first warm up with a light weight for 15 to 20 reps. He'd then pyramid up in weight with each set until he reached 700 to 800 pounds. Although he's tried vertical and horizontal presses, he eventually came to rely on the 45-degree leg press. A typical workout would consist of 4 working sets of leg presses.

With regards to technique, Lee would use a medium 12 to 18-inch foot stance, and keep the knees wide as he lowered down. For those new to the sport he cautions against bouncing the knees off the chest as it's a great way to crunch ribs (not to mention the cheat you get from using your knees as springs). Lee would never lock out at the top as the amount of weight being used could seriously damage the knees. Lee has seen some pretty foolish leg pressing in his days. Guys using 1500-plus-pounds, but only moving it six to eight inches. Or doing a rep and then locking out for a couple of seconds rest. Lee always performed leg presses with a complete range of motion and with a nonstop-pumping-type motion.

2. Squats – With his legs already pre-exhausted from heavy leg pressing, Lee didn't need to go superheavy on squats. He'd typically do 4 sets, starting with 185 pounds and working up to 315 for 12 to 15 reps. This may not seem like much weight for a pro bodybuilder, but after 4 sets of leg presses, and his technique of going nearly to the floor, 315 pounds for up to 15 reps was more than enough. Although considered primarily a thigh builder, Lee found squats to be

181

Lee came to rely on the 45-degree leg press.

equally effective as a hamstring exercise. The key of course is lowering slow and controlled. This forces the hamstrings to contract as a counterbalance to the quads. The result is well-rounded leg development.

3. Leg Extensions – Only after his thighs and knees were completely warmed up from the previous two exercises would Lee move on to leg extensions. He'd typically do 3 sets of 10 to 12 reps using medium weight. One thing many bodybuilders do to cheat is rock back and forth in the chair. Lee feels this is defeating the purpose of the exercise and more importantly is putting undue stress on the knees.

With 11 to 12 solid sets of thighs out of the way, Lee would move on to hamstrings. His workout consisted of just two exercises, lying leg curls and stiff-leg deadlifts.

1. Lying leg curls – To hit the semitendinosus and semimembranosus, Lee did 5 sets of 10 to 15 reps of this exercise. The key is to keep the butt down on the bench. many bodybuilders in their attempt to lift more weight throw their rears in to the air and rock back and forth. But this is as defeating as swaying back and forth on barbell biceps curls. It does wonders for the ego, but little for the muscle in question. For variety Lee liked to point his toes in and out on this exercise. He found this shifted the stress back and forth between inner and outer hamstrings.

2. Stiff-leg deadlifts – To hit the large biceps femoris, Lee did 5 sets of 10 to 15 reps. Although the name suggests the legs should be locked out straight, Lee recommends a slight bend at the knees. he also urges that the lower back be kept slightly arched. Rounding the back puts great stress on lower back ligaments.

Lee performed the previous workout in under 60 minutes. Although not a follower of Mike Mentzer's Heavy Duty in the purest sense (one set to failure), Lee believed in quality not quantity. Get in, get it over, get outta there. It's that simple.

Calves

Lee realized early in his career that he would never be able to match the likes of Haney, Christian, and DeMey, on the mass front. There was no way he could carry 240-plus pounds on his small frame. Instead he set out to create the most perfectly balanced physique possible. For many he accomplished just that, and his shape at the 1989 and 1990 Mr. Olympias only confirmed that a great, under 200-pound bodybuilder could hold his own with a great, over 200-pound competitor.

One area where Lee took the lead over most competitors was calves. They had the size, shape, and balance that most bodybuilders could only dream about.

Lee typically started his calf training with toe presses on the leg press. With his toes about four to six inches apart, Lee pressed the platform out until his knees were locked. He'd then flex only at the ankle, pushing the weight up and down with just his calves. For variety he'd alternate between a parallel stance with his feet and one where his toes pointed outward. Lee relied on this exercise to hit the large, upper gastrocnemius part of the calf. But occasionally he'd bend his knees slightly to shift the stress to his soleus. On most days he'd do 4 or 5 sets, alternating between heavy weight for low reps (6 to 8) and moderate weight for high reps (15 to 20).

Next up Lee moved a pure soleus exercise like seated calf raises. Unlike straight-leg calf exercises, toe position doesn't make that much difference on seated calf raises, so Lee keeps his pointing straight ahead. Given the fiber make up of the soleus, Lee found it best to keep the reps in the higher, 15 to 20 range. Again it was 4 or 5 sets.

For his third exercise Lee would move on to standing calf raises. Given the amount of weight being used on this exercise, Lee always did seated raises and toe presses first. That way he was sure his calves were fully warmed up. The slightest bounce or jerk with 500 or more pounds of weight could easily rip the Achilles tendon.

As with every calf exercise, the key to standing raises is full range of motion. Lee would go for the maximum stretch at both the top and bottom. If this wasn't possible he would decrease the amount of weight being used. Lee typically did 4 or 5 sets of standing calf raises.

> **"A champion doesn't just have big arms and a big chest. He's developed proportionately all over, and that means calves too."**
>
> – Lee Labrada

Lee was heavily influenced by the writings of Mike Mentzer, in that fewer all-out sets are more productive than 20 or more low volume sets.

Lee's fourth exercise is not really an exercise but a technique. Between every set of the previous exercises, Lee would stretch. Sometimes he'd keep his feet on the machine's block and stretch, other times he'd adopt the familiar runner's stretch against a wall with one knee bent and the other back with the leg kept straight.

We should leave the last word on calf training to Lee. "If you want calves you have to work for them. Put in the time. Put in the effort. Prioritize your calves. And don't baby yourself. Go full bore. Be tough!"

Back

Lee divided his back into three regions, lats, upper back and traps, and lower back. For his lats Lee used to start with a rowing movement, usually seated pulley rows. He would normally use the narrow, triangle-shaped attachment, although for variety he would occasionally switch to a short straight bar. If he used the straight bar he would pull it to his chest. But for the triangle bar he would bring it to the top of his abs. No matter which bar he would hold it for a second or two, and arch his chest and squeeze his shoulder blades together. On most days Lee would do 3 sets of 10 to 12 reps.

At his best Lee carried 180 almost flawless pounds on his 5'6" frame.

After pulley rows Lee usually moved on to lat pulldowns to the chest. Unlike most bodybuilders, Lee found a wide grip never gave him the feel in his lats that he was after. instead he used a medium grip, about shoulder width. Lee would also alternate between a regular straight bar and the short bar with the loops on each end. Again it was 3 sets of 10 to 12 reps.

For his third exercise Lee almost always did one-arm dumbell rows. With one hand and knee resting on a flat bench, Lee would pull the dumbell up to his waist. You guessed it, 3 sets of 10 to 12 reps.

To finish off his lats, Lee would alternate between T-bar and barbell rows. No matter which one, Lee would always keep his lower back slightly arched and knees slightly bent. With a shoulder-width grip, Lee would pull the bar or the plates to his upper lats.

"First of all, I treat my back a little differently than my other muscle groups. As you know I never do more than ten sets for any muscle group, and for smaller muscles groups like biceps I usually one do between six and eight sets. But the back consists of so many different muscles that I felt I had to do more sets than usual to train it properly."
– Lee Labrada on back training.

Lee got into pro body-building to win, and wasn't about to let anyone get the better of him if he could help it.

On all previous exercises Lee used the reverse pyramid training style. After one or two warm-up sets he would put on his heaviest weight and reduce it gradually with each set.

To hit his traps Lee made dumbell shrugs his number one exercise. One variation he employed was to keep his palms facing forward, rather than back or to the sides. He found this little trick tended to put more stress on his traps. From here Lee would shrug straight up and down, no rolling of the shoulders, which adds little or nothing to the movement. On a typical day Lee would do 5 to 6 sets of between 10 and 12 reps.

To finish off his back training, Lee would hit the often neglected spinal erectors. He would either do back extensions or stiff-leg deadlifts for 3 sets of 15 reps.

Abs

When you weigh between 180 and 190 in contest shape, and you're surrounded by 240 pounders, you quickly realize that there's no way you'll ever beat such monsters on their own terms. You have to highlight your physique's best points, and show the judges that there's more to bodybuilding than just beef.

Lee Labrada found himself in the previous scenario many times during the late '80s and early '90s. With the likes of Lee Haney on one side and Mike Christian on the other, Lee sometimes felt like a shrub in a forest of California Redwoods. Now, he could have been content to merely stand on the same stage with these guys. But those that know Lee, know that's not his character. He got into pro bodybuilding to win, and wasn't about to let anyone get the better of him if he could help it.

The end result of such determination was the building of a physique that many experts feel came as close to physical perfection as humanly possible. Few bodybuilders can be described as having no weaknesses, but Lee came close. Like Frank Zane and Bob Paris, Lee's physique was the perfect blend of symmetry, muscularity, and balance. And while many of the 240 pounders were stumbling around the stage, Lee brought posing to a new level.

On two occasions (1989 and 1990) Lee came damn close to taking the Mr. Olympia from Lee haney. Only Haney's overall size and champions status gave him the nod over the slightly sharper Labrada.

One of the muscle groups Lee knew he could match if not beat the mass-monsters on were abs. That's one area that size is not important. In fact the smaller the midsection the better.

Lee was always known for his moderate set/ high intensity training methods. He averaged about 9 to 10 sets for larger muscle groups, and 6 to 8 for smaller groups like biceps and triceps. Lee trained abs on Monday, Wednesday, and Friday. If you could sum up Lee's ab training it would be simple and intense.

The center of Lee's ab training was the crunch. He alternated two styles of his favorite exercise. During one workout he'd use weight and do 15 to 20 reps, and the next he'd do them with just his bodyweight and go to failure. No matter which version, Lee would do 3 sets in total, and aim for a minimum of 100 reps. If he used weight it would be a 25 pound plate held across his forehead. Then as he got tired he'd move the plate down to his chest. The physicists among you will recognize that moving the weight close to or away from the midsection, will change the leverage.

With regards to speed, Lee again alternates. If he uses weight, he does his reps in a faster, more explosive style. But if it's just bodyweight he does the reps ultra slow.

After 3 sets of crunches, Lee twists his knees to one side and does twisting crunches. Again he alternates sets with and without weight. He does 3 sets on each side.

For his third exercise, Lee does hanging leg raises or decline bench reverse crunches.

With regards to the hanging leg raises, this is an exercise that despite its poor ab kinesiology, Lee finds very effective for his lower abs. If you go by the book, hanging leg raises are supposed to mainly hit the hip flexors. But like most bodybuilders, Lee prefers to go by how the exercise actually feels, not how it's supposed to feel. Again he did 3 sets for a total of 100 reps.

If Lee did reverse crunches he'd use a 30-degree decline bench and reach back behind and grab the leg supports. He'd then draw his legs toward his upper body, keeping the knees bent at all times. He'd never go to a complete lockout at the bottom.

Lee started his own line of supplements called Labrada Nutrition and it is one of the largest supplement manufacturers in the world.

As a final comment, Lee's total ab workout consisted of just 9 sets, three times a week. That's 27 sets in total. This was less than some of his fellow competitors did in one workout. Yet Lee developed great abs and they didn't. The difference is that Lee realized that direct ab training is only one of the three variables necessary for developing a great midsection. The other two are diet and aerobics. No matter how great the abs, they are useless to a bodybuilder if covered by a layer of fat. And the way to get rid of fat is to put the body in a calorie deficit, either by taking fewer calories in, or burning more off.

Biceps

Lee's biceps were never as peaked as Robby Robinson's or Albert Beckles'. They lacked the overall mass of Schwarzenegger's and Sergio Oliva's. But Lee Labrada's biceps were full and defined and looked like two bronzed softballs gleaming in the sun.

What made Lee's biceps even more astounding was how he got them. When other bodybuilders were working on their 15th or 20th set, Lee was in the showers drying off! Lee did a total of 6 to 9 sets for biceps twice a week.

Lee did a total of 6 to 9 sets for biceps twice a week.

Having read his other training routines you should be realizing by now that Lee followed a modified form of Mike Mentzer's Heavy Duty training style. He picked two or three exercises for most muscle groups and did 6 to 12 sets in total, going to absolute failure on each set. For a large muscle group like legs or back he may go up to 12 sets in total, but for a muscle as small as biceps, 6 to 9 sets was the norm.

Being a student of kinesiology Lee also realized that the biceps are heavily involved in just about every back exercise. So even when he's not training biceps directly with curls, they are getting a good workout from back training.

Lee typically started his biceps training with concentration curls, doing 3 sets of 10 reps each arm. He then followed with standing or preacher barbell curls for another 3 sets of 10. On some days that would be his entire biceps routine. But periodically he'd add on two or three sets of alternate dumbell curls at the end.

For variety, Lee sometimes alternated the order of the previous exercises. Or instead of ending with the alternate curls he'd switch to hammer curls to target the brachialis and forearms.

Lee was never a fan of pyramiding his sets – starting light and adding weight with each set and dropping the reps. Instead he did one warm-up set, added on his workout weight for a set of ten, and then dropped the weight by ten percent for his next set. Finally he'd drop it another ten percent for his last set.

Lee's rational was that pyramiding prevents you from using the maximum weight possible. All those initial sets tire out the muscle. But by doing one warmup, the muscle is still fresh and capable of handling the maximum amount of weight.

At an early age, Rich Gaspari knew he wanted to be a bodybuilder.

Rich Gaspari

Rich was born in New Brunswick, New Jersey, on May 16, 1963. At an early age he knew that he wanted to be a bodybuilder: "You know, it was kind of weird. Wanting to be a bodybuilder was something that was in my head when I was ten years old. When I was a little kid, I used to always look at the comic books and see the Charles Atlas ads. I even sent away for the course because I wanted to get big. I also sent away for the Weider thing they used to have in the comic books. The father of a friend of mine collected old *Muscle Builder* magazines, and I used to stay friends with this kid just so I could go to his basement and read them. I'd look for hours at pictures of Arnold, and Franco, and Frank Zane, and Dave Draper, and to me it was like, 'Wow! These people are like Superman,' and I wanted to some day, if I could, look like that."

That day came, and as far as the judges were concerned, he was Superman! Rich became one of the dominant personalities of the 1980s. On no less than three occasions he took Lee Haney to the wire at the Mr. Olympia, placing second. Rich had the slight edge in sharpness but just couldn't match the Atlantan's overall muscle mass. Although Rich didn't fair well in the '90s, his record is still impressive:

1983 Junior Nationals – NPC, overall winner
   Junior Nationals – NPC, heavyweight, 1st
   Nationals – NPC, heavyweight, 5th
1984 Nationals – NPC, light heavyweight, 1st
   World Amateur Championships – IFBB, light heavyweight, 1st
1985 Night of Champions – IFBB, 2nd
   Olympia – IFBB, 3rd
1986 Los Angeles Pro Championships – IFBB, winner
   Olympia – IFBB, 2nd
   World Pro Championships – IFBB, winner
1987 Grand Prix France – IFBB, winner
   Grand Prix Germany (2) – IFBB, 2nd
   Grand Prix Germany – IFBB, winner
   Olympia – IFBB, 2nd
1988 Grand Prix England – IFBB, 2nd
   Grand Prix France – IFBB, winner
   Grand Prix Germany – IFBB, winner

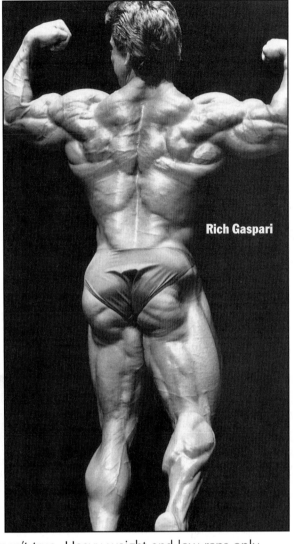

Rich Gaspari

Back

As many bodybuilders discover, all-out training has its drawbacks. Eventually the body's joints and soft tissues start rebelling and say "that's it, we've had enough." Rich Gaspari found this out the hard way when years of heavy pressing finally led to a triceps tear. In fact it not only kept him out of the 1992 Mr. Olympia, but in many respects ended his competitive career.

One of the things Rich noticed after switching training styles was that the old notion that high reps were useless for musclebuilding wasn't true. Heavy weight and low reps only stimulate some muscle fibers, whereas high reps hit other types of muscle fibers and stimulate capillary production. Rich found that by cycling his training between heavy and light he not only made great improvements in his physique but also reduced the degree of overtraining that often accompanied long-term heavy training. Rich also found that fewer sets could accomplish just as much as the high-volume training he engaged in for years.

"I used to be an all-out lifter – I would lift as heavy as I could and do 8 to 10 reps. Lifting that way caused me to incur a lot of injuries, mostly muscle tears. Now I kind of cycle my training, going heavy for three weeks, then doing three weeks of moderate training followed by three weeks of high rep training."

– Rich Gaspari, top '80s competitor, commenting on how injuries forced him to modify his training style.

As an example the "old" Rich Gaspari often did up to 35 sets for his back, but starting in the early '90s he reduced the total number of sets and to use his own words "started training more intelligently."

The old Rich rarely bothered to warm up either. But nowadays he'll do a couple of high-rep sets of cable exercises before moving on to is primary back exercises.

Rich's first back exercise was often front lat pulldowns. On most days he did 3 to 4 sets, with the rep range being determined by the cycle he was in. Rich has noticed over the years that this was an exercise that many bodybuilders performed in very sloppy style. Many people lean way too far back and turn the exercise into a rowing type motion. These same individuals also sway back and forth using way too much body momentum to keep the weight moving. Rich says that if you have to rock back and forth you have too much weight on.

Another tip Rich adds is to pull the elbows back as far as possible when the bar reaches the chest. This way the shoulder blades get fully contracted leading to maximum lat stimulation.

After an upper lat movement like pulldowns, Rick usually moved on to a lower lat exercise. For convenience he often stayed where he was at and switched from a straight bar to a small, triangle-shaped bar. This time he would lean back slightly as he pulled the bar down to his mid-chest. But leaning does not mean swaying. Once his torso was in the desired position, he would keep it there. He wouldn't rock back and forth just to keep the weight moving. Rich typically did 3 or 4 sets of narrow pulldowns.

After his two pulldown exercises, Rich moved on to a basic rowing movement like barbell rows. To get a maximum stretch Rich did his rows while standing on the end of a flat bench. He also used a cambered bar to get the maximum range of motion (for those not familiar with this bar, it looks like and over-sized EZ-curl bar, and is mainly used for doing bench presses).

To finish off his upper back, Rich did a vertical row exercise like the Hammer row machine. To add a bit of extra intensity he often did drop sets or forced reps on this exercise.

To hit his lower back, Rich alternated between stiff-leg deadlifts, good mornings, or back extensions (on the hyperextension machine). Again it was 3 or 4 sets of low, moderate, or high reps, depending on the phase of his training.

Rich became one of the dominant personalities of the 1980s.

John Terilli

John Terilli was a fixture on the pro scene in the late '80s and early '90s. This native of Australia developed a reputation for his outstanding muscularity and symmetry. John never made a huge impact in the IFBB, but he won the NABBA Universe title in 1982 and 1994. After retiring from bodybuilding John hosted his own show *Ask Mr. Universe* on the radio. Here's his short, but impressive competitive record:

1980   World Amateur Championships – IFBB, light heavyweight, 6th
1982   Universe – NABBA, medium, 1st
1983   Grand Prix Las Vegas – IFBB, 2nd
        Night of Champions – IFBB, 5th
1984   World Pro Championships – IFBB, 8th
1985   Night of Champions – IFBB, 6th
1986   Los Angeles Pro Championships – IFBB, 6th
        Olympia – IFBB, 9th
        World Pro Championships – IFBB, 5th
1988   Niagara Falls Pro Invitational – IFBB, 6th
1989   Arnold Classic – IFBB, 13th
        Grand Prix France – IFBB, 12th
        Grand Prix France – IFBB, 13th
        Grand Prix Sweden – IFBB, 11th
1991   Mr. Australia – IFBB, tall, 2nd
1992   Ironman Pro Invitational – IFBB, 13th
        Ironman Pro Invitational – IFBB, 16th
1993   Ironman Pro Invitational – IFBB, 18th
        Universe – Pro, NABBA, 2nd
1994   Universe – Pro, NABBA, winner
1995   Universe – Pro, NABBA

After retiring from body-building John hosted his own show *Ask Mr. Universe* on the radio.

Arms

In recent years trainer extraordinaire, Charles Poliquin, has garnered a great deal of attention with his one-day arm cure. Well, despite the publicity Charles has received, he wasn't the first to apply it to his training techniques. Australian bodybuilder, John Terilli, often employed such madness in his arm training 15 to 20 years ago. As he says "the best shock ever applied to my arms happened when I took a barbell into the house and did a set for biceps and a set for triceps every half hour for the whole waking day."

"People are always trying to associate me with mysterious happenings. There's nothing mysterious about my disappearance. I went back to Australia for family reasons, and then I saw the great opportunities that Australia offered in real estate and business, and I decided to stay."

– John Terilli, 1982 Mr. Universe winner, demonstrating that there's more to some pro bodybuilders than a great physique.

"Sometimes I did it two days in a row. It used to work like magic. I won't even bother to tell you how much I used to gain. You wouldn't believe it and neither would anybody else."

The reason John resorted to such drastic measures was that his arms were always one of his more stubborn bodyparts, but like anybody else he had to learn by trial and error. And such trial and error led to his arm workouts becoming simpler not more advanced. Once he found the right exercise combinations and intensity, his arms took right off.

His typical arm workout involved a few sets of alternate dumbell curls with light weights and lots of squeezing, and then either EZ-bar curls or barbell curls. He sometimes reversed the order, but always used heavier weights for barbell exercises than for dumbell exercises. Then close to a show he added some sort of one-arm cable or dumbell work.

For triceps he did either lying or standing triceps extensions with a straight bar, an EZ-bar, or even a cable. Then it was on to pushdowns using a rope or straight bar. To finish off John did one-arm cable extensions.

For most of the previous exercises, John did 2 to 4 sets of 6 to 15 reps. Even though the foundation of his workouts was straight sets and reps, John would occasionally perform forced reps and giant sets. For example, for triceps he might do one set of lying EZ-bar extensions, a set of narrow presses, one set of pushdowns, and finishes off with dumbell kickbacks. As John adds "the more I feel it, the better pump I get, and consequently the more growth I get."

Gary Strydom

Gary Strydom has the word focus for a middle name. Even the very public breakup of his marriage could not stop him: "Bodybuilding has given me a lot in life, but I've always had to make many sacrifices because of it. The choices I made in favor of bodybuilding may seem harsh to some, but really I'd made my choice long before I met Alyse. I made my choice for bodybuilding ten years ago in South Africa, and if I hadn't been so committed to the sport, I probably wouldn't have gone to the States, and would never have met Alyse.

So by making the choice I did, I don't feel that I let Alyse down. It wasn't as if I dropped a bombshell on her by changing my priorities from those I had when I first met her

I knew I had to pick myself up: I was the only person who could do it. No one was going to do it for me! Having resolved the crunch issue of where my future lay was proof, even to me, of how important bodybuilding was to Gary Strydom, and this new realization caused me to become even more dedicated toward reaching my goals."

Many in the sport assumed Gary was being groomed to be the sport's next superstar. He had it all, looks, size, marketability, but

Gary Strydom had it all, looks, size and marketability.

after a couple of disappointing Mr. Olympia outings, Gary left the IFBB for Vince McMahon's new WBF federation. Gary was the undisputed star of that short-lived experiment, but when it folded, Gary never really made much of an impact back in the IFBB, His last contest was the 1996 New York Night of Champions.

When the WBF folded, Gary never really made much of an impact back in the IFBB.

Here's his competitive record:

1984 USA Championships – NPC, heavyweight, 1st
1986 Nationals – NPC, overall winner
        Nationals – NPC, heavyweight, 1st
1987 Night of Champions – IFBB, winner
1988 Chicago Pro Invitational – IFBB, 2nd
        Olympia – IFBB, 5th
1989 Arnold Classic – IFBB, 3rd
        Grand Prix France – IFBB, winner
        Grand Prix Germany – IFBB, 2nd
        Grand Prix Melbourne – IFBB, winner
        Grand Prix Spain (2) – IFBB, 2nd
        Grand Prix Spain – IFBB, 2nd
        Grand Prix Sweden – IFBB, winner
        World Pro Championships – IFBB, 2nd
1990 Grand Prix England – IFBB, 2nd
        Grand Prix Finland – IFBB, 3rd
        Grand Prix France – IFBB, 2nd
        Grand Prix Germany – IFBB, 4th
        Grand Prix Italy – IFBB, 3rd
        Houston Pro Invitational – IFBB, 2nd
        Ironman Pro Invitational – IFBB, 4th
1991 WBF Grand Prix – WBF, winner
1996 Night of Champions – IFBB, 12th

The last word goes to Gary: "The sport of bodybuilding has a lot of good people in it; fans, promoters and competitors. I'd just like to thank those many good people who stood by me, and boosted my morale just when I needed it most."

"The secret of growth is to make as many different muscle fibers as possible contract at any given moment. The attainment of that facility is possible only through intense mental concentration, and has nothing to do with strength levels. You can't mentally concentrate on fiber contraction to the required degree if you're constantly heaving and cheating vast poundages through a range of partial movements."

– Gary Strydom, former top pro bodybuilder, commenting on the key to muscle growth.

Gary Strydom and
Mike Christian

Arms

During his days chasing the Mr. Olympia title, Gary followed a four-day training cycle, working out twice a day, with the fifth day off. He normally trained biceps and triceps on the same day, hitting biceps in the morning and triceps later in the evening.

Each arm session he would do two or three exercises, rarely exceeding 12 sets in total. He mixed up the sequence on a regular basis, varying the angle of attack from workout to workout.

A typical set of exercises for triceps and biceps would look like this:

Triceps
Close-grip bench presses
Lying triceps extensions
Pushdowns
One-arm cable pushdowns

Biceps
Alternate dumbell curls
EZ-bar curls
Preacher curls
Dumbell concentration curls

Gary would normally rest about 45 to 60 seconds between sets, doing 3 sets of each exercise.

To give an example of how Gary performed each exercise, let's take a closer look at dumbell curls.

Gary would stand in front of a mirror holding two medium-sized dumbells. He'd then start repping with one arm while keeping the other stationary. When he could no longer execute another rep with this arm, he'd switch and do the same for the other. According to Gary this singular action allowed the brain to concentrate on one arm at a time without flip-flopping from side to side the way most people do. After Gary reached positive failure on the second arm, he'd return to the first and do half reps until even this was not possible. He'd then repeat for the second arm. If this was not enough he'd go back to the first arm and try and lift the dumbell. Although it rarely moved, he squeezed and contracted his biceps muscles as hard as possible. Only when he couldn't physically hold onto the dumbell would he finally put it back on the rack.

Gary was never a slave to reps and sets, preferring instead to go to absolute failure, no matter how long it took. Typically he'd be holding the dumbells for five or six minutes. Gary found such training produced great results but he warns beginners about jumping into this level of intensity. A couple of workouts at this level would burn out most newcomers.

For triceps Gary's main focus was changing the angle of attack as frequently as possible. He found pushdowns great for hitting the triceps from any angle desired. In fact there were occasions where his entire triceps routine consisted entirely of pushdowns. He'd do a couple of sets of straight-bar pushdowns, a few rope pushdowns, and then finish off with one-arm pushdowns. Of course on other days he'd throw in such standbys as lying extensions and narrow presses.

Tom Platz – The Golden Eagle

Tom Platz can best be described as the owner of the most famous pair of legs in bodybuilding. They're simply incredible! In fact, most agree that the only reason Tom didn't win more contests was because his legs were so huge they seemed out of proportion to the rest of his body (which was massive as well). There is not a single bodybuilder alive today who has a pair of legs that can rival Tom's.

Tom was born in Oklahoma in 1955 to a Polish Catholic family. He grew up in the steel town of Pittsburgh, which he considers his hometown. Tom was an altar boy, and feels that the discipline of his Catholic upbringing prepared him for his chosen career. That and the strong work ethic so common in immigrant communities propelled Tom on his journey to pursue his own American dream.

Tom Platz feels that the discipline of his Catholic upbringing prepared him for his chosen career.

He trained hard, and soon began competing:

1974   Teen Mr. America – AAU, 2nd
1976   Mr. America – AAU, short, 3rd
1977   Mr. America – AAU, short, 2nd
1978   Mr. America – AAU, short, 2nd
      World Amateur Championships – IFBB, overall winner
      World Amateur Championships – IFBB, middleweight, 1st
1979   Olympia – IFBB, lightweight, 8th
1980   Night of Champions – IFBB, 12th
      Olympia – IFBB, 9th
      Universe – Pro, IFBB, 2nd
      World Pro Championships – IFBB, 2nd
1981   Olympia – IFBB, 3rd
1982   Olympia – IFBB, 6th
1984   Olympia – IFBB, 9th
1985   Olympia – IFBB, 7th
1986   Olympia – IFBB, 11th
1987   Detroit Pro Invitational – IFBB, 6th

Tom has also had a film career:
Book of Love (1990) … bodybuilder
Who Killed Johnny Love? (1998) … Emcee
8 Heads in a Duffel Bag (1997) … Hugo
Twins (1988) … Granger son #1[1]

Take a look at Tom's pillars of power.

In the early 1990s Tom became a sort of spokesman for Vince McMahon's WBF bodybuilding federation. This didn't endear him to the Weider camp as he helped recruit many of the IFBB's top stars including Aaron Baker, Gary Strydom, Mike Christian, and Mike Quinn. When the WBF folded after just two seasons, Tom started focusing his energy on business interests, and today he's a successful businessman. "My parents instilled in me that if you're going to do something, give it your all! And that principle has dominated my bodybuilding efforts. I won't deny that to a certain extent bodybuilding is an ego trip; not all ego, but everything you do in your life is in some way associated with your ego. To feel good about myself I have to be successful in what I do. And that does not make me better than anyone else. Deep inside I have the need to be able to get up every morning and feel good about my existence. I have to train hard, I have to feel that I have accomplished something. Every day in the gym I like to 'put out' and feel good. That way I win every day."

Reference:
(1) http://us.imdb.com/M/persn-exact?Platz%2C+Tom

Thighs

Talk about great chest development and the names Schwarzenegger, Ferrigno, and Nubret, come to mind. Discuss huge arms and you have Coleman, Coe, and Priest, to name just a few. For shoulders look no further than Mike Matarazzo, Paul Dillett, and Mike Christian. But if the topic in question is legs, one name alone stands (no pun intended!) way above the rest, the Golden Eagle, Tom Platz.

With all due respect to DeMayo, Cutler, and Tim Belknap, few dispute the fact that in his prime, Tom Platz had the greatest legs of all time. In fact a couple of years ago, new leg monster, Paul DeMayo challenged Tom to drop his pants at an exhibition. Despite being out of competition for ten years, Tom took up the challenge and proceeded to display a set of legs that caused DeMayo's heart to flutter. After all those years Tom's legs still had the size and muscularity that other bodybuilders only dream about.

It's not surprising that the owner of bodybuilding's undisputed greatest set of legs started his leg training with squats. For those who have any doubt that squats only build large butts and wreck knees, take a look at Tom's pillars of power. That's what years of squatting will do for you. Still interested? Read on.

Before hitting the humungous weights for which he'd become famous, Tom did a warmup. Now warming up for Tom was a little bit different than what the rest of us mortals go through. On numerous occasions Tom would put 225 on the bar and, are you ready for it, perform nonstop squats for 5 to 10 minutes. Notice we said minutes not reps. It seems even Tom's warmup was from another dimension.

By this point most bodybuilders would be either throwing up or heading for the shower, but Tom is just getting ready to train his legs. He would proceed to do 8 to 10 sets of

Few dispute the fact that in his prime, Tom Platz had the greatest legs of all time.

rock-bottom squats, pyramiding up in weight and down in reps. To show you just how impressive those thighs of his were, Tom regularly went up to 600 pounds for 20 reps, and 700 for 10 reps.

For most bodybuilders 10 sets of such madness would be enough for their thighs, but Tom considered this phase one. He then moved on to hack squats for 5 sets, again pyramiding up in weight, down in reps. Tom considered this to be the exercise that put the great sweep on his massive thighs. On a typical day Tom would average 10 to 15 reps on his sets of squats.

By now Tom had down upward of 15 sets for his thighs, but he still wasn't finished. To really make sure those quads of his were begging for mercy, Tom ended his workout with 5 to 8 sets of leg extensions, averaging 10 to 15 reps per set.

Although long retired from competition, Tom Platz's legs still inspire millions. Even by today's growth hormone-inflated standards, no bodybuilder has become more synonymous with great legs than the Golden Eagle.

History's first black Mr. America, Chris Dickerson.

Chris Dickerson

It was while on a trip to California in 1963 that bodybuilding discovered Chris Dickerson. He saw a picture of Bill Pearl on the cover of a Weider magazine and decided to visit Bill's new gym in Inglewood. The first person Chris saw when he entered the door was the Mr. Universe winner himself. That fateful meeting not only set Chris on the road to his 1982 Mr. Olympia win, but also cemented the roots of a friendship that endures to this day.

Following Bill's advice to the letter, Chris rose rapidly through the bodybuilding ranks. In 1970 he became history's first black Mr. America. Chris kept a low profile during most of the '70s, but by the early '80s he was the top bodybuilder in the world. Only Arnold's and Franco Columbu's 1980 and 1981 controversial wins kept Chris from being a three-time Mr. Olympia winner.

For those wondering if it's too late to made a career in bodybuilding, look to Chris for inspiration. He won the Mr. America at 30, turned pro at 40, and won the Mr. Olympia at 43. Here's his competitive record:

1966 Junior Mr. USA – AAU, winner
      Junior Mr. USA – AAU, most muscular, 1st
      Mr. Atlantic Coast – AAU, overall winner
      Mr. Eastern America – AAU, overall winner
      Mr. New York State – AAU, overall winner
      Mr. North America – AAU, 2nd
1967 Junior Mr. America – AAU, 4th
      Junior Mr. America – AAU, most muscular, 5th
      Mr. America – AAU, 6th
      Mr. America – AAU, most muscular, 4th
      Mr. California – AAU, winner
1968 Junior Mr. America – AAU, 3rd
      Mr. America – AAU, 3rd
      Mr. America – AAU, most muscular, 3rd
      Mr. USA – AAU, winner
      Mr. USA – AAU, most muscular, 2nd
1969 Mr. America – AAU, 2nd
1970 Junior Mr. America – AAU, winner
      Junior Mr. America – AAU, most muscular, 1st
      Mr. America – AAU, winner
      Mr. America – AAU, most muscular, 1st
      Universe – NABBA, short, 1st
1971 Universe – NABBA, short,1st
1973 Pro Mr. America – WBBG, winner
      Universe – NABBA, overall winner
      Universe – NABBA, short, 1st
1974 Universe – Pro, NABBA, overall winner
      Universe – Pro, NABBA, short, 1st
1975 Universe – Pro, PBBA, 2nd
      World Championships – WBBG, 2nd
1976 Olympus – WBBG, 4th
      Universe – Pro, NABBA, 3rd
      Universe – Pro, NABBA, short, 2nd
1979 Canada Diamond Pro Cup – IFBB, 2nd
      Canada Pro Cup – IFBB, winner
      Grand Prix Vancouver – IFBB, 2nd
      Olympia – IFBB, lightweight, 4th
1980 Canada Pro Cup – IFBB, winner
      Florida Pro Invitational – IFBB, winner
      Grand Prix California – IFBB, winner
      Grand Prix Louisiana – IFBB, 2nd
      Grand Prix Miami – IFBB, winner
      Grand Prix New York – IFBB, winner
      Night of Champions – IFBB, winner
      Olympia – IFBB, 2nd
      Pittsburgh Pro Invitational – IFBB, 2nd
1981 Grand Prix California – IFBB, winner

Tom Platz and Chris Dickerson

Besides bodybuilding, Chris' other great love is opera.

Besides bodybuilding, Chris' other great love is opera, and there are those who say he could have had a bigger career as an opera singer than bodybuilding.

Shoulders

It's said that the three muscle groups you can't hide onstage are the abs, shoulders, and calves. Every pose you hit will highlight any weaknesses in these areas. When Chris Dickerson first walked into Bill Pearl's gym in the 1960s, the natural development of his chest made his shoulders look small and narrow. Bill took one look and set Chris on the road to the Mr. Olympia.

For the first couple of months, Chris's entire shoulder routine consisted of front military presses. Only after he had laid down a good foundation did Bill add in dumbell presses and lateral raises.

Over the years, and there have been many of them, Chris has modified his shoulder routine many times. But no matter what combination of exercises, Chris always performs at least one pressing movement and one lateral exercise in his routine.

Another point Chris is a stickler on is injury prevention. As the shoulders are involved in most upper body exercises, they are often overstressed and very susceptible to injuries. Chris always did two or three warm up sets on each exercise before attempting anything heavy.

The following is Chris's shoulder routine during his heyday in the early '80s:

1. Seated behind-the-head presses   6 sets of 12 to 8 reps
2. Standing dumbell lateral raises   6 sets of 8 to 10 reps
3. Seated dumbell presses   6 sets of 8 reps
4. Bent-over lateral raises   6 sets of 12 to 15 reps
5. Upright rows   4 sets of 10 to 12 reps.

Chris kept a low profile
during most of the '70s, but
by the early '80s he was the
top bodybuilder in the world.

Chapter 6

The 1990s

If commercialism summarizes the 1980s, then technology must surely best describe the '90s. From DVD players and digital cameras, to home computers and e-mail, technology has transformed how we look at the world. The Internet alone has revolutionized how humans communicate with one another. It had the same impact in the '90s as television's introduction in the late '40s and early '50s.

No sooner had Lee Haney captured his eighth-straight Mr. Olympia title in 1991, when his successor was waiting in the wings. The second place finisher that year was 235-pound Dorian Yates of Birmingham, England. The following year he strolled onstage weighing 260 pounds and began his own streak of six consecutive Mr. Olympia wins. Not only was Dorian the heaviest Mr. Olympia ever, but he was also the first non-American resident to capture the title (Arnold, Sergio, Franco, and Samir Bannout, were all living in the US when they captured their titles). With his rugged physique and working class Brit personality, Dorian was a popular champion. Dorian dominated the sport for most of the decade, despite stiff challenges from such greats as Flex Wheeler, Nasser El Sonbaty, and Kevin Levrone. With a series of nagging injuries taking their toll, Dorian finally retired in 1997.

Most pundits assumed one of the front runners would inherit the crown with the lad from across the pond out of the scene. But such was not the case. From Arlington, Texas, came 255-pound Ronnie Coleman who stole the whole show in 1998 and again in 1999. Ronnie

Joe Weider and Dorian Yates

was one of those bodybuilders who hung around the top ten position for a couple of years and never appeared to be a threat to the top five. But starting in 1997 he added about 25 pounds to his physique and jumped right into the fray. (To finish in September of 2000.)

Besides the passing of the Sandow statue from Haney to Yates to Coleman, the other major event of the '90s was the revolution in the supplement industry. After decades of a virtual monopoly by Joe Weider, dozens of new supplement companies came on the scene, all vying for a slice of the enormous supplement pie. Such names as Twin Lab, EAS, MuscleTech, MET-Rx, and Formula One, are now as well known as Weider. In fact EAS has outsold Weider for most of the decade.

It wasn't just the volume of supplement sales that characterized the decade, but also the quality. After a decade of mainly nutrient products, which don't make much difference unless the individual is deficient to begin with, bodybuilders now had over-the-counter products that actually boosted athletic performance. This revolution in ergogenesis, included such products as creatine, glutamine, and pro hormones. The end result was amateur bodybuilders developing physiques that rivaled most of the pro bodybuilders of the '60s and '70s.

Here are some of the bodybuilders and routines that made the last decade such an exciting time in bodybuilding history.

Paul DeMayo

Paul DeMayo was born in Malden, Boston, in 1967. When he burst on the scene in 1993, images of Tom Platz came to mind. Paul's legs brought back memories of the leg king himself, and it wasn't long before magazines and fans had nicknamed him "Quadzilla."

Paul's first contest was the 1987 Teenage Massachusetts, in which he won the heavyweight and overall title. His first major win was the 1991 Junior Nationals.

Amy Fadhli, Paul DeMayo and Mia Finnegan

Paul cites Dorian Yates as his primary idol, and despite following different training styles, has managed to build a physique very similar in density to the six-time Mr. Olympia.

Paul spent a short period in jail in the late 1990s, but since his parole has vowed to realize his dream as one of the best bodybuilders in the world. Here's his competitive record:

Not since Tom Platz has a bodybuilder exhibited such a gruesome set of thighs as Paul DeMayo.

Legs

They call him Quadzilla, and for good reason. Not since Tom Platz has a bodybuilder exhibited such a gruesome set of thighs! When this guy does the "walk," even other pro bodybuilders stop to take a peak, DeMayo's quads are that large.

What's ironic is that while most people have to spend years busting their hump for an extra inch or two on the thighs, DeMayo discovered early on that his thighs grew no matter what he did. In fact DeMayo is tired of answering questions on how he built his thighs. He'd rather talk about muscle groups that were stubborn to build, like chest. "If

"Early on in my leg training I used to always train thighs and squat first in my workouts, but I noticed that my quads were overpowering my hamstrings and calves something fierce. So I switched to training calves first, then hamstrings and quads last."

- Paul DeMayo, USA National Champion commenting on how his rapid thigh growth forced him to modify his approach to leg training.

**Paul
"Quadzilla"
DeMayo**

you wanna talk about chest, that's something that I built up from nothing, but legs for me are primarily genetic."

As Paul starts his leg workout with calves, it only makes sense to begin here. Paul's first calf exercise is that old standard, standing calf raises. Although it varies, Paul usually uses the Flex machine for this exercise. It's not surprising that his main complaint is the "limited" weight on the stack. "I just wish it was heavier coz it only goes up to 500 pounds."

Paul does 4 sets of about 20 to 25 reps on each set of standing calf raises. You don't realize just how impressive that is until you discover that Paul's using between 400 and 500 pounds on each set. Paul utilizes the minute to minute and a half between sets to stretch the calves.

For variety Paul does 2 sets with his feet straight, and 2 sets with the toes pointing inward. He doesn't perform the heel to heel version, and unlike most bodybuilders, Paul doesn't keep the legs completely locked out straight. Instead he keeps the knees slightly bent.

Paul's second exercise for calves is incline standing raises on the Icarian machine. Again he does 4 super intense sets. Unlike the straight version, Paul doesn't count reps on incline raises. Instead he throws 260-300 pounds on the machine and bangs out as many reps as he can. Once again he alternates toe position, 2 sets in, and 2 sets straight ahead.

To finish what's left of his calves, Paul does 4 sets of seated calf raises on the Flex machine. "I start with three plates and a 25 for as many reps as I can. Depending on how I feel, the most I'll go up is another plate." Paul usually does 15 reps per set but he's first to admit that he's not a slave to numbers. "I don't know for sure, I never count."

After a short break, it's on to hamstrings. Paul's first hamstring exercise is what he feels is the "granddaddy" of hamstring exercises, lying leg curls. He does lying leg curls till failure and works the reps until, to use his own words "my hamstrings feel like they've been through hell."

After lying leg curls, Paul moves on to the standing leg curl on the Flex machine. "I usually do them using about 60 or 70 pounds. I know that doesn't sound heavy, but it feels heavy when you're doing them separately."

Paul uses a slow rep tempo on standing curls and stops for a split second to squeeze at the top. He does 3 sets with the same weight and again, doesn't become a slave to rep numbers. Unlike many bodybuilders who will keep training when their form starts slipping, Paul terminates the set as soon as his technique begins to suffer. "I'm more interested in training my muscle than ego."

To finish hamstrings Paul does 3 to 4 sets of stiff-leg deadlifts. With his hamstrings already suffering from 6 to 8 sets of curls, Paul doesn't need to go ultra heavy on stiff-legs. He takes a moderate weight and does 15 to 20 reps in a slow and controlled motion. No bouncing or jerking for Quadzilla.

With his calves and hamstrings punished, it's time to inflict some suffering on his Quads. Early in his career, Paul used the "king" of leg exercises, squats, to put some serious beef on his thighs. On a typical leg day Paul would go up to 505 pounds for 8 to 12 reps. As he couldn't squat flat-footed, Paul would elevate his heels on a two-by-four block of wood. Once he had more mass in his thighs than most bodybuilders could only dream about, Paul backed off the squats and switched to isolation exercises.

Nowadays Paul's first quad exercise is hack squats on a Flex machine. After one or two warm-up sets with two plates a side, Paul puts four plates on each side and does 4 quality sets. "Since I'm gifted genetically I don't need that much weight. I have the muscle there. I just wanna stimulate my quads and develop the muscle maturity. Believe me, I could go heavier if I wanted to, but I don't."

After hacks, it's on to Icarian or Cybex leg extensions. As with hacks, Paul opts for quality over quantity. He usually puts about 100 pounds on the machine and bangs out 3 or 4 sets of as many reps as possible. Depending on how he feels, he may throw in an 80-pound set to finish off leg extensions.

One exercise Paul doesn't employ in his quad training is leg presses. He found that a combination of lower back pain plus stomach compression, made the exercise unsuitable for him. Still, he's quick to add that the exercise will put some serious meat on your thighs if it meets your individual genetics.

Paul uses moderate weights, with good exercise form and little cheating.

Triceps

You'd think given the amount of meat hanging from his shirtsleeves, that Paul DeMayo would be throwing around some huge poundages in his workouts. But for the most part, Paul uses moderate weights, with good exercise form and little cheating. He uses moderate reps (about 10 per set) and averages three to six exercises per muscle, depending on its size. For a medium muscle group like triceps he averages 9 to 12 sets in total.

"His triceps were beyond the ham-like stage. They were full-grown boars. In the biceps pose they hung down like the belly of an overfed great white shark."

– Greg Zulak, regular *MuscleMag International* contributor giving a visual commentary on 1994 NPC National's Champion, Paul DeMayo.

As Paul constantly changes his exercise combinations, it's difficult to nail down a precise triceps' routine. He has a list of six or seven exercises and he picks three or four during each workout. At one time he did heavy weight/ low rep sets, but not any more. Nowadays if he can't get at least 10 reps, he'll reduce the weight for the next set.

His first exercise is often triceps pushdowns using either a straight or bent bar attachment. For some reason he gets little or nothing out of rope pushdowns. He uses a false grip and makes a determined effort not to lean forward and push the weight down with his upper body. Paul starts with 70 pounds for 20 reps, moves up to 90 for about 15, and then adds ten pounds per set for another 3 or 4 sets, eventually working up to 135 pounds. This may not seem heavy for a guy that weighs 275 pounds in the off-season, but Paul responds that sure he could go up to 200 pounds or more, but for what? He's training his triceps not his ego.

With his elbows warmed up from the pushdowns, Paul switches to lying EZ-bar extensions for his second exercise. He'll start with about 90 pounds for 15 reps, and then add 25 pounds and do another medium set for 15 reps. Then depending on how he feels Paul will do the next 3 sets as follows: 125 for 10, 135 for 10, and 155 for 10. Again he uses a false grip, and lowers the bar to his forehead using no body momentum, just triceps power. Paul feels this exercise has ruined the elbows of many promising bodybuilding careers and all because the individuals were using too much weight.

For his third exercise, Paul often does 45-degree triceps extensions using a cable machine. Unlike pushdowns, Paul prefers using the rope on this exercise. He found a straight bar puts too much pressure on his wrists. This is another exercise where many bodybuilders get too caught up in the amount of weight they are using, and have to rock the torso back and forth just to keep the weight moving. Depending on the machine (some have two pulley wheels, some have three wheels) Paul will use from 70 to 130 pounds for 3 sets of 12 to 15 reps.

On most days Paul stops triceps with his third exercise, but like many, there are days when he has a bit of extra energy and drive, so he adds a fourth exercise. As he considers this fourth movement a finishing exercise, he likes to pick an exercise that he can train the arms one at a time, usually one-arm dumbell extensions or one-arm cable pushdowns. If it's dumbell extensions he'll do 3 sets of 10 to 12 reps using a 45 or 50 pound dumbell. Likewise he doesn't get too carried away on the cable pushdowns, and uses just enough weight (30 to 50 pounds) to allow 12 to 20 reps in strict style.

Biceps

Although known for his freaky legs – hence the nickname Quadzilla – Paul DeMayo also has a pair of the largest arms around. Paul's biceps are round and high-peaked, not long and baseball-

Although known for his freaky legs – Paul DeMayo also has a pair of the largest arms around.

"You don't realize how big his arms are until you see him standing next to a man who has true 20-inch arms. When someone's 20-inchers suddenly look small by comparison, you realize how truly huge DeMayo's big guns are."
– Greg Zulak commenting on the incredible arms of Paul DeMayo.

shaped like Larry Scott's. But it's not just the peak that makes Paul's biceps so special, it's their thickness and fullness. His upper arms are thicker than many people's thighs.

All the fantasizing aside, your first question is how did Paul build those mothers? You'd probably expect him to say from curling 120-pound dumbells and 250-pound barbells, right? Well believe it or not, Paul considers himself a "moderate-weight" man. He believes in strict style with lots of constant tensing and squeezing while in the contracted position. In looking at Paul's biceps routine, the first thing that comes to mind is simplicity. His usual approach is just three biceps exercises for 3 sets each. That works out to just 9 working sets in total. He tries to keep the reps in the 8 to 10 range with each set. He uses moderate weights and tries to rest just 45 seconds between each set.

Paul prefers to train biceps after chest, not back like most bodybuilders. He found that his biceps are too fatigued from back exercises to do them justice. But as chest training consists of pushing rather than pulling, his biceps are still fresh.

Paul cites Dorian Yates as his primary idol.

Paul usually starts his biceps training with perhaps the greatest arm builder there is, standing barbell curls. He starts light, around 70 pounds for a smooth 12 reps. For most this would be strictly a warm-up set, but Paul performs the exercise in such a slow manner that it not only warms the muscle up, but actually contributes to development. Paul's next set consists of 100 pounds for another set of 10 to 12 reps. Again it's ultra slow and strict.

For his third set he stays with 100 pounds and does another perfect 12 reps. We know 100 pounds sounds like nothing for a guy weighing 275 in the off-season, but remember many of those bodybuilders claiming 200-plus pound barbell curls are rocking back and forth, and throwing their bodyweight into the movement. With Paul there is no swinging, bouncing, or cheating the weight up.

Paul's second exercise is alternate dumbell curls. For variety Paul either stands or sits down, depending on how he feels that day. As his biceps are warmed up from the barbell curls, he jumps right into his workout weight of 60 pounds. As before he does 10 to 12 reps in ultra strict style.

To finish off the DeMayo monsters, Paul does 3 sets on the Hammer Strength preacher machine. Typically he uses four 25-pound plates for sets of 12 to 15 reps per set.

There you have a typical Paul DeMayo biceps routine. Occasionally he'll add in a couple of sets of cable or concentration curls, but the previous three exercises comprise the bulk of his training.

Shoulders

Paul considers his delts (along with chest and back) his worst bodypart. In reality his torso muscles are not that bad, in fact they're incredible, but it's just that his arms are so bloody huge that they tend to dwarf the surrounding muscle groups. It was for this reason Paul cut back on his arm training to concentrate on his torso muscles. And as the delts are one muscle group that you can't hide on stage (the abs and calves being the other two) you can be sure they received their fair share of torture over the past couple of years.

Paul's arms are so huge that they tend to dwarf the surrounding muscle groups.

Paul starts his shoulder routine with a pressing exercise, usually seated dumbell presses. After one warm-up set he jumps to a pair of 100's and does about 10 strict reps in strict style for a full range of motion. Two more sets follow, 120's for 10 reps and 130's for 10 – in all just three working sets.

His second exercise is the press behind the head using the Hammer Strength machine. With his shoulders already warmed up from the dumbell presses, Paul jumps right to 225 pounds for 3 sets of 10 reps. Again strict style, no cheating, no half reps.

With front delts out of the way, Paul turns his attention to side delts, doing 3 sets of standing dumbell side laterals. You'd expect to see him swinging up 70's or 80's, but he prefers to stay around the 50- to 55-pound mark for sets of 10. He really tries to concentrate on his side shoulders as the front delts and traps can dominate on this exercise if you get sloppy.

To hit the rear delts, Paul heads to the rear delt machine and does 3 sets of 10 reps. Again strict style is the order of the day.

On some days Paul will stop with the rear delts, but occasionally he'll do 3 sets of alternate front raises to finish off his front and side shoulders. He uses a pair of 45's for 3 sets of 10 reps.

That ends a typical shoulder workout for Paul, but since he likes to train traps with shoulders (as most bodybuilders do), he does two additional exercises. His first trap exercise is usually barbell upright rows for 3 sets of 10 reps using 110 to 135 pounds. He follows the uprights with 3 sets of machine shrugs using 405 pounds for 15 reps.

Chest

By now you should be getting the message that Paul DeMayo doesn't use monstrous poundages when he trains, and his chest workouts are no exception. He's a bodybuilder, not a powerlifter trying to set records in the bench press.

Paul's chest workout by most standards is fairly simple. It consists of four exercises for 4 sets each, with reps in the 8 to 10 range. Paul rarely uses cheating or loose form in his training, preferring to maintain strict form at all times. He rests approximately 45 seconds between sets, just long enough to catch his breath and begin the next set.

Paul usually starts his chest workout with barbell incline presses. He's convinced that too many bodybuilders spend too much time on flat presses and fail to work the all-important pec-delt tie-in. Paul starts with 135 pounds as a warmup and then goes 225 for 10, 315 for 10, 315 for 8. To make sure his inner chest

Paul rarely uses cheating or loose form in his training, preferring to maintain strict form at all times.

receives its share of the load, Paul uses a medium grip. He also stops just short of a lockout, doing so gives the chest muscle a momentary rest. Finally Paul keeps a slight arch in his lower back so his upper chest does most of the work. Keeping the back flat only shifts most of the stress to the front delts.

Paul's next exercise is the incline dumbell press. As he's already warmed up from the incline barbell work, Paul jumps right to the 130-pounders for his first 2 sets of 8 reps. He then does 2 dropsets using 120 and 55-pound dumbells. Again he keeps the reps in the 8 to 10 range.

With two exercises for upper chest out of the way, Paul now moves on to lower and outer chest work. He starts with Hammer Strength presses. He does the first 3 sets with about 275 pounds for 8 to 10 reps. He'll then drop the weight to 225 and do a final set of 10 reps.

To finish off his chest, Paul does cable crossovers, but using his own unique style. Instead of bringing the handles down at about a 45-degree angle, he brings them across in front of his face. He does this not so much to be different but because he honestly finds he gets a better feel in his chest muscles. Who are we to argue? In any case it's 4 sets of 8 to 10 reps, using around 60 pounds on the stack.

Back

When he stepped on stage at the 1994 NPC Nationals, it didn't take the judges or audience long to decide the winner. Paul DeMayo had finally, to use a bodybuilding term, "dialed it in." In other words he timed things perfectly and arrived on contest day in the best shape of his life. Not only did he retain his nearly 260 pounds of muscle mass, but he was ripped to shreds.

One of the muscle groups Paul needed to work on early in his career was his back. Like most bodybuilders he assumed the key was lifting as much weight as possible. With judges and friends alike telling him he needed to bring up his back, Paul re-evaluated his training. As he was already doing the primary exercises for his back, there wasn't much room for improvement there, so he adopted a different approach. He dropped the weight on most exercises and concentrated on isolating the back muscles with as little secondary muscle involvement as possible.

Paul usually starts his back workouts with 3 sets of chinups as a warmup. On most days he'll use just his bodyweight, but occasionally he'll add a few pounds around his waist. With his back fully warmed Paul performs the following exercises:

Dennis was 19 when he first realized that bodybuilding was what he wanted to do.

1. Reverse-grip barbell rows   4 sets of 10 to 12 reps
2. Seated cable rows   4 sets of 10 to 12 reps
3. Hammer machine rows   4 sets of 10 to 12 reps
4. Front pulldowns   4 sets of 10 to 12 reps
5. Close-grip pulldowns   4 sets of 10 to 12 reps
6. Back extensions   4 sets of 10 to 12 reps

Paul is constantly stretching his lats between sets. He is not concerned about how much weight he is lifting either. He picks a weight that is heavy enough to stimulate his back muscles without requiring him to sacrifice good form. Finally, even though Paul "averages" 10 to 12 reps per set, he's not a slave to numbers. He goes to positive failure. Whether that happens at the 10th or 15th rep, he's not that fussy.

Dennis Newman

We come across very few people in life who leave an indelible impression on us. Dennis is one of them. Most of us in the bodybuilding community are well aware of Dennis' tragic story of being diagnosed with leukemia right after his '94 USA win. The news hit the bodybuilding world hard – from fans to bodybuilders, to writers and publishers. In fact many of us thought Dennis would never set foot onstage again. Everyone felt for Dennis, not because he was one of the sport's fastest-rising stars, but because this illness struck (as it so often does), such a decent human being.

Dennis Allen Newman Jr. was born in Fort Hood, Texas, on January 4, 1970, but grew up in Northern California. A natural athlete, he played in his first football league at the age of nine! He continued playing football right through high school. At the age of 14 he took up both surfing and lifting weights. At the age of 16, he became a bit more serious about bodybuilding: "When I was 16 years old, I was able to join a gym at the local mall and I wanted to further my training with more equipment that my high school didn't have. There was a personal trainer at this gym – an older guy named Malen – and he helped everybody, me included. I really paid attention to everything he said. He taught me an awful lot about training – what to do and how to do it. Before meeting Malen, I used to just train my upper body and I didn't bother with my legs, but he got me into doing squats and leg presses and all that other stuff. I gradually got involved and I entered my first bodybuilding contest at Fort Ord (a military base) when I was 16 … and I won!"

His early success continued, and at 19 he was on the cover of bodybuilding magazines. Yet with celebrity comes a dark side, fans that don't know when to back off: "… At first the fame was exciting and great, but then I found another side of bodybuilding … I had certain people harassing me and other people telling me things and just freaking me out. You know

> **"I think you have to keep changing the approach so your muscles never get used to any one workout."**
>
> – Dennis Newman, National champ commenting on his approach to training.

Size, shape, cuts, and those movie star good looks – Dennis Newman has it all.

what I mean? … I had homos calling me up at the gym and saying all this weird stuff. You have to remember that coming from a small town you don't encounter anything like that. It really shocked me to say the least. I don't have anything against homos – what they do is their business – but they were trying to make me feel like shit! … I was 19 and I think I had more of a male than female following. Now they don't mess with me, and I try to look back and laugh at it."

It was his friend and mentor, Lou Zwick, who helped Dennis adapt to this strange new world: "Lou helped me a lot in dealing with that situation though. He coached me through it. If I hadn't had anyone to help me through that period, I probably wouldn't have continued with bodybuilding. In fact, I know I wouldn't have continued with bodybuilding … Lou was sort of my guide. He made sure that I did the right kind of contests to help me keep winning, and he helped to make me more knowledgeable about the sport. He taught me how to deal with situations that would make most normal people trip out. But I was so hooked into bodybuilding – with the training and the way I looked and all that stuff – which even if I didn't pursue it as a career I still would train. I didn't really plan to make bodybuilding my profession. It just worked out that way with winning all the contests. I was 19 when I realized that bodybuilding was what I wanted to do."

Here's his competitive record:

1989 California Championships – NPC, teen, 1st
1993 Nationals – NPC, heavyweight, 2nd
1994 USA Championships – NPC, overall winner
        USA Championships – NPC, heavyweight, 1st
1998 Ironman Pro Invitational – IFBB, 7th
1999 Toronto Pro Invitational – IFBB, 18th
2000 Ironman Pro Invitational – IFBB, 13th

When asked what he would change about bodybuilding, Dennis answered: "We don't get enough money. We're supposed to be professional athletes, and considering what we do to

Dennis is a firm believer that you need to employ many different variables to achieve ultimate size and muscularity.

our bodies, we get next to nothing. In order to prepare for our contests we should be paid a lot more, especially if the supplement companies are making millions of dollars, hand over fist. For example, a company makes $25 million and pays the contracted athlete $50,000. It isn't right. They don't give the bodybuilder enough compensation for selling and endorsing the product that made all the money in the first place."

Training Philosophy

With his cancer in remission Dennis is now concentrating on regaining the form that won him the 1994 USA Championships. When he was sending shudders up the spines of other amateur bodybuilders, Dennis displayed a physique that was as close to perfect as humanly possible. You know, size, shape, cuts, and those movie star good looks. In essence the complete package.

Dennis normally trained on an eight-day on/ one-day off routine, splitting the body over four workouts. Instead of going four-on, one-off, he would go eight-on, one off. A typical muscle breakdown would be as follows:

Day 1 – chest and delts
Day 2 – legs
Day 3 – back
Day 4 – arms

As with most top bodybuilders Dennis is a firm believer that you need to employ many different variables to achieve ultimate size and muscularity. During a typical workout Dennis would employ light weight, high reps, heavy weight, low reps, slow training, fast training. "No two of my workouts are ever exactly the same," he says.

A quick glance at his 240- to 250-pound physique and you can probably guess that Dennis prefers free weights over machines for building mass. Of course there are exercises that require the use of machines. But if there's a free weight exercise that can mimic a machine, you can nearly bet that that's the one he'll use.

Another Newman must is strict form and full range of motion. He's not a big believer in half or quarter reps with outrageous poundages. As soon as muscles other than the targeted muscles need to be employed, Dennis decreases the weight.

Back

Now that you have his training philosophy, it's time to take a look at one of his back routines. We say "one of" because Dennis constantly changes things around. On days when he wants to give the lats priority, he begins with wide-grip chins supersetted with cross-bench dumbell pullovers. Dennis prefers to chin on the Parrillo Performance swivel-grip chinning machine, which allows him to supinate his biceps and twist his hands to work his lats more effectively. This machine also allows him to vary his grip width.

Dennis usually begins with one set of 10 to 15 reps using no weight. Each rep is performed in a slow, deliberate fashion, with no jerking or bouncing. After the first set with no weight, Dennis starts adding plates around his waist with a chinning belt. He increases

Dennis displayed a physique that was as close to perfect as humanly possible.

the weight trying to get 8 to 10 hard reps per set. Despite the increased weight and fatiguing muscles, Dennis tries to keep his form as strict as possible. Don't forget that after each set of chins Dennis is throwing in a set of dumbell pullovers. Besides the extra stretch in his lats, Dennis finds pullovers pre-exhaust the lats so they tire out before the biceps when doing chins. This is something beginners should keep in mind as often the biceps give out first on pulldowns and chins.

After chins Dennis moves on to wide-grip front pulldowns, once again supersetted with cross-bench pullovers. The nice thing about pulldowns is that if his biceps are beginning to fatigue he can drop the weight and concentrate on his lats. With chins the lightest he could go is his bodyweight, which during the off-season could be 260 to 270 pounds!

After 7 or 8 supersets of pulldowns and pullovers, Dennis moves on to exercises that hit the center of his back. The first exercise is usually T-bar rows. For safety and effectiveness Dennis performs T-bar rows with his head up, back slightly arched not rounded, and knees slightly bent.

Next up is another superset combination, this time barbell rows and bent-over dumbell laterals. Although most bodybuilders only perform bent-over laterals with their shoulder routines, Dennis finds that by bending the elbows more and keeping the arms closer to the body, he can shift most of the focus to the upper lats and rhomboids. In many respects this exercise is half way between a regular bent-over lateral raise and a dumbell row. Dennis performs 8 to 12 reps during both exercises, going to failure on both.

As we mentioned the previous is just one of the many routines Dennis performs for his back. He regularly switches exercises to keep the muscles guessing. On one day he may throw in straight arm pushdowns as his pre-exhaust exercise. Or he may add seated cable rows as his primary upper back and rhomboid movement. One thing is certain, now that he's conquered leukemia, the pro ranks better be prepared for the return of the bodybuilder who has it all.

Biceps

When Dennis starts with biceps his first exercise is normally the barbell preacher curl with the straight bar. He considers this to be a supreme mass builder when done correctly, and no less an authority than former Mr. Olympia Larry Scott agrees. Larry did preacher curls almost exclusively for years and developed two of the greatest biceps in bodybuilding history.

Dennis warms up for 2 sets and then piles on the plates, working up to 135 or 140. He does 2 sets of 10 reps with a wide grip, followed by 2 sets of 10 reps with a medium grip. He usually keeps the weight the same for all 4 sets, but there are days when he'll pyramid up in weight until he's just able to get 6 reps.

Dennis likes to follow preacher curls with alternate dumbell curls. Because his biceps are well warmed up from the preachers, he doesn't waste much time warming up. He jumps right to a set of 75-pounders and does 10 near perfect reps. He then drops the weight about five pounds per set until he has completed four good sets averaging 10 reps per set. Dennis is careful to use strict form and supinates the palms on each rep. Dennis learned this from watching and reading about Arnold's training back in the '70s.

With two good mass builders out of the way, Dennis moves on to two shaping and peaking movements. His third exercise is either spyder curls or cable preacher curls. No matter which one, he starts with the heaviest weight first and works down with each successive set.

Dennis needs the assistance of a training partner to help keep him anchored to the floor when doing triceps pressdowns.

For his final exercise, Dennis almost always does one-arm dumbell concentration curls. Dennis does them seated with his elbow resting on his inner thigh. On typical day Dennis will do 4 sets of 8 to 10 reps of concentration curls.

Triceps

Dennis usually follows biceps training with triceps. He finds all the biceps work serves as a good warm up for his elbows.

His first exercise is a good basic mass builder like lying EZ-bar extensions. Dennis does two light warmup sets and then pyramids up in weight, doing 3 hard sets of 10 to 12 reps. Where technique is concerned, Dennis lowers the weight to his skull, not to the top of his head or behind the head like many bodybuilders do. He's also careful to keep the upper arm and elbows pointing directly at the ceiling for every rep.

Dennis' second triceps exercise is triceps pushdowns, or as Dennis does them triceps pressdowns. Instead of locking his elbows and upper arms to his sides like most bodybuilders, he lets them flare out so that he is pressing the bar down in a similar manner to a narrow press. Dennis is extremely strong on this exercise and uses between 300 and 400 pounds. Even with his off-season weight going up to 260 to 270 pounds, Dennis needs the assistance of a training partner to help keep him anchored to the floor.

For variety Dennis sometimes does pushdowns with a rope and performs them in the conventional elbows locked to the sides manner. In either case he does 4 sets of 10 to12 reps.

Dennis' third exercise is either reverse-grip pushdowns or lying dumbell triceps extensions. If he uses reverse pushdowns he does 4 sets of 10 to 12 reps. As the bar touches his forehead at the top and thighs at the bottom, Dennis squeezes hard and pauses for a split second to give his triceps a good contraction. Given the nature of this exercise, Dennis uses medium weight and employs very strict form.

If Dennis opts for lying dumbell extensions he'll again do 4 sets of 10 to 12 reps. He starts with a 45-pound dumbell and works up to around 60 pounds. Dennis performs this exercise one arm at a time and lowers the dumbell to his ear, keeping his elbow pointed at the ceiling at all time.

To finish off his triceps Dennis likes to throw in a "rep out" movement. His favorite is bench dips and as his triceps are pretty fatigued by this point, he finds his bodyweight is ample. Dennis doesn't count reps on this exercise. Instead he just keeps going until he can't do another rep.

We should add that Dennis frequently changes around the order of the previous exercises. The next day he comes into the gym he may start with rope pushdowns and then move on to lying EZ-bar extensions. He may even throw in a couple of new exercises like dumbell kickbacks and seated one-arm extensions. For Dennis variety is definitely the key to continued growth.

Shoulders

When asked what was the most important variable in bodybuilding, the pump, heavy weights, or intensity, Dennis replied, "all three." From one look at his physique it seems he's a man of his word. Dennis has that lucky combination of good looks, great size, and near-perfect symmetry.

One of his most outstanding muscle groups is his delts, and readers will no doubt be happy to hear that Dennis has had to cut back on his shoulder training because in his own words "they have a tendency to get too big and out of proportion with my other muscles." Oh, to have to endure such burdens!

Dennis trains shoulders after chest. This not only allows him to hit his chest a bit harder, but also warms his delts up. He usually starts shoulder training with dumbell side laterals. He'll start with one light warm-up set, and then jump to a heavy weight for a set of 10 to 12 reps. Then he'll pyramid up in weight for another three sets. On the final set this works out to a set of 75-pound dumbells for 10 to 12 reps. He keeps his small fingers out and his thumbs down at the top of the exercise, thus putting most of the stress on the side delts.

One of Dennis' most outstanding muscle groups is his delts.

After side laterals it's on to bent-over laterals. Again he does 4 sets of 10 to 12 reps using about a 50-pound dumbell.

For his third exercise Dennis does the exercise most bodybuilders start with, behind-the-head barbell presses. Dennis' rationale is that his front delts have already been hit hard with his various chest exercises. He doesn't need to subject them to 250- to 300-pound barbell shoulder presses. Instead he'll put about 180 pounds on the bar and do 4 sets of 10 to 12 reps in near-perfect style.

To finish off his shoulders, Dennis does two trap exercises – shrugs and upright rows. Again it's 4 sets of 10 to 12 reps of each.

A few words on Dennis' training techniques. He only rests about 30 seconds between sets, and limits supersets, trisets, and other advanced techniques to his pre-contest training. For most of the year he does straight sets to positive failure.

Bruce Patterson

Bruce Patterson was born in Sackville, New Brunswick, Canada, on October 4, 1972. By his late teens Bruce had gained as much muscle mass as most far more experienced bodybuilders. A write up in *MuscleMag International* likened his potential to a young Arnold. Weighing 230 to 240 pounds in contest shape, Bruce has developed a reputation as a crowd pleaser, and his posing exhibitions are always a hit. Bruce hasn't quite made the impact on the pro scene that was expected, but the guy's still only 28 years old. Another couple of pounds and a few more years and he may take his place in the top ten. Here's what he's done so far:

1995   Canada Pro Cup – IFBB, 19th
1997   Canada Pro Cup – IFBB, 13th
        Ironman Pro Invitational – IFBB, 9th
        San Jose Pro Invitational – IFBB, 10th
1999   Ironman Pro Invitational – IFBB, 20th
        Night of Champions – IFBB
        Bruce Patterson, a phenomenal young bodybuilder with a great future ahead of him.

Back

Bruce prefers to train on a three-on/ one-day off double-split routine. In other words he trains the whole body over three days, but hits the gym twice a day, once in the morning and once at night. This type of schedule allows him to hit just one muscle at a time. And what a punishing it gets!

Bruce has developed a reputation as a crowd pleaser, and his posing exhibitions are always a hit.

Most workouts last from 45 to 60 minutes, employing anywhere from 6 to 10 sets total per muscle group. Although not pure heavy duty in the Mentzer sense, Bruce's workouts are a long way from the high volume workouts performed by many bodybuilders. Bruce likes to train heavy and brief. He's tried supersets, dropsets, and other "pumping" techniques, but prefers good old-fashioned straight sets with heavy weight. "I can't even get a decent pump unless I lift some heavy iron."

Like most bodybuilders who train heavy, Bruce is a stickler for strict style. He doesn't believe in sacrificing form just for a few extra reps or pounds on the bar. With the exception of a few cheat reps at the end of a set of barbell curls, Bruce performs all his sets in strict form and a full range of motion.

With Bruce's back reminiscent of Franco Columbu's, let's see how he built it.

Generally speaking Bruce usually does four or five exercises for about 4 sets each. Now before you point out that this would be an example of high volume training, (and didn't we just say Bruce doesn't subscribe to this?) keep in mind that of the 4 sets per exercise, two are warm-up sets and two are heavy training sets. So he's really only doing 8 to 10 all-out sets for his back.

Bruce likes to start his back training with a basic power movement like wide-grip chins. Weighing over 250 pounds means he doesn't need to attach much weight around his waist. Bruce usually does 12 reps on the first set, followed by sets of 10, 8, and 4 to 6 reps respectively.

After chins it's on to narrow-grip pulldowns. The first two sets are usually performed with about 180 pounds for 15 reps. He then throws the stack on (300 pounds) and bangs out 1 or 2 sets of 8 to 10 reps.

With the widening exercises out of the way, Bruce moves on to the thickening movements. His first exercise is seated cable rows. The first set is the standard warm-up set of 15 reps with, in this case about 150

Bruce prefers good old-fashioned straight sets with heavy weight.

pounds. Then he puts the pin at the bottom of the stack (250 to 300 pounds) and does one all-out set of 6 to 8 reps. On most days one such set is adequate, but occasionally he'll do a second.

Bruce's second rowing movement is usually one-arm dumbell rows. For the first 2 sets he uses a 100-pound dumbell for 12 to 15 reps. He then finishes off with a 140 pounder for 6 to 8 reps. Rather than pull the dumbell straight up and down, Bruce likes to perform the exercise as if sawing wood. That is stretching the dumbell slightly forward at the bottom of the movement.

To finish off his back training, Bruce likes to perform Dorian Yates' favorite, reverse-grip bent-over barbell rows. Although this version doesn't quite hit the center lats like the standard version, most bodybuilders find it does a better job targeting the lower lats. As his lats are fully warmed up by now, Bruce only does one light warm-up set on this exercise, usually a 20-rep set using 135 pounds. He then puts a respectable 285 pounds on the bar and does 2 sets of 6 to 8 reps.

The previous is a typical Bruce Patterson back workout. Of course the next time he comes into the gym he may change the sequence of exercises. For those not achieving much success on the high volume approach to training, give Bruce's high-intensity back workout a try.

Shoulders

A typical Bruce Patterson shoulder workout will see him do one isolation exercise for each head of the deltoid – front, side, and rear – and one heavy pressing movement for overall shoulder mass and power. Most bodybuilders include traps with their shoulders but Bruce has reached the point now where his traps grow from the indirect stimulation they receive from the regular shoulder exercises. So this means you won't see Bruce doing many sets of shrugs and uprights when he's in the gym.

Like most bodybuilders who train heavy, Bruce is a stickler for strict style.

It's hard to give an exact Patterson shoulder workout as he constantly changes things around, but the following is one that he was observed performing during the mid-'90s.

Bruce liked to start shoulder training with rear delts. These small muscles tend to be neglected by many bodybuilders, but Bruce realized early on, that great rear delts go a long way in moving you up the competitive ladder. Bruce prefers the rear-delt machine to hit these muscles. It allows him to go heavy and isolate the rear delts without putting undue stress on his lower back. He does his first set with a medium weight for 15 reps. He then increases the weight and does what he calls a medium warm-up set. Now he gets serious. He increases the weight substantially so he can just manage 8 reps in good style. If he found the 8 reps easy he'll increase it for the next set, but if the 8 was a struggle he'll stick with it for another set.

For his second exercise, Bruce does another rear delt movement, this time lying one-arm dumbell laterals. Most bodybuilders do these for the side shoulders, but Bruce has found that if he leans forward slightly and starts the dumbell in front of him and not to the side, he can put most of the stress on his rear delts. He normally does 3 sets of 8 to 10 reps using a 30 pound dumbell. Rather than do 3 straight sets for one shoulder, he alternates back and forth.

For his third exercise Bruce likes to do a basic power movement. One of his favorites is the Hammer Strength pressing machine. He'll put two 45-pound plates on each side and do 3 sets of 6 to 10 reps, taking each set to total failure. Unlike many pressing machines this one allows the user to work the shoulders through a full range of motion.

Bruce's next exercise is often one-arm side laterals to punish his side delts. Bruce typically uses a 50- to 60-pound dumbell and does 3 sets of 8 to 10 reps on each side, again taking each set to failure.

Unlike many bodybuilders, Bruce doesn't rotate his hands as he lifts the dumbells to the sides. The familiar "pouring water from a jug" doesn't seem to offer him any extra stimulation, so he just brings the dumbells up to shoulder height while trying to keep his palms parallel to the floor.

To finish off his shoulders, Bruce includes 3 sets of 8 to 12 reps of alternate front raises. Many bodybuilders find their front delts get enough stimulation from the heavy presses and chest exercises. But Bruce wants as much shoulder mass as possible. Let's face it, when your goal is to one day slug it out with the likes of Levrone, Dillett, and Coleman, you need every muscle fiber enlarged to the maximum.

Lee prefers to rely on diet and aerobics to shed bodyfat, not light weights and high reps.

Lee Priest

Lee Priest was born in Newcastle, Australia, in 1972. Bodybuilding success came early to Lee as he won the Sydney Classic at 13 years of age. Within three years he had won the Mr. Australia contest three times.

But this was only a hint of things to come as Lee packs an unheard of 220 pounds on his 5'4" frame. And this is in contest shape! He easily goes up to 260 to 280 pounds in the off-season.

Lee is without doubt proportionally one of the largest bodybuilders competing today. Here's his outstanding contest record:

"How can anyone pack so much beef onto such a small frame?"

– Greg Zulak, former *MuscleMag International* editor commenting on the Australian wonder, Lee Priest, pound for pound one of the most massive bodybuilders in history.

1989	Mr. Australia – IFBB, overall winner
1990	Mr. Australia – IFBB, overall winner
	World Amateur Championships – IFBB, 4th
	World Amateur Championships – IFBB, lightweight, 4th
1993	Niagara Falls Pro Invitational – IFBB, 9th
1994	Arnold Classic – IFBB, 7th
	Ironman Pro Invitational – IFBB, 4th
	Night of Champions – IFBB, 12th
	San Jose Pro Invitational – IFBB, 7th
1995	Arnold Classic – IFBB, 9th
	Florida Pro Invitational – IFBB, 4th
	Ironman Pro Invitational – IFBB, 3rd
	South Beach Pro Invitational – IFBB, 4th
1996	Ironman Pro Invitational – IFBB, 4th
	San Jose Pro Invitational – IFBB, 6th
1997	Arnold Classic – IFBB, 7th
	Grand Prix Czech Republic – IFBB, 5th
	Grand Prix England – IFBB, 6th
	Grand Prix Finland – IFBB, 9th
	Grand Prix Germany – IFBB, 3rd
	Grand Prix Hungary – IFBB, 3rd
	Grand Prix Russia – IFBB, 9th
	Grand Prix Spain – IFBB, 3rd
	Ironman Pro Invitational – IFBB, 2nd
	Olympia – IFBB, 6th
	San Jose Pro Invitational – IFBB, 4th
1998	Olympia – IFBB, 7th
1999	Ironman Pro Invitational – IFBB, 6th
	Olympia – IFBB, 8th
2000	Night of Champions – IFBB, 5th

Lee is without doubt proportionally one of the largest bodybuilders competing today.

Biceps

Not many bodybuilders standing just 5'4" can stand next to such behemoths as Paul Dillett, Nasser El Sonbaty, and Ronnie Coleman, and trade shots, but Australia's Lee Priest is one notable exception. Like Franco Columbu before him, Lee hasn't let something as trivial as height stand

"To say that Lee Priest had some genetic talent for bodybuilding is an understatement. He progressed so fast that he was already competing at the Mr. Universe when he was only 17. Most of your current Mr. Universe and Mr. Olympia competitors were just picking up a weight for the first time at that age, or at best, were still novice bodybuilders."

– Greg Zulak, former *MuscleMag International* editor, commenting on Australian wonder kid, Lee Priest.

in his way. Lee packs as much muscle mass on his frame as many bodybuilders half a foot or even a foot taller. A tipped 220 pounds would be respectable for most six-foot bodybuilders, but when it's packed on someone less than five-and-a-half-feet tall, well folks, you have to see it to believe it!

Lee often follows the popular four day on/ one day off training routine. His split goes as follows:

Day 1 – chest and biceps
Day 2 – shoulders and triceps
Day 3 – back
Day 4 – legs

Notice that Lee likes to alternate a large pushing muscle group (chest) with a smaller pulling muscle (biceps). Over the years he discovered that his recovery abilities went up when he switched to this format. Conversely when he trained triceps after chest, he couldn't do them full justice as chest training had exhausted them. Likewise he no longer combines biceps with lat training. No matter how strict your training style, lat exercises also tire out the biceps.

These days Lee prefers basic movements for 6 to 8 reps with heavy weight. Typically he does three to four exercises per muscle group for about 5 to 7 sets per exercise. Even though he lives in Venice California, and has access to the best training equipment in the world, Lee relies on barbells and dumbells to make up the bulk of his training. He's what Greg Zulak calls a "bodybuilder's bodybuilder."

Given that Lee has two of the largest guns seen anywhere on the pro bodybuilding circuit (cannons is probably a better description), let's take a detailed look at his arm training.

Lee packs as much muscle mass on his frame as many bodybuilders half a foot or even a foot taller.

Lee normally begins his biceps training with straight barbell curls. After a couple of light warm-up sets he pyramids up the weight to about 220 pounds for 6 reps. For those not impressed by these numbers, keep in mind that this is Lee's competitive bodyweight!

With regards to technique, Lee has his own views. "Going one hundred percent strict just limits the weight too much. You can't go really heavy if your form is 100 percent strict." Through years of experience Lee has learned how to cheat the weight up and still keep maximum tension on his biceps. He then lowers the weight in strict style. Another Priest philosophy is that the straight bar is much better for building the biceps than the EZ-curl bar. He insists that anyone trying to put some serious beef on their arms should stick to the straight bar.

After standing barbell curls, Lee moves on to standing preacher curls. Most bodybuilders prefer to do this exercise sitting down, but Lee finds he can get better leverage and use more weight by standing up. Also he finds his front delts get too involved when he does seated preacher curls.

Lee starts preacher curls with 100 pounds for a warm-up set of 10 reps, and then pyramids up 10 pounds for each of the next 5 sets. Eventually he's grinding out 6 reps with 150 pounds on the bar.

With 12 or 13 sets under his belt, you'd think Lee would be finished with his biceps, but such is not the case for the Hercules from down under. Next up it's seated alternate dumbell curls. He performs this exercise one arm at a time. By this we mean he doesn't have one arm going up as the other is going down. Instead he makes one complete rep before switching arms. He usually starts with a pair of 60s for 6 to 8 reps, and then pounds out 3 more sets using a pair of 70s.

To finish off his biceps, Lee will either do seated one-arm concentration curls, or standing Icarian cable curls. With his biceps still suffering from the previous 15 to 17 sets, Lee only needs a 30-pound dumbell to work with on his concentration curls.

After his last set of biceps curls, Lee hits a few poses in the mirror to check his progress. At this point many other gym members, pros and amateurs alike, stop what they're doing a take a peek. In many respects it brings back memories of Arnold hitting a chest pose or Franco flexing the lats, back at the old Gold's Gym in the '70s. Lee's biceps are that good.

Lee likes to conclude his triceps training with a couple of check poses in the mirror.

Triceps

Until Lee Priest came on the scene it was assumed that Sergio Oliva's famous hands over head pose would never be duplicated. But Lee has brought about a re-evaluation of this view. With the possible exception of Britain's Ernie Taylor, Lee has the largest, most muscular set of triceps of any pro. What's ironic is that he usually only employs two exercises in the off-season to build them.

Lee's favorite triceps exercise is two-arm dumbell extensions, also called a dumbell French press. After a few warm-up sets using 40 to 50 pounds, Lee grabs a 120-pound dumbell and does a set of 15 reps. He then goes up 20 pounds per set until he's forcing out 6 reps with a 200-pound monster. All told Lee performs 8 to 10 sets of dumbell French presses.

To finish off those slabs of meat hanging off his upper arms, Lee does seated one-arm dumbell extensions. With his triceps semi-exhausted from those 200-pound French presses, Lee only needs to use 40 to 45 pounds on this exercise. He usually does 5 to 7 sets in total, averaging 10 to 15 reps per set.

As with biceps, Lee likes to conclude his triceps training with a couple of check poses in the mirror. Once again more stares, more drooling. But it's this sort of admiration that makes the Aussie tick.

Shoulders

As with most muscle groups, Lee favors heavy basic exercises to train shoulders. He also prefers straight sets and heavy weight, to supersets, trisets and other exotic techniques. Generally he'll pick four exercises for a muscle group and do 5 sets per exercise. He doesn't vary his routine much either. He may occasionally do dumbell presses instead of barbell presses, but for the most part he sticks to basic exercises. He doesn't do a lot of cable stuff or machine exercises either.

Lee favors heavy basic exercises to train shoulders.

A typical deltoid workout for Lee usually has him beginning with seated behind-the-head presses. Besides hitting pretty much the whole deltoid region, Lee finds them excellent for the traps. After two light warmup sets, Lee will do 5 work sets, pyramiding the weight up the first 3 sets, and keeping it the same for the last 2 sets. He usually keeps the reps in the 6 to 8 range.

Lee usually trains with a training partner so as soon as his partner has done his set, Lee starts his. This gives a nice tempo to the workout. It also allows them to handle some heavy poundages without fear of getting trapped with the bar across their necks.

As you might expect from someone who likes to train slow and heavy, Lee moves the weight over a full range of motion, from the base of his neck to almost complete lockout. He doesn't do the short, fast, constant tension reps that are popular with so many bodybuilders these days.

For his second delt exercise, Lee does dumbell side laterals. He favors the two-arm version over the one-arm version. He does 5 sets of 6 to 8 reps, again pyramiding up the weight with each set. He uses fairly strict form for most of his reps, but will resort to a slight cheat to keep the weight moving on his last couple of reps. Being the experienced bodybuilder he is, Lee has learned how to cheat and keep the stress on his side delts. Most bodybuilders who cheat end up shifting most of the tension to their front delts.

Exercise number three is the bent-over dumbell lateral. Once again Lee does 5 sets of 6 to 8 reps of this all-important rear delt builder. As with side laterals, Lee does most of the reps in strict style and then cheats a couple toward the end.

To finish off his shoulder and pack some serious Aussie beef on his traps, Lee does 5 sets of shrugs. The format is the same as the other exercises, pyramid up in weight the first 3 sets, and then keep it the same for the last 2 sets.

The previous is Lee's standard shoulder routine. Occasionally he'll substitute upright rows for the barbell shrug. And to use his own words "once in a blue moon" will triset barbell presses, dumbell side laterals, and bent-over laterals. But this is rare. He finds trisetting limits the weight he can use, and Lee is one bodybuilders who loves putting plates on bars!

As a final word, Lee follows the previous "slow and heavy" philosophy year round, even during his precontest phase of training. He prefers to rely on diet and aerobics to shed bodyfat, not light weights and high reps.

Lee Priest – you have to see him to believe him.

Forearms

The first thing Lee will tell you in an interview is that his massive forearms owe some of their existence to great genetics. At 38 his mother took second in the Ms. Australia contest, and just a few years ago his great grandfather broke both legs while doing 700 pound leg presses (the platform slipped and crushed both ankles). The boy from down under couldn't have chosen a better family to get tied up with.

Great genetics or not, Lee worked his butt off to get his world-class forearms. He prefers training forearms with back as he believes, and quite correctly, the forearms play a bigger role in rowing movements than curling exercises. Lee also believes the key to steel-chord forearms is high reps using as much weight as you can handle. For him this means 25 reps per set.

Lee believes in the high volume approach for forearm training. He picks four exercises and does 5 sets of each. That works out to 20 sets in total. But the results have been worth it as his forearms are in perfect balance with his freaky upper arms.

Lee starts his forearm workout with what he feels is the best mass builder of them all, hammer curls. Lee grabs a set of dumbells in the familiar palms-facing-in direction, and alternates raising and lowering the weight. Five sets of 25 reps is the norm.

Next up Lee moves on to twists. Lee alternates between machine rotations and dumbell twists for this exercise. If he uses the dumbells he'll rest his forearms on the edge of a flat bench, and rotate his hands as far as possible in both directions.

Exercise three is the standard barbell wrist curl. Again Lee rests his forearms on the edge of a flat bench and curls the weight back as far as he can, bending only at the wrists. His forearms never leave the bench. He then lowers the bar to the tips of his fingers.

To finish off those Popeye-like forearms, Lee bangs out 5 sets of standing barbell reverse curls.

Lee says the key to getting the most out of forearm training is to squeeze and forcefully contract the forearm muscles at the top of each exercise.

Flex Wheeler

Few bodybuilders have generated the amount of controversy that Flex has. His outstanding body (230-plus pounds in contest shape) is often dwarfed by his ego. Yet he is an articulate man, and a practical one. To Flex, bodybuilding is a serious vocation:

"Let me ask you: How do you get up every day and go to work? How do you get up, say at 7 am every day, every week, every month, every year? How do you do it man? You do it because that's your job. In that respect things are no different for me than for anyone else. It's my job, my profession. It's earning money for me. It's how I feed my family. I don't want to sit out a year and watch other guys make money."[1]

Kenneth Martin Wheeler was born in Fresno, California, on August 23, 1965. Fresno was a very prejudiced town to grow up in at the time. Flex was a racial minority in the schools he attended. With the racial tensions was the menacing presence of gangs: Cripps, Bloods, Stoners and the F-14s. Flex wasn't athletic in high school, and by grade 11 he weighed 98 pounds, soaking wet. By the time he graduated he weighed 135. He became heavily involved in both bodybuilding and Tae-Kwon-Do. Despite winning a big martial arts competition, Flex decided to concentrate on bodybuilding. His decision paid off, as his competitive record clearly shows:

Flex cites Robby Robinson, Lee Haney, and Lee Labrada as being early idols.

1989   California Championships – NPC, light heavyweight, 1st
        Nationals – NPC, light heavyweight, 5th
1990   Junior Nationals – NPC, heavyweight, 2nd
1991   Nationals – NPC, heavyweight, 2nd
        USA Championships – NPC, heavyweight, 2nd
1992   USA Championships – NPC, overall winner
        USA Championships – NPC, heavyweight, 1st
1993   Arnold Classic – IFBB, winner
        Grand Prix England – IFBB, 2nd
        Grand Prix France – IFBB, winner
        Grand Prix Germany – IFBB, winner
        Ironman Pro Invitational – IFBB, winner
        Olympia – IFBB, 2nd
1995   Arnold Classic – IFBB, 2nd
        Florida Pro Invitational – IFBB, winner

It was from Lee Labrada that Flex learned that posing should be treated with the same respect as training and dieting.

	Grand Prix Spain – IFBB, 5th
	Ironman Pro Invitational – IFBB, winner
	Olympia – IFBB, 8th
	South Beach Pro Invitational – IFBB, winner
1996	Arnold Classic – IFBB, 2nd
	Canada Pro Cup – IFBB, 2nd
	Florida Pro Invitational – IFBB, winner
	Ironman Pro Invitational – IFBB, winner
	Night of Champions – IFBB, winner
	Olympia – IFBB, 4th
1997	Arnold Classic – IFBB, winner
	Ironman Pro Invitational – IFBB, winner
	San Jose Pro Invitational – IFBB, winner
1998	Arnold Classic – IFBB, winner
	Ironman Pro Invitational – IFBB, winner
	Olympia – IFBB, 2nd
1999	Grand Prix England – IFBB, 2nd
	Olympia – IFBB, 2nd
	Professional World Cup – IFBB, 2nd
2000	Arnold Classic – IFBB, winner
	Grand Prix Hungary – IFBB, winner
	Ironman Pro Invitational – IFBB, 2nd

Only the presence of Dorian Yates and Ronnie Coleman has kept Flex from being a three-time Mr. Olympia winner.

Flex cites Robby Robinson, Lee Haney, and Lee Labrada as being early idols. In fact it was Robby who told Flex to keep an eye on Labrada as despite his short size, Labrada had a reputation for being perhaps the most complete bodybuilder of his generation. It was from Labrada that Flex learned that posing should be treated with the same respect as training and dieting. The results paid off as Flex has gained an excellent reputation himself for "dialing it in" when it comes to contest preparation.

A lot of people have been hard on Flex, but no one more so than Flex himself. While he may not like the judges' decision (and he often doesn't), he doesn't try to delude himself either: "My biceps were superior. I always had big arms and was known for my big guns. They were big – and everything else was skinny. I even had a sunken chest."

"What did I do about it? I looked in the mirror and critically appraised myself, assessing and acknowledging what was good, what wasn't, and what needed a lot more work.

Finally I started wearing shorts and tights so that my weak bodyparts would show. That was rough on the ego! But I had to admit to my weak bodyparts and start to train them with priority, not leaving them for last or just doing a couple of sets, but doing them first, concentrating on them and training them when I was at my freshest and most rested."[1]

And don't ask him about how much weight to lift: "Weights don't mean crap. It's the workout that counts. It's your intensity and concentration, your form and the number of reps that count. It's never, never the weight, but always the intensity. If you're trying to do a leg press with 400 pounds say, but you can hardly move it, how much better it would be to cut the weight back to 300-something and be able to do 20 good reps where you control the weight."[1]

Reference:

1) http://www.bodybuilder.org/profiles/wheeler.php3

Back

It was just after winning the 1989 NPC California Championships that Flex Wheeler started concentrating on bringing his back development up to par. Even though he had one of the smallest and tightest midsections around, he still felt his lats needed the extra width and thickness that separates winners from the rest of the pack.

Flex's first back exercise is usually medium-width chinups. He finds chins not only add the extra width he needs, but warm the back up for the heavier movements that come later.

He begins chins with a full stretch at the bottom and ends with a full contraction at the top. Unlike many bodybuilders who swing back and forth to cheat extra reps, Flex performs each and every rep in immaculate style. Flex does 5 sets of chins, trying to grind out 10 to 12 reps per set.

Flex is one of the few who can stand next to Dorian Yates and Ronnie Coleman and trade back shots!

Flex's second back exercise is single arm cable pulldowns to the side. As this is a seldom seen exercise in gyms, a detailed description is needed. Stand in the same position as for cable crossovers and grab one side of a high pulley. Walk over to the opposite side and grasp the supporting post with the free hand. Pull the handle down and in toward the rib cage, bending at the elbow until it is completely against the rib cage.

Flex performs 5 sets of 10 to 12 reps of this exercise, alternating sides with no rest in between.

Next up on Flex's itinerary is bent-over barbell rows. Given his flexibility, Flex likes to stand on a 6" to 8" short bench so he can get a full range of motion at the bottom. Strict style on this exercise is a must and Flex is careful to keep his knees slightly bent and lower back slightly arched. Over the years Flex has discovered that by keeping the torso about 45 degrees to the floor, he can target the areas of the back that he wants.

"When I started competing on the national level I realized that I had to have a bigger back onstage. You are up against so many guys who are incredible and even if they lack symmetry, almost all of them have great backs."

– Flex Wheeler, twice Mr. Olympia runner-up commenting on the point at which he started taking back training seriously.

Flex has two of the largest guns on the scene.

On a typical day Flex starts at about 175 pounds and works up to 300. Once again he performs 5 sets of 10 to 12 reps.

For his fourth exercise Flex performs close-grip seated cable rows. He usually starts with about 170 pounds and works up to the whole stack. Unlike some bodybuilders who stretch completely forward, Flex only leans forward just slightly past vertical. As he pulls the handle into his lower rib cage, he arches his back and squeezes his shoulder blades together. As expected he does his customary 5 sets of 10 to 12 reps.

For mere mortals the previous four exercises would suffice, but Flex is no mere mortal. To really bring out the width in his back, he adds seated pulldowns behind-the-head as a fifth exercise. Unlike the medium width grip he uses on chins, Flex takes as wide a grip as possible on pulldowns. During the exercise he keeps his torso as vertical as possible, and arches the lower back ever so slightly. Even though many bodybuilders find behind-the-head pulldowns hard on the shoulder joint, Flex has never had any problems. In fact he discovered that puling to the front just doesn't seem to give him the same degree of back contraction as puling behind.

Well there you have it, the back routine that has made Flex Wheeler one of the top bodybuilders in the world, and one of the few who can stand next to Dorian Yates and Ronnie Coleman and trade back shots!

Biceps

It's not surprising that many patrons of Gold's Gym in the early '90s, mistook gossip about "Twin Peaks" as referring to Flex Wheeler's biceps and not the zany TV show of the same name. But when you have two of the largest guns on the scene, causing confusion becomes a way of life.

Charles Clairmonte, Flex Wheeler and Michael Francois

But there's no confusing what Flex Wheeler has protruding from his arm sleeves. To the list of Arnold, Coe, Beckles, Robinson, and Coleman, must be added the name of Ken "Flex" Wheeler. In contest shape his biceps rise like two lost peaks of the Rocky Mountain chain.

What makes Wheelers' biceps so impressive is that they have it all, size, shape, and fullness. The fact that the separation between his biceps and triceps is near perfect hasn't hurt him either.

As with most pros, Flex varies his exercises on a regular basis. On some days he'll go for more basic size movements, while on others it's isolation exercises to bring out refinement. Here's a typical example of the latter.

Flex's first exercise on what he calls his peaking day, is usually seated concentration curls. With his elbow braced on the inside of his thigh, Flex will lower the weight to just short of a lockout, and then raise it all the way up to eye level. Four sets of 7 to 12 reps is the order of the day.

Next up Flex moves on to one-arm alternate dumbell curls. Even though most bodybuilders consider these more of a mass than peak builder, Flex finds that supinating his hands as he curls up, helps bring out the peak in his biceps. Again he'll do 4 sets of 7 to 12 reps. To finish off his biceps, Flex does 4 sets of one-arm cable curls.

Although this routine is more of a refining workout than for building mass, Flex is quick to add that he goes as heavy as possible. He doesn't subscribe to the "isolation days are for light weights" theory. Twin Peaks was cancelled long ago, but every time Flex Wheeler steps on stage bodybuilding fans get a look at two of the highest peaks around.

Triceps

Given the size and shape of his biceps, it's not surprising Flex Wheeler has had to pay special attention to his triceps. Flex was lucky in that growing up in California he was constantly surrounded by world-class competitive bodybuilders. One of the pieces of advice he took to heart was that symmetry and balance are what separates good bodybuilders from great bodybuilders. When he discovered that his biceps seemed to respond faster than his triceps, he revamped his triceps routine to bring them in line.

A typical Flex Wheeler triceps routine will see him start with one-hand seated dumbell extensions. He sits on the bench with his feet shoulder width apart, torso straight, and his left hand grabbing the inside of his left leg for support. Flex holds his right elbow straight up, point-ing at the ceiling, and lower his forearm and the dumbell down to the base of his neck. Without pausing, he extends his arm to the outstretched position. He does 4 sets of 10 reps, using from 50 to 75 pounds.

For his second exercise, Flex moves on to lying EZ-bar extensions or skull crushers. With his upper arms kept perfectly straight, Flex lowers the bar to the top of his head. He then pushes it back to a full locked-out position. Flex typically uses from 100 to 175 pounds for 4 sets of 10 reps. Given the safety concerns of this exercise, Flex tries to have a spotter standing behind him in case something goes wrong.

For his third triceps exer-cise, Flex does v-bar pushdowns on the lat pulldown machine. He finds he can get a slightly better contraction in his triceps

> One of the pieces of advice Flex took to heart was that symmetry and balance are what separates good bodybuilders from great bodybuilders.

by using the V-shaped bar as opposed to a rope or straight bar. He'll typically use about 135 to 150 pounds and do 4 sets of 10 reps.

To finish off his triceps, Flex prefers a total isolation movement like one-arm reverse cable pushdowns. Flex finds this exercise great for hitting the long head of the triceps. The key, he says, is to keep tension on the muscle at all times. This means raising the handle in a slow and controlled manner. Letting the weight fly up to the starting position only loses you half the benefit.

Besides the previous exercises, Flex also includes the following in his training on a regular basis: bench dips, kickbacks, and two-arm dumbell extensions (while sitting straight up).

To Flex Wheeler,
bodybuilding is a
serious vocation.

Troy Zuccolotto

Troy Zuccolotto was born in Long Beach, California on July 9, 1961. Always athletic, he played football, baseball and basketball. In his junior and senior years he got sick with mononucleosis. He got very thin, leading him to take up weight lifting. Unlike his peers, he didn't take up drinking: "In high school I hung around with all the jocks, because that's what I was. I always had lots of confidence. I wasn't one of those shy, quiet kids with an inferiority complex … I never drank at all. I got into health so early in high school, even before everyone else got into drinking and partying, that I never did. I used to take orange juice to parties and drink that. I think the people really respected me for that because they knew what I was trying to accomplish. They never made fun of me …"

Today Troy runs his Youth Tech Wellness Center in San Clemente, California.

Nor did the judges:

1981   California Gold Cup Championships – teen, 1st
1986   Nationals – NPC, heavyweight, 7th
1987   Nationals – NPC, heavyweight, 3rd
1988   North American Championships – IFBB, heavyweight, 2nd
        USA Championships – NPC, heavyweight, 2nd
1989   Nationals – NPC, overall winner
        Nationals – NPC, heavyweight, 1st
1991   WBF Grand Prix – WBF, 13th
1994   Chicago Pro Invitational – IFBB, 18th
        Night of Champions – IFBB, 17th

With his blond hair, blue eyes, boyish good looks and massive muscles, it's no surprise that Troy has done some TV appearances, including *Doogie Howser, M.D., Full House,* and commercials.

Today Troy runs his Youth Tech Wellness Center in San Clemente, California. And what is Troy's greatest strength? "I have a positive outlook. I'm goal-oriented. I'm the type of person who sets a goal and no matter how long it takes or what it takes, I will never give up until I do achieve it. I'm not just all talk. If I say I'm going to do something, I do it."

Legs

In a sport where great upper bodies are a dime a dozen, it's nice to see a bodybuilder who put as much effort into developing an outstanding set of wheels. In the case of Troy, the effort paid off as he displayed one of the best pair of legs on the bodybuilding scene in the early 1990s.

Troy takes a different approach than most bodybuilders to leg training. Instead of starting with the big, showy muscles like quads, he starts each leg workout with calves. This philosophy is no doubt one of the reasons why Troy was famous for his calves during his competitive days.

"The first time I saw Troy Zuccolotto in person was at Vodak Hawkin's Blocks Gym in Placentia, California. Zuke was riding a stationary bike. He was very quiet and nonflamboyant, dressed in a nonconspicuous T-shirt and spandex shorts. But what calves! Their astonishing size, thickness, and density were eye-boggling if not mind-boggling."

– Rosemary Hallum, former *MuscleMag International* contributor, commenting on the first time she saw Troy Zuccolotto's legs up close.

Troy takes a different approach than most bodybuilders to leg training. Instead of starting with the big, showy muscles like quads, he starts each leg workout with calves.

During a typical calf workout Troy would select two exercises and perform 4 to 5 sets of 15 to 20 reps. The next time he hit calves he would pick two different movements.

If he picked seated and standing calf raises, he would start with the seated version first. To get a full contraction he would go all the way up on the ball of his feet and then stretch all the way down. A typical workout would see him pyramid up to about 200 pounds and then work down the other side so to speak.

After seated calf raises it was on to standing calves. Given the greater strength potential in this exercise it's not surprising to hear that Troy worked up to over 500 pounds for reps. For variety he would then throw in a strip set or two. Then after every set he would stretch his calves for 10 to 20 seconds.

Another popular Zuccolotto calf combo was donkey raises and toe presses. During the late '80s and early '90s, Troy often worked out with top superstar, Shawn Ray, and the two were a fixture at Gold's Gym in Fullerton at the time. But donkey calf raises was one exercise where Troy relied on heavier beef to stress his calves. Troy usually picked on the heavier members in the gym, in most cases off-season heavyweight bodybuilders or football players. One tip Troy offers to readers is that to obtain the maximum benefit from your partner's weight, you should have them sit as close to your hips as possible. If they sit too far forward, the upper body torso muscles are doing much of the lifting. Not to mention the extra stress it's putting on your spinal column. After 4 or 5 sets to failure, Troy moves on to the toe press on the leg press machine.

This exercise is one of Troy's favorites as he can go really heavy, often up to 1000 pounds or more. Although kinesiologists say it doesn't make much difference, Troy likes to vary his foot position. On some sets he points the toes in, while on others he makes a V-stance and points them outward. As with his other calf exercises Troy usually does 4 to 5 sets of 15 to 20 reps.

After calves, Troy moves on to thighs, another muscle group he's got in abundance. He usually starts with leg extensions as a warmup. At one time he'd head straight for the squat rack, but a series of knee problems means he has to watch things these days. Instead of the usual 8 to 12 reps performed by most bodybuilders, Troy likes to do 3 to 4 sets of, get this, 50 reps! He's a firm believer in high reps for the legs.

Once he's satisfied his knees are fully warmed he hits the squat rack. Troy starts with a set of 30 reps using 135 pounds and then adds a 45-pound plate to each side with each successive set. He decreases the reps by five with each set until he's squeezing out 500 pounds for a set of 10.

To target different parts of his thighs, Troy alternates putting a block of wood under his feet on one day, and not the next. Troy's also a great believer in constant tension. He doesn't lock out at the top and pause for a second or two like some bodybuilders. Instead every rep is up and down in a piston-like motion.

Troy's positive outlook is his greatest strength.

Troy's third leg exercise is barbell lunges. He does 12 to 15 reps on each leg, starting with 135 and working up to no more than 185 pounds. For those who have never done this exercise before, Troy recommends starting with an empty bar or even a broomstick. The key to the entire exercise is balance and it makes far more sense to lose your balance with no weight on the shoulders than having 180 to 200 pounds across your back.

To finish off his thigh training, Troy goes back to the leg extension machine and does an additional 4 sets. This time around he goes a bit heavier, doing 30 reps on the first set and then going 20, 15, and 10 respectively.

Although Troy does hamstrings on a separate day, we'll discuss his routine here for convenience.

The mainstay of Troy's hamstring workout is lying leg curls. As with thighs he prefers doing slightly higher reps than most, usually in the 25 to 30 range. He does 5 to 6 sets going from 50 to 150 pounds. He noticed that since he switched to a higher rep scheme his hamstrings have become fuller with more separation.

Troy's second and final hamstring exercise is the stiff-leg deadlift. Troy usually performs this exercise while standing on a two-inch block of wood. Troy cautions that the name of this exercise is misleading as you should never perform this exercise completely stiff-legged. Always keep a slight bend at the knee to reduce the stress on the lower back. During a typical workout Troy will do 4 sets of stiff-legs going from 135 up to 225 pounds. He keeps the reps in the 15 range but it usually depends on how fatigued his hamstrings are from the lying leg curls.

Arms

When it comes to arms, Troy can be considered a certified instructor. His guns stretch the tape to over 21 inches, and that folks is in contest condition.

Troy always began his arm training with one or two light, warm-up sets before jumping in to the killer sets. He always went to

Troy always began his arm training with one or two light, warm-up sets before jumping in to the killer sets.

positive failure on every set, and pyramided up in weight. Then he'd drop the weight to the same as his starting weight. Typically Troy did three to four exercises for both biceps and triceps. The fourth set was optional, though, depending on how he felt. There are days when 9 sets will suffice to burn the muscles out. But on others he needed that fourth exercise to finish the job. Troy offers the following advice to beginners when it comes to arm training: "If you feel you need a little more then go for it, but remember that the arms are a relatively small muscle group and can be easily overtrained."

Here's a typical arm routine that helped Troy capture the prestigious 1989 US Nationals:

Biceps

1. Seated dumbell curls	3 sets of 7 to 10 reps
2. Preacher curls	3 sets of 7 to 10 reps
3. Cable curls	3 sets of 7 to 10 reps
4. Standing barbell curls	3 sets of 7 to 10 reps

Triceps

1. Cable pushdowns	3 sets of 7 to 10 reps
2. French curls	3 sets of 7 to 10 reps
3. Kickbacks	3 sets of 7 to 10 reps
4. Bar dips	3 sets of 7 to 10 reps

Shawn Ray

Shawn Irvin Ray is one of the top bodybuilders competing in the world today. With his almost flawless 210 pounds of proportioned muscle mass, he consistently beats opponents who outweigh him by 50 pounds or more.

Shawn's first major contest was the 1983 Teenage Orange Classic in California where he placed second at the age of 17. His first major win was the 1987 NPC Nationals. Shawn's early heroes were John Brown, Mike Christian, and Chris Dickerson. He admired John and Mike for their total devotion to the sport, especially at contest time. Dickerson was an obvious idol given their similar sizes and bone structures. When Chris won the 1982 Mr. Olympia, Shawn realized that a smaller refined bodybuilder could hold his own and even beat larger less proportioned competitors. By the early 1990s Shawn had established himself as one of the top five bodybuilders in the world; a distinction he holds to this day. Here's his impressive competitive record:

1984 Mr. Los Angeles – AAU, teen, 1st
1985 Teen Nationals – NPC, overall winner
1987 Nationals – NPC, overall winner
        Nationals – NPC, light heavyweight, 1st
1988 Night of Champions – IFBB, 4th
        Olympia – IFBB, 13th
1990 Arnold Classic – IFBB, disqualified
        Ironman Pro Invitational – IFBB, winner
        Olympia – IFBB, 3rd
1991 Arnold Classic – IFBB, winner
        Olympia – IFBB, 5th
1992 Olympia – IFBB, 4th
1993 Olympia – IFBB, 3rd
1994 Olympia – IFBB, 2nd
1996 Arnold Classic – IFBB, 5th
        Ironman Pro Invitational – IFBB, 3rd
        Olympia – IFBB, 2nd
1997 Olympia – IFBB, 3rd
1998 Olympia – IFBB, 5th
1999 Olympia – IFBB, 5th

Shawn Ray, together with such body-builders as Frank Zane, Lee Labrada, and Bob Paris, has developed one of the most perfectly balanced physiques in history.

Shoulders

Like most bodybuilders early in their careers, Shawn's initial goal was enlarging the size of his deltoids. As one old saying goes, you can't shape something you don't have!

These days Shawn has a different approach to shoulder training. He has most of the size he needs, so the emphasis is more on balance and symmetry, what shawn calls the finishing details. Shawn is a stickler for strict form and always relies on full range of motion for his exercises. He firmly believes his near-perfectly-balanced physique is the result of such training. He rarely does negative sets, cheat sets, or other advanced techniques becoming vogue these days.

Shawn is a stickler for strict form and always relies on full range of motion for his exercises.

One thing that may surprise many readers is that Shawn trains shoulders instinctively. When he walks into a gym he doesn't know the exact sets, reps, or sequence of exercises. He finds such training keeps him motivated and allows him to attack the muscle group from every conceivable angle, instead of becoming a creature of habit. Another advantage is that he can train by himself or work in with somebody else and follow his routine.

As Shawn is paying more attention to his side delts these days, he usually starts his shoulder workout with single arm cable laterals. He uses a medium to light weight and performs 3 sets of 20 reps in ultra-strict fashion.

After single arm lateral raises Shawn goes over to the dumbell rack and does 4 sets of 10 to 15 reps of standing dumbell laterals, pyramiding the weight up with each set. How heavy he goes depends on how strong he feels that particular day. He doesn't always opt for heavy weights. Instead he prefers to do higher repetitions in strict form. He rarely if ever goes below 10 reps.

Shawn's third delt exercise is seated bent-over laterals. He sits on the end of a bench and leans forward so that his face is almost touching his knees. He holds the dumbells parallel to the floor, and with his palms facing his cables raises straight out to the sides and up, being careful to squeeze the rear delts at the top.

> **"As I grew, and I fell out of football and into bodybuilding, I set out to make my shoulders as big and as wide as possible. I wasn't concerned with balance and symmetry in those days, just to get big – period."**
>
> – Shawn Ray, top bodybuilding pro, explaining his approach to shoulder training early in his career.

After bent-over laterals, Shawn moves on to seated presses behind-the-head. For variety Shawn alternates between the Smith machine and a regular barbell. Again he does 4 sets of 10 to 15 reps, pyramiding the weight with each set. He never goes below 10 reps, but occasionally throws in a drop or descending set.

To finish off his shoulder training Shawn does dumbell shrugs. He usually goes up to 120-pound dumbells, and this is one of the few exercises where he likes to use a set of straps to get a better grip. On a typical shoulder day, Shawn will perform 4 sets of 10 to 12 reps. Unlike most bodybuilders who hold the dumbells by their sides, Shawn holds them in front end to end as if he were holding a barbell.

For variety Shawn uses a number of different styles and techniques when training back.

"The only thing that's changed lately in my training is the order in which I do exercises. I'm not interchanging the order, and I'm not following any rules or any guidelines when it comes to what order they should be done in. A lot of people think that there's a certain order that you should stick to. I'll start with exercises that most people usually finish with."

– Shawn Ray, one of bodybuilding's greatest stars, commenting on exercise order.

There you have it, a shoulder routine from one of bodybuilding's greatest stars. Give it a try and watch your shoulders grow!

Back

Shawn often starts his back workout with one-arm dumbell rows – an exercise that most people leave toward the end of their routine. Shawn does one warm-up set, and then does 4 sets of 10 to 12 reps. For variety Shawn uses a number of different styles and techniques. The standard version is with one knee braced on a bench, but Shawn also does them standing up with his free hand supporting his weight. He finds he can get a better stretch this way, particularly when he lets the dumbell move forward slightly at the bottom.

Shawn's second exercise is also another so-called "finishing" movement, close-grip pull-ins. The movement consists of attaching a close-grip handle or rope to a lat pulldown machine. Instead of locking his knees under the pad of the pulldown machine, Shawn stands up with his knees slightly bent. He then grabs the handle or rope, locks his elbows into a 90-degree angle, and drags or pulls the weight down using only his lats. Rather than pull the handle or rope down with a rowing type movement, Shawn concentrates on pulling it down using an arcing motion. On a typical day Shawn will do 4 sets of 10 to 12 reps.

Shawn's third exercise is what most people start their back workouts with, lat pulldowns. To fully utilize the exercise's effectiveness, Shawn will alternate pulling to the front one day, and pulling behind the head the next. Unlike many who load up the machine and do partial reps, or worse use so much body momentum that the lats get little or nothing out of it, Shawn keeps his upper body stationary and performs each rep using full range of motion. Pulldowns are one exercise that Shawn finds higher reps more productive, usually in the 15 range.

For his fourth exercise, Shawn does seated cable rows, a movement Shawn feels that most people abuse. "People abuse this exercise and the abuse comes from using too much weight. This is an exercise that you don't need to use a whole lot of weight on to feel properly." Shawn performs seated rows in the style taught to him by 1982 Mr. Olympia, Chris Dickerson. The goal is to picture yourself rowing a boat. As you row back the goal is not so much to pull the shoulders back as stick or thrust the chest forward. Shawn has tried different pulling techniques over the years with pulling to the upper stomach/lower rib cage being the most productive.

At that point most bodybuilders would call it a back workout and either move on to another muscle group or leave the gym. But remember Shawn is after the complete package. Realizing that a well-developed lower back will not only earn you points on stage but also prevent injuries, Shawn concludes his back workout with a couple of exercises for his spinal erectors.

Shawn's two favorite lower back exercises are regular deadlifts and straight-leg deadlifts. Shawn feels both exercises don't get performed as often as they should, as they are very taxing. And let's face it, they don't build the big showy muscles. But if you hope to compete some day, you'll need great lower back development. If you don't believe us, check out pictures of Shawn, Dorian Yates, or Ronnie Coleman.

If Shawn is doing conventional deadlifts he'll do reps in the 10 to 12 range, but prefers slightly higher reps, say 15, on the straight-legs. In both cases he'll do four quality sets.

Sonny Schmidt, Shawn Ray and Lee Labrada.

Legs

In this age of 1000-pound squats and 2000-pound leg presses, it's refreshing to read about a bodybuilder who stays true to the fundamental principles of the sport, using weights to train the muscles and not the ego. Shawn Ray is one such individual and together with such body-builders as Frank Zane, Lee Labrada, and Bob Paris, has developed one of the most perfectly balanced physiques in history.

It may surprise many to learn that Shawn's favorite leg exercise is not squats or leg presses. No, Mr. Ray considers himself king of the lunge. It's not that he doesn't do squats or leg presses, he does. But Shawn feels lunges are the one movement that has done the most to add contest-winning detail to his thighs.

Shawn usually begins his leg workout with 3 sets of medium-weight leg extensions to warm up the thighs. He keeps the reps in the 20 to 25 range.

Next up it's his much-loved lunges. Shawn feels that this one exercise not only adds mass to his thighs, but adds separation between the four quad heads as well. In addition he considers them tops for bringing out the separation between his thighs and hamstrings.

Shawn normally does 5 sets of about 20 reps on lunge, but sometimes he'll add in drop sets and go up to 50 reps a set.

After lunges, as if his thighs needed it, Shawn moves on to squats. He'll alternate between front and rear squats depending on the time of the season. With back squats he can go heavier so he utilizes them during the off-season. As front squats are more of an isolation movement he'll do them in the months leading up to a contest. Again technique and quality plays a more important role than weight. Shawn uses a moderate weight and keeps the reps in the 15 to 20 range and does 4 or 5 sets. He uses a medium shoulder-width stance and makes a slight V with his feet. As he's not into partial reps, Shawn squats all the way down until his ass is nearly touching the floor.

Shawn Ray considers himself king of the lunge.

To finish off his quads, Shawn will do three breakdown sets of leg extensions. he'll do 200 pounds for 10 reps, 150 for 10, and finally 100 pounds for 10 reps. He repeats this three times.

After a short rest and time to grab a few gulps of water, Shawn begins his hamstring training. He starts with stiff-leg deadlifts, and we mean stiff-leg. Shawn is one of the few bodybuilders who takes the name to heart. Unlike most, he doesn't keep any bend in the knees. His legs are locked out straight. For an extra stretch he stands on a block and keeps his feet shoulder width apart. Typically he'll do 5 sets of 15 to 20 reps.

Shawn's chest training is very instinctive. He doesn't follow any set routine.

To finish off his hamstrings Shawn does 6 sets of lying leg curls. The first 4 sets are straight sets for 15 reps, but the last two are done in drop-set fashion.

The previous is a typical Shawn Ray precontest workout. During the off-season he keeps things a bit more basic, doing 4 sets of 12 to 15 reps of leg presses, squats, and leg extensions. For hamstrings he'll alternate lying leg curls with stiff-leg deadlifts.

Chest

By his own words, Shawn's chest training is very instinctive. He doesn't follow any set routine, and on any given day will pick four exercises and do 4 or 5 sets of each. Usually it's one warmup and 3 solid sets of 8 to 12 reps.

After witnessing the upper pec development of 1983 Mr. Olympia, Samir Bannout, Shawn decided to make incline work a priority in his training. So even though he constantly changes around the exercises, he tries to start his chest workout with some sort of incline movement.

A typical Shawn Ray workout will begin with incline dumbell presses. Shawn varies the angle between 25 and 45 degrees to hit different parts of his upper chest. He rarely does drop, negative, or forced reps, preferring to do 4 straight sets of 8 to 12 reps.

After incline dumbell presses, Shawn likes to move on to flat dumbell flyes. To use his own words, "I try to picture that I'm hugging a fat lady." While the analogy may not appeal to most, it works for Shawn and forces him to do flyes in the proper, arcing type motion. With a slight bend at the elbows Shawn lowers the dumbells down until his upper arms are slightly below parallel with the floor. He then presses up and inward until the dumbells are just short of touching at the top.

For his third exercise, Shawn may do flat barbell presses. Like all his exercises, Shawn does flat barbell presses with a smooth, fluid like motion. He refuses to bounce the bar off his chest just to lift a few extra pounds. Once again it's four good sets of 8 to 12 reps.

To finish off his chest, Shawn likes to do weighted dips. To keep the stress more on the chest than triceps, Shawn performs dips with his elbows out wide and his chin on his chest. He also does slightly higher reps on this exercise, going for quality 12 to 15 per set.

As we said at the beginning, Shawn likes to constantly vary things. The next day he may start with barbell inclines, move on to dumbell inclines, and then finish with barbell presses and cable crossovers.

Shawn's approach to training has resulted in one of the greatest physiques currently on the bodybuilding scene. Over the past decade he has placed in the top five in just about every

Shawn usually trains biceps before triceps as he found over the years his triceps responded much faster to training than his biceps.

contest he's entered. And we are talking about dozens of shows here. Shawn is a threat to win every contest he enters, and many feel it's only a matter of time before the Mr. Olympia is his.

Arms

Given Shawn's attention to detail, it's not surprising he has two of the most pro-portioned arms on tour. No, they'll never be 23 inches. Shawn doesn't have the height or bone structure to carry such mass. On the other hand his 20-inchers look darn big on his 5'7" frame. And when it comes to balance, many of those bigger-armed bodybuilders out there can't hold a can-dle to this former Arnold Classic winner.

Shawn usually trains biceps before triceps as he found over the years his triceps responded much faster to training than his biceps. He also hits both muscles twice a week, alternating a heavy and light workout.

On his heavy day, one of the exercises he'll do is standing preacher curls. Shawn prefers the standing position as it allows him to add in a bit of body momentum toward the end of the set. He also uses a medium grip as when he goes wide it affects his wrists. On a typical day Shawn will do 4 sets of 8 to 10 reps.

One technique Shawn utilizes in his training is visualization. When training legs, he visualizes Tom Platz's legs. If it's shoulders, Mike Christian becomes the focus. And it's not surprising that when Shawn trains biceps, Arnold's monstrous hams come to mind.

After preacher curls, Shawn moves on to standing alternate dumbell curls. He'll go from 45- to 70-pound dumbells on this exercise, doing 4 sets of 8 to 10 reps. Like many bodybuilders, Shawn supinates his wrists on the way up. He also completes one full rep with each arm before switching. This is slightly different than most bodybuilders who have both arms moving at the same time, in a one up, one down, type motion.

To finish off his biceps on heavy day, Shawn pounds out 4 sets of standing barbell curls. As his biceps are reaching fatigue at this point, Shawn only needs to put 110-120 pounds on the bar to get the results he wants.

For triceps, Shawn usually starts with reclining extensions using an EZ-curl bar. He does one set as a warmup, and then 4 heavy sets of 8 to 10 reps. Typical weight for Shawn will be three or four quarters on each side of the bar (180 to 220 pounds). He lowers the bar to his forehead, and then extends to straight above his eyes.

After EZ-bar extensions, Shawn moves on to dumbell kickbacks. This is sort of Shawn's equivalent of lunges. As we mentioned earlier, Shawn swears by lunges for his legs even though most bodybuilders skip them. The same is true about dumbell kickbacks. Most bodybuilders either avoid them, or throw them in a few months before a contest. But Shawn finds they're great for bringing out the all-important horseshoe look of the triceps. Once he gets the arm to the locked-out position, he flexes as hard as he can, pretending he's onstage. As with most of his exercises, Shawn will add in a tiny bit of body momentum for the last couple of reps. He does 4 sets of 8 to 10 reps.

To finish off his triceps, Shawn moves on to what he considers the best overall triceps exercise, pushdowns. He alternates between a straight bar and rope to vary the angle of attack so to speak. Again it's 4 sets of 8 to 10 reps.

You will notice from looking at Shawn's two routines that he finishes off with two exercises that most bodybuilders start with, barbell curls and triceps pushdowns. But Shawn's not one for conformity. After nearly 20 years of training, Shawn has discovered by trial and error what works best for him. It's a piece of advice that he feels all bodybuilders should heed.

Over the past decade Shawn has placed in the top five in just about every contest he's entered. Shawn is a threat to win every contest he enters, and many feel it's only a matter of time before the Mr. Olympia is his.

Selwyn Cotterill

Although he only competed for five years or so, England's Selwyn Cotterill helped usher in the 250-plus pound club that became the norm in the 1990s. Standing 6'2" and weighing 255 pounds in contest shape (280 in the off-season), Selwyn was one of the more imposing bodybuilders during the later '80s and early '90s.

Selwyn Cotterill was cast in the move *Over the Top*.

Selwyn took up weight training as a way to increase his power in boxing. Initially he only half-heartedly hoisted the iron, but upon the death of his mother, he turned to weight lifting as an outlet.

Besides his brief bodybuilding career, Selwyn was an accomplished arm wrestler and won the open class at the British Championships. The win qualified him for the World Championships in Las Vegas where Sylvester Stallone just happened to be in town recruiting for his movie *Over the Top*. Selwyn's physique immediately caught Rambo's eye, and before he knew it, was cast in the movie.

Here's Selwyns short but impressive career:

1985   World Games – IFBB, heavyweight, 6th
1986   European Amateur Championships – IFBB, heavyweight, 7th
1988   Grand Prix England – IFBB, 12th
1989   Niagara Falls Pro Invitational – IFBB, 6th
        Night of Champions – IFBB, 12th
1990   Grand Prix England – IFBB, 4th
        Grand Prix Holland – IFBB, 5th
1991   Arnold Classic – IFBB, 12th
        Ironman Pro Invitational – IFBB, 11th
        Ironman Pro Invitational – IFBB, 12th
        Musclefest Grand Prix – IFBB, 8th
        Pittsburgh Pro Invitational – IFBB, 8th
1992   Grand Prix England – IFBB, 10th
        Grand Prix Germany – IFBB, 13th
1993   Grand Prix France – IFBB, 12th
        Grand Prix France – IFBB, 13th
        Grand Prix Germany (2) – IFBB, 10th
        Grand Prix Germany – IFBB, 16th
        San Jose Pro Invitational – IFBB, 12th

Back

Selwyn is the first to acknowledge that his back has always been one of the easiest muscles to develop. In fact, as many readers will be sickened to hear, he often limits his back training to once a week to keep it from growing out of proportion with the rest of his physique.

A typical session will see Selwyn doing 4 sets 8 to 12 reps of four different exercises. For variety he likes to vary the order around so that the muscles don't become stale. As might be expected he is careful to perform each exercise in a strict, rhythmic style. The following are Selwyn's five favorite back exercises. He usually chooses four to make up a given back workout.

1) Lat Pulldowns – Selwyn alternates front pulldowns with pulldowns behind the head. He finds the behind the head version better for hitting the upper lats and rhomboids, while the front pulldown emphasizes the lower lats. Selwyn starts lat pulldowns with his arms in the fully stretched out position and pulls down until the bar is touching either his collarbone or base of the neck.

"I turned to find the colossal heavyweight looming over me, blocking out the sun's rays. My squint-eyed gaze scanned the Cotterill silhouette; giant traps exploded from his neck to merge with coconut-like delts bulging from his T-shirt."

– Peter McGough, *MuscleMag International* contributor, giving his first impressions of one of the sport's true giants, England's 280-pound Selwyn Cotterill.

2) T-Bar Rows – Selwyn prefers T-bar rows to the standard barbell row. After grabbing the handles Selwyn sets his torso just short of parallel with the floor. He then pulls upward until the plates touch his chest. he then slowly lowers until his arms are in the starting, locked-out position. One mistake Selwyn frequently sees in the gym is guys loading so much weight on the bar that they need to swing the upper body up and down to keep it moving. If you can't move the weight with your lats and arms, forget it he says. Not only are you wasting your time but also you are running the risk of doing some serious lower back damage.

3) Seated Pulley Rowing – Another Selwyn favorite, seated rows allow him to give his lats a great stretch. In the seated position he grabs the handles and with the legs slightly bent, leans forward until he can feel the stretch in his lats. He then starts pulling the handles toward his lower rib cage

Selwyn is the first to acknowledge that his back has always been one of the easiest muscles to develop.

and at the same time brings his torso perpendicular to the floor. As the handles start nearing his rib cage, Selwyn arches his chest and squeezes his shoulder blades together. After a split second pause he leans forward until his arms are in the stretched out position.

4) Straight-Arm Push Downs – Selwyn finds this exercise great for isolating the upper lats, and he often uses it first in his program to pre-exhaust the lats. For those not familiar with the exercise, stand in front of a pulldown or triceps machine and grab the bar with a shoulder-width grip. With the arms held slightly above the head, step back until the plates you are lifting are one or two inches above the stationary plates. Slowly push down until the bar reaches the thighs (or the plates hit the top of the column). Slowly raise to the starting position. Be sure to keep the arms locked straight at all times. You'll discover that the body tries to cheat by bending the arms and bringing the triceps into play.

5) Chins – No matter what routine Selwyn follows for his back, he always incorporates some form of chinups. Selwyn's favorite grip is the narrow V-bar handle, but he will throw in wide and reverse grip for variety. No matter what the version, he stretches completely out at the bottom and arches his chest and squeezes the shoulder blades together at the top.

Although he didn't make a huge impact on the pro scene, Selwyn was always one of the bigger, more popular bodybuilders on stage during the early 1990s. And at the heart of his physique was one of the best backs in the business.

Chest

There are a number of bodybuilders who upon starting their chest workouts, seem to cause many gym members to stop their own workouts and have a good look. First to come to mind are Arnold, Lou Ferrigno, Lee Haney, and Ronnie Coleman. All four are famous not only for their chest development but their overall size. Another bodybuilder who tended to make the "colonists" sit up and take notice was British and European champion, Selwyn Cotterill. Even though he didn't win any major shows in his career, his workouts in gyms in Europe and North America during the early and mid 1990s, tended to draw a few stares and gasps.

With all the power and grace of a Nimitz-class aircraft carrier at flank speed, Selwyn hoisted some pretty incredible weight during his chest workouts. His first exercise was usually the barbell incline press. He did 5 sets of 6 to 10 reps, going from, are you ready, 205 up to 500 pounds. To keep his body from moving, Selwyn

Selwyn hoisted some pretty incredible weight during his chest workouts.

kept his feet wide apart. The barbell would move up and down in a rthymic manner, and he'd lower it to just below his collarbone.

Selwyn's second exercise was usually incline dumbell flyes. He called them "arch" flyes as he kept a slight arch in his back to maximize chest stimulation and minimize shoulder involvement. As expected Selwyn used some frightening weights on this exercise, going from 90s up to 150s. Again he did 4 sets of 6 to 10 reps.

For his third exercise Selwyn moved on to decline barbell presses. Unlike most that bring the weight down to the lower chest, Selwyn preferred to lower it to the mid-chest. He found by doing so he could bring in some of the upper chest muscle fibers as well. With a slight arch in his back Selwyn did 4 sets of 6 to 10 reps, going from 300 to 450 pounds.

To finish off those slabs of meat that Selwyn called his chest muscles, he would do 4 sets of cable crossovers. He would do 2 sets standing directly in between the machine's uprights, and then 2 additional sets standing about six inches in front of it. As with every other chest exercise, Selwyn didn't wimp out on this one either and he routinely put the stack (200 pounds at the gym he usually trained at) on for sets of 10.

Gunter Schlierkamp

Perhaps it was Gunter's strict, traditional upbringing that helped prepare him for the sport that has become his lifelong passion.

Few pros can match the awesome size and shape of Germany's Gunter Schlierkamp. The gentle giant (6'1", 285 pounds) is a true champions in anyone's book! He has had to work incredibly hard for all that he has achieved in his life, and bodybuilding has been no exception. Perhaps it was Gunter's strict, traditional upbringing that helped prepare him for the sport that has become his lifelong passion.

Gunter was born in the village of Olfen, in Nordrhein-Westfalen, Germany. Growing up on a farm, Gunter led an idyllic childhood. His father was not interested in his children becoming educated. He wanted to see his children go to work, earn money and become independent. Yet Gunter found himself drawn in a different direction.

"At 16 I was not happy with the way I looked, so I decided to take up weight training. I was muscular and strong, but I wasn't happy with my shape. I worked as a machinist in a factory at the time. After a few months of training and seeing how quickly I got results, I began to take bodybuilding seriously and within a few years I felt ready to compete."

He was right!

1990   German Championships – overall winner
        German Championships – junior, tall, 1st

1992   European Amateur Championships – IFBB, heavyweight, 1st
        German Championships – heavyweight, 1st

1993   World Amateur Championships – IFBB, heavyweight, 1st

1994   Grand Prix England – IFBB, 8th
        Grand Prix Germany – IFBB, 8th
        Olympia – IFBB, 19th

1995   Canada Pro Cup – IFBB, 2nd
        Grand Prix Ukraine – IFBB, 10th

1996   Arnold Classic – IFBB, 11th
        Night of Champions – IFBB, 11th
        San Jose Pro Invitational – IFBB, 9th

1997   Canada Pro Cup – IFBB, 6th
        Ironman Pro Invitational – IFBB, disqualified
        Night of Champions – IFBB, 9th
        San Jose Pro Invitational – IFBB, 11th

1998   Grand Prix Finland – IFBB, 6th
        Grand Prix Germany – IFBB, 6th
        Night of Champions – IFBB, 10th
        Olympia – IFBB
        San Francisco Pro Invitational – IFBB, 9th
        Toronto Pro Invitational – IFBB, 6th

1999   Arnold Classic – IFBB, 9th
        Ironman Pro Invitational – IFBB, 5th

2000   Arnold Classic – IFBB, 6th
        Ironman Pro Invitational – IFBB, 4th

**Train hard and stay hungry.
– Gunter Schlierkamp**

And the last word goes to Gunter: "Train hard and stay hungry. You will see me on stage for many years because I won't stop until I win the Mr. Olympia crown – and I will never give up. Finally, a sincere thank you to all my fans. I couldn't do it without you."

Shoulders

Standing 6'1" and weighing a solid 275 to 280 in contest shape, Gunter is easily one of the largest competitors in any bodybuilding contest he enters. And while never quite cracking the top six in the world rankings, nevertheless he's a standout in any line up with his shoulder width.

Gunter's shoulder routine consists of five exercises that hit the delts from all angles. Typically Gunter does 3 sets per exercise increasing the weight and decreasing the reps with each successive set. In his contest preparations Gunter trains with high reps using moderate weight. In the off-season he goes lower volume using heavy weight for fewer reps. Normally he does 3 sets per exercise with reps in the 8 to 12 range. In the precontest season he'll do the first sets for 15 reps, followed by one set of 10 to 12 reps, and one set of 6 to 8 reps.

Standing 6'1" and weighing a solid 275 to 280 in contest shape, Gunter is easily one of the largest competitors in any bodybuilding contest he enters.

We should add that Gunter is a firm believer in thoroughly warming up the shoulder region. He's seen too many shoulder injuries over the years from bodybuilders jumping right into heavy training. The following are Gunter's favorite shoulder exercises.

1. Seated presses behind the head – Gunter uses this old standby to hit his front and side heads. He warms up with 135 pounds for 20 reps, and then increases and decreases the weight in the following manner: 205, 255, 255, and 205. Given the susceptibility of the small rotator complex to injury, Gunter does behind-the-head presses in ultra slow and strict style. You may get away with sloppiness on dumbell laterals, but not barbell pressing movements.

2. Upright rows – To hit the front and side delts and to bring in the traps, Gunter does 3 sets of upright rows. He starts with 95 pounds for 15 reps, and works up to 135 for a set of 10. Gunter prefers the barbell to dumbells and cables on this exercise. This is another exercise that Gunter feels must be performed in good style.

3. Seated dumbell presses – To hit the front and side delts a tad harder, Gunter does 3 sets of seated dumbell presses. He finds by using dumbells he can get a greater range of motion; something that works the muscle better, but should not be attempted until the muscles are fully warmed up. That's why he does them third in his routine after barbell presses and upright rows. During a typical workout Gunter will go from 100- to 140-pound dumbells on this exercise.

4. Front cable raises – To finish off his front delts, Gunter grabs a low pulley handle in one hand and raises it forward and across in front of his body to shoulder height. He'll usually start with 40 pounds for a set of 15 reps and work up to 100 pounds for a set of 6 to 8 reps.

5. Seated bent-over laterals – Not one to neglect his rear delts, Gunter finishes off shoulders with 3 sets of seated bent-over laterals. He prefers sitting as despite his best intentions, seems to swing and cheat slightly while standing. Others may derive something out of cheating, but not Gunter. Everything is by the book.

Dorian continues
to perplex fans
with his amazingly
quiet manner.

Dorian Yates – The Shadow

Dorian Yates was born in a small village called Hurley in Staffordshire, just outside of Birmingham, England on April 19, 1962. Life should have been easy, but it wasn't. At the age of 13 his father died, and times were hard. Dorian began to run with a rough crowd:

"… It's more like a youth culture thing. When I was a teenager, skinheads and mods were popular. Our gangs were more about codes of dress, not like organized killing with people shooting each other over territory… I was a skinhead. I had a shaven head, skinhead clothes, steel-toed boots, all the gear. It was a cultural statement. Over here skinhead means racist. Over there it's about fashion and doesn't have anything to do with race … We'd go to clubs and pubs where everyone would meet. The place would be full of punk rockers and skinheads. There were not many places we could get in because we were bad for business, so we'd go to certain hangouts – places where everyone like us would congregate – and then maybe there'd be a party with some gig with the groups. My social life was concentrated around all that. At other times I was on my own a lot."

"I guess loneliness is why people get into gangs. They become like a family. I think it's the same reason kids get into gangs in the US. Kids have no father and no family background that teaches them how to conduct themselves. They have no support, so they drift and are open to anything where they feel they'll have a sense of belonging."

"Everyone asks me what sort of person he is because he seems so cryptic. I always tell them that he's actually very funny. Dorian has a really dry sense of humor. He'll make a joke and he doesn't laugh. He just sits there stone-faced while everyone else laughs. I like him because he's a gentleman. He's a good champion. He doesn't criticize anyone. I think that when you're a champion you don't need to do that."

– Paul Dillett, describing Dorian Yates.

At the age of 19, Dorian was arrested and sent to a detention center. He was taught a trade and given the opportunity to try powerlifting. It was while powerlifting that the bodybuilding bug bit. Within six years he went from a seventh at the World Amateur Games to winning the New York Night of Champions. His placing second to Lee Haney at the 1991 Mr. Olympia was just a hint of things to come. Starting in 1992 and continuing for the next six years, Dorian was the undisputed top bodybuilder in the word. Here's his incredible competitive record:

Dorian Yates

1985   World Games – IFBB, heavyweight, 7th
1990   Night of Champions – IFBB, 2nd
1991   Grand Prix England – IFBB, winner
         Night of Champions – IFBB, winner
         Olympia – IFBB, 2nd
1992   Grand Prix England – IFBB, winner
         Olympia – IFBB, winner
1993   Olympia – IFBB, winner
1994   Grand Prix England – IFBB, winner
         Grand Prix Germany – IFBB, winner
         Grand Prix Spain – IFBB, winner
         Olympia – IFBB, winner
1995   Olympia – IFBB, winner
1996   Grand Prix England – IFBB, winner
         Grand Prix Germany – IFBB, winner
         Grand Prix Spain – IFBB, winner
         Olympia – IFBB, winner
1997   Olympia – IFBB, winner

Dorian continues to perplex fans with his amazingly quiet manner. Perhaps we're too used to bodybuilders venting in magazine interviews, but Dorian maintains a uniquely British stoicism.

"Well, I think I'm almost a contradiction – different from a lot of the guys. The general public perception of bodybuilding is that it is an egotistical, narcissistic sport. Maybe it is, but I never approached it from that point of view. I felt very proud when I was on the stage at the Olympia competing in front of people who understood what it took for me to get there, and what I'd been able to achieve. I was never into trying to get people's adulation. I never walked around in a tank top and never wanted people to notice me or adore me. I didn't ever build my body for that reason. I did it for myself ... A lot of people have been critical of my nonarrogant approach. I know that Americans are accustomed to equating superior athletic ability with a kind of ultra confident, borderline-arrogant personality, but I'm not like that."

But how did he get his nickname, the Shadow?

"He (Peter McGough) gave me that name just before I won the novice competition. There was a lot of talk about this guy from Birmingham who was pretty good. No one had ever seen me before, so in their eyes I just materialized and won. Then I disappeared again back into my own world. I'd do that ... show up, compete, and then disappear. Shadows come and go. They're there one moment and then gone. Peter was interested in this side of my character, so he named me the Shadow because I was seldom seen."

Although retired from competition, Dorian has dived headfirst into the supplement field. If he approaches this latest endeavor with the same zest he had for bodybuilding, rest assured we'll be seeing the Shadow for many years to come!

Chest

Besides his incredible physique, Dorian Yates set the tone for training techniques in the 1990s. Being heavily influenced by the writings of Dr. Arthur Jones and Mike Mentzer, you wouldn't find Dorian spending three hours in the gym doing 25 to 30 sets per bodypart. No, the "Shadow" usually picked two exercises for a muscle group, and did just 4 to 6 sets total. While not adhering to Heavy Duty in the classical sense (one set to failure), nevertheless Dorian was a firm believer that most bodybuilders are overtrained from doing too many low intensity sets. To illustrate his approach, let's use chest training as an example.

> **"Although my arms and calves responded fairly quickly when I first started training, my chest was pitifully weak with no pec muscle to speak of at all. I used to dream of having massive bulbous pecs like those of Arnold."**
>
> – Dorian Yates, Six-time Mr. Olympia commenting on how like many beginner bodybuilders, he used Arnold as an early form of inspiration.

Dorian typically started his chest training with a couple of light dumbell exercises just to warm up the shoulder joint. He then picked a basic exercise to hit the lower and outer chest. On most days it would be flat barbell presses or decline barbell presses. Dorian would then do 2 to 3 light warm-up sets to prepare the chest and shoulders for his workout sets. Where most bodybuilders do 4, 5, even 10 sets of bench presses, Dorian did just 2 all-out sets to failure, for reps in the 5 to 8 range. And that was it. No depleting the recovery reserves with lighter rep out sets.

After his flat or decline presses, Dorian would attack the upper chest with incline barbell presses. As his chest was fully warmed up by now from the flats, Dorian went right into the incline for 2 heavy sets of 5 to 8 reps. Again no lighter rep out sets at the end.

To finish his chest Dorian usually did flat or slightly inclined (about 20 degrees) dumbell flyes. As this was his last chest exercise, Dorian would sometimes

For those not getting any results from their training, try cutting your routine in half, and then see what happens.
– Dorian Yates

do a drop set after initially doing 8 to 10 reps to failure. Once more Dorian only did 2 sets of this exercise.

There you have it, the total chest workout of one of bodybuilding's greatest stars. We are going to leave the final word to Dorian: "For those not getting any results from their training, try cutting your routine in half, and then see what happens."

Dorian trains all three leg muscles during the same workout.

Legs (Thighs)

It was shortly before winning his third Mr. Olympia, that the rumors started circulating about how Dorian had abandoned his patented high-intensity style of training in favor of the traditional high-volume style. It didn't take the "working-class Brit" long to respond that such rumors were utter rubbish. It was true a couple of injuries forced him to modify his training, but 20 sets per bodypart, forget it!

Dorian's leg training is a perfect example to illustrate how he modified his training. Dorian trains all three leg muscles during the same workout. For those that claim this is too much muscle mass to train during the same workout, Dorian responds that his routine is so brief that he's in and out of the gym in under an hour. You won't catch him hanging around for hours doing endless sets and reps. Get in, get it done, get out, that's his motto.

Dorian starts leg training with 3 sets of leg extensions. This exercise not only pre-exhausts the thighs, but also warms up the legs for the heavier movements to come. He does the first set light for 12 to 15 smooth reps. The second is medium-intense for 10 to 12 reps. Finally he finishes off with one all-out set to failure for 8 to 10 reps.

In the past Dorian would go as heavy as possible on each of these sets using a loose sort of style. But those injuries we mentioned earlier forced him to lower the weight slightly and do things in a much slower manner.

After leg extensions Dorian moves on to either leg presses or Smith Machine squats. If he starts with leg presses, he'll do 2 medium intensity sets for 12 to 15 reps, and then one balls-to-the-wall set for the same number of reps.

If he chooses squats, he'll use a fairly narrow stance to maximize thigh involvement and reduce butt involvement. He'll also keep his feet forward a tad to reduce the stress on his knees. As with leg presses it's 2 medium and 1 heavy set of squats for 12 to 15 reps.

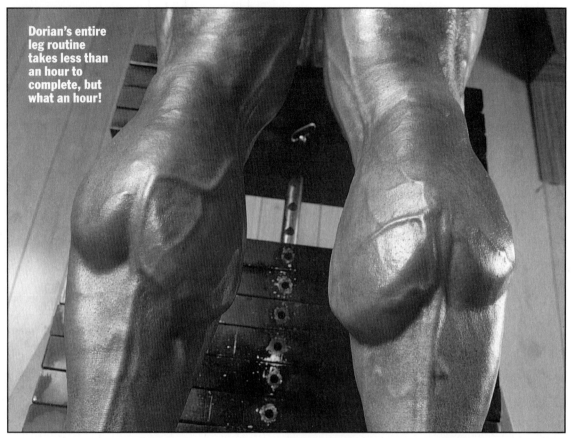

Dorian's entire leg routine takes less than an hour to complete, but what an hour!

Dorian usually finishes off his thigh training with hack squats. As his thighs are nearly wasted by this point, he does just 1 heavy set, keeping the reps in the 12 to 15 range. To minimize the stress on his knees, Dorian keeps his feet medium wide and points his feet outward.

Hamstrings

To compliment his massive thighs, Dorian gives equal attention to his hamstrings. He starts with 2 sets of lying leg curls, doing the first set as a warm up for 12 to 15 reps, and the second set using as much weight as he can handle for 10 to 12 reps.

Dorian's second hamstring exercise is the stiff-leg deadlift. Dorian points out that if you perform deadlifts properly there shouldn't be much stress on the lower back. The big mistake most bodybuilders make is to go all the way down to the toes. This forces you to round the lower back, putting tremendous pressure on the spinal column. Dorian bends forward until his torso is just short of parallel with the floor. He does 1 set of 10 to 12 reps.

Calves

Dorian's calf routine is as simple as it is effective. He starts with one medium-weight set of standing calf raises for 12 to 15 reps, and then does one all-out set for 12 reps to absolute positive failure. With his gastrocnemius exercise out of the way, Dorian moves on to seated calf raises to hit the soleus or lower part of the calf. Again it's one medium and one heavy set.

Dorian's entire leg routine takes less than an hour to complete, but what an hour! For those who wonder about Dorian's training intensity, just check out his video, *Blood and Guts*. If that doesn't get the training juices flowing you're clinically dead!

Thierry Pastel

Thierry Pastel was born on the French island of Martinique in the West Indies and moved to France when he was 24. Thierry was lucky in that early in his career he obtained the advice of bodybuilding great, Serge Nubret.

Thierry's first major win was the WABBA World Championships in 1984. He won numerous titles with the WABBA before switching to the IFBB in 1989. Despite being outweighed by 50 pounds or more by most competitors, Thierry established a reputation as one of the best "pound for pound" bodybuilders in the world. With two of the largest arms of any bodybuilder competing, and a midsection to match, Thierry won the Holland Grand Prix in 1990. Here's his record:

1984   World Championships – WABBA, winner
1985   World Championships – WABBA, professional, 4th
1986   Universe – Pro, NABBA, 4th
          World Championships – WABBA, professional, 1st
          World Championships – WABBA, professional, 4th

Thierry established a reputation as one of the best "pound for pound" bodybuilders in the world.

1989   Grand Prix England – IFBB, 5th
          Grand Prix France – IFBB, 5th
          Grand Prix Germany – IFBB, 7th
          Grand Prix Holland – IFBB, 8th
          Grand Prix Spain (2) – IFBB, 7th
          Grand Prix Spain – IFBB, 7th
          Grand Prix Sweden – IFBB, 6th
1990   Grand Prix France – IFBB, 3rd
          Grand Prix Holland – IFBB, winner
          Night of Champions – IFBB, 9th
1991   Arnold Classic – IFBB, 5th
          Grand Prix Denmark – IFBB, 4th
          Grand Prix England – IFBB, 6th
          Grand Prix Finland – IFBB, 3rd
          Grand Prix Italy – IFBB, 4th
          Grand Prix Spain – IFBB, 4th
          Grand Prix Switzerland – IFBB, 3rd
          Ironman Pro Invitational – IFBB, 4th
          Musclefest Grand Prix – IFBB, 2nd
          Night of Champions – IFBB, 4th
          Olympia – IFBB, 8th
          Pittsburgh Pro Invitational – IFBB, 3rd
1992   Arnold Classic – IFBB, 6th
          Chicago Pro Invitational – IFBB, 2nd
          Grand Prix England – IFBB, 6th
          Grand Prix Germany – IFBB, 6th
          Grand Prix Holland – IFBB, 3rd
          Grand Prix Italy – IFBB, 6th
          Ironman Pro Invitational – IFBB, 4th
          Night of Champions – IFBB, 4th
          Olympia – IFBB, 10th
          Pittsburgh Pro Invitational – IFBB, 3rd

Shoulders

It's not surprising that someone who trained under the guidance of the great French body-builder, Serge Nubret, could at times be a tad unorthodox in his training. Serge was known to frequently go off the main path himself. But as Thierry explains, "My body talks to me and tells me what I need to do."

During his heyday in the early to mid '90s, Thierry was known as one of those "pound for pound" type of guys. The phrase first originated with boxing great, Sugar Ray Robinson, and refers to smaller competitors who were so great that if they were scaled up to the heavyweight class, they would easily win. Thierry was one such bodybuilder. Despite his rather diminutive height (about 5'2"), Thierry was proportionally one of the biggest bodybuilders competing, much the same as Lee Priest is now. In particular Thierry's arms and shoulders easily rivaled those of the taller bodybuilders.

Although he did almost any combination of shoulder exercises known to man during his workouts, all were variations of two basic movements: presses and dumbell raises. By pressing at different angles, or raising dumbells in different directions, Thierry could hit any part of his delts he wanted.

Although Thierry did almost any combination of shoulder exercises during his workouts, all were variations of two basic movements: presses and dumbell raises.

"Concentration is the most important thing – to think about the muscle, and to do the exercise without cheating. If you use your mind you can shape the body any way that you want."

– Thierry Pastel, French bodybuilder, commenting on the importance of the mind to bodybuilding success.

Using that great instinct we mentioned earlier, Thierry would start his routine with exercises to hit the part of the shoulders he felt needed more work. For example if he felt front delts needed extra work, he would start with seated dumbell presses. Occasionally he would substitute a barbell, but he found the greater range of motion allowed by the dumbells did more for his front delts. With regard to reps and sets, Thierry comes from the old school of high volume. For most exercises he did 5 or 6 sets of 12 to 20 reps. Again this is different than most bodybuilders who usually keep the reps under 12, but Thierry found that the higher reps with moderate weight seemed to offer the most muscle stimulation.

After front delts, Thierry moved on to side shoulders. Once again Thierry did things slightly different. Most bodybuilders do side laterals while standing, and add a little body momentum to keep the weight moving. Thierry preferred to do them while seated and without so much as a degree of body swing "your muscles have to do the movement, not gravity and momentum."

Thierry Pastel, owner of one of the greatest sets of abs in bodybuilding history.

Even though he was partial to dumbells, Thierry liked to do bent-over cable laterals for his rear delts. He found that cables allowed much the same degree of freedom of dumbells without the restrictions of most machines.

Although he did seated presses to hit his front delts, Thierry usually added a second exercise to target the front shoulders. In most cases it was front lateral raises. As expected Thierry had his own variation to this exercise. Where most bodybuilders raise their arm parallel to the floor and stop, Thierry would raise the dumbells right over his head until nearly vertical with the floor.

For his traps, Thierry was blessed with good old genetics. He rarely did any direct trap exercises. He found his traps grew from his pressing and lateral movements. Occasionally he added in upright rows, but for the most part, Thierry's traps were like some bodybuilder's forearms or calves, they grew by merely looking at a weight!

Abdominals

Unlike the costume that came complete with abs used by the various actors who portrayed Batman, Thierry Pastel's abs are very real. In fact to most who witness them for the first time, the term unreal comes to mind. What made Thierry's abs the best onstage during the early 1990s was a genetic abnormality that gave him that very elusive fourth row of abs just below his chest.

Aside from his all-important diet, Thierry trained abs just like every other muscle group – hard! A typical ab workout lasted at least 45 minutes, but Thierry often relied on the mirror to determine how long to train a particular muscle. On some days 10 sets might suffice, while on others his body tells him to do 60.

Thierry generally does four ab exercises per workout, but order was not that important. For the sake of argument, let's say he started with leg lifts. He'd lie on a flat bench with his hands grabbing the side of the bench next to his head. With a slight bend at his knees he would then raise his legs up almost vertical with the floor, and then lower them back down until his feet were about six inches from the floor. Thierry typically did 5 sets of 50 to 100 reps. He never used extra weight as he found that by going slow and controlled he could put as much tension as he needed on his abs.

For his second ab exercise, Thierry would do crunches with his legs across a flat bench. On some days he'd do them straight, while on others he'd twist from side to side to give the obliques a bit of extra work. Again he did 5 sets of 50 to 100 reps.

Another exercise Thierry almost always included in his training was the hanging leg raise from a chinup bar. Once again he'd alternate straight leg raises with twisting versions. This was one exercise Thierry never counted reps on. Instead he'd train to failure, be it 35, 50, 100, even 200 reps or more. To Thierry concentration was far more important than being a slave to reps.

To finish off that great midsection of his, Thierry often did rope crunches. He'd do these while kneeling down grabbing an overhead cable. He'd then contract his abs, bringing his torso down until it touched the ground. Thierry adds that the key to this exercise is concentrating on the abs and not allowing the spinal erectors to take over. This is one exercise where extra weight is a must, and Thierry would normally use about 50 pounds on the machine.

There you have it, the ab routine of Thierry Pastel, owner of one of the greatest sets of abs in bodybuilding history. Give it a try and watch your midsection disappear!

Triceps

When you talk about the largest arms in bodybuilding, such names as Arnold, Sergio, Coleman, and Ferrigno, come to mind. All four had or have arms have easily passed the 20-inch mark. In fact 22 to 23 inches is probably closer to the truth. But the problem with making up such lists is that only overall size is taken into account. With few exceptions there's no way a five-foot bodybuilder can develop the arm size of a six-footer. But if we use proportions, then the shorter bodybuilder is on equal footing (or arming!).

Take French bodybuilder, Thierry Pastel. During his competitive days in the early to mid '90s, his arms approached if not actually made the 20-inch mark. By any standards these were huge guns. But what's more remarkable is that Thierry stood just 5'2". Like Lee Priest today, Thierry's

A typical triceps workout might start with reverse-grip pushdowns. Thierry found this exercise great, both as a warmup, and as an excellent inner triceps movement.

Start

arms appeared gargantuan on his short frame (to Priest's credit his arms probably measure 21 to 22 inches and rank right up there with Coleman, Wheeler, and company, despite his height).

Nailing down an exact routine that Thierry used to build his triceps is difficult, as he was a great follower of the instinctive principle. When he went into the gym the odds were good to excellent he would do something different than the previous day.

When interviewed by *MuscleMag* in the early '90s, Thierry and his translator, bodybuilding legend, Serge Nubret, said that a typical triceps workout might start with reverse-grip pushdowns. He found this exercise great, both as a warmup, and as an excellent inner triceps movement. He used about a nine-inch wide grip, and pushed down to a complete lockout position. Dragging sets and reps out of Thierry was like pulling teeth as he frequently changed those around as well. After repeated prodding by *MuscleMag* contributor, T.C. Luoma (one of the founders of the popular bodybuilding site, Testosterone.net), Thierry said that a typical day would see him do 5 to 6 sets of 12, 16, or 20 reps.

Another favorite Thierry triceps exercise was bench dips. He would place two benches about four feet apart and put his hands and feet about shoulder-width apart on each bench. He would then lower down as far as he could comfortably go, and then push up to an arms-locked

Finish

out position. Thierry found this exercise great for packing meat on the entire triceps muscle. As he uses an extremely slow tempo, he doesn't place any weight on his lap like most bodybuilders who use a much faster speed, often bouncing at the bottom. Thierry preferred to use slow speed to make up for heavy weight. Not only did he find it more effective, but also it greatly reduced the risk of injury.

To finish off his triceps, Thierry liked to do a one-arm isolation movement like dumbell extensions. Again he used a medium weight for 15 to 20 reps in ultra slow motion.

As a final comment of Thierry's triceps training, he did his utmost to complete the previous routine in 30 minutes or less. He found that training for anything over that amount of time had the opposite effect, and he'd lose the great triceps pump he had developed.

Sonny Schmidt

Sonny was born in New Zealand and now lives in Australia. His ancestry is a mixture of Samoan, English and German. He attributes his incredible musculature to genetics:

"I have a very good shape. I always have had. It's genetics. All my family has a good shape with large calves … My dad and uncles are very big – 300 to 400 pounds – and several in the family are between six and seven feet tall."

Now when you've naturally got a killer body, why bother lifting weights? Sonny explains how he got into bodybuilding:

"I wasn't interested in bodybuilding then. At the time when I played football, some of my friends would go to the gym. They'd say, 'You have a good body, you have everything – nothing is missing. You should try bodybuilding.' But I said, 'No, I'm happy the way I am. The girls love me the way I am."

Then Sonny hurt his shoulder playing football. "That's the reason I went to the gym. The doctor said he wanted to operate on my shoulder, and I was scared. I went to the gym to see if I could help my shoulder without an operation. The gym instructor looked me up and down, saying, 'You've been training before.' I told him I'd never been in a gym in my life. 'Are you sure?' he asked. … The more I got to the gym, the more I liked it. And the more I liked it, the hungrier I got!"

He turned the stage into his personal buffet:

During his best years, Sonny Schmidt had two of the largest and most complete sets of delts on the pro scene.

1989	Grand Prix Melbourne – IFBB, 7th
	World Pro Championships – IFBB, 8th
1990	Niagara Falls Pro Invitational – IFBB, 8th
	Night of Champions – IFBB, 6th
1991	Grand Prix Denmark – IFBB, 2nd
	Grand Prix England – IFBB, 5th
	Grand Prix Finland – IFBB, 6th
	Grand Prix Italy – IFBB, 3rd
	Grand Prix Spain – IFBB, 3rd
	Grand Prix Switzerland – IFBB, 5th
	Niagara Falls Pro Invitational – IFBB, 2nd
	Night of Champions – IFBB, 2nd
	Olympia – IFBB, 6th
	San Jose Pro Invitational – IFBB, 2nd
1992	Arnold Classic – IFBB, 3rd
	Grand Prix England – IFBB, 3rd
	Grand Prix Germany – IFBB, 3rd
	Grand Prix Holland – IFBB, 4th
	Grand Prix Italy – IFBB, 3rd
	Olympia – IFBB, 7th
	Pittsburgh Pro Invitational – IFBB, 2nd
1993	Arnold Classic – IFBB, 8th
	Arnold Classic – IFBB, 9th
	Grand Prix England – IFBB, 4th
	Grand Prix Finland – IFBB, 4th
	Grand Prix France (2) – IFBB, 8th
	Grand Prix Germany (2) – IFBB, 3rd
	Grand Prix Spain – IFBB, 2nd

Sonny works his delts with seated dumbell presses.

	Olympia – IFBB, 8th
1994	Arnold Classic – IFBB, 10th
	Grand Prix England – IFBB, 10th
	Grand Prix France – IFBB, 10th
	Grand Prix Germany – IFBB, 8th
	Grand Prix Germany – IFBB, 9th
	Grand Prix Italy – IFBB, 8th
	Grand Prix Spain – IFBB, 7th
	Ironman Pro Invitational – IFBB, 6th
	Olympia – IFBB, 10th
1995	Grand Prix England – IFBB, 7th
	Grand Prix France – IFBB, 7th
	Grand Prix Germany – IFBB, 5th
	Grand Prix Russia – IFBB, 7th
	Grand Prix Spain – IFBB, 7th
	Grand Prix Ukraine – IFBB, 7th
	Olympia – IFBB, 13th
	Olympia, Masters – IFBB, winner
1996	Olympia, Masters – IFBB, 2nd
1997	Olympia, Masters – IFBB, Masters 40+, 2nd
1998	Arnold Classic – IFBB, Masters, 2nd
	Masters Arnold – IFBB, 2nd
1999	Olympia – Masters, IFBB, 3rd

And the last word goes to Sonny:

"I'm a pro now. I didn't think I'd come this far. I just want to do well and not embarrass myself."

Shoulders

In this age of bodybuilders competing only once or twice a year, Sonny Schmidt was in a class by himself. Throughout most of the 1990s, Sonny averaged 8 to 10 contests a year, and was finally rewarded for his efforts with the 1995 Masters Mr. Olympia title. This was in addition to a host of 2nd and 3rd place finishes at numerous Grand Prix events.

Like the country that created him, Sonny trained hard and heavy. Let's face it, any country founded by convicts rarely turns out wusses. And folks, Sonny Schmidt is no wuss!

During his best years, Sonny had two of the largest and most complete sets of delts on the pro scene. His first exercise was that old standby, behind-the-head barbell press. Sonny was a great believer in pyramiding and would start with 135 pounds for 15 reps as a warmup, and then work up to 250 pounds for 8 reps. And these weren't half reps either. Sonny brought the bar all the way down to the base of his neck and then extended to just short of locking out. If he tired before getting the desired number of reps, he'd have a training partner help him with a couple of forced reps.

At this point most bodybuilders would switch to some sort of lateral movement, but not Sonny. Grabbing a set of heavy dumbells he did seated dumbell presses, or more specifically Arnold presses. Again he pyramids up the weight doing 4 to 5 sets in total.

As soon as Sonny started to bounce or cheat during and exercise, he'd terminate the set and drop the weight.

With 8 to 10 heavy sets of lateral raises out of the way, Sonny finally relents and starts his lateral movements. First up was usually standing dumbell laterals for his side delts. Raising the dumbells to shoulder height, Sonny would normally do 4 sets of 10 reps.

Not being a big fan of machines, Sonny usually skipped reverse pec decks and instead did bent-over dumbell laterals for his rear delts. Given the tendency for the larger traps and lats to take over, this was one exercise where Sonny used slightly less weight and concentrated on working his rear delts. Once more he usually did 4 sets of 12 reps.

With all three delt heads given a good going over, Sonny turned to his traps. The first exercise was usually upright rows, and is the only exercise in his shoulder routine that he made use of a machine. Grabbing a short bar connected to a low pulley, Sonny would do 4 sets of 10 to 12 reps of upright cable rows.

To finish off his traps, Sonny did perhaps the most basic trap movement there is, barbell shrugs. You'd think that given his philosophy on training – heavy – Sonny would go all out on barbell shrugs. But that just wasn't the case. True he hoisted some heavy poundages, but like bent-over laterals, barbell shrugs are an easy exercise to cheat on. Most bodybuilders put far too much weight on the bar and bounce up and down using their thighs and lower back. Sonny on the other hand would use just enough weight to stimulate the traps. As soon as he started to bounce or cheat, he'd terminate the set and drop the weight.

"I've been sadly misled. For years I've thought that the Great Barrier Reef referred to Australian bodybuilder Sonny Schmidt's impossibly wide shoulders. I also thought that all this talk about the vast, barren Australian Outback was a tribute to Sonny's massive lats. And to top it off, I thought down under was an area of Sonny that only hormonally active schoolgirls talked about in hushed whispers. Imagine my embarrassment when I found out that all those terms had to do with Australian geography!"

– T.C. Luoma, former *MuscleMag International* contributor, and current editor of the online magazine Testosterone.net.

Vince Taylor

Vince was born in Havre de Grace, Maryland. In his youth and into high school he excelled in sports like football, basketball, and track and field. He also began using weights. But his talents went unrecognized. "In high school, it didn't really matter how well I did in sports because I never got any positive recognition for it. Because of the school I attended most of the publicity went to the kids of fairer skin. We (meaning blacks) broke the records, but the fair-skinned kids got the publicity and the scholarships. There was institutionalized prejudice, but I just rolled with it. It was aggravating at the time, but I really didn't see what it was about and the widespread effects it would have on me."

After high school, Vince was approached by several college scouts: "Sure I had offers from several colleges. But none of them were very enticing because they were really just loans. Out of a need for direction I chose a small school, which was a big mistake. It was Durham Business College (DBC) and ironically it was located between two big universities, Duke and North Carolina Central."

"DBC had written me about a basketball and track team and I knew I could study to be a lab technician there along with playing sports, so I decided to go … I still remember the cab ride to DBC. We drove past NC Central and I saw how big it was and started getting excited about going to school. So I asked the cab driver if that was it, and he said, 'No, yours is further down the road.' I'll never forget this. Then he pulls into a driveway in a rundown area and I start getting the idea that DBC isn't what I'd expected. The whole complex couldn't have been bigger than the third room at Gold's Venice and it looked as if it should have been condemned …"

Vince is another of those pro bodybuilders who has few, if any weaknesses.

"They didn't have a basketball team. They didn't have a gym. They had to go somewhere else to play games. The bus was broken down. The track was just a backyard with a fence around it. They had nothing. But it took me two and a half months to get sick enough to leave."

Still, Vince bounced back. He went to work for Coca-Cola as a line technician in a bottling plant. He worked his way up to Quality Control, but while visiting his brother in Germany, he decided it was time to move. He pumped gas by day and partied by night. The day part changed when he got a job as a weapons specialist, but the good times continued. In 1983 Vince met John Brown and saw him compete.

"...John drove the audience crazy, especially the women, and that's when I realized I needed to get some muscles of my own if I was really gonna run women..."

"John told me I had the potential to be good in bodybuilding; I just needed to work at it. I'll never forget this. John told me that there were three things I needed to do if I was gonna be good in bodybuilding. Train big, eat big, and sleep big. I went home that night, about an hour later, and started eating."

Vince started competing three months later:

1983   Mr. Berlin – 1st

1987   Mr. America – AAU, medium, 1st
        Nationals – NPC, light heavyweight, 4th

1988   Nationals – NPC, overall winner
        Nationals – NPC, light heavyweight, 1st

1989   Grand Prix England – IFBB, 2nd
        Grand Prix Finland – IFBB, 2nd
        Grand Prix Holland – IFBB, 4th
        Night of Champions – IFBB, winner
        Olympia – IFBB, 3rd

1991   Arnold Classic – IFBB, 3rd
        Grand Prix Denmark – IFBB, winner
        Grand Prix England – IFBB, 2nd
        Grand Prix Finland – IFBB, winner
        Grand Prix Italy – IFBB, winner
        Grand Prix Spain – IFBB, winner
        Grand Prix Switzerland – IFBB, winner
        Ironman Pro Invitational – IFBB, 5th
        Olympia – IFBB, 3rd
        Pittsburgh Pro Invitational – IFBB, winner

1992   Arnold Classic – IFBB, winner
        Ironman Pro Invitational – IFBB, winner
        Olympia – IFBB, 6th
        Pittsburgh Pro Invitational – IFBB, winner

1993   Arnold Classic – IFBB, 3rd
        Grand Prix France – IFBB, 2nd
        Grand Prix Germany – IFBB, 2nd
        Ironman Pro Invitational – IFBB, 3rd
        San Jose Pro Invitational – IFBB, winner

1994   Arnold Classic – IFBB, 2nd
        Grand Prix France – IFBB, 2nd
        Grand Prix Germany – IFBB, 2nd
        Ironman Pro Invitational – IFBB, winner

1995   Grand Prix England – IFBB, winner
        Grand Prix France – IFBB, winner
        Grand Prix Germany – IFBB, 2nd
        Grand Prix Germany – IFBB, 6th
        Grand Prix Russia – IFBB, 2nd
        Grand Prix Spain – IFBB, 2nd
        Grand Prix Ukraine – IFBB, winner

Vince Taylor

Houston Pro Invitational – IFBB, 2nd
Niagara Falls Pro Invitational – IFBB, winner
Night of Champions – IFBB, 2nd
Olympia – IFBB, 5th
1996   Arnold Classic – IFBB, 4th
Grand Prix Czech Republic – IFBB, 4th
Grand Prix England – IFBB, 6th
Grand Prix Germany – IFBB, 6th
Grand Prix Russia – IFBB, 3rd
Grand Prix Spain – IFBB, 6th
Grand Prix Spain – IFBB, 7th
Grand Prix Switzerland – IFBB, 5th
Olympia – Masters, IFBB, winner
San Jose Pro Invitational – IFBB, 3rd
1997   Arnold Classic – IFBB, 5th
Grand Prix Czech Republic – IFBB, 7th
Grand Prix England – IFBB, 7th
Grand Prix Finland – IFBB, 6th
Grand Prix Germany – IFBB, 9th
Grand Prix Hungary – IFBB, 9th
Grand Prix Russia – IFBB, 6th
Grand Prix Spain – IFBB, 8th
Olympia, Masters – IFBB, overall winner
1998   Arnold Classic – IFBB, 3rd
Arnold Classic – IFBB, Masters, 1st
Masters Arnold – IFBB, winner
1999   Arnold Classic – IFBB, 6th
Olympia, Masters – IFBB, winner

Vince's triceps training tends to be a bit more specialized, as they don't grow as easily as his biceps.

By the early '90s Vince was starting to slip in the pro rankings. He could still give the younger guys a moment's pause or two, but he realized that beating the likes of Coleman, Wheeler, and Yates was probably not going to happen any more. But like golf and tennis, Joe Weider thought the time was right for a Master's contest, and so the 40-plus generation now get a chance to strut their stuff at the Master's Mr. Olympia contest. Vince has won the last three Master's Mr. Olympia's and also the Master's Arnold Classic contest.

The last word goes to Vince: "… Lee haney told me I looked great … I have a hard time accepting compliments … But when Haney told me that, it changed a lot for me because I think he's the greatest."

Biceps and Triceps

Vince is another of those pro bodybuilders who has few, if any weaknesses. His torso and leg development is excellent, and as for his arms and calves, well the words outstanding and phenomenal get thrown around quite often.

Because of a biceps injury suffered in the late 1980s, and the fact that his arms grow so easily, Vince does very little biceps work. Often the secondary work he gets from his upper back work is sufficient. When he does train them, he sticks to three basic exercises.

Vince battles it out with Robby Robinson.

Vince is a big believer in rest pause, which he calls "double sets." He'll pick a weight that just allows 12 reps, stop for a few seconds to catch his breath, and then do a second set trying to duplicate the same number of reps.

Vince trains biceps with back on the second workout day. Beginning with a resistance-free movement (usually curls with a broomstick) he warms up the muscles and associated connective tissues.

The first exercise is bent-forward concentration curls. Using a dumbell he'll either curl the dumbell straight up to the shoulder, or across the chest. On a typical day Vince will do 5 double sets of about 10 to 12 reps.

Vince's next exercise is a cable movement, usually single-arm, cross-the-body curls. On this exercise, Vince prefers to pyramid the weight up with each set.

To finish off his biceps, Vince will grab a light dumbell, and do ultra slow, concentration curls. Although he did them early in his career, Vince doesn't do barbell curls any more. With all the mass he needs, combined with the previous biceps injury, he finds cables and dumbells less stressful, and perhaps more important, add much better quality to his biceps.

Triceps training tends to be a bit more specialized, as his triceps don't grow as easily as his biceps. He usually trains triceps on the first day after chest training. Again, he utilizes 5 double sets per exercise for 10 to 12 reps.

To start his triceps training Vince does 5 sets of standard triceps pushdowns on the cable machine.

Vince's second exercise is actually a combo, one-arm pushdowns with a palms-up and palms-down grip. He stands sideways to the machine and takes a handle in the opposite hand. He then brings his hand down and out across his body. After a few seconds rest he reverses his grip and tries to do another 10 to 12 reps.

Vince's third exercise is dumbell French presses. He finds the dumbells less stressful on the wrists and seems to hit the triceps a bit better.

To finish off, Vince does 5 sets of triceps kickbacks. On this exercise he likes to pause for a half second in the locked out position.

Vince Taylor, Kevin Levrone and Paul Dillett

Vince Comerford

He stood 5' 4 1/2" tall and weighed 180 pounds, with 19" arms in contest shape (over 20" in the off-season). Match those arms with 26-inch thighs, bulging 18-inch calves, a thick and shapely chest of nearly 50 inches and a tiny waist of only 27 inches, and you have the kind of physique that inspires the legend of the Blond Myth.

Vince Comerford was born in West Seneca, New York, a small town just outside of Buffalo, New York, on December 27, 1961. Vince grew up dedicated to baseball, soccer and wrestling, and excelled at all three. Unbelievably, he never touched a weight until he was 19 years old. At the time he weighed only 140 pounds and had enrolled at Delhi Ag & Tech College, majoring in architecture, partly because they had a tremendous wrestling program. While wrestling in a tournament Vince made it all the way to the semi-finals only to suffer a broken ankle. That knocked him out of the tournament and led him into weight training.

His wrestling coach suggested that Vince lift weights while his ankle healed to help maintain his upper body strength. He immediately fell in love with the pump, especially in his arms. Even before he took up weight training, Vince says he used to get a pump from his wrestling:

"I would just fill up with blood. And it felt great but it hurt my wrestling because I would tighten up. But when I broke my ankle and started weight training, it gave me another avenue to express my competitiveness. That's basically how I got into bodybuilding."

He began to work out with a couple of local bodybuilders who trained at the weight room. Naturally, he fell in love with training and then there was no going back to wrestling. He began to enter contests, and before long had established himself as one of the greatest under-200-pound bodybuilders of all time:

1984	Mr. America – AAU, short, 9th
1985	Mr. USA – AAU, short, 1st
1986	Mr. America – AAU, short, 3rd
1987	Nationals – NPC, middleweight, 1st
1989	Grand Prix US Pro – IFBB, 2nd
	Night of Champions – IFBB, 3rd
1990	Grand Prix England – IFBB, 8th
	Grand Prix Finland – IFBB, 11th
	Grand Prix France – IFBB, 11th
	Grand Prix Germany – IFBB, 6th
	Grand Prix Holland – IFBB, 18th
	Grand Prix Italy – IFBB, 8th
	Houston Pro Invitational – IFBB, 4th
	Ironman Pro Invitational – IFBB, 3rd
	Pittsburgh Pro Invitational – IFBB, 6th
1991	WBF Grand Prix – WBF, 7th

Biceps and Triceps

It was just after placing second at a proessional championship in Los Angeles, that a writer dubbed Vince Comerford the "Blond Myth." Some suggested it was because of Vince's resemblance to early 1950s Mr. Universe, Jack Delinger, but more than likely it was because in some poses, Vince brought back memories of the original "Myth," Sergio Oliva.

Vince blasts out one more rep.

Like Lee Priest today, Vince had proportionally two of the largest arms on the scene during the late '80s and early '90s. Vince preferred to work biceps and triceps together, alternating a biceps movement with a triceps exercise, and then back to biceps.

He usually worked arms on the second workout of the first and fifth training days. He began with standing barbell curls, starting first with four light, warm-up sets, and progressing to four drop sets. A typical drop set would involve 10 reps in good style, followed by two drop sets of 4 to 6 reps each.

Next up it would be triceps pushdowns on the cable machine. Vince would do one, light warmup set, and then do two all-out sets, increasing the weight with each set. For the final two sets he would decrease the weight and go to positive failure.

After pushdowns it was back to biceps for 45-degree incline curls. Vince typically did 4 to 5 sets of incline curls for 12 reps on each.

To finish off arms, Vince would normally do either close-grip bench presses or lying triceps presses. He would use as much weight as possible for 5 sets of 8 to 12 reps. Depending on the day he would either pyramid up in weight, or start heavy and drop the poundage with each successive set.

Back

For Vince, back training depended on two variables; location and complexity. Because most back muscles are not that visible when they're being trained, they tend to get passed over in favor of the more showy muscles like chest and biceps. Vince recognized early on that unless you do some creative mirror rearranging, you can't rely on sight to train the back, you must go by feel.

Vince also knew that the back wasn't just made up of two major muscles like the chest (pectorals major and minor), it consisted of many different areas such as the lats, rhomboids, teres, traps, and the spinal erectors. In fact the last muscle group is the one Vince feels is the key

Vince performed T-bar rows with strict form.

to the whole back. "What people have to realize is the origin of the back is the lower back, and it branches up into your lat area, center back, and then up into the rhomboids. Before you can build the upper part, you have to build the lower part."

Given the previous, it's not surprising to hear Vince began every back workout with lower back training in the form of hyperextensions. He would do 4 or 5 sets of 15 to 20 reps of this all-important exercise, squeezing all the way up, and all the way down.

Another slight variation that separates Vince from the norm, is that he always does a few light biceps curls before hitting the heavy back exercises. Vince witnessed some gruesome biceps tears over the years, and most were not from direct biceps training but from back training. How often have you heard of bodybuilders tearing a biceps tendon from reverse-grip barbell rows? Vince had no intentions of being one of them so he always warmed the little buggers up first.

With his lower back and biceps fully warmed up, Vince would begin the exercise bombardment. His first exercise was either T-bar or bent-over rows. If it was the latter he usually used the Smith machine. Vince found that with the regular barbell, any shift in balance put unwanted stress on his lower back. He found the Smith machine more stable.

Vince performed both exercises in a similar manner, knees slightly bent, torso just short of parallel with the floor, lower back slightly arched. He also concentrated on keeping the abdominals flexed as they help take the stress off the lower back. Typical sets and reps for Vince were 5 sets of 8 to 12.

With a basic power movement out of the way, Vince moved on to wide-grip pulldowns to the front. As he pulled down he kept the chest high and squeezed his shoulder blades as close together as possible to maximize muscle stimulation. Vince usually used straps on this exercise (in fact he uses straps on most of his back exercises). Again it's 5 sets of 8 to 12 reps.

To further torture his back, Vince moved on to seated pulley rows as his third exercise. Vince prefers the V-bar on this exercise and kept his knees slightly bent to minimize lower back stress. As he pulled the bar into his lower rib cage, Vince once again squeezed his shoulder blades together and stuck his chest forward. On this exercise Vince liked to add a drop set in at the end. You guessed it, 5 sets of 8 to 12 reps was the norm.

To finish off his upper back, Vince moved on to one-arm dumbell rows. He put his knee on a slight incline, and braced his torso by resting his free hand on the bench. As this was his finishing upper back exercise Vince limited the weight to a 100-pound dumbell and did 4 sets of 10 reps.

After all this, Vince went back to the back extension apparatus, and did 4 more sets of hyperextensions.

For variety Vince often rearranged the previous exercises starting with the pulldowns before the heavy rows. But he always did the back extensions last.

Nimrod King

Nimrod King was born in Port-of-Spain, Trinidad, on February 11, 1965. His family moved to Concord, Ontario (just north of Toronto) when he was seven. He had three brothers and one sister. Like all youngsters, Nimrod played sports – mostly football, soccer and track and field. The day that changed his life forever was the day he picked up his brother's 38-pound dumbell and started doing curls and various exercises with it. He was 12 years old! Within only a few months he was doing as many as 33 sets just for biceps, so great was his determination to get big and muscular. When he started high school he trained every morning before classes in the school weight room. At age 17 he joined Gold's Gym in Mississauga, Ontario and within a couple of years Nimrod was one of the best bodybuilders in Canada. He sported 20-inch arms and a body to match!

Nimrod's record is one of the best ever set by a Canadian:

1988 North American Championships – IFBB, overall winner
      North American Championships – IFBB, heavyweight, 1st
1989 Grand Prix US Pro – IFBB, winner
      Niagara Falls Pro Invitational – IFBB, 2nd
      Night of Champions – IFBB, 2nd

Nimrod King

1990 Arnold Classic – IFBB, disqualified
      Grand Prix England – IFBB, 3rd
      Grand Prix Finland – IFBB, 2nd
      Grand Prix France – IFBB, 4th
      Grand Prix Germany – IFBB, 2nd
      Grand Prix Italy – IFBB, 2nd
      Houston Pro Invitational – IFBB, 5th
      Ironman Pro Invitational – IFBB, 6th
      Pittsburgh Pro Invitational – IFBB, 5th
1991 Grand Prix Denmark – IFBB, 6th
      Grand Prix England – IFBB, 10th
      Grand Prix Finland – IFBB, 5th
      Grand Prix Italy – IFBB, 6th
      Grand Prix Spain – IFBB, 5th
      Grand Prix Switzerland – IFBB, 7th
      Olympia – IFBB, 15th
1992 Niagara Falls Pro Invitational – IFBB, 3rd
      After retiring from competition Nimrod has gone on to great success as a contest promoter. To reach Nimrod King you can call him at (519) 735-1225.[1]

Reference:
1) http://www.optimumfitness.com/npcsched.html

Biceps and Triceps

It's not surprising someone whose last name is King would have two of the largest arms in bodybuilding. When he competed back in the early '90s, Nimrod made it a point to flex his 21-plus inch guns whenever possible.

Like Vince Taylor, Nimrod preferred to train biceps and triceps on separate days. He'd normally train biceps in the morning after his back workout, and then hit triceps in the evening after shoulders.

Nimrod was unique among pro bodybuilders in that he did 15 to 25 reps per set. Most bodybuilders would consider this cardio training, but Nimrod found by trial and error, high reps gave him both the size and separation he was after.

Another King idiosyncrasy was that he used the same poundage on all sets of an exercise. He'd pick a weight that allowed 20 to 25 reps in ultra strict style, and then do 4 to 5 sets.

Nimrod usually started with incline hammer curls on a 45-degree incline bench. Using an alternating style, Nimrod would do 4 sets of hammers for his biceps and brachialis.

For his second exercise Nimrod would do medium-grip barbell preacher curls. He found these excellent for the lower biceps.

Nimrod's third and final biceps exercise was seated concentration curls with the upper arm braced against the inner thigh. Out of all the exercises, Nimrod attributes this one the most for developing his baseball-sized biceps.

The next evening Nimrod would hit the gym to hit his triceps, beginning with 5 sets of triceps pushdowns. The first set was a warmup set, and then a slightly heavier weight was used for 4 sets of 15 to 25 reps.

It's not surprising someone whose last name is King would have two of the largest arms in bodybuilding.

Nimrod's second triceps exercise was lying dumbell extensions. Nimrod found the dumbells both easier on his wrists and offered a greater range of motion, than the straight or EZ-curl bars. As with incline curls for biceps, Nimrod considered lying dumbell extensions his primary triceps mass builder.

To isolate his triceps, Nimrod next moved on to one-arm cable pushdowns. Nimrod would hold his elbow and upper arm tight against his body and forcefully lockout at the bottom.

For his fourth and final triceps exercise, Nimrod did behind-the-head rope extensions. Using the all-familiar rope, Nimrod would hold one end in each hand and lean forward so he was facing away from the machine. Again he extended to a locked out position for 4 sets of 15 to 25 reps.

Thighs

"I believe in going for the burn. Those extra five to ten reps mean a lot. They bring out the cuts, the density and striations. Just going from 15 to 20 reps or from 20 to 25 reps can mean the difference between building good legs and great legs." – 1988 North American Bodybuilding Champion, Nimrod King, outlining his philosophy on high-rep training.

You'd think that with legs larger than many people's waists, Nimrod King would have spent years squatting with Tom Platz-sized weights. But in reality Nimrod was a high-rep man, and he was never a fan of poundages that limited him to the traditional 6 to 8 reps. Nimrod rarely if ever did any leg exercises for less than 20 reps per set. For him the burn, intensity, and pump achieved from a set is far more important than the actual weight used.

A typical workout saw Nimrod start with squats and do 4 sets of 20 to 25 reps. He did one set as a warmup, increased the weight for another set, and continued adding weight for another three sets. The weight used on his last three sets was around 315 pounds. For those who regularly squat 400 to 500-plus pounds for the traditional 6 to 8 reps, give Nimrod's style a try and see what pain is really all about!

After squats, Nimrod moved on to leg presses. But he had his own variation on this. Nimrod preferred to do leg presses, one leg at a time. He did 3 sets for each leg, averaging 20 to 25 reps each.

Following leg presses Nimrod moved on to leg extensions. This was one exercise Nimrod liked to employ an advanced training technique, usually rest-pause. He would pick a weight that allowed 15 reps to failure. He'd then get up, walk around for 10 seconds or so, and then hop back on the machine and force out another 12 reps. Once again he'd wait about 10 seconds and try an additional 10 reps. Nimrod considered all this part of one set. He'd typically put himself through four to six cycles of such madness. This alone worked out to 12 to 16 sets!

Most bodybuilders would be sick of the leg extension by now, but Nimrod did an additional 3 sets of leg extensions, this time one leg at time. Again the reps were 20 to 25 per set.

Calves

Nimrod is first to admit that his calves were never his strongest point. At one point they were so weak he had a friend design a special 45-degree calf machine that allowed him to get a greater stretch. He put it in his home and trained with it every other day for about two years. He figured he did thousands of sets and tens of thousands of reps, but the results were worth it as he put a solid two inches on his calves.

With a good foundation laid Nimrod cut back on his calf training. But Nimrod's idea of cutting back still meant doing more calf work in a day than most bodybuilders do in a week.

Nimrod usually started his calf training with toe presses on the Nautilus leg press machine. Even though he considered this his warmup exercise, Nimrod did 7 sets of 25 reps. Nimrod's warmup rivals most bodybuilders' entire calf workout!

After toe presses Nimrod moved on to seated calf raises. Eight sets of 20 to 25 reps usually sufficed.

For his third exercise, Nimrod went back to toe presses, but this time on the 45-degree leg press machine. He did 6 sets of 25 reps.

To finish off his calves, Nimrod did 3 sets of standing calf raises, averaging 20 to 25 reps per set. Do the math and you see Nimrod did 24 sets for his calves during a typical workout. The pump in his lower legs at this point had to be seen to be believed.

Chest

With the possible exception of Lee Haney or Bertil Fox, few bodybuilders competing in the 1980s had thicker pectorals than Canada's Nimrod King. When Charles Glass and George Butler, in their groundbreaking book *Pumping Iron*, talked about the chest muscles being the "bear's hugging muscle," they could have been referring to Nimrod. But it wasn't always this way.

At one point Nimrod's chest was one of his weak points. But over a two-year period it went from mediocrity to excellence. Nimrod attributed the improvement to two changes. First, he split up his muscle groups differently so his chest workout was separated from shoulders and triceps. When he trained chest with shoulders and triceps Nimrod found that he would deliberately hold back on chest just so he had enough energy to train the other two muscles. But as soon as he set improving his chest as a priority, he realized that nothing less than 100 percent intensity would cut it. So he split things up, training chest with calves in the morning, and shoulders and triceps later in the evening. The second change was to switch from low to medium and high reps. When he first started training, Nimrod followed the advice of more experienced bodybuilders, and that meant heavy weight for sets of 5 to 10 reps, but it wasn't long before he realized that this sort of rep-scheme wasn't working for him. So he lowered the weight and increased his rep to 15 to 25. In a matter of weeks he noticed his chest size and muscularity had increased dramatically.

Like most bodybuilders Nimrod incorporated a great deal of variety into his chest training. From barbell flats and inclines, to dumbell flyes and cable crossovers, he did them all. And Nimrod would never be mistaken for a disciple of Mike Mentzer! A typical chest workout consisted of six or seven exercises for 4 or 5 sets each.

Nimrod usually started his chest training with the granddaddy of all chest exercises, flat barbell presses. But instead of trying to bench press 400 or 500 pounds, Nimrod would pick a weight that allowed anywhere from 15 to 25 reps. He'd then do 5 sets using a short, piston-like motion, trying to keep the tension constantly on the pecs.

Nimrod's second exercise was usually the incline barbell press, again for 5 sets of 15 to 20 reps. He used the same short, nonlockout style as on the flats. His rest interval was between 30 and 60 seconds.

For his third exercise, Nimrod went back to a flat bench and did dumbell flyes. He would bring the dumbells as low as possible, getting a full stretch in his chest muscles. Then it was back up to the top of the exercise using a hugging type motion. Nimrod typically did 3 sets of 12 to 15 reps of this exercise.

To give his chest muscles, serratus, and rib cage a good stretch, Nimrod followed flat flyes with cross-bench dumbell pullovers. Three sets of 12 reps was the norm.

After pullovers, Nimrod moved on to cable crossovers to hit the inner chest. Depending on the day, Nimrod did anywhere from 3 to 6 sets. This is one of the few exercises Nimrod liked to incorporate an advanced training technique, in this case rest-pause. He'd pick a weight and do 12 reps, wait about ten seconds and then do another 5 to 10 reps, and wait another ten seconds and finish off with as many reps as possible. he'd consider this one set, and do one or two rest-pause sets in this manner.

To finish off his inner chest, Nimrod added in two sets of 15 reps of pec deck flyes. As with most of his chest exercises, Nimrod used a short, quick tempo on pec decks.

After inner chest, Nimrod moved on to decline flyes, doing 4 sets of 15 reps. After experimenting with different angles, he finally settled on a 30-degree decline angle.

To finish off his chest, Nimrod did 2 sets of vertical machine presses. He did the first set for about 17 reps, and the second one for 15 reps. Nimrod found vertical presses an excellent finishing movement as it tended to hit the overall chest, and give it a good final pump.

At one point Nimrod's chest was one of his weak points. But over a two-year period it went from mediocrity to excellence.

Shoulders

During his heyday in the late '80s and early '90s, few bodybuilders carried the degree of shoulder muscle mass as the Canadian colossus, Nimrod King. He was right up there with such other mass-monsters of the time as Mike Christian, Lee Haney and Bertil Fox.

Nimrod started his shoulder training by doing three warm-up sets on a Universal pressing machine. He's do high reps, 15 to 20, to get the blood in there.

Nimrod's first heavy shoulder exercise was the behind-the-head barbell press. We should explain the word "heavy" as Nimrod preferred to do high reps on most of his exercises, with 15 to 25 being the norm. Even though he'd use as much weight as possible on his exercises, the high reps necessitated using less weight than if he was doing reps in the more typical 8 to 12 range.

Nimrod normally did 3 sets of barbell presses, doing 15 to 20 reps per set. When doing the exercise, Nimrod placed particular emphasis on the lowering part of the movement. He always brought the bar right down to his neck. But he never locked all the way out at the top. He found locking out shifted much of the stress from his delts to his triceps. He preferred a non-lock, piston-type motion to keep the tension on his delts.

After barbell presses, Nimrod moved on to barbell upright rows. Again he did 3 sets of 15 reps. He found this exercise great for the front and side delts, and the traps. Nimrod paused for a split second at the top of the exercise to reduce the momentum that easily builds up during this exercise.

After uprights came 3 sets of seated dumbell side laterals. Nimrod found doing this exercise in the seated position worked best, and like uprights, paused for a split second at the top to give the muscles an extra degree of contraction, and to keep him honest. That is no cheating!

After seated laterals came 4 sets of dumbell shrugs. This was the only direct trap exercise Nimrod performed, as he was one of those lucky bodybuilders whose traps seemed to grow just by doing the other shoulder exercises. A good tip Nimrod passes on to beginners is to try to touch the traps off the ears as you shrug the shoulders up. When you find yourself going deaf, you know you're well on your way!

Aaron Baker

To finish off his shoulders, Nimrod gave his rear delts a good going over. Rather than perform the traditional standing, bent-over version, Nimrod found lying face-forward on an incline bench worked best. Given the importance of great rear-delt development to competitive bodybuilding, Nimrod did an extra set of this exercise, doing 4 sets all told. Once again the reps were kept in the 15 range.

Aaron Baker

Aaron was born in Flint, Michigan on November 9, 1960. At an early age, his parents split up and he moved with his mother and siblings to Winston-Salem, North Carolina. At the age of six, he became fascinated by Batman. This inspired him to take an interest in comic book super-heros, particularly their muscular physiques. At the age of 15 he took up weight training, mostly to build up his body to impress the girls.

After graduating high school, Aaron signed up for a four-year enlistment in the US Army. He served in the US and Korea. Of his time in the arms,

Quite possibly one of the most underrated bodybuilders in the world – Aaron Baker.

Aaron says: "I would never do it again, but as far as growth and experience go, I think it was invaluable. It instilled in me a lot of discipline and principles that are valuable in life."

Near the end of his army service, Aaron made several pilgrimages to the Mecca of bodybuilding, Gold's Gym in Venice Beach, California. Yet it would be three years later, in 1985, when Aaron would return to the gym to train.

With or without Gold's Gym, Aaron was training, and getting results. He racked up an impressive amateur record and then did the unthinkable, he defected to Vince McMahon's rival WBF federation. After the federation folded Aaron went back to the IFBB. Many assume that Aaron's lack of success, despite his near-perfect physique, is because of his time spent in the WBF. It seems Aaron is being forced to pay his dues. No less an authority than *MuscleMag International's* Greg Zulak has said that Aaron is the most underrated bodybuilder in the world. Here's his record:

1981   Junior Mr. USA – AAU, light heavyweight, 5th
1983   California Classic – NPC, light heavyweight, 12th
1986   Nationals – NPC, light heavyweight, 4th
1987   USA Championships – NPC, heavyweight, 5th
1989   Nationals – NPC, heavyweight, 2nd
        North American Championships – IFBB, heavyweight, 3rd
        USA Championships – NPC, heavyweight, 4th
1990   USA Championships – NPC, overall winner
        USA Championships – NPC, heavyweight, 1st
1991   WBF Grand Prix – WBF, 6th
1993   Night of Champions – IFBB, 12th
        Pittsburgh Pro Invitational – IFBB, 9th
1994   Arnold Classic – IFBB, 6th
        Grand Prix France – IFBB, 9th
        Grand Prix Germany – IFBB, 8th
        Ironman Pro Invitational – IFBB, 3rd
        Olympia – IFBB, 12th
        San Jose Pro Invitational – IFBB, 6th
1995   Arnold Classic – IFBB, 6th
        Florida Pro Invitational – IFBB, 2nd
        Ironman Pro Invitational – IFBB, 2nd
        Olympia – IFBB, 9th
        South Beach Pro Invitational – IFBB, 2nd
1996   Grand Prix Czech Republic – IFBB, 7th
        Grand Prix England – IFBB, 11th
        Grand Prix Germany – IFBB, 10th
        Grand Prix Russia – IFBB, 6th
        Grand Prix Spain – IFBB, 9th
        Grand Prix Switzerland – IFBB, 6th
        Olympia – IFBB, 11th
1997   Arnold Classic – IFBB, 9th
        Ironman Pro Invitational – IFBB, 4th
1998   Arnold Classic – IFBB, 7th
        Ironman Pro Invitational – IFBB, 3rd
        Olympia – IFBB

Keep on doubting me because I can't wait to prove you wrong.
– Aaron Baker

The last word goes to Aaron: "I'd just like to thank all of the fans who have supported me from the very beginning. I'd like to apologize to any fans who have written me that I haven't gotten back to, as at times I have been very busy and have neglected that side of the business. It doesn't mean I take their support lightly, and I really wish I could contact everyone back and thank them personally for their notes and letters of support and encouragement. I'd also like to thank the people who said I'd never make it, because without their doubt I might not be here. Keep on doubting me because I can't wait to prove you wrong!"

Triceps

In his workouts Aaron typically trains triceps with biceps and delts. He uses the priority principle, training delts first, then biceps, and finally triceps. It's not that his shoulders and biceps are weak, but when compared to his enormous triceps, they need a tad more work.

Aaron comes from the new school of training, when it comes to volume. Where most bodybuilders are hitting their triceps with 15 and 20 sets, Aaron does just 6 to 8 total sets. Now either everyone else is overdoing it, or Aaron is undertraining, who knows? But take a look at Aaron's triceps and it's hard not to be convinced he's on to something.

"It's no secret that Aaron has some of the most titanic tris ever to be sunken into the back of an upper arm. In fact when you take a good close look at his triceps, they appear to be improperly labeled coz he looks to have more than three distinct sections to that bodypart."

– *MuscleMag* contributor, Jason Mathas, commenting on the great triceps development of one of bodybuilding's most underrated stars, Aaron Baker.

Check out Aaron's triceps.

Aaron's favorite triceps exercise is lying EZ-bar extensions. Lying on a flat bench, Aaron lowers the bar to just behind his head, and then extends it to above his eyes. He starts with 95 pounds for 15 to 20 reps as a warmup, and then proceeds to do 2 to 3 sets of 8 to 12 reps using 130 to 140 pounds. Keep in mind these are rough numbers, particularly with regards to the reps. Aaron won't terminate a set just because he reached a given rep number. He'll always go to failure.

Aaron's second exercise is push-downs on the Icarian machine. Once again he'll do a light warm-up set for 15 to 20 reps, and then work up to 130 pounds for 2 sets of 10 to 12 reps.

Another exercise that frequently gets thrown into the mix is one-arm dumbell extensions. With his elbow kept pointing at the ceiling, Aaron will warm up with a 40-pound dumbell and then move up to a 50 for one set of 12, a 60 for one set of 10, and finally a 70 for 10 to 12 reps.

These three exercises usually form the bulk of Aaron's triceps routine, but occasionally he'll add dips on the Cybex machine. Given that his 240-plus pound

Don't be afraid to try new techniques and exercises.
– Aaron Baker

bodyweight is nowhere near heavy enough, Aaron will strap 100 to 120 extra pounds around his waist and crank out 4 sets of 10 to 12 reps, or whatever he can get on that day.

Back

Aaron's philosophy on back training is quite simple; train the way he has to to get the job done. He does whatever it takes to get the most out of himself. As with most muscle groups, Aaron's back training doesn't revolve around lifting the maximum weight possible. He only uses enough weight to get 10 to 12 ultra strict reps.

Aaron's first back exercise is wide-grip front chins. He considers this exercise to be the best overall back exercise, and the one that has done the most to give him a back that helped earn him the nickname "Batman."

Aaron pulls his body up until the bar touches his chest, usually around collarbone level. At the top of the movement he pauses for a second, and then lowers back down to just short of a lockout with his arms. Aaron does 4 sets of 8 to 10 reps of chins.

Aaron's second exercise is usually lat pulldowns to the front. He does 4 sets going from 200 pounds up to 350 pounds. Again he pulls the bar to his collarbone. Despite the weight used, Aaron uses little or no body momentum to keep the weight moving.

With his two primary upper back and width movements out of the way, Aaron next moves on to exercises for his lower lats. Grabbing the lat bar with a narrow, reverse (palms facing up) grip, Aaron starts with 4 sets of narrow pulldowns. Although he is slightly stronger on this version of pulldowns, he uses the same weight as wide pulldowns since his lats are already pre-exhausted from the chins and wide pulldowns.

To finish his back, Aaron will do either seated cable rows or front pulldowns with a narrow, standard (palms facing down) grip. As this version of the pulldown is very similar to the previous, we'll focus on the seated row. This biggest mistake bodybuilders make on seated rows is putting too much weight on the machine and yanking with the lower back. There's none of that for Aaron. He uses just enough weight to work his lats, and if he has to start getting sloppy to keep the weight moving, he'll stop the set and lighten the weight. As he pulls the bar in to his lower rib cage, Aaron squeezes his shoulder blades together and arches his chest forward. He finds this is the best way to get full contraction in his back muscles, and also to keep the stress off the lower back.

Aaron's final words to beginners are to experiment and see what works best for you. Just because he has found the previous to be the most productive routine for him, doesn't mean it will do the same for you. Don't be afraid to try new techniques and exercises.

Shoulders

In the early 1990s as he was recovering from his stint in Vince McMahon's short-lived WBF organization, Aaron decided to link up with Mike Mentzer, former Mr. Universe and promoter of the Heavy Duty style of training. Aaron had gotten into a rut and decided something radical was needed to break him out of it. Initially he made great gains by following Mike's training methods, but soon differences in nutrition and training led him to go back on his own. But even though he no longer trains with Mike he still loosely follows Mike's central training philosophy – short and intense!

Aaron's current delt routine may seem almost simplistic for a top pro bodybuilder, but the results speak for themselves. He doesn't do too many exercises, and he keeps the total number of sets to 8 to 10. He's also modified his rep range from 6 to 8 to 12 to 15. There are days when he even goes up to 25 reps per set.

Typically Aaron will do a warm-up set or two of seated dumbell presses and dumbell laterals or side raises. Then, depending on his mood, will either start with presses followed by laterals, or he'll do presses and laterals in pre-exhaust superset fashion. He usually alternates this training format on an every-other-day basis.

Let's use the superset format as an example. Aaron will do a set of 60-pound laterals to positive failure, and then without resting grab the 125-pounders and do the dumbell presses.

There are times when his strength levels are higher so he'll use a 70-pound lateral for the side raises. He always shoots for 15 to 20 reps on the laterals, and 12 to 20 on the dumbell presses.

For variety Aaron sometimes substitutes the side delt machine in place of the dumbells. In this case he goes for 20 to 25 reps and uses the whole stack, sometimes with an extra 45-pound plate attached. That folks, means side laterals with over 300 pounds for 20 or more reps.

To his his rear delts, Aaron does bent-over dumbell laterals. Again he only does 2 sets of 15 to 20 reps, but he uses heavy weights – 70-pound dumbells to be precise. He doesn't need to do any warm-up sets as his shoulders are fully warmed from the preceding presses and side laterals.

The previous is usually all Aaron does for his delts, but occasionally he'll throw in 2 sets of barbell upright rows. Aaron doesn't make direct trap work a regular part of his training as he's one of the lucky ones whose traps seem to grow merely by looking at weight.

Counting warm-up sets and all, Aaron's total shoulder routine is just 8 sets. But given the weight he's using and intensity he employs, those eight sets are as draining as most bodybuilders 15 to 20 sets. And one look at Aaron's shoulder development is all the proof you need.

Aaron's traps seem to grow merely by looking at weight.

Milos (Mishko) Sarcev

Milos Sarcev, or Mishko as he prefers to be called, was born in Yugoslavia. Growing up he wasn't allowed to go out by himself, other than for soccer games or basketball games, until he was 17. His life consisted of going to school, coming home, doing his homework, and going to bed.

Milos Sarcev is one of the more proportioned pros on the scene.

In addition, both of Mishko's parents were doctors. His father was a psychiatrist who believed that bodybuilders were exhibitionists. As a result, Mishko met with severe family disapproval. He wore baggy clothes to conceal his developing body. But as if Mishko's parents weren't enough of a hurdle, he didn't have any weights!

"He likes lots of variety in his arm training. For him every workout is different – different exercises, different sets and reps and even different training principles."

– Greg Zulak, commenting on the training philosophy of Yugoslavian pro bodybuilder, Milos Sarcev.

"When I started training, which was September 18, 1981 – I remember because I kept a diary – we had to build a lot of our own weights from cement. We also trained for like four hours a day, thinking that the more we trained, the faster we would grow."

And grow he did!

1991	Grand Prix Denmark – IFBB, 5th
	Grand Prix England – IFBB, 9th
	Grand Prix Finland – IFBB, 4th
	Grand Prix Italy – IFBB, 7th
	Grand Prix Spain – IFBB, 7th
	Grand Prix Switzerland – IFBB, 6th
	Niagara Falls Pro Invitational – IFBB, 4th
	Night of Champions – IFBB, 11th
	Olympia – IFBB
	San Jose Pro Invitational – IFBB, 3rd
1992	Arnold Classic – IFBB, 8th
	Chicago Pro Invitational – IFBB, 5th
	Grand Prix England – IFBB, 8th
	Grand Prix Germany – IFBB, 10th

Grand Prix Holland – IFBB, 12th
Grand Prix Italy – IFBB, 10th
Ironman Pro Invitational – IFBB, 6th
Niagara Falls Pro Invitational – IFBB, 4th
Night of Champions – IFBB, 5th
Olympia – IFBB, 16th
Pittsburgh Pro Invitational – IFBB, 4th
1993   Chicago Pro Invitational – IFBB, 3rd
Grand Prix England – IFBB, 5th
Grand Prix Finland – IFBB, 3rd
Grand Prix France (2) – IFBB, 3rd
Grand Prix Germany (2) – IFBB, 5th
Grand Prix Spain – IFBB, 4th
Niagara Falls Pro Invitational – IFBB, 3rd
Night of Champions – IFBB, 5th
Olympia – IFBB, 11th
Pittsburgh Pro Invitational – IFBB, 3rd
1994   Grand Prix England – IFBB, 8th
Grand Prix France (2) – IFBB, 6th
Grand Prix Germany – IFBB, 4th
Grand Prix Italy – IFBB, 4th
Grand Prix Spain – IFBB, 4th
Olympia – IFBB, 13th
1995   Canada Pro Cup – IFBB, 3rd

Milos enters most of the major bodybuilding shows each year.

Houston Pro Invitational – IFBB, 5th
Niagara Falls Pro Invitational – IFBB, 4th
Night of Champions – IFBB, 6th
1996   Canada Pro Cup – IFBB, 3rd
Florida Pro Invitational – IFBB, 3rd
Night of Champions – IFBB, 4th
1997   Canada Pro Cup – IFBB, winner
Grand Prix Czech Republic – IFBB, 8th
Grand Prix England – IFBB, 8th
Grand Prix Finland – IFBB, 8th
Grand Prix Germany – IFBB, 7th
Grand Prix Hungary – IFBB, 7th
Grand Prix Russia – IFBB, 7th
Grand Prix Spain – IFBB, 9th
Night of Champions – IFBB, 2nd
Olympia – IFBB, 10th
Toronto Pro Invitational – IFBB, winner
1998   Grand Prix Finland – IFBB, 5th
Grand Prix Germany – IFBB, 5th
Night of Champions – IFBB, 11th
Olympia – IFBB
San Francisco Pro Invitational – IFBB, 5th
Toronto Pro Invitational – IFBB, 7th
1999   Arnold Classic – IFBB, 5th
Grand Prix England – IFBB, 5th
Ironman Pro Invitational – IFBB, 2nd
Night of Champions – IFBB, 5th
Olympia – IFBB, 10th
Professional World Cup – IFBB, 5th
Toronto Pro Invitational – IFBB, 2nd

Milos really likes to mix up his workout. No two workouts are ever the same.

When asked what was the best thing that ever happened to him, Mishko replied: "Coming to the United States."

Arms

It's hard to believe someone weighing 235 to 240 pounds in contest shape can be considered "light" but that's how far bodybuilding has evolved (or regressed depending on your point of view). Milos as most people call him, is one of the more proportioned pros on the scene. He's also one of the most consistent competitors, entering most of the major bodybuilding shows each year.

Despite being a product of the 1980s and 1990s, Mishko doesn't subscribe to the "overtraining" preaching of some experts. For him, there is no such thing as overtraining, only under eating and undersleeping. "Come on now, 6 sets for biceps and maybe 10 sets for chest! That's ridiculous."

Even though he trains seven days a week, he normally splits his body up four ways and trains on the traditional four-day cycle, but without the off days normally taken. He usually does 25 to 40 sets for a muscle, even smaller groups like biceps and triceps. Speaking of which, for biceps he usually starts with heavy barbell curls or dumbell curls and finishes with concentration curls and cable curls. On triceps he starts with such basic power movements as close-grip bench presses and dips, and finishes with pulley work and kickbacks.

Mishko really likes to mix up his workout. He changes his routine all the time, so no two workouts are ever the same. He may do straight bar curls, preacher curls, concentration curls and pulley curls one workout, and EZ-bar curls, alternate curls, one-arm preacher curls, bent-over barbell curls, and one-arm pulley curls the next. By changing his exercises so frequently, not only does he avoid boredom, but he also shocks the muscle and prevents plateaus and staleness. Variety keeps his interest and enthusiasm up. With regards to weight, once again variety plays the biggest role. Some days it's heavy and some days it's light.

When Milos trains back he includes the full spectrum of back exercises.

A typical Mishko arm workout goes something like this. He'll start with triceps and do 8 sets of close-grip presses, pyramiding down to 4 reps on his heaviest set. He'll then do 4 sets of seated French presses, followed by 4 sets of lying EZ-bar extensions. Next up is 4 sets of triceps pushdowns using a rope, followed by 4 sets of overhead extensions using an EZ-curl bar. To finish off Mishko would do 4 sets of pushdowns using a rope, followed by 4 sets of triceps kickbacks. Do the math and it adds up to 32 sets! He averages 4 to 10 reps on the heavy exercises, and 12 to 20 on the isolation movements.

Mishko hits biceps with the same amount of volume. He may start with barbell curls for 6 to 8 sets of 6 to 8 reps. He'll then do 5 sets of standing dumbell curls and 5 sets of cable curls. To finish off he may do 5 sets of concentration curls and 5 sets of one-arm cable curls.

Back

Early in his career Milos made the same mistake as many beginning bodybuilders. He neglected to train his back with the same intensity as his chest, arms, and shoulders. Unlike most bodybuilders who neglect back training because it's a muscle they can't see, Milos assumed his was in good shape from many years of competitive judo. But it wasn't long before his mistake caught up with him. Sure his back had good strength, but in bodybuilding poses it lacked thickness and width.

Initially Milos stuck with basic exercises like chins and barbell rows. This wasn't so much out of planning as necessity. The gym he trained in lacked any fancy equipment so he was forced to make do with these simple but effective exercises. But in a way this was a godsend as these exercises are probably two of the best movements for adding both width and thickness to the back.

With increased success in bodybuilding has come access to the best gyms in the world. Nowadays when he trains back Milos includes the full spectrum of back exercises. He alternates heavy with light movements, and routinely switches around his exercises. He also makes use of just about every grip possible. For example on pulldowns he'll go from wide to narrow to reverse, all in the same workout. He takes the same approach with chinups, alternating grips and attachments (straight chinup bar, v-bar, etc.).

In a typical back workout, Milos will start with chins or pulldowns for 5 to 6 sets, alternating grips. he'll then move on to a basic rowing exercise, usually one-arm rows or barbell rows, again for 3 sets of 8 reps. If it's barbell rows he alternates from a standard to a reverse grip.

For his third exercise, Milos heads to the seated rowing machine. This is one exercise where Milos feels technique is much more important than weight. For this reason he keeps the weight moderate and does higher reps (usually in the 15 range) in ultra-strict style.

Here's a typical Sarcev back routine:

1. Chinups – 3 sets of 8 reps with 90 pounds attached.
2. Chinups – 1 set of 15 reps using bodyweight.
3. Barbell rows – 3 sets of 8 reps.
4. Barbell row reverse grip – 3 sets of 8 reps.
5. Pulldowns – 3 sets of 8 reps.
6. Reverse grip pulldowns – 3 sets of 8 reps.

Milos and Milomar Sarcev

7. Dumbell rows – 3 sets of 8 reps with a 180-pound dumbell.
8. Seated cable rows – 2 sets of 15 reps.
9. Back extensions – 3 sets of 8 reps using 45-pound plate.
10. Back extensions – 2 sets of 15 reps using bodyweight.

Shoulders

Although he doesn't quite have the muscle mass of some of the other bodybuilders on the pro circuit, there's no disputing that Milos Sarcev has one of the most balanced physiques around. And one of the primary reasons for this is his wide, wide, shoulders. Milos was blessed with having a wide shoulder girdle, and when you put a set of melon-sized delts on top of that, the result is a set of shoulders that keep getting those yard-wide descriptions.

Milos will do at least one exercise for each delt head. He usually starts with a front delt exercise, alternating barbell and dumbell presses on a monthly basis. He does barbell presses to the front as after about 15 years of behind-the-head presses his shoulders started causing problems. Whether barbell or dumbell he does 3 sets of 6 to 8 reps.

Milos Sarcev and
Nasser El Sonbaty

With a basic power movement out of the way, Milos finishes off his front delts with an isolation exercise like front dumbell raises. He typically does 2 sets of about 15 reps using a 30- or 35-pound dumbell.

Milos adopts the same approach for his side delts. He'll start with a basic movement like dumbell side laterals and do 3 sets of 6 to 8 reps. And then do an isolation movement like cable laterals for 2 sets of 15 reps. Milos prefers to perform both the previous exercises one side at a time.

To hit his rear delts, Milos does 3 heavy sets of bent-over dumbell laterals. Again he uses a weight that just allows him to complete 6 to 8 reps. He alternates between the standing and seated version of this exercise. His isolation movement for rear delts is some sort of bent-over cable lateral, 2 sets of 15 reps each.

On some days Milos will finish shoulder training with heavy shrugs. But as the traps also fit in well with back exercises, Milos may wait until he trains back to do his shrugs. It all depends on how he feels.

Markus Ruhl

History shows that Paul Dillett won the 1999 New York Night of Champions contest, but the real crowd pleaser was Germany's Markus Ruhl. In eight years Markus has gone from a 140-pound soccer player to a 280-pound behemoth. From a mild-mannered, Volkswagen and Audi salesman, to one of the most popular bodybuilders in the world. To many he is the next stage in bodybuilding evolution. With his 2000 Toronto Pro Cup win, and second place finish at the 2000 New York Night of Champions, Markus has established himself as the one to watch in future contests. Here's what he's done in a few short years:

1997	Grand Prix Germany – IFBB, 10th	
1998	Night of Champions – IFBB, 9th	
1999	Grand Prix England – IFBB, 7th	
	Night of Champions – IFBB, 4th	
	Olympia – IFBB, 12th	
	Professional World Cup – IFBB, 7th	
2000	Night of Champions – IFBB, 2nd	
	Toronto Pro Invitational – IFBB, winner	

> **"To be the biggest you can be you must use the heaviest weights possible on every exercise."**
>
> – Markus Ruhl, German pro bodybuilder, offering some simple but effective advice.

Shoulders

Markus Ruhl's deltoids are among the largest on the current pro bodybuilding scene. Each cannonball-sized delt seems to be the size of an average NBA basketball. Walking through a door for this guy takes a few minutes of prior planning. Yet, as frightening as they are, Markus uses just three exercises to build them.

For his first exercise Markus does seated dumbell presses. Given the weight he will eventually work up to, he always starts with 2 or 3 light warm-up sets. He starts with the 50s for 30 fast, non-lockout reps. He then does 10 sets in pyramid fashion, working from the 50s (respectable workout weight for many bodybuilders) all the way up to the 150s or 175s, depending on how he feels that day. His reps usually range from 10 to 12 for the mid-weights, down to 4 or 5 for the monsters.

280-pound behemoth Markus Ruhl.

After inflicting severe punishment with the seated presses, Markus moves on to standing dumbell lateral raises. If the poundages on the previous exercise sound impressive, get a load of what he's using for lateral raises. He starts with 50-pound dumbells for 20 reps, and works up to, are you ready for it, 120-pounders for sets of 8! Most readers would consider 120-pound dumbells respectable pressing weight, but Markus is using it for strict lateral raises. What could the guy lift if he decided to loosen up his style?

Markus Ruhl's deltoids are among the largest on the current pro bodybuilding scene.

As Markus finds his rear delts get enough stimulation from his back training, he rarely does bent-over laterals. Instead he bombards his front and side delts with a third exercise, usually front military presses. As expected Markus does his presses with weight that most people would squat with. Starting with 135 pounds for 20 fast reps, Markus works up to 365 to 405 for sets of 6 to 8.

Markus usually trains traps with back, but as most bodybuilders finish their shoulder training with this muscle group, well discuss them here. Markus starts his trap training with barbell shrugs. The first set is done as a warmup and consists of 20 easy reps with 135 pounds. Markus then does additional sets adding a set of 45's with each set. Once he reaches 585 he does 2 to 3 sets for 8 to 12 reps. Markus always uses wrist straps once he passes the 225-pound mark as he wants his traps to receive most of the stimulation.

To finish his traps, Markus heads to the far end of the dumbell rack and begins dumbell shrugs. Starting with the 95-pounders for 20 reps, he works up to the 175-pounders. In all he'll typically do 6 to 8 sets of dumbell shrugs.

Arms

Markus trains his arms just once a week, but what a workout! For biceps he starts with barbell curls. The first set is usually 95 pounds for a quick set of 30. He then pyramids up to 250 pounds for 4 to 6 reps. In all Markus blasts his pythons with 10 to 12 sets of standing barbell curls.

You'd think 12 sets of barbell curls would suffice, but Markus is only a third of the way there. His second exercise is standing alternate dumbell curls, starting with 50 pounds for his patented 20 reps, and working up to 110's or 120's for 6 to 8 sets of 6 to 8 reps. How many readers use that weight for flat dumbell presses, let alone dumbell curls? Not many we are sure.

To finish off those 23-plus-inch monsters, Markus does 5 to 6 sets of concentration curls. On a typical day Markus will work up to 120 or 130 pounders for sets of 6 to 8 reps. The result is two of the highest peaked biceps on the planet.

Markus usually trains triceps on a separate day, and tosses around as much weight as when he trains biceps. Markus starts with two arm seated dumbell extensions. The first set consists of a 50 pounder for 30 quick reps, followed by 9 more sets pyramiding up the weight to a 160-pound dumbell. Given the susceptibility of the elbow joint to injury, Markus is careful not to bounce at the bottom of the movement.

For his second exercise Markus performs lying EZ-bar extensions or skullcrushers. This is another exercise that has to be seen to be appreciated. Markus will start with a human-like 110 pounds for 20 reps and work up to a bench press sized 275 pounds for 6 reps. These are by no means loose behind-the-head reps either. Markus lowers the weight in strict style to his forehead.

To finish off his gargantuan horseshoes, Markus does 6 to 8 sets of cable pushdowns. He normally uses the stack (200 pounds in the gym where he works out) for 6 to 8 reps.

Craig did his first bodybuilding show after the legendary Lee Labrada told him that he would do well in competition.

Craig Titus

From June 1995 until June 1996, Craig Titus had a year that (for most people), would culminate with a gunshot wound to the head! He was brought up on drug charges just prior to the '95 USA, lost the USA to Phil Hernon and stormed offstage. Disaster further reared its ugly head when Titus sustained a gnarly pec tear, had surgery, was engaged to be married and then deftly dumped by his girlfriend for prizefighter Vinnie Pazienza. Did that stop Craig? Not likely; when you're that big nothing can stop you.

Craig Michael Titus was born in Wyandotte, Michigan on January 14, 1967. In high school, Craig competed on the wrestling team. He weighed 132 pounds soaking wet. Upon graduation, he became determined to put on muscle via weight training.

"Even he is not immune to the powerful allure of building big biceps. You know the kind I mean – those Schwarzeneggerian inhumanly engorged excuses for human flesh that blow our collective minds whenever a big-arm champ hits a single or double biceps pose."

– Greg Zulak, *MuscleMag International* contributor commenting on USA amateur champion, Craig Titus.

Craig's determined to be a mover and shaker in the sport of bodybuilding.

When Craig graduated from high school he was 5'6" and 140 pounds. Once he started weight training and seeing results, he was hooked. By the age of 21, he was 5'9" and 185 pounds. Craig did his first bodybuilding show after the legendary Lee Labrada told him that he would do well in competition.[1] Lee's statement was prophetic:

1988   NPC Houston Bodybuilding Championships – 1st middleweight and overall
1989   NPC Houston Bodybuilding Championships – overall
1990   NPC Western Cup – overall
         Tournament of Champions – NPC, heavyweight, 3rd
1991   Ironman Championships – NPC, overall winner
1993   USA Championships – NPC, heavyweight, 4th
1994   Nationals – NPC, heavyweight, 2nd
         USA Championships – NPC, heavyweight, 2nd
1995   USA Championships – NPC, heavyweight, 2nd
1996   USA Championships – NPC, overall winner
         USA Championships – NPC, heavyweight, 1st
2000   Arnold Classic – IFBB, 10th
         Ironman Pro Invitational – IFBB, 8th
         Night of Champions – IFBB, 11th
         Toronto Pro Invitational – IFBB, 5th

Today Craig is back, and he's determined to be a mover and shaker in the sport of bodybuilding. And a more hard-nosed businessman you won't find: "Let me straighten out all the grand illusions that amateur body-builders have, thinking that they are going to sign million dollar contracts as soon as they become pros in the IFBB. I think that's the biggest misconception that these young bucks have, coming up in the sport. The fact of the matter is, giving a contract to a novice pro is somewhere in the ballpark of $30-40,000 a year. Or even in some cases much less. I myself was fortunate to sign an above-average deal with MET-Rx right after turning pro in 1996, where I was making $60,000 the first year, and $72,000 the second year on a two year deal. I have been a pro for over three years now and I recently signed a two-year deal with Sports One Inc. for even more money. I am also signed with a Max Muscle clothing contract. Both of these endorsements did not come to me. I had to hustle and go out and get them. But remember, it took three years to end up at this financial situation ... I charge $2000 for guest posing and I will make an effort to attend the prejudging for that price. For a guest appearance at a gym grand opening, nutritional store or doing an expo I charge $1200. To do a seminar

Don't sell yourself short. – Craig Titus

along with the appearance I charge $1500 or I take the door cover charge if the promoter thinks it is a better deal. All expenses paid, airfare and hotel, $70 a day for food, and no hotel without room service is accepted. This brings me to something that really pisses me off! If you're a pro, charge as a pro for your time. A $1000 fee is fine to guest pose when you're an amateur, but as a member of the IFBB don't cut yourself short. Stick to your guns and get your money. Every time a pro guest poses for $1000, it lowers the worth of professional bodybuilders ..."[2] – Craig Titus, a name we'll be hearing for years to come!

References:
1) http://www.bodybuilder.org/profiles/titus.php3#interview
2) http://members.xoom.com/_XMCM/CraigTitus/speaks4.htm

Biceps

Craig is like most bodybuilders in that he loves to see huge, freaky biceps. And over the last couple of years he has evolved the methods and routine that have added nearly two inches to his already freaky arms. Believe it or not, one of the reasons he failed to make much progress in the past was undertraining. He had totally bought into the argument that the biceps are a small muscle and don't need lots of sets to grow, so he only did 8 or 9 sets for them. Unfortunately not much happened in the growth department either. It was only when he increased his sets for biceps to 15 or 16 that his arms started to enlarge big time.

Craig is the first to admit that Mike Mentzer's theory of high intensity, low sets, may work for some, but not him. It was only after reading an article by Mike Matarazzo about higher sets for the biceps, and incorporating it into his own training that his arms finally started growing. Before he switched his arms were a respectable 18 3/4 inches, but now they easily go over the 20-inch mark.

Craig likes to train biceps as the second half of his Day 1 split routine. In the mornings he'll blast chest, and then come back later in the evening and do biceps. In a typical biceps session, Craig will pick four exercises and do 4 sets of each for 9 to 12 reps. Let's say he starts with barbell curls, he'll do the first set with 135 pounds for 12 reps, and then go 155 for 11, 165 for 10, and 185 for 9. At least that's his goal, but there are days when he can only manage 5 or 6 reps on the last set, so his training partner helps him reach 9 reps. Craig's style on barbell curls is very strict, although he will do a few cheat reps on the last couple of reps to complete the set.

Over the last couple of years Craig has evolved the methods and routine that have added nearly two inches to his already freaky arms.

Craig's second biceps exercise is often seated preacher cable curls. Again he does 4 sets of 9 to 12 reps. Listing weight is impossible as different machines have different leverages. A hundred pounds on one machine may be "heavier" than 150 pounds on another, depending on the machine's design. Whatever the weight, he picks enough so that he can only get 12 reps on the first set, and then pyramid up so he loses one rep per set.

For his third exercise, Craig will stand up and do straight bar cable curls. This is one of Craig's favorite movements and he particularly likes the feel it incurs in his biceps. Again he adds weight with each set for 4 sets of 9 to 12.

To finish off Craig will do 3 sets of dumbell concentration curls. This is the only time Craig deviates from his normal 4 sets of 9 to 12 eps. As this is a finishing movement, Craig does 12 to 15 reps. He does concentration curls in the standard way, elbow of the working arm braced against the inside of the knee.

The previous is just one biceps workout that Craig uses to pound his guns. The next workout he might start with 4 sets of standing alternate dumbell curls as his primary power movement. Then he might switch to standing cable curls for another 4 sets of 9 to 12 reps. For his third exercise he will do preacher curls. As last time he did cable preacher curls, this time he will use a straight barbell. To finish off he will replace one-arm dumbell concentration curls with one-arm cable curls.

The previous seems like a lot of biceps work, but keep in mind Craig trains biceps just once every five days. That's sufficient time for his arms to recover for the next brutalizing.

Shoulders

Craig Titus is another of those bodybuilders who equates stronger muscles with bigger muscles. His rationale is the stronger he gets the bigger he'll get. It's for this reason that you'll see the guy training with weights that impress powerlifters and the biggest bodybuilders. The end result has been the coveted US Nationals crown and his pro card.

A typical shoulder workout for one of bodybuilding's newest stars begins with seated presses on the Smith machine. Craig gave up barbell presses as they were playing havoc with his rotator muscles. By using the machine he doesn't have to worry about balancing just pushing the weight up. His first set is usually 135 pounds for 10 reps, followed by 225 for 12, 275 for 11, 295 for 10, and 315 for 9.

After Smith presses it's on to the BodyMaster's rear delt machine. Craig does 4 sets of 12 to 9 reps, using the entire 25-plate stack.

Craig goes to positive failure when performing dumbell shrugs.

Recognizing the importance of rear delt development to a competitive bodybuilder, Craig does bent-over dumbell laterals as his third shoulder exercise. The reps are again kept in the 12 to 9 range, and typical weight is a set of 90-pound dumbells. Craig prefers the standing version of this exercise to the seated version as he can use a bit more weight.

To hit his side delts, Craig moves on to dumbell side laterals. Using a 60-pound dumbell, Craig will do 4 sets going 12, 11, 10, and 9 reps respectively.

To finish off his side delts and warm up his traps, Craig does barbell upright rows as his fifth exercise. He'll do 2 sets using about 185 pounds, and then drop back to 155 pounds for an additional 2 sets. Again the reps are kept in the 9 to 12 range.

Next up it's 4 sets of dumbell shrugs using the colossal 180-pound dumbells. On this exercise Craig uses wrist straps and doesn't count reps. Instead he goes to positive failure. On some days this happens at the 10 to 12 range, while on others he may get 15 or 20.

To finish off those amazing traps, Craig does 4 sets of either Smith machine or Hammer Strength shrugs. Once again he keeps the reps in the 9 to 12 range.

Ronnie Coleman

Like Arnold, Haney, Dorian before him, Ronnie Coleman is currently the undisputed top bodybuilder in the world. With Mr. Olympia titles to his credit, Ronnie has raised the bar to a new level, and is daring everyone else to come get him.

Despite reaching the pinnacle of bodybuilding success, Ronnie still maintains his job as an Arlington Texas patrolman. And one look at the guy and you see why he doesn't need a badge to earn a troublemaker's respect. Nor a gun, not when you've got huge guns on each arm. But it's not hard to garner a little respect (actually a lot of respect) when you stand 5'11 and carry 260 pounds of muscle! Bad guys call him Sir, but we call him the Fortress.

Ronnie Coleman was born in Bastrop, Louisiana May 13, 1964. At the age of 13 he started training with weights. In high school he was asked to join the powerlifting team. Before joining he weighed 178 pounds. He went up to 181 pounds, but that does not describe his increase in lean muscle, which was impressive. He was so good at football in college that he was almost drafted into the pro ranks. But a serious neck and back injury kept him out of the last few games of the season.

Ronnie recovered, and became serious about bodybuilding. This was no surprise, as he had long ago learned that popularity was proportional to muscle size:

"I did become popular once I got to high school, though, because of my muscularity. As a matter of fact they held a contest at my college called the Mr. Physique. You had to get onstage and hit a few poses. I didn't know much about bodybuilding but entered and won it anyway!"

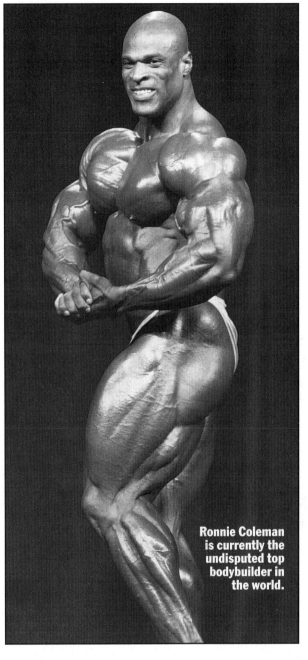

Ronnie Coleman is currently the undisputed top bodybuilder in the world.

We know that the judges liked him, look at these results:

1990   Nationals – NPC, heavyweight, 3rd
1991   Nationals – NPC, heavyweight, 4th
         World Amateur Championships – IFBB, heavyweight, 1st
1992   Chicago Pro Invitational – IFBB, 11th
         Night of Champions – IFBB, 14th
         Olympia – IFBB, 16th
         World Amateur Championships – IFBB, light heavyweight, 3rd

1993   Chicago Pro Invitational – IFBB, 6th
        Grand Prix France – IFBB, 4th
        Grand Prix Germany – IFBB, 6th
        Niagara Falls Pro Invitational – IFBB, 6th
1994   Grand Prix France – IFBB, 3rd
        Grand Prix Germany – IFBB, 3rd
        Olympia – IFBB, 15th
        San Jose Pro Invitational – IFBB, 4th
1995   Canada Pro Cup – IFBB, winner
        Grand Prix France – IFBB, 4th
        Grand Prix Russia – IFBB, 6th
        Grand Prix Ukraine – IFBB, 3rd
        Houston Pro Invitational – IFBB, 6th
        Night of Champions – IFBB, 3rd
        Olympia – IFBB, 11th
1996   Canada Pro Cup – IFBB, winner
        Florida Pro Invitational – IFBB, 2nd
        Grand Prix England – IFBB, 5th
        Grand Prix Germany – IFBB, 5th
        Grand Prix Spain – IFBB, 5th
        Night of Champions – IFBB, 2nd
        Olympia – IFBB, 6th
1997   Arnold Classic – IFBB, 4th
        Grand Prix Czech Republic – IFBB, 4th
        Grand Prix England – IFBB, 5th
        Grand Prix Finland – IFBB, 3rd
        Grand Prix Germany – IFBB, 5th
        Grand Prix Hungary – IFBB, 6th
        Grand Prix Russia – IFBB, winner
        Grand Prix Spain – IFBB, 7th
        Ironman Pro Invitational – IFBB, 3rd
        Olympia – IFBB, 9th
        San Jose Pro Invitational – IFBB, 6th
1998   Grand Prix Finland – IFBB, winner
        Grand Prix Germany – IFBB, winner
        Ironman Pro Invitational – IFBB, 10th
        Night of Champions – IFBB, winner
        Olympia – IFBB, winner
        San Francisco Pro Invitational – IFBB, 2nd
        Toronto Pro Invitational – IFBB, winner
1999   Grand Prix England – IFBB, winner
        Olympia – IFBB, winner
        Professional World Cup – IFBB, winner

Ronnie is one cop that you won't find hanging out in a donut shop!

Of course, there a few cynics who think that bodybuilders are big, but not all that strong. They should try training with Ronnie: "I've deadlifted 750 pounds, squatted 585 for ten, 645 for four, and I've benched 475 for one."

Ronnie is one cop that you won't find hanging out in a donut shop! But if you do catch him cheating on his diet, just remember to call him Sir. And God help you if you've eaten the last cruller!

Shoulders

Ronnie Coleman is the first to admit that lifting heavy has its drawbacks, especially when it comes to shoulder training. It's nice to be able to brag about your behind-the-head barbell press, but a shoulder injury, no matter how small, does nothing for your pro bodybuilding career. After much experimenting Ronnie discovered that his shoulders responded best to high volume, high intensity, training, based mainly on cables and dumbells. He also learned the key to continued success is to frequently change exercises. At present he does two shoulder routines, usually on Thursday and Saturdays. The following program is his Saturday's routine.

"I've always been athletic, so that helps. I played football, basketball, and baseball in high school and Grambling State University in Louisiana. I also ran track, did the discuss and shot put, and was on the powerlifting team."

– Ronnie Coleman, Mr. Olympia, giving some insight into his athletic versatility.

Ronnie usually starts with 3 sets of down-the-rack dumbell lateral raises. His first set is 25 reps using 30 pounds. He then goes 40 pounds for 15, 50 pounds for 10, and 60 pounds for 8 reps. After a short rest, Ronnie repeats the giant set using the same weights for the same reps. The big mistake Ronnie sees others making on this exercise is too much rocking back and forth. Ronnie makes sure to maintain excellent form on each and every set.

Ronnie's next exercise is one-arm dumbell laterals. Holding a dumbell in each hand, Ronnie raises one dumbell to shoulder height, pauses, and then returns to the starting position.

Kevin Levrone, Ronnie Coleman and Flex Wheeler

Only after he has completed 12 reps with one arm will he start the other. Ronnie typically does 3 sets of 12 reps using a 40-pound dumbell.

To increase the size of his front delts, and also bring out the separation between his front delts and upper chest, Ronnie does 3 sets of front barbell raises. Ronnie uses a 60-pound barbell for this exercise and grabs it with an underhand (as if doing a biceps curl) grip. He slowly raises until his arms are parallel with the floor and then lowers until the bar is just short of his thighs.

To hit the famous Coleman rear delts, Ronnie performs bent-over cable laterals. He uses a cross-cable grip (the left hand holding the right cable handle and vice versa) and once again raises until his arms are no higher than shoulder height. Once again he does 3 sets of 12 to 15 reps.

Biceps

Not since Arnold Schwarzenegger has a Mr. Olympia sported such mountainous peaks. Even Dorian Yates and Lee Haney, with their combined 14 Mr. Olympia wins, could not stand next to Ronnie coleman in a front double biceps pose.

Ronnie comes from that most cursed school that the rest of us call "favorable genetics." This means he adds inches to his arms by merely sniffing a barbell. Where other bodybuilders spend years trying to force another inch on the almighty guns, Ronnie seemingly gains arm

Ronnie had to cut back on his arm training to once a week.

mass by thinking about it. In fact it has reached the point now that he has cut back on arm training to just once a week. He doesn't want them to get too big you know!

A typical Coleman biceps' routine will consist of four exercises done for 3 sets of 8 to 10 reps. As with most bodyparts, Ronnie stays true to his bodybuilding fraternity, and uses moderate weights. "With biceps the important part is not what you lift but how you lift. Form is crucial."

Ronnie seldom uses cheating, forced reps, or negatives in his training and his rationale for staying away from ponderous poundages in his training is that he wants to avoid injuries at all costs.

Ronnie likes to start with the bench press of biceps exercises, standing barbell curls. Ronnie uses a shoulder-width grip on curls, and slowly raises the bar until his upper arms are about 45 degrees from the horizontal. He then lowers to just short of touching his thighs. In this day of 200-plus pound barbell curls, it's refreshing to see someone of Ronnie's stature doing his sets using between 110 and 135 pounds. But when you witness those sets you see why. Each and every rep is slow, deliberate, and controlled. There's not an ounce of

When Ronnie Coleman does barbell curls, each and every rep is slow, deliberate, and controlled. There's not an ounce of body momentum.

body momentum. No swinging, no bouncing, no jerking. Ronnie's biceps are getting the full benefit of the weight.

Ronnie's second exercise is usually standing alternate dumbell curls. After hitting both biceps together with barbell curls, Ronnie likes to isolate each separately. Again he only uses moderate weight, in this case 35-pound dumbells. At the top of the movement Ronnie pauses for a split-second to give the biceps an extra degree of contraction.

For his third exercise, Ronnie performs 3 sets of one-arm dumbell concentration curls. Ronnie takes a page form Arnold's book on this one and prefers to stand up and lean slightly forward, as opposed to most bodybuilders who do the exercise while sitting on the edge of a bench. Ronnie's only variation from Arnold's style is to rest his elbow on his inner thigh, as opposed to Arnold's letting his arm hang loose. As he lifts the dumbell, Ronnie supinates his palms so his little finger is slightly higher than his thumb at the end of the movement. As with alternate curls, Ronnie also likes to hold the contraction at the top for a second or two. This not only gives the biceps an extra degree of tension, but also helps cut down on any swinging that usually accompanies fast reps.

To finish off perhaps the greatest guns currently on the bodybuilding scene, Ronnie heads to the cable machine and forces out 3 sets of one-arm cable curls. Ronnie uses about 60 pounds on this exercise and curls the handle up to just short of his chin. As always his rep speed is slow and controlled.

From looking at the previous we see that Ronnie has done more than just four biceps exercises. There is a method to his madness so to speak. The first two exercises, barbell and alternate dumbell curls, are pure mass builders, while the last two, concentration and one-arm cable curls, are shaping and refining movements. The end result is two of the meanest arms ever to hold the Sandow statue.

Triceps

Ronnie realized early on that he would need to pay particular attention to his triceps given the incredible growth potential of his biceps. When you are blessed with perhaps the largest biceps on the Mr. Olympia stage, it's an absolute must that equal attention be given to the triceps. In this regard Ronnie has excelled as his horseshoes are now garnering nearly as much attention as his biceps.

Check out the intensity of Ronnie's shoulder workout.

Ronnie usually starts his triceps training with pushdowns. He finds that this exercise is not only a good overall triceps movement, but also warms the triceps up for the later dumbell exercises. Ronnie uses about 80 pounds for the first set of 25 to 30 reps, and then pyramids up in weight for three additional sets until he's doing 200-plus pounds for 10 to 15 reps. He then does one burn out set of 20 to 30 reps using about 100 pounds.

To hit the long head of the triceps, Ronnie performs overhead cable extensions as his second exercise. After one light warm-up set, Ronnie does 3 sets of 15 reps.

Exercise number three is one-arm dumbell extensions. Again it's one light warm-up set followed by 3 heavier sets of 10 to 12 reps using a 60-pound dumbell. This is one exercise that can be stressful on the elbow joint, so Ronnie rarely starts his triceps with it. He always does pushdowns or cable extensions first.

Ronnie's final exercise is triceps kickbacks. Given that his triceps are fatigued at this point, he doesn't need to use a heavy dumbell, 30 to 35 pounds for 3 to 4 sets of 10 to 15 does the trick. The key to this exercise is ultra strict form. The body will constantly try to cheat by swinging the upper arms and rocking the torso. The only thing that should be moving on this exercise is the forearm, with the elbow acting like a hinge.

Legs

With perhaps the most awesome upper body on the pro scene, it only makes sense to devote extra attention to keeping the legs in balance. Ronnie has found by trial and error that year-round heavy training is not the most productive. By cycling heavy with light to medium training, Ronnie not only reduces the risk of injuries, but also keeps the muscles guessing. On heavy days he keeps the reps in the 6 to 8 range, while light days are done for sets of 30 (usually in drop sets of 10).

Mr. Olympia's first leg exercise is usually squats. He'll start with a set of 10 using 135 pounds, and add a pair of 45's with each successive set. The result is 225 for 10, 315 for 10, 405 for 10, 495 for 10, and yes, 585 for 8 reps. For those not impressed, try squatting nearly 600 pounds for 8 reps after five previous sets. Further, these are not half-assed reps either. Ronnie goes all the way down, below parallel, almost to the floor.

For his second exercise, Ronnie heads to the leg press machine and works up to 1125 pounds for 15 reps. This number is not chosen arbitrarily as the machine he uses can only hold 12 plates a side. But there are days when the strength is there so he'll add on a couple of plates on top and maybe a training partner for good measure, and do sets of 10 (it works out to about 1305 pounds).

Ronnie's third leg exercise is hack squats. Again some hefty poundages are thrown around starting with 315 for 10 reps and working up to 765 pounds for 10 reps. As with squats and leg presses, hacks are done for a full range of motion, all the way down and up just short of a lock out. For variety Ronnie likes to vary his foot position to target different parts of his thighs.

The previous is just one routine Ronnie uses to blast his quads. Some days he and his training partner will start with leg presses and do three triple drop sets. They'll then do the same thing on the hack and leg extension machines. For those who didn't do the math that works out to 27 sets for their thighs! As Ronnie says, "You don't walk normal for a while."

By cycling heavy with light to medium training, Ronnie not only reduces the risk of injuries, but also keeps the muscles guessing.

To hit hamstrings, Ronnie usually starts with standing leg curls for 4 sets of about 15 reps. Unlike most of his other exercises, Ronnie uses the same weight on all 4 sets.

Next up it's 4 sets of 10 to 12 reps on the lying leg curl.

Finally Ronnie will finish off hamstrings with stiff-leg deadlifts. On some days he'll make it his third exercise, while on others he'll superset stiff-legs with lying leg curls.

Close to a contest Ronnie performs the previous exercises in triple-drop fashion. And he'll also add in lunges. Ronnie has his own version of lunges. Instead of the standard stationary lunge, Ronnie will lunge forward for a distance of 50 yards, and then lunge back for the same distance. Remember this is after the abuse his thighs and hamstrings suffered only minutes earlier. But the results are worth it as Ronnie has become famous for his hamstrings.

Back

Until Ronnie Coleman came on the scene, the best backs on the pro scene belonged to Flex Wheeler and Dorian Yates. With Yates' retirement in 1997, most assumed that the back poses would easily be snatched up by Flex Wheeler. But then along came Arlington's biggest police officer, and Flex had his work cut out for him. It's no exaggeration to say Ronnie has one of the greatest backs in bodybuilding history.

Ronnie always begins back training by warming up and stretching. Not only does this help prevent injuries, but in fact gives him better development.

The first thing we should point out is that Ronnie rarely does the same exercises in the same order. Depending on the areas of the back he wants to hit, the equipment available, or the mood he's in, Ronnie frequently changes things around. If he starts with close-grip pulldowns he'll strap his hands to the bar and sit down leaning back at a 30-degree angle. The first thing he'll do is stretch the lats out fully at the top, and then pull the handle down to his chest. Ronnie keeps his chest high and squeezes his shoulder blades together at the bottom. On a typical day Ronnie will do about 4 sets of 12 to 15 reps. Depending on the gym, he'll use the stack, or the stack plus an additional 25 to 50 pounds.

Ronnie's second back exercise might be wide grip pulldowns. With the exception of the wide grip, Ronnie's technique is the same as the close-grip version, chest forward and high, squeezing at the bottom, full stretch at the top. Again Ronnie does 4 sets of 12 to 15 reps using the stack or more.

With two width exercises out of the way, Ronnie moves on to seated rows for central back thickness. Ronnie starts with his knees bent, feet positioned on the machine's pad. He then leans forward so his torso is about 45 degrees to the floor. As he starts pulling back, Ronnie arches his chest and starts squeezing his back muscles so that by the time his torso is vertical and the bar touching his rib cage, his shoulder blades are nearly touching. As guessed he does 4 sets of 12 to 15 reps.

Ronnie's fourth exercise is T-bar rows. For this exercise Ronnie wears a pair of gloves and a weight lifting belt. With his knees slightly bent, torso about 45 degrees to the floor, Ronnie pulls the bar up to his lower rib cage. As with most back exercises he fully stretches his lats at the bottom. Typically he'll work up to six plates for 4 sets of 12 to 15 reps.

A fifth lat exercise is chinups or pullups. If he started with this exercise he'd add extra weight around his waist, but if it's the last exercise in the rotation, his bodyweight will suffice (that's about 280 pounds in the off-season!). Ronnie uses a wide grip on pullups and leans back slightly as he pulls his body up to bar height. Four sets of 12 to 15 reps is the norm, but it all depends on how tired his lats are from the previous exercises.

Mr. Olympia,
Ronnie Coleman.

Henderson Thorne

Henderson Westerman Thorne was born in Bridgetown, Barbados, on March 21, 1961. Henderson is the oldest child in a family of four (one younger brother and two younger sisters). Growing up in Barbados he had a strict Catholic upbringing. He attended a boy's school and wore a school uniform. He was expected to get good grades in school and to be well behaved. His father believed in the old adage, "spare the rod and spoil the child." Henderson recalls it, though, as a mostly happy and pleasant childhood. Many of his spare hours were spent with his boyhood chums roaming the island's beautiful beaches and enjoying the warm tropical waters. Compared to the Canadian winters he now endures, it was like living in a paradise.

Henderson discovered bodybuilding by accident.

He participated in many sports in Barbados, especially cricket, soccer and track and field. He had a naturally muscular body and a good build, but at that time he didn't lift weights at all.

His father's decision to uproot the family and move to Toronto, Ontario when Henderson was just 14 created a severe culture shock. Arriving in Toronto in the dead of winter, without even a winter coat, he didn't know quite what to expect. As the plane taxied in, he saw snow for the first time. "We came in the winter. I remember looking out the window of the plane and thinking, 'Boy, why does everybody up here smoke?' Because in the winter when it's cold you can see your breath, but I thought everybody was smoking."

Henderson discovered bodybuilding by accident. An injury to his shoulder had forced him to quit football. He had never lifted weights before, and he started lifting to strengthen his shoulder. Football became a distant memory, and bodybuilding a way of life:

1988   North American Championships – IFBB, light heavyweight, 3rd
1989   World Games – IFBB, light heavyweight, 1st
1990   Niagara Falls Pro Invitational – IFBB, 6th
       Night of Champions – IFBB
1991   Musclefest Grand Prix – IFBB, 9th
       Niagara Falls Pro Invitational – IFBB, 5th
1992   Chicago Pro Invitational – IFBB, 4th
       Grand Prix England – IFBB, 13th
       Grand Prix Germany – IFBB, 7th
       Grand Prix Holland – IFBB, 9th
       Grand Prix Italy – IFBB, 8th
       Niagara Falls Pro Invitational – IFBB, 2nd

Night of Champions – IFBB, 6th
Olympia – IFBB, 14th
1993 Chicago Pro Invitational – IFBB, 5th
Niagara Falls Pro Invitational – IFBB, 7th
Night of Champions – IFBB, 6th
Pittsburgh Pro Invitational – IFBB, 6th
1994 Ironman Pro Invitational – IFBB, 8th
Niagara Falls Pro Invitational – IFBB, winner
Night of Champions – IFBB, 9th
Olympia – IFBB, 19th
San Jose Pro Invitational – IFBB, 10th
1995 Arnold Classic – IFBB, 10th
Canada Pro Cup – IFBB, 10th
Houston Pro Invitational – IFBB, 8th
Niagara Falls Pro Invitational – IFBB, 8th
San Jose Pro Invitational – IFBB, 6th
1996 Canada Pro Cup – IFBB, 10th
Ironman Pro Invitational – IFBB, 9th
1997 Canada Pro Cup – IFBB, 5th
Ironman Pro Invitational – IFBB, 8th
Night of Champions – IFBB, 8th
1998 Night of Champions – IFBB, 15th
Toronto Pro Invitational – IFBB, 10th
1999 Toronto Pro Invitational – IFBB, 6th
2000 Toronto Pro Invitational – IFBB, 13th
Henderson Thorne, the Canadian menace on the American stage!

Shoulders

Despite never having won any of the big contests on the pro circuit, Henderson is known as one of the most consistent pros out there. He has been competing since 1988, and there have been few contests where the guy was in nothing but top shape.

Henderson's training can best be described as intense and straightforward. Nothing fancy, nothing off the wall. You rarely find him doing such advanced techniques as supersets, trisets, forced reps, or negatives. Just basic exercises for straight sets and reps. Generally he picks a weight that he can handle for 6 to 10 reps and does 3 to 4 sets. To give an example of Henderson's honest approach to training, let's look at his shoulder routine.

"I used to run track and played soccer and football in high school, so my legs were always pretty strong and muscular, even before I took up bodybuilding."

– Henderson Thorne, pro bodybuilder, responding to an interviewer's question about always having strong legs.

Henderson is known as one of the most consistent pros out there.

"I don't like to spend hours in the gym training. I seldom spend more than an hour on a workout, and many of my workouts are only 30 to 45 minutes. If you're spending three hours in the gym you're probably talking more than training."

– Henderson Thorne,
Canadian pro bodybuilders,
offering good advice to those who
spend hours in the gym. Quality
counts far more than quantity.

Henderson's training can best be described as intense and straightforward.

Having witnessed so many shoulder injuries over the years, Henderson always starts his shoulder training with a good warmup. He usually grabs a set of 2 1/2 pound plates and does a couple of quick sets of front, side, and rear lateral raises. This gets the blood into the muscles and helps prepare them for what they are about to receive.

Henderson trains similar to late '80s early '90s great Mike Ashley, in that he alternates three different workouts, light, medium, and heavy.

On his heavy workout he generally starts with a heavy basic movement like seated behind-the-head barbell presses. He pyramids up in weight until he can just manage 6 reps. Each rep is full, going all the way up and down. He doesn't do short, constant tension reps. He does his smoothly and strictly with no cheating. A typical Henderson workout will look like this:
Behind-the-head barbell presses
135 x 10
225 x 8
245 x 6
275 x 6

If he's feeling particularly strong that day he might go up to 315 for a heavy triple, but this usually happens on every fourth workout or so.

Next up it's seated dumbell presses. As his shoulders are fully warmed up from the barbell presses, he jumps right to the 90 pounders. He pyramids up in weight from the 90's to the 140's and 150's for sets of 6 to 8 reps. Henderson does his dumbell presses with his palms facing forward at all times. He finds the rotation employed by some bodybuilders too awkward on his shoulders.

To finish off his delts, Henderson moves on to barbell upright rows. He starts with 135 pounds for 10 reps, and then goes up to 155 for 8, and then finishes with 175 pounds for 2 sets of 6 to 8 reps.

Henderson's medium day consists of more isolation exercises with reps in the 8 to 12 range. After a light warmup he begins with one-arm raises to the sides, working up to a

Henderson is not a slave to conformity.

60-pound dumbell for 4 sets of 10 to 12 reps. Henderson follows the "pouring water from the jug" approach on laterals unlike the dumbell presses, where he doesn't like to rotate his wrists. This keeps the elbow high and puts maximum tension on the side delts.

To hit the rear delts, Henderson usually makes bent-over dumbell laterals his second exercise. He'll typically use a pair of 60s for 4 sets of 10 to 12 reps.

Even though this is his medium day, Henderson always makes it a point to do seated dumbell presses as his third exercise. The only difference is that he only goes up to a pair of 90s for 4 sets of 8 to 10 reps.

To finish off shoulders on this day, Henderson does 4 sets of reverse grip dumbell shrugs. He finds this type of grip hits the traps a little lower on the back than the standard overhand variety. Henderson typically uses 150 pounders for sets of 8 to 10 reps.

Again we see a straightforward, no nonsense workout that can be done in about 45 minutes. Are you getting the picture yet?

On to Henderson's third or light routine – for variety and to give his shoulder joints a rest from the heavy dumbell and barbell movements, he likes to employ a lot of cable work in this routine. His first exercise is one-arm cable laterals, which he does for 4 sets of 12 to 15 reps, alternating back and forth between left and right sides.

His second exercise is again cable raises, but this time he does them to the front, holding a short, straight bar with both hands. Henderson faces away from the machine with the cable between his legs. He raises upward until the bar is above his forehead, and then returns so that the moving plates stop just short of the remaining stack.

For his third exercise, Henderson hits the rear delts with 4 sets of reverse pec flyes. Unlike most that sit down on the machine's seat, Henderson prefers to remain standing. Again he does sets in the 12 to 15 range.

To finish his delts Henderson heads to the Icarian press machine and bangs out 4 sets of 12 to 15 reps using the stack (250 pounds) plus an additional 45 pounds. That folks is nearly 300 pounds for high reps after the other three exercises.

The last movement Henderson usually does on light day is machine shrugs on the bench press station on the old Universal machine. On most days he adds an extra 180 pounds to the machine's 225 pounds and executes 4 sets of 12 to 15 reps.

Although Henderson usually alternates the three previous workouts, he's also a great believer in the instinctive training principle. If his shoulders are telling him to skip a heavy workout in favor of a lighter, more isolated one, then that's what he'll do. Henderson is not a slave to conformity.

Back

Henderson Thorne is one of those body-builders who looks as if he could lift a building. He has that thickly muscled look that only comes from hoisting heavy weights over long periods of time. To quote Greg Zulak "this guy's definitely no muscle-pumper."

Henderson's back is especially one of his strongest points, both in appearance and function. His lats are wide and thick. His traps look like softballs laid on top of his shoulders. And those two spinal erectors of his run up his back like two pythons. You get the picture.

It's difficult to give an exact Henderson Thorne back workout as he does three different routines, heavy, medium, and light. He finds adding in a light day gives his joints and soft connective tissues a break, and also cuts down on the chance of overtraining. He also finds that by doing three different routines he can hit the back from every conceivable angle. Finally no matter what type of routine he follows he always uses wrist straps. Straps allow him to handle heavier weights and get those last couple of muscle-stimulating reps.

A heavy day for Henderson is one which the reps will be lower than on his light or moderate day. He does more sets too. Whereas on a light day he might keep the reps in the 12 to 15 range, on the heavy day he will

Henderson's back is especially one of his strongest points, both in appearance and function.

aim for 6 to 8 reps per set. He stays with basic exercises and does less cable work. Because of the weight being used he'll rest longer between sets too, about three minutes, sometimes a bit longer on deadlifts and rows.

No matter what day, heavy, light or medium, Henderson always starts his back workout with wide-grip chins. This exercise serves as both a warmup and to add width to his lats. Although not in the Roy Callender mold (40 sets or more!) Henderson lives chins, and will do 6 to 12 sets a workout. Some days he'll do six sets and move on to his other back exercises, and then throw in six more at the end. On other days he'll bang out 12 straight sets. A typical rep range is 8 to 10 per set. Sometimes for a bit of extra tension he'll strap a 35-pound plate around his waist. Many bodybuilders think that chins and pulldowns are interchangeable – that they are identical – but Henderson disagrees. He's convinced that chins are the superior lat-building exercise.

In the past Henderson usually followed chins with deadlifts – very heavy deadlifts. He'd typically do 5 sets of 6 to 8 reps, pyramiding up in weight. Henderson credits heavy deadlifting with not only thickening his whole back, but also improving his squat. At one point he was stuck at 400 pounds for 10 reps on the squat, but after adding heavy deadlifts to his routine, his squat went up to 700 pounds for 8 reps and 800 pounds for a triple. It's to the point now that he considers 600-pound squats for 10 reps his maintenance phase!

A few words of advice from Henderson on deadlifting. He always uses straps and keeps his back slightly arched at all times. As soon as you relax the spinal erector muscles and allow the lower back to round, most of the stress is shifted to the spinal column, particularly the ligaments. Henderson also recommends that you keep your head up and don't pull the weight with a jerking motion. Do the reps smoothly.

At present Henderson only deadlifts once or twice a month. His second back exercise therefore is usually T-bar rows. He does 6 to 8 sets of T-bars, adding a plate with each set until he's up over 300 pounds. Once again he keeps the reps in the 6 to 8 range. Henderson considers T-bars (and the closely related barbell rows) a must for bodybuilders wishing to put some serious beef on their middle backs.

For his third exercise, Henderson heads to the lat pulldown machine. As he did chins to add width to his upper lats, he relies on pulldowns for the lower lats. He accomplishes this by switching from a wide to narrow grip, using the familiar triangle-shaped bar normally used for seated rows. Once again Henderson's strength comes true on this exercise and he'll go up to 300 pounds for 8 to 10 reps per set. These are strict reps by the way. You won't find him swinging back and forth using body momentum. At the bottom he pulls his elbows down and back as far as they'll go.

The previous is a good example of what Henderson calls his heavy day. The next time he comes into the gym he'll follow his moderate routine. As on his heavy day he will start with chins, but with two differences, he'll do 6 to 8 sets instead of 10 to 12. And he doesn't add extra weight around his waist either. The reps are kept in the 8 to 10 range and his form is smooth and controlled.

Porter Cottrell and Henderson Thorne

For his second exercise Henderson does barbell rows. He finds this exercise great for hitting the entire back, and next to chins probably the greatest back exercise there is. He'll typically do 5 to 6 sets, pyramiding up the weight each set. Here are some average poundages: 225 for 10, 315 for 8, 365 for 8, 385 for 6, and if everything feels good, 405 for 5 or 6.

To get that all-important stretch at the bottom, Henderson stands on a block. He also uses straps to prevent his forearms from becoming the weak link in the chain.

After barbell rows it's on to one-arm rows, again 5 sets of 8 to 10 reps, working up to a 150 pound dumbell. With one hand and knee braced on a flat bench, Henderson pulls the dumbell as high as possible, and lowers all the way down to give the lats a good stretch. This is one of the few exercises where Henderson will use a little body swing to keep the weight moving. But just enough to get past his sticking point. He still relies on his lats to do most of the work.

If he did deadlifts the previous back workout and not T-bars, he'll do 5 sets of T-bars as his third back exercise. Again it's 5 sets of 6 to 8 reps, but he keeps the weight a bit lighter than on his heavy day.

For his fourth exercise Henderson does 4 sets of seated cable rows. For variety he alternates between the narrow, triangle-shaped bar, and the straight bar. In either case it's sets of 10 to 12 reps using between 225 and 250 pounds.

To finish off his moderate day Henderson will do 4 or 5 sets of lat pulldowns to either the front or rear. Depending on the day his weight will range from 225 to 250 pounds, for sets of 10 to 12 reps.

Dumbell rows are one of the few exercises where Henderson will use a little body swing to keep the weight moving.

Henderson's light day relies more on cable work and less on barbell work. He also keeps the reps slightly higher, usually in the 12 to 15 range. The pace is faster too, 60 to 90 seconds instead of his normal two to three minutes.

As expected his first back exercise is wide chins. He does just 4 or 5 sets on light day, keeping the reps in the 12 to 15 range. He finds the higher reps with just his bodyweight still gives the lats a good workout without the same draining effect that heavy weight and lower reps has on his recovery system.

Seated cable rows are next, and again the weight is kept light. Henderson's primary goal on light day is to give the lats a good pump, and 4 or 5 sets of 12 to 15 reps does the job.

To finish his lats he does 4 or 5 sets of 10 to 15 reps of lat pulldowns using light to moderate weight. Occasionally if he's in the mood he may throw in a couple of sets of one-arm cable or dumbell rows. But most light days his entire back workout consists of 12 to 15 sets.

For those of you following the same back workout, month in, month out, give Henderson's rotating routine a try. It might be just what you need to get those back muscles growing again.

Legs

Henderson used to marvel at the photos of Arnold and Dave Draper in *Muscle Builder* magazine (forerunner of today's *Muscle and Fitness* magazine) squatting with 405 pounds for sets of 8 to 12 reps when he was growing up. To the 15-year-old Henderson, these 250-pound behemoths seemed like supermen.

Using the previous as inspiration, Henderson intensified his leg training and it wasn't long before he was using over 600 pounds for 10 reps on the squat. Not bad when you consider Henderson only weighs around 220 pounds in the off-season.

Henderson typically trains quads by themselves on the morning of leg day, and then comes back later at night to do hamstrings. He usually starts with 6 to 8 sets of medium-weight leg extensions, averaging 12 to 15 reps per set. Doing leg extensions first serves two purposes for Henderson, it warms up his thighs for the heavy squats he'll do later, and it pre-exhausts his thighs so he doesn't need to go super heavy on the squats.

After the extensions, Henderson moves to the two core exercises of his thigh routine, squats and 45-degree leg presses. He starts with squats, and pyramids up in weight in the following manner:

225 pounds for 15 reps
315 pounds for 12 reps
405 pounds for 10 reps
495 pounds for 10 reps
600 pounds for 10 reps

The last set depends on how he feels. Some days he'll end off with 495 pounds.

After squats it's on to leg presses. Henderson is a firm believer in high reps on leg presses and rarely does less than 25 reps a set. In fact he usually averages 50 reps per set, and this is with 750 to 800 pounds on the machine. And if this is not enough to impress you, Henderson does his reps in nonlockout style. This means no rest for the entire set. Oh, did we tell you he puts himself through 6 sets of such madness?

To really shock his thighs, Henderson may do drop sets on this exercise. He'll put on over 1000 pounds and bang out 25 or 30 reps, have a partner or two strip off a couple of plates, do another 20 or 30 reps, strip off still more weight, and do another 25 or 30 reps. By the time he's finished he will have done 100 reps or more.

Another training technique is to do rest-pause sets. He'll put 1000 pounds or so on the machine and go to positive failure, which usually happens around the 30-rep mark. He'll then lock out his legs, pause for ten seconds or so and then continue for another 15 to 20 reps.

To finish off his thighs (as if squats and leg presses in such training style was not enough) Henderson goes back to the leg extension for another 6 sets of 8 to 10 reps, this time using heavier weight.

When he comes back later in the evening Henderson proceeds to inflict similar punishment on his hamstrings. First he'll start with 5 sets of stiff-leg deadlifts doing about 10 to 12 reps per set. Then it's on to lying leg curls for 6 sets of 10 to 12 reps. Finally, he'll do standing leg curls for 8 to 10 reps.

For variety Henderson will sometimes do drop and rest pause sets on both leg curl exercises.

Andreas Munzer

Andreas is one of those individuals who achieved bodybuilding immortality by dying. His ability to appear onstage, massive and shredded, is almost as legendary as his last drug cycle. He kept his personal life, and his family history, intensely private. He was certainly a man of contrasts. Though almost secretive about himself, he was very public in displaying his body, and the judges were impressed.

Andreas ate, slept, and lived bodybuilding to the extreme.

Andreas was born in Graz, Austria (same birthplace as Arnold). His first introduction to bodybuilding came in 1981 when he missed the bus home and while waiting for the next one, wandered into a gym. A short workout got him hooked and within two years the 175-pound Andreas had won the middleweight division of the Austrian Championships. In 1989 Andreas won the heavyweight division at the World Championships while weighing 210 pounds.

During his short competitive pro career Andreas developed a reputation for coming into the show literally shredded. To quote many a writer "Andreas has cross striations on his cross striations." Unfortunately Andreas ate, slept, and lived bodybuilding to the extreme. And just looking immortal doesn't make you immortal. Andreas died in 1996. There's no need to go into the details of his death. While genetics has not been ruled out, the evidence suggests Andreas died from complications associated with the cocktail of bodybuilding drugs he was taking. Here's his short, but impressive competitive record:

1986   European Amateur Championships – IFBB, middleweight, 6th
1987   World Amateur Championships – IFBB, light heavyweight, 3rd
1988   World Amateur Championships – IFBB, light heavyweight, 3rd
1989   Olympia – IFBB, 13th
       World Games – IFBB, heavyweight, 1st
1990   Arnold Classic – IFBB, 3rd
       Grand Prix Germany – IFBB, 3rd
       Olympia – IFBB, 9th
1991   Arnold Classic – IFBB, 9th
       Ironman Pro Invitational – IFBB, 3rd
       Olympia – IFBB
       Pittsburgh Pro Invitational – IFBB, 4th

Andreas Munzer is still regarded as having perhaps the most ripped physique ever to hit the posing platform.

Triceps

Although he's been dead for over five years, Andreas Munzer is still regarded as having perhaps the most ripped physique ever to hit the posing platform. Munzer's contest shape was such that one creative journalist coined the term "Munzered" to describe any bodybuilder who got his or her bodyfat percentage down in the 1 to 2 percent range. Unfortunately as events later confirmed, Andreas was using more than just good eating habits to achieve such muscularity. And he paid the ultimate price with his death.

If there was one muscle group that displayed Munzer's muscularity to its utmost, it was his triceps. Most bodybuilders are happy to get longitudinal separation between the three triceps heads. But Munzer set a new standard by having cross striations visible on each individual head!

Of course there's more to great triceps than having a low bodyfat percentage, you need some quality muscle mass there to begin with, and in this regard Andreas was no slouch either. Andreas would start a typical triceps routine with a good mass builder such as narrow-grip bench presses. Using an 8 to 10 inch grip, Andreas would lower the bar to his lower rib cage and then push it back up to an arms-locked out position. At the top he would stop for a split second and squeeze his triceps.

"I worked for eight hours a day. My bus would go home two hours after I left work. I had two hours time, and I thought what should I do with this time? So I found a gym and went for two hours to train, for fitness only, not bodybuilding. I trained for a year and I made progress, and that was motivation for me. And in two years my friend said, 'You have very good structure. Why don't you go into competition?' So I went into the competition."

– The late Andreas Munzer, telling T.C. Luoma about how he got involved in competitive bodybuilding.

Andreas' next exercise was usually triceps pushdowns. Again he would use a narrow grip and try to keep his wrists straight. The big mistake Andreas saw in gyms across the world was bodybuilders using too much weight and throwing their bodyweight into the movement. Andreas always kept his body straight, elbows locked to his sides, and most important used little or no body swing.

For his third exercise Andreas liked to do one-arm dumbell extensions. The key on this one is to keep your elbows pointed at the ceiling at all times. As soon as you start swaying the upper arm back and forth the lats, rear delts, and traps start coming into play.

To finish off his triceps, Andreas did parallel bench dips. Given that his bodyweight was not enough resistance, Andreas would have a training partner place a couple of 45-pound plates across his lap. He'd then do 8 or 10 reps, and have his partner remove a plate and he'd try to force out another 6 to 8 reps. Once he couldn't do any additional reps, Andreas would have his partner remove the final plate and he'd rep out to failure using just his bodyweight.

Mohamed dropped soccer to devote himself to bodybuilding.

Mohamed Benaziza

Mohamed Benaziza was born in Lyons, France in 1965, and grew up in his parents' native Algeria. His first sport was soccer. He had speed and determination, but he was 5'3 and 118 pounds. To compete against taller, heavier players, Mohamed took up weights. He never became a great soccer player. Instead, he became the first man in history to qualify for the Olympia after competing in only one contest!

"Every time he's appeared since that show, he's gotten more muscular and impressive. This last year he won five out of six European Grand Prix contests!"

– The late Don "Ripper" Ross, commenting on the late Mohamed Benaziza during his heyday back in 1991.

Having no coaches or personal trainers in Algeria, the young athlete had to rely on bodybuilding books and magazines for training information. He was amazed at the massive muscularity of the men in these publications. Responding quickly to daily workouts, his muscles grew so large that his soccer coach worried that Mohamed's soccer ability might be adversely affected. That was a prophetic observation. Mohamed dropped soccer to devote himself to bodybuilding.

At that time Algeria had few gyms and no bodybuilding stars for guidance. Mohamed moved to France, where he trained under Mr. Universe winner, Gerard Buinoud. After eight years of working out, Mohamed had packed on 30 pounds of muscle! His record speaks for itself:

1987   World Amateur Championships – IFBB, lightweight, 1st
1988   Grand Prix France – IFBB, 8th
         Olympia – IFBB, 11th
1989   Grand Prix Finland – IFBB, 3rd
         Grand Prix France – IFBB, 4th
         Grand Prix Germany – IFBB, 3rd
         Grand Prix Holland – IFBB, 2nd
         Grand Prix Spain (2) – IFBB, 4th
         Grand Prix Spain – IFBB, 4th
         Grand Prix Sweden – IFBB, 5th
         Olympia – IFBB, 5th
1990   Grand Prix England – IFBB, winner
         Grand Prix Finland – IFBB, winner
         Grand Prix France – IFBB, winner
         Grand Prix Germany – IFBB, winner
         Grand Prix Holland – IFBB, 2nd
         Grand Prix Italy – IFBB, winner
         Night of Champions – IFBB, winner
1991   Arnold Classic – IFBB, 11th
         Ironman Pro Invitational – IFBB, 9th
1992   Arnold Classic – IFBB, 2nd
         Grand Prix England – IFBB, 4th
         Grand Prix Germany – IFBB, 2nd
         Grand Prix Holland – IFBB, winner
         Grand Prix Italy – IFBB, winner
         Olympia – IFBB, 5th
         Pittsburgh Pro Invitational – IFBB, 7th

Mohamed was a great believer in flexing.

         Unfortunately, Mohamed was also known to some as "The Pharmacist." While anabolic steroids are ruthlessly vilified in the press, the truly deadly drugs in our sport are diuretics. Striated muscles are readily revealed by dehydrated skin. But the human body is composed of water, and the delicate biochemical reactions necessary for life depend on the amount of water present. Mohamed competed for the last time in 1992. According to witnesses, immediately after the contest Mohamed went back to his hotel room where he seemed to "freeze and fall over, dead." Efforts by fellow pro bodybuilder Porter Cottrell, a trained firefighter and paramedic, to revive Mohamed were in vain.

         It has been claimed that his autopsy revealed that he had over 300 different drugs in his system. While this seems incredible even by bodybuilding standards, nevertheless it was a tragic end to a career that had burst onto the stage with such incredible promise. Not counting Lee Haney's two Mr. Olympia wins, Mohamed was the top bodybuilder in 1990, and although he had a poor year in 1991, was back to winning form in 1992. His presence is sorely missed.

Legs

Attempting to pick out a "best" bodypart on the Algerian Atlas is difficult. He packed as much muscular bodyweight as humanly possible on his diminutive 5'3" frame. Still, few could argue that his legs were among the best in bodybuilding history. To many it seemed the Second Coming of Tom Platz.

With a perfect balance between quad, hamstring, and calf size, these areas were also huge. Not only that, but the separation between the three muscles was such that you could lose a quarter down there. It's hard to believe that Mohamed's legs were once his worst bodypart.

When he began bodybuilding, Mohamed's calves were decently developed from years playing the world's favorite sport, soccer. But his thighs, as he put it "were like noodles!" After a while his upper body started improving, but legs remained a problem. It was only after moving to France and obtaining the advice of 1981 Mr. Universe, Gerald Biunoud, that Mohamed's legs caught up with his upper body. Buinoud took one look at the Algerian Atlas and saw the potential, but he also recognized that Mohamed needed some major work with his legs. The result was a program consisting of heavy squats, leg presses, and deadlifts. Within a couple of years Mohamed's hard work had paid off as he won the World Championships.

Up until his death, Mohamed still relied on the advice he received from Gerald

It's hard to believe that Mohamed's legs were once his worst bodypart.

Buinoud, heavy basic movements in the off-season for sets of 8 reps, and lighter refining movements for 12 to 15 reps in the precontest phase.

Mohamed preferred to split his leg training into thighs in the morning, and hamstrings and calves later in the day. Quad training always began with several minutes of stretching and a few warm-up no-weight squats. He'd also hold on to a stationary upright and do a couple of high-rep sissy squats. Finally he'd perform two or three light sets of leg extensions. All this warming up may seem unnecessary, but Mohamed witnessed so many knee injuries in his career that he vowed he wouldn't be one of them.

As expected, Mohamed's first leg exercise was full squats. And we mean full squats, the type where your ass nearly touches the floor. Mohamed would pyramid up in weight, doing 8 to 12 reps per set, depending on the season.

Mohamed's second leg exercise was leg presses on the 45-degree machine. Unlike most bodybuilders who use a wide V-stance while pressing, Mohamed kept his feet close together. He found this hit more of the lower, outer thighs, while the squats took care of the inners. Again it was 5 sets of 8 to 12 reps.

To finish off his thighs, Mohamed went back to the leg extension machine and did 5 sets of 8 to 12 reps. At the top of the exercise he held the contraction for a split second.

Like all great bodybuilders, Mohamed was a great believer in flexing. Sure it satisfies the ego, but it's also a great way to bring out extra detail and separation between muscles. Mohamed always concluded his thigh training by going to the nearest mirror and hitting a few leg shots. He'd first flex one leg, hold it for a forceful contraction, and then switch legs.

To start his afternoon hamstring workout, Mohamed again spent a couple of minutes stretching and warming up. His first exercise was lying leg curls. This was one exercise where he followed a high-rep scheme year round, doing 6 sets of 12 to 15 reps. To isolate his hamstrings, Mohamed made a determined effort to keep his butt and hips from bouncing into the air. This is a mistake many bodybuilders make in order to get a few extra reps.

To finish his hamstrings, Mohamed did 4 to 6 sets of standing leg curls. As this exercise is similar to concentration curls for biceps, Mohamed did each rep as strictly as possible.

Mohamed realized early on that the key to a great pair of legs, in fact the key to a great physique, is calf development. His first exercise was usually standing calf raises for 8 sets of 20 to 40 reps. As with squats, Mohamed pyramided up in weight with each set.

To finish his calves, Mohamed repeated the same rep and set scheme for seated calf raises.

Back

Despite his death nearly ten years ago, people still talk of the Algerian Atlas and his powerful physique. To quote the late Don Ross, "Mohamed's mighty back looks like a topographical atlas in bold relief … three-dimensional mountains and valleys atop the thickest set of spinal erectors ever seen."

The rugged thickness that was Mohamed's physique reflected his training preference – lots of heavy basic exercises in the off-season using heavy weights for no more than 8 reps per set. At his best (about 180 pounds at a diminutive 5'3" in height) Mohamed was capable of deadlifting over 600 pounds.

Mohamed trained back on the morning of his third and sixth training days. He changed the routine or added or replaced exercises every two months. Here's a typical off-season back routine Mohamed followed while tearing up the bodybuilding circuit in the early 1990s:

Mohamed competed for the last time in 1992.

1. Weighted chins behind the neck – He would do one or two bodyweight warm-up sets and then do 6 sets of 8 to 10 reps with weight attached to a chinning belt.

2. T-bar rows – With his torso in a bent position, knees slightly bent and lower back slightly curved, Mohamed would pull the bar to his midsection. There would be no jerking or yanking the bar off the floor either. He typically did 5 sets of 8 to 10 reps.

3. Seated pulley rows – On the low pulley machine Mohamed would start in the stretched-forward position and pull the narrow bar into his lower rib cage for 5 sets of 8 to 10 reps.

4. Deadlifts – These were done while standing on a bench or platform to allow for a greater stretch. For the first workout of the week he would use heavy weight and do 5 sets of 5 to 6 reps, while later in the week he'd lower the weight and do 5 sets of 8 to 10 reps.

5. Shrugs – During the off-season Mohamed added shrugs to his program. He preferred the barbell and shrugged the weight straight up and down with little rolling of the shoulders. He typically did 5 sets of 10 to 12 reps.

When preparing for a contest Mohamed would start including more isolation exercises and use medium weight for slightly higher reps. He also reduced the rest interval between sets and had a training partner help him with a couple of forced reps. Here's a typical precontest back routine that Mohamed followed:

1. Pulldowns behind head – Mohamed used a wide grip on this exercise, touching the traps with the bar. He normally did 6 sets of 12 to 20 reps.

2. Wide grip pulldowns to the front – Mohamed did this exercise more as a rowing movement than a straight pulldown. He would lean back until his torso was about 45 degrees to the floor and pull the bar to mid-chest. He did 5 sets of 10 to 12 reps.

3. Close-grip pulley rows – Although an off-season movement, Mohamed found seated rows great for the center and lower lats. He did 5 sets of 10 to 12 reps.

4. Straight-arm pushdowns – Using a regular pulldown machine, Mohamed would stand in front of the machine and grab the bar with a shoulder-width, arms locked-out straight grip. He then pushed the bar down until it touched his thighs, and returned to the starting position with his arms stretched above his head.

5. Hyperextensions – To hit his lower back during the precontest season, Mohamed replaced deadlifts with back extensions using a plate behind his head. He typically did 5 sets of 25 to 30 reps.

6. Posing – Although not measured in sets and reps, Mohamed always finished off his pre-contest back training with a series of back shots. He would hit a familiar bodybuilding pose, both compulsory and free round, and hold it for five to ten seconds. He'd then switch to another pose and repeat. Mohamed found posing not only gave him the muscle control he needed onstage, but also etched in the fine details that gave his back that freaky look.

Mike Francois

Michael Francois was born in Dubuque, Iowa, in 1965. He attended Catholic college in Dubuque with the full intention of becoming a priest. He was such a serious and dedicated student that his bishop sent him to Columbus, Ohio to study theology and to complete his studies there. It was a four-year program and upon graduation in his fourth year he was to be ordained as a priest. That was his intention, something he felt comfortable with, and he had the full support and backing of his family. Then the unexpected happened. During Christmas of his third year he met a beautiful

Mike
Francois

Flex Wheeler, Mike Francois and Charles Clairmonte

young woman named Shannan Irvin. For the first time in his life Michael questioned his conviction that his purpose in life was to become a priest. Things became more complicated when Michael and Shannan fell in love. Since Roman Catholic celibacy laws prevent priests from marrying, Michael was forced to make the most difficult decision of his life – whether to pursue his path to the priesthood or to pursue his by now serious relationship with Shannan. After much soul-searching he chose to pursue his relationship with Shannan. They were married May 11, 1991, just weeks before he would have been ordained, had he chosen to complete his studies.

While Michael had been dedicating himself to spiritual matters, he had also been very athletic. He played football, baseball, did some wrestling and ran track. He also lifted weights. At the age of 20 he went to his first physique contest, and was so inspired that he took up bodybuilding. The rest is history:

1987   Mr. Springfield – overall winner
1988   Upper Mid-West – 5th
1990   Mr. Ohio – overall winner
          Mr. Ohio – heavyweight, 1st
1992   USA Championships – NPC, heavyweight, 3rd
1993   Nationals – NPC, overall winner
          Nationals – NPC, heavyweight, 1st
          USA Championships – NPC, heavyweight, 2nd
1994   Chicago Pro Invitational – IFBB, winner

Night of Champions – IFBB, winner
1995   Arnold Classic – IFBB, winner
Olympia – IFBB, 7th
San Jose Pro Invitational – IFBB, winner
1996   Olympia – IFBB, 10th
1997   Arnold Classic – IFBB, 3rd
Olympia – IFBB, 11th
San Jose Pro Invitational – IFBB, 3rd

We would like to be able to say Mike is currently one of the top bodybuilders in the world battling it out for the Mr. Olympia title, but fate intervened. In the late 1990s Mike was diagnosed with colitis, and required surgery just to stay alive. As of this writing he has lost much of his once famous muscle mass, but maintains a positive outlook in life. He still attends the occasional contest and loves talking to fans.

> **"Mike is definitely of the school of thought that heavier and slower training is better than high reps and lighter training. He also has drastically cut back on the number of sets he does for a muscle. For instance, for a small muscle like biceps or triceps, he rarely does more than nine sets – and never more than 12."**
>
> – Greg Zulak, commenting on the training approach taken by Arnold Classic winner, Mike Francois.

Triceps

When he was creating havoc on the pro scene during the mid 1990s, Mike trained triceps after deltoids. He found shoulder training warmed up his triceps and prepared them better than if he started training them cold. He would do just one or two warm-up sets and jump right in.

During a typical triceps workout, Mike would start with either lying triceps extensions (skullcrushers) or pushdowns. If it was skullcrushers he would use an EZ-curl bar and do them on a flat or decline bench. He'd also vary his lowering technique, bringing the bar down to his forehead or all the way behind to the bench. Mike always locked his arms out straight at the top of the exercise. Mike typically did 3 sets of 8 to 12 reps.

Although since retired from bodybuilding due to his bout with colitis, Mike still influences millions with views on high-intensity training.

Mike's next exercise was behind-the-head rope extensions. As he'd be fully warmed up by now, he would jump right into his heavy weight doing 3 sets of 8 to 12 reps. We should add that if Mike's first exercise was incline EZ-bar extensions, he wouldn't do rope extensions as he found the two exercises very similar. Instead he'd do some heavy triceps pushdowns.

To finish off his triceps, Mike did an isolation movement like dumbell kickbacks or rope pushdowns. Again it was usually 3 sets of 8 to 12 reps.

As you can see Mike sort of followed the fewer sets, higher-intensity, style of training. For most bodybuilders, 9 sets total for a muscle group would be a warmup. But Mike found by putting everything into these sets, his triceps grew as much as he wanted. Grew so well in fact that for a time in the mid '90s, he was the favorite to win the Mr. Olympia, having won the Arnold Classic and New York Night of Champions.

Although since retired from bodybuilding due to his bout with colitis, big Mike still influences millions with views on high-intensity training.

Mike varied his training by doing different exercises, changing exercise order, and modifying his set/rep schemes.

Biceps

Mike is another bodybuilder who feels most people overtrain their arms. With one or two exceptions, virtually all back exercises heavily involve the biceps. For this reason Mike modified his program so that he only trained his biceps directly once every ten days or so. He also varied his training by doing different exercises, changing exercise order, and modifying his set/rep schemes.

Given Mike's preference for training heavy, it's not surprising that he always did an extensive warmup before attempting maximum poundages. He always did at least two warm-up sets of each exercise to get some blood into the muscle.

Mike was a great believer in the concept of pyramiding, and added weight with each set. He also liked to train with a partner who could spot him on those final hard reps. And for big Mike there were many of those. Besides safety, Mike found training with a partner set a good tempo to the workout. Mike would rest only as long as it took his partner to complete a set, and then they'd switch.

Now to Mike's biceps training specifics. He typically selected four exercises and did an average of four hard sets of each. Of course this was the routine he followed later in his career when his goal was refinement rather than adding extra mass. During his "growing days" Mike did fewer exercises, lower reps, about 5 to 8, and fewer sets, about 10 to 12.

Mike often began his biceps routine with standing barbell curls. He preferred the straight bar as the EZ-curl bar didn't quite give him the same feeling in his biceps. He would typically do 4 sets of 12 reps, using a medium-width grip. Mike's style on barbell curls could best be described as loose. He would do 4 to 6 reps in perfect style, and then add just enough body momentum to keep the weight moving. But remember he cheated to increase the load on his biceps, not reduce it. He also incorporated negative training into his workouts. As soon as the barbell was in the up position, he'd start lowering it as slow as possible.

With 4 sets of this all-important basic biceps exercise completed, Mike moved on to preacher curls. Mike preferred using the EZ-curl bar on this exercise, proving the old adage that "everyone is different." He also narrowed his grip. Given the extra tension placed on the lower biceps, particularly the biceps tendon region, Mike rarely, if ever, cheated on this exercise. Instead he sort of did them in a concentration curl style. That is, slow and controlled with no bounce or jerking at the bottom. Again he did 4 sets of 10 to 12 reps.

After 8 quality sets of barbell work, Mike moved on to dumbells, and his third exercise was that old faithful, alternate dumbell curls. He would do his normal 4 sets of 12 reps using 60-pound dumbells. At the top of the exercise he would pause for a split second and squeeze his biceps. He also liked to supinate his hands on this exercise as well, rotating his hands from a palms in to a palms up position, at the top of the exercise.

To finish off those Arnold Classic-winning guns of his, Mike liked to do 4 sets of 12 reps of a one-arm isolation exercise such as dumbell concentration curls or cable curls.

If he did cable curls he would stand side on to the machine and bring the cable across his body, supinating his hands and squeezing as he lifted, especially toward the top.

If he did concentration curls he'd sit on the end of a bench and rest his elbow on the inside of his knee. Toward the end of the set, he would reach over with his free hand and spot himself for a few extra reps.

The previous is but one example of a Mike Francois biceps routine. On some days he changed things by varying the order of the exercises. On others he'd substitute exercises. For example he may replace the preachers with a machine curl, or the alternate dumbell curls with incline dumbell curls.

Mike has lost much of his once famous muscle mass, but maintains a positive outlook in life. He still attends the occasional contest and loves talking to fans.

Bob Paris

Bob Paris was born in Columbus, Indiana in December 1959. He had a typical mid-west upbringing, including joining the Boy Scouts, canoeing, backpacking, and playing football. It was this last passion that first brought Bob to the weight room: "I was about 17 and I wanted to put on a little size for football. I stumbled onto this Universal machine in a little room in my high school. I began playing with it, and everything felt really good. I felt my muscles work in a way they never had before, so it became a real positive addiction."

"After a time I started noticing the bodybuilding magazines, and a light bulb went off over my head. Up to that point I had looked on weight training as a really intense hobby, not realizing that there was a sport involved around it."

Bob's parents were not thrilled about his choice of sports. "In the beginning they thought the sport was kinda weird. I think that what I had to do was have my own self-beliefs, and do what was right for me. If I had tried to please everyone, I would have stagnated."

After graduating from high school, Bob continued lifting weights and went away to college, but after a semester and a half he realized he wasn't happy. After some soul searching he knew what he really wanted to do was be a bodybuilder and an actor: "So I packed everything up in an old beat-up car and took off for the west coast. I trained at Gold's in Venice for about two weeks before my money ran out. Then I moved to Orange County and got a job. I still trained, but my efforts were directed toward setting up my life. I'm very goal-oriented, in fact, I'm singularly goal-oriented. It was difficult for me to pursue both acting and bodybuilding when I wanted to take them both seriously. I found that I had to do one or the other."

Bob Paris

"When I began working out, I found it almost impossible to make my back sore. The visual connection that's so easy to get with other bodyparts was missing when I trained my back, so what I did was memorize how my back worked by studying it in the mirror when I wasn't exercising it. I then burned the image of it into my mind so that I could easily call up a mental picture of what was happening during a back workout. It was almost like watching my back in a mental imagery."

– Bob Paris, US National Champion, outlining his approach to back training.

His tenacity paid off:

1982　Mr. California – NPC, light heavyweight, 2nd
　　　Nationals – NPC, heavyweight, 4th
　　　North American Championships – IFBB, heavyweight, 3rd
　　　USA Championships – NPC, heavyweight, 3rd
1983　Nationals – NPC, overall winner
　　　Nationals – NPC, heavyweight, 1st
　　　World Amateur Championships – IFBB, overall winner
　　　World Amateur Championships – IFBB, heavyweight, 1st
1984　Olympia – IFBB, 7th
1985　Olympia – IFBB, 9th
1986　Los Angeles Pro Champions – IFBB, 7th
　　　World Pro Championships – IFBB, 6th (1)
1988　Chicago Pro Invitational – IFBB, 5th
　　　Grand Prix England – IFBB, 6th
　　　Grand Prix France – IFBB, 4th
　　　Grand Prix Germany – IFBB, 6th
　　　Grand Prix Greece – IFBB, 6th
　　　Grand Prix Italy – IFBB, 3rd
　　　Grand Prix Spain (2) – IFBB, 4th
　　　Grand Prix Spain – IFBB, 5th
　　　Niagara Falls Pro Invitational – IFBB, 3rd
　　　Night of Champions – IFBB, 3rd
　　　Olympia – IFBB, 10th
1989　Arnold Classic – IFBB, 5th
　　　Grand Prix France – IFBB, 3rd
　　　Grand Prix Germany – IFBB, 6th
　　　Grand Prix Melbourne – IFBB, 3rd
　　　Grand Prix Spain (2) – IFBB, 3rd
　　　Grand Prix Spain – IFBB, 3rd
　　　Grand Prix Sweden – IFBB, 4th
　　　Night of Champions – IFBB, 4th
　　　Olympia – IFBB, 14th
　　　World Pro Championships – IFBB, 3rd
1990　Night of Champions – IFBB, 14th
1991　Arnold Classic – IFBB, 16th
　　　Grand Prix Italy – IFBB, 5th
　　　Ironman Pro Invitational – IFBB, 10th
　　　Ironman Pro Invitational – IFBB, 11th
　　　Musclefest Grand Prix – IFBB, 3rd
　　　Olympia – IFBB, 12th
1992　Chicago Pro Invitational – IFBB, 10th

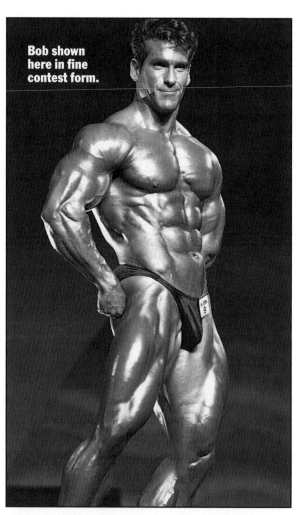

Bob shown here in fine contest form.

What wisdom has Bob gathered from his years in bodybuilding? "If there's a secret out there, it's that there are no secrets. It's hard work, commitment, determination, and persistence. Those are the keys. Other than those things, I would stress feel. That's an absolutely essential factor in training. I work very, very hard in the gym, but I have to feel the muscle in order to be satisfied with the workout. For the most part, I get such intense contractions when I train that I'm usually sore for days afterward."

"Also, learning to perfect the exercise is very important. If you don't perfect the exercise, you're going to injure yourself. I've walked into gyms all around the world and seen people doing things with dumbells and barbells that I wouldn't wish on my worst enemy. A lot of times, if I'm training somebody, I'll start him on what I call a rehearsal workout. That's where I have the client take almost no weight at all, maybe a broomstick or very, very light dumbells, and teach him how to do the exercise properly. If you do an exercise the right way, you'll get a whole lot more out of it, and you'll be able to perfect your physique instead of making a pile of mud."

No discussion of Bob Paris would be complete without mentioning his decision to reveal the fact that he is gay. Most of us respond, "Who cares?" But at the time that Bob went public there was and still is strong anti-gay prejudice. How did it affect Bob as a bodybuilder?

When performing seated rows Bob used visualization, pretending to be in a boat crew rowing to the finish line.

"In bodybuilding there's a common ground among athletes. It doesn't matter what your skin color is, what your sexuality is, what your ethnicity is, what your religion is, or what your income is. What does matter is your physique, and that's the common denominator."

Back

It's not surprising to hear that Mr. Symmetry used an analytical approach when designing his back workouts. The back is like the delts in that it's such a complex muscle group that one or two exercises won't hit the whole are. You need exercises for width, exercises for thickness, something for the spinal erectors, and something for the traps. Although a typical Paris back workout did not include exercises to hit every muscle group just described, Bob was sure to hit the whole area over a couple of back sessions. It's for this reason that it's difficult to outline one Paris back workout. Instead we'll focus on his favorite exercises.

Bob usually started his back training session with some sort of width exercise, usually front pulldowns. For variety he used different grips on the straight bar (wide, narrow, and reverse), and also different attachments (long straight bar, palms facing inward bar, and narrow V bar). Bob also made a point of concentrating on his back muscles as he pulled the bar down. Too many bodybuilders pull with their biceps on this exercise, and the result is little or no back stimulation. Bob typically did 4 or 5 sets of pulldowns, alternating heavy (6 to 8 reps) days, with light (25 to 30 reps) days.

Another Paris favorite is pulldowns behind the head. On this exercise Bob would lean forward and pull his elbows as far back as possible. This insured his lats were working in line with the action of the machine.

For central back thickness, Bob relied on such exercises as seated pulley rows and dumbell rows. On seated rows he again used visualization, pretending to be in a boat crew rowing to the finish line. Even though

Bob generally worked his back twice over seven to ten days.

he leaned forward on the exercise, he never let the tension shift from his upper to lower back. Likewise when pulling back toward vertical, he pulled with his arms and lats, not his lower back. This is another exercise Bob saw being abused over and over again by bodybuilders more concerned with how much weight they could lift.

The fourth movement Bob included in his back routine was dumbell rows. Bob always kept one knee and free hand on a bench for support. Rather than pulling the weight straight up, Bob let it drift slightly forward at the bottom, much the same as if sawing wood. He found this gave the lats an extra degree or two of stretch.

Bob generally worked his back twice over seven to ten days. From trial and error he found any more than this led to overtraining. Another thing he rarely did was forced reps. He considered this (and other advanced techniques) to be one of the most abused training methods seen in gyms. He feels most beginners and intermediates should only do forced reps on one or two sets, every second or third workout. any more places too much stress on the individual's recovery system.

Hard work, commitment, determination and persistence paid off for Bob.

Kevin Levrone

Born in Baltimore, Maryland, in 1966, Kevin has been involved in weight training for the better part of 15 years. His brothers and cousins got him started when he was 12, and they trained at home for years before Kevin joined a real gym. During those early years he competed in powerlifting and racked up impressive lifts like a 600-pound bench press and an 800-pound squat!

After winning his class at the 1990 Colossus powerlifting meet, Kevin happened to notice the bodybuilding contest held that same day. "My friends talked me into entering the physique show, so I went down to Sears and got a pair of posing trunks, threw them on and shaved down backstage, went out there – and won! It was a local Baltimore show, and I had seen some of the competitors backstage, so I thought I could win, I just went out and hit shots. I didn't know what I was doing

It was obvious that all the heavy lifting had given Kevin his incredibly muscular physique, and winning his first show with such ease caused him to gravitate into bodybuilding competition. His talent soon became apparent:

Kevin is undisputedly one of the top five bodybuilders in the world today.

1991   Junior Nationals – NPC, heavyweight, 2nd
        Nationals – NPC, overall winner
        Nationals – NPC, heavyweight, 1st
1992   Chicago Pro Invitational – IFBB, 3rd
        Grand Prix England – IFBB, 2nd
        Grand Prix Germany – IFBB, winner
        Night of Champions – IFBB, winner
        Olympia – IFBB, 2nd
1993   Grand Prix England – IFBB, 3rd
        Grand Prix Finland – IFBB, 2nd
        Grand Prix France (2) – IFBB, 5th
        Grand Prix Germany (2) – IFBB, winner
        Grand Prix Spain – IFBB, 3rd
        Olympia – IFBB, 5th

1994   Arnold Classic – IFBB, winner
        Grand Prix England – IFBB, 2nd
        Grand Prix France (2) – IFBB, winner
        Grand Prix Germany – IFBB, 2nd
        Grand Prix Italy – IFBB, winner
        Grand Prix Spain – IFBB, 2nd
        Olympia – IFBB, 3rd
        San Jose Pro Invitational – IFBB, winner
1995   Grand Prix England – IFBB, 2nd
        Grand Prix Germany – IFBB, winner
        Grand Prix Russia – IFBB, winner
        Grand Prix Spain – IFBB, winner
        Olympia – IFBB, 2nd
1996   Arnold Classic – IFBB, winner
        Grand Prix Czech Republic – IFBB, 2nd
        Grand Prix England – IFBB, 4th
        Grand Prix Germany – IFBB, 3rd
        Grand Prix Russia – IFBB, 5th
        Grand Prix Spain – IFBB, 4th
        Grand Prix Switzerland – IFBB, 3rd
        Olympia – IFBB, 3rd
        San Jose Pro Invitational – IFBB, winner
1997   Arnold Classic – IFBB, 8th
        Grand Prix Czech Republic – IFBB, winner
        Grand Prix England – IFBB, winner
        Grand Prix Finland – IFBB, winner
        Grand Prix Germany – IFBB, winner
        Grand Prix Hungary – IFBB, winner
        Grand Prix Russia – IFBB, 2nd
        Grand Prix Spain – IFBB, winner
        Olympia – IFBB, 4th
1998   Grand Prix Finland – IFBB, 2nd
        Grand Prix Germany – IFBB, 2nd
        Night of Champions – IFBB, 2nd
        Olympia – IFBB, 4th
        San Francisco Pro Invitational – IFBB, winner
        Toronto Pro Invitational – IFBB, 2nd
1999   Arnold Classic – IFBB, 2nd
        Grand Prix England – IFBB, 3rd
        Olympia – IFBB, 4th
        Professional World Cup – IFBB, 3rd
2000   Arnold Classic – IFBB, 3rd

Kevin's arms are now among the largest and perfectly balanced on the pro circuit.

Kevin is undisputedly one of the top five body-builders in the world today. He's also quite the musician and when not on the pro circuit tour, can be seen onstage with his rock band, *Full Blown.*

331

Shoulders

Variety is the word that best describes Levrone's approach to weight training. He likes hitting a bodypart different ways with heavy poundages. When it comes to training his championship deltoids, he goes right to his favorite exercise, seated dumbell presses. He does 4 sets of 12 reps in the following manner:

100 pounds – 12 reps
120 pounds – 12 reps
130 pounds – 12 reps
150 pounds – 12 reps

    Given the size of those weights, it's not surprising to hear Kevin employs a training partner to help him hoist the dumbells into starting position. This is Kevin's favorite mass builder and he uses an adjustable incline bench set in the upright position. Kevin locks out on each rep and usually sticks to straight sets, although occasionally he'll add in a forced rep or two.

    To finish his front delts, Kevin moves on to front dumbell raises. Again it's 4 sets of 12 reps. He uses a 50-pound dumbell for each set, and raises his arms until the dumbell is in line with his forehead. He keeps his palms facing down at all times.

    With front delts out of the way, it's on to rear delts. Although most bodybuilders prefer bent-over dumbell raises, Kevin prefers cables. Kevin stands between two upright cable machines and with his right hand reaches over and grabs a handle connected to the left pulley.

If your shoulders are lagging behind, give Kevin's routine a try.

Likewise he grabs the right handle with his left hand. Bending over so his torso is about 45-degrees with the floor, Kevin raises out and up until his arms are parallel with the floor. Once again he does 4 sets of 12 reps.

    To finish off his delts, Kevin does standing side laterals. Again he prefers cables over dumbells, and uses 30 to 40 pounds for 4 sets of 12 reps. He prefers to do them one arm at a time as he finds he can get a better contraction in his side delts.

"It's those shoulders and particularly Levrone's monstrous delts, that seem to be the bodypart which most impresses muscle fans seeing him in competition for the first time."
– Editors of *MuscleMag International*, commenting on one of the top bodybuilders in the world today, Kevin Levrone.

Kevin is also quite the musician and when not on the pro circuit tour, can be seen onstage with his rock band, *Full Blown*.

Levrone's delt program is as simple as it is effective. Nothing glamorous like the latest machines or advanced training techniques. Yet he has two of the largest shoulders on the Mr. Olympia stage. If your shoulders are lagging behind, give Kevin's routine a try. Who knows, maybe getting back to basics is what more of us really need.

Biceps

Twenty-one, twenty-two, twenty-three inches, only Kevin Levrone knows for sure just how large those suckers are. What we are talking about are those gargantuan hams that Kevin calls arms protruding from his shirt sleeves. Together with such other mass-monsters as Nasser El Sonbaty, Paul Dillett, and Dorian Yates, Kevin helped set the standard for modern bodybuilding.

Like most bodybuilders these days, Kevin likes to incorporate free weights, machines, and cables, into his workouts. Barbells will lay down a good foundation, but Kevin feels you need the full spectrum of exercises to build true winning quality. But even this approach may need tinkering with. A number of years back, Kevin noticed his arms weren't responding the way they should, despite the battering he regularly subjected them to. Many bodybuilders would have kept slugging away with the same routines, over and over, but Kevin adopted a different strategy. He devised a biceps routine based almost entirely on dumbells. The radical approach paid off as Kevin's arms are now among the largest and perfectly balanced on the pro circuit.

Kevin starts his priority biceps' routine with the tried and true, alternate dumbell burls. He performs the exercise sitting down so as to limit the amount of body momentum. Kevin's witnessed far too many bodybuilders rocking back and forth while standing up. He's after bigger biceps not an enlarged ego. Kevin prefers to keep the palms facing upward at all times, rather than the traditional supination (wrist rotation) version. It's not that he has anything against supinating, it's just that it doesn't do much for him. A typical workout will see Kevin do 4 sets of 12 to 15 reps of this important mass builder.

For his second exercise Kevin moves on to incline curls. Again he prefers alternating his arms, rather than lifting both at the same time. And like seated curls, prefers not to supinate his hands as he lifts. Kevin pyramids up in weight for 4 sets of 10 to 6 reps.

Kevin Levrone
and Paul Dillett

Kevin's third exercise is one-arm preacher curls. He prefers the one-arm version over the two-arm version as it allows him to concentrate on each biceps separately. Again it's 4 sets of 10 to 6 reps in pyramid fashion.

It's only after he has done the three previous dumbell exercises that Kevin switches to a cable exercise. Kevin does 3 sets of standing cable raises using the same weight for 10 to 15 reps. Kevin has his own style on this exercise. Instead of facing the cable machine like most, he turns around and raises the cable between his legs. He finds that this technique keeps the stress on his biceps for a longer period of time.

Victor Richards

Victor Richards was born in San Diego in 1964. Vic actually lived in many different countries growing up, including Nigeria and Morocco. His father was a physician and the Richards family traveled often. Needless to say, Victor is blessed with an incredible genetic gift for building muscle. He says that all Richards' men are naturally huge and muscular and notes that his younger brother, who doesn't train with weights, is 240 pounds and very muscular too.

In high school Vic played football, soccer and ran track. He started to weight train at the age of 15 and loved it from the first time his meaty hands wrapped around a barbell. By then he already had 17-inch arms. Although he didn't know a lot about training or diet, he knew that he liked to train and was very dedicated. While his friends were out getting high or drunk he was in the gym training.

By the time he was 16 he weighed 225 pounds. People already assumed that he was a bodybuilder because he was so large and muscular. Unlike so many other beginners, however, Victor didn't start to train with the aspiration of becoming a bodybuilder.

"I started training without any idea of what competitive bodybuilding was. I trained for fun and because working out gave me a sense of inner peace." That inner peace produced an exterior that amazed fans:

1982   American Cup Contest – 2nd
1983   Los Angeles Championships – NPC, teen, 1st
1984   California Gold Cup Classic – 1st
1989   Mr. Barbados – 1st
1992   Nigerian Championships – 1st and overall

As with Greg Kovacs today, Vic Richards was one of the most popular bodybuilders in the late 1980s and early 1990s, despite rarely competing at the pro level. Most bodybuilding fans are impressed with beef, and Vic carried more of it than most. He didn't need to compete to be popular, and was constantly in demand for posing exhibitions and seminars.

Victor continues to train and develop his body to it's full potential. And bodybuilding fans all over the world continue to be amazed!

Victor didn't start to train with the aspiration of becoming a bodybuilder.

Back

With more muscle on his back than most bodybuilders have on their entire bodies, it's hard to believe the guy never even won a national contest. Instead he built one of the largest, most muscular bodies of all time, and used his immense popularity to become one of the most sought after posers and seminar speakers in the early '90s.

Given the amount of surface area Vic had to work for his back, he preferred to split his training over two workouts. In the morning he would do his upper back and pulldown movements and then come back later in the day and do middle and lower back with rowing

Victor became one of the most sought after posers and seminar speakers in the early '90s.

"His back is so thick that he must be the standard from which all other backs are judged. His lats, although a bit high, are wide. His traps are like two basketballs stuffed under his skin, and his lower back is so thick you can stick your hand into the groove between the spinal erector muscles up to your wrist."

– Greg Zulak, commenting on the size of one of the most popular, noncompetitive bodybuilders of the early 1990s, Victor Richards.

movements. In addition, if by chance he failed to complete his evening workout, he'd come back bright and early the next morning and do so.

Vic comes from the old school of training, high volume using large numbers of sets for each exercise. Where many bodybuilders perform 10 to 15 sets for their entire back routine, Vic does that many per exercise.

His first exercise was usually lat pulldowns to the neck. Vic rarely counted sets or reps but observers guessed 12 to 15. Vic was a traditionalist in that he preferred to pyramid up in weight with each set. then when he reached a weight he felt comfortable with he'd do 4 or 5 sets with it. He'd then start reducing the weight and do some higher-rep sets. Typically rep ranges were 5 to 8 for heavy sets and 10 to 20 for light sets.

After he feels he has done enough pulldowns to the neck, he switches to front pulldowns. This is one of Vic's favorite and strongest exercises, and it was nothing to see him hoisting the stack (300 pounds in most gyms) plus a couple of extra plates attached. He started with a wide grip and moved his hands closer as his lats started tiring. In other words as his lats tired he compensated by bringing more biceps into play. As with pulldowns behind the head, Vic averaged 10 to 15 sets of front pulldowns.

You'd think at this point he'd be finished with pulldowns, but not a chance. Replacing the straight bar with a small triangle-shaped attachment, Vic would now do 10 to 15 more sets of narrow pulldowns. Again he'd vary the reps between 5 and 20.

With 35 to 45 sets of pulldowns completed, Vic would move on to a small muscle like triceps. But then later in the day he'd come back for round two.

The three rowing movements Vic relied on were one-arm dumbell rows, seated cable rows, and bent-over barbell rows. Depending on his mood and energy level he would do anywhere from 6 to 15 sets of each exercise, with the reps varying between 5 and 20. For variety he frequently alternated the sequence of exercises.

As with the pulldowns done earlier, Vic uses wrist straps on his rowing exercises. Let's face it, when you are using 180-pound dumbells for one-arm rows and 405 pounds for barbell rows, holding on becomes a chore all by itself.

Dave Palumbo

Dave hasn't made a name for himself on the pro circuit yet, but with his competitive weight in the 250-plus pound's range, it's probably only a matter of time before he cashes in a big show.

Dave is known to many as the "thinking man's bodybuilder" because he dropped out of medical school in the last year. He is also the author and founder of the S.M.A.R.T. Personal Training course. Besides competitive bodybuilding Dave has established a reputation as one of the industry's best writers, and he has numerous articles online and in print. Here's Dave's amateur results:

1994	Junior USA – NPC, heavyweight, 3rd
1995	Junior Nationals – NPC, heavyweight, 1st
	USA Championships – NPC, heavyweight, 7th
1996	Nationals – NPC, heavyweight, 4th
	USA Championships – NPC, heavyweight, 7th
1997	Nationals – NPC, heavyweight, 5th
	USA Championships – NPC, heavyweight, 6th
1998	Nationals – NPC, superheavyweight, 8th
	North American Championships – IFBB, heavyweight, 6th

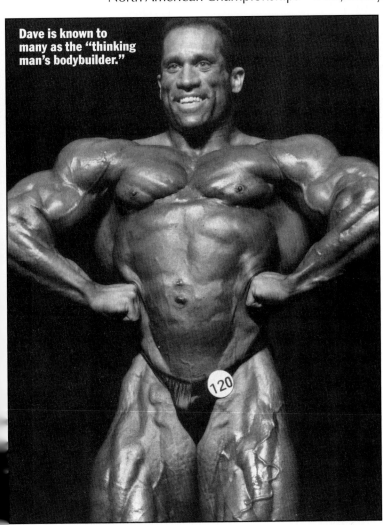

Dave is known to many as the "thinking man's bodybuilder."

Shoulders

Using that great intelligence that saw him come within an inch of graduating from med school, Dave constructed his shoulder workout with a great deal of thought, deliberation, and brain work. Rather than just rely on straight sets and reps, Dave utilizes such advanced techniques as supersets, trisets, negatives, and periodization.

"Besides being the thinking man's bodybuilder, Dave is also one of the biggest bodybuilders on the amateur circuit. Density is his personal hallmark, and it fails to evade any portion of his beefy body. This guy is thick, thick, thick, and hard, hard, hard!"

– *MuscleMag International* writer, Lori Grannis, commenting on one of the sport's new beef kings, Dave Palumbo.

Dave usually starts his shoulder training with an all-around shoulder builder. For years the exercise of choice was military presses, and he'd work up to 315 pounds for 6 reps. But such weight started creating havoc with his shoulder joints, so now he uses dumbell presses instead. By using dumbells he can move his arms through the shoulder's normal range of motion. He also uses considerably less weight, opting for 70- to 80-pound dumbells. For example he'll typically start with 25- or 30-pound dumbells for a quick warm-up set, and then move up to the 70s or 80s. As Dave is a firm believer in quality over quantity, he does just two sets, rather than the standard three to five performed by most bodybuilders.

For his second exercise Dave likes to hit the side delts with dumbell side laterals. Dave alternates between two-arm laterals, and the one-arm version leaning away from a post. In either case he does one warm-up set and then proceeds to do two intense workout sets.

To hit his massive front delts, Dave moves on to front raises. But rather than just rely on one version, he has three in his arsenal. Two versions involve the use of a straight barbell. In one variation he'll use a slightly less than shoulder-width grip, and for the other he'll go slightly wider than shoulder-width. A third form of raises is the familiar dumbell version. Even on dumbell raises, Dave likes to shake things up. Instead of keeping the palms facing down at all times, he slowly rotates his hands until the thumbs are pointing outward, nearly to a biceps curl position. Again he does 2 sets of 10 to 14 reps. This is one exercise where he may do a drop set, using a heavy weight for 7 or 8 reps and then dropping to a light weight for 6 to 8 more reps.

Another exercise Dave uses in his shoulder training is upright rows. As he does shrugs and deadlifts on a regular basis (also great trap and shoulder builders), Dave only does uprights every second or third workout. In fact there are times when he may go a month without doing uprights in his shoulder routine. Dave prefers the barbell to cables and dumbells for uprights and typically does 2 sets of 4 to 6, or 12 to 16 reps.

To hit the rear delts, Dave does what he calls high pulley reverse cable crossovers. Instead of grabbing the low pulleys on a crossover machine, Dave holds onto the upper handles, using an opposite-side grip (i.e. left-hand grabs right·handle, and vise versa). He then pulls the handles down to the sides until his arms are parallel with the floor. He then raises back up until the moving weights are about an inch from the remaining stack. He does 2 sets of 8 to 10 reps.

Dave constructed his shoulder workout with a great deal of thought, deliberation, and brain work.

Chris Cormier

Chris has established himself as one of the top bodybuilders in the world.

Broderick Christopher Cormier was born August 19, 1967. Chris was heavily into sports through high school and before. Pop Warner football and track led to junior high school football and track and high school football and track. During his high school years, he got into competitive BMX racing. When he started, he was ranked 779th in his conference. by the end of that same year, he had moved up to 73rd.

But BMX had to make way for wrestling. He ended up placing fourth in the state in the 167-pound class. In fact, he won a wrestling scholarship to Cal State, Bakersfield. And all this time, he was playing football, too. After high school, he went to Bakersfield on the wrestling scholarship. But Chris graduated from high school at 16, and collegiate wrestling took its toll on his relatively immature body. He had to have a knee operation, made it through one season, came home to rest, and couldn't return.

Next, he played college football. His knee bothered him intermittently, but he made All Conference anyway. During this same time, he'd been training with weights too. In Palm Springs, California, his hometown, the Palm Springs Muscle Classic began in 1983. He attended that show and every other. One high school teacher mentioned that he thought Chris should get into this sport and compete. And compete he did!

1987   Teen Nationals – NPC, light heavyweight, 1st
1991   USA Championships – NPC, heavyweight, 4th
1993   USA Championships – NPC, overall winner
         USA Championships – NPC, heavyweight, 1st
1994   Arnold Classic – IFBB, 4th
         Grand Prix France – IFBB, 7th
         Grand Prix Germany – IFBB, 6th
         Ironman Pro Invitational – IFBB, 2nd
         Olympia – IFBB, 6th
1995   Grand Prix England – IFBB, 5th
         Grand Prix France – IFBB, 5th
         Grand Prix Germany – IFBB, 4th
         Grand Prix Russia – IFBB, 5th
         Grand Prix Spain – IFBB, 4th
         Grand Prix Ukraine – IFBB, 4th

Night of Champions – IFBB, 4th
Olympia – IFBB, 6th

1996   Grand Prix Czech Republic – IFBB, 8th
Grand Prix England – IFBB, 8th
Grand Prix Germany – IFBB, 7th
Grand Prix Russia – IFBB, 8th
Grand Prix Spain – IFBB, 8th
Grand Prix Switzerland – IFBB, 8th
Olympia – IFBB, 7th

1997   Canada Pro Cup – IFBB, 3rd
Grand Prix Czech Republic – IFBB, 2nd
Grand Prix England – IFBB, 2nd
Grand Prix Finland – IFBB, 2nd
Grand Prix Germany – IFBB, 6th
Grand Prix Hungary – IFBB, 8th
Grand Prix Russia – IFBB, 4th
Grand Prix Spain – IFBB, 6th
Night of Champions – IFBB, winner
Olympia – IFBB, 8th
Toronto Pro Invitational – IFBB, 3rd

1998   Arnold Classic – IFBB, 5th
Grand Prix Finland – IFBB, 4th
Grand Prix Germany – IFBB, 4th
Olympia – IFBB, 6th

1999   Arnold Classic – IFBB, 3rd
Ironman Pro Invitational – IFBB, winner
Olympia – IFBB, 3rd

2000   Arnold Classic – IFBB, 2nd
Ironman Pro Invitational – IFBB, winner

If you really want to see power in motion, then witnessing a Cormier leg workout is a must.

With his 2000 Ironman win over Flex Wheeler, Chris has established himself as one of the top bodybuilders in the world. He is now one of the favorites to inherit the Mr. Olympia crown if Ronnie Coleman retires or loses his edge.

Legs

Chris has always been known as one of the stronger members of the sport. But with his 2000 Ironman win over favorite Flex Wheeler, Chris has also established himself as one of the top bodybuilders around.

If you really want to see power in motion, then witnessing a Cormier leg workout is a must. Chris credits good genetics with helping him achieve such leg size and strength. He was blessed with proportionally short legs so building muscle mass was easier than someone with longer legs. He also attributes his athletic background with laying a good foundation, especially in his hamstrings. In fact when he started training his legs with regularity, he found his hamstrings jumped way ahead of his thighs. When bodybuilders with less favorable genetics started beating him because of their better leg development, Chris realized it was time to get serious. And for those who wonder what Chris' idea of serious is, how about leg presses with 1000 pounds for 15 reps?

Here's a typical Chris Cormier leg workout that he used to build those incredible pillars of power.

1) Leg presses   8 sets of 15 to 20 reps, going from 315 to 1000 pounds
2) Leg extensions   6 sets of 15 to 20 reps
3) Machine squats   4 sets of 15 to 20 reps or
4) Hack squats   6 sets of 15 to 25 reps, going from 200 to 1000 pounds

Hamstrings
1) Standing leg curls   5 sets of 25 reps
2) Lying leg curls   5-6 sets of 15 to 25 reps
3) Stiff-leg deadlifts   3 sets of 15 reps

Abdominals

Like most National's winners, Chris Cormier thought he was ready to walk through the pro ranks. But one look backstage at such behemoths as Yates, Sonbaty, and Levrone, and Chris realized that this was a different ballgame altogether. But there was one area where he felt he could match if not beat most competitors and that was the midsection. Through a combination of great genetics and diligent training, Chris had developed a phenomenal midsection. But what was good for the Nationals would have to be even better to combat Yates and Co.

Through a combination of great genetics and diligent training, Chris had developed a phenomenal midsection.

Chris normally trains abs three times a week. He usually starts with 5 sets of ab crunches on a machine doing 25 reps per set. Chris prefers the machine as it not only seems to target his abs better, but he can adjust the tension.

Chris' second exercise is rope crunches. Chris grabs a rope behind his head and kneels down facing away from the cable machine. He then bends forward until his abs are fully contracted. For beginners Chris adds that you have to focus on the abs. The hip flexors try to take over on this exercise. Not to mention the natural tendency to rock up and down using body momentum. As with crunches Chris does 5 sets of 25 reps.

To finish off one of the best midsections in the business, Chris does 5 sets of what he calls frog kicks. The more common name is reverse crunches. Chris sits on the end of a bench and draws his knees into his torso.

Dave Fisher

Dave Fisher was born in Montreal, Quebec, Canada, on February 1, 1964. He grew up on the Canadian Prairies, and started weight training as a teenager: "I started training in my basement. My father had a Weider weight set which has a real interesting story behind it. The story is he bought his weight set while we were in Montreal, and he went right to Ben Weider's house to buy it."

It was a good purchase, and those weights produced a champion:

1991	North American Championships – IFBB, light heavyweight, 2nd
1992	North American Championships – IFBB, light heavyweight, 2nd
1995	Arnold Classic – IFBB, 11th
	Florida Pro Invitational – IFBB, 5th
	Ironman Pro Invitational – IFBB, 6th
	Niagara Falls Pro Invitational – IFBB, 17th
	San Jose Pro Invitational – IFBB, 8th
	South Beach Pro Invitational – IFBB, 5th
1996	Canada Pro Cup – IFBB, 8th
	Florida Pro Invitational – IFBB, 6th
	Night of Champions – IFBB, 14th
1999	Night of Champions – IFBB, 18th
	Toronto Pro Invitational – IFBB, 9th
2000	Ironman Pro Invitational – IFBB, 16th

Dave's classical physique is what the male body should look like.

Given the emphasis on pure mass these days, it's difficult for a 230-pound Dave Fisher to beat 280-pound Markus Ruhl or Nasser El Sonbaty. But for many fans, Dave's classical physique is what the male body should look like.

The last word goes to Dave. When asked if he could change anything, he answered: "I wish I had a college degree. But I always hated high school so much that when I got out of high school the thought of going to university for another three or four years was too much. I despised it. Now when I look back I wish I had a college degree to prove I can do more than just lift weights, that I also have a brain. I have the ability, I know. I could have had a degree. I consider myself a fairly smart person – no genius, but I am intelligent. It would be nice to have the degree to show that intelligence."

Legs

Dave follows the traditional four-day split in his training, hitting chest and biceps on day one, back and triceps on day two, shoulders and traps on day three, and legs on day four. Then he takes a day or two off depending on how he feels. Of course off for Dave means still coming into the gym and doing cardio and calves or abs. Let's take a look at his leg program.

Dave usually starts with hamstrings as he feels this is a weak area. He picks two exercises like lying leg curls and seated leg curls. At one time he did four different hamstring exercises but soon came to the realization that he was grossly overtraining his hamstrings. Typical sets on the lying leg curl would be: 1 x 20 reps with 50 pounds, 1 x 20 reps with 60, 1 x 20 reps with 80, and 2 x 15 reps with 120. These are precontest weights, and during the off-season Dave will work up to 150 pounds on this exercise.

On the seated leg curl Dave prefers higher reps, and does up to 30 reps per set. He averages 3 to 4 sets of this exercise.

With hamstrings out of the way Dave moves on to inflict some punishment on his thighs. Dave starts by doing 5 to 6 sets of 12 to 15 reps of leg presses. During the off-season he'll go up to over 1000 pounds, but during his precontest phase he keeps things in the 750 to 800 range.

On the seated leg curl Dave prefers higher reps.

"Every time I've competed I've strived to improve on something from the last show, and eventually I ended up with a body that was ready to win the Big One. Sometimes it's done in five years, other times 16. Whatever your situation, or whatever genetic potential you have, if you want it bad enough you'll get it!"

– Dave Fisher, former *MuscleMag* contributor and IFBB pro, revealing his mindset.

With his thighs fully warmed up, Dave moves on to his second thigh exercise, squats. He starts with 315 pounds for a couple of sets of 10 to 12 reps, and then drops to 225 for an additional 2 sets of 12 to 15 reps. Once again these are precontest weights, and Dave will go up to 450 to 500 pounds in the off-season.

To finish off his quads, Dave does 2 sets of leg extensions with 100 pounds for 20 reps each.

Biceps

It's amazing the number of bodybuilders who have had strict style forced on them after sustaining one or more injuries. In Dave's case it was a series of biceps injuries that forced him to totally redesign his biceps' workouts. But like many body-builders, Dave discovered that his biceps not only regained their preinjury form, they actually surpassed it. Now Dave's not sug-gesting you go out and injure yourself to reboot your system, but there is a lesson to be learned here.

A series of biceps injuries forced Dave to totally redesign his biceps' workouts.

The first change Dave made was to lighten his workout poundages and concen-trate more on the task at hand. Another change was to drop any exercise that put unwanted stress on his biceps. For example he reduced the amount of barbell work he did and substituted cable work instead. He also altered the order of his workouts. Often injuries are the result of doing the same exercises over and over. Such repetitive training can wear down even the largest and strongest muscles.

Something else Dave does nowa-days that tended to get short-shifted in the past is a good warmup. For biceps this means doing two or three light sets of dumbell curls before moving on to anything else.

Here are three different routines Dave uses to build two of the most complete biceps on the pro circuit.

Routine A
1. Standing barbell curls	4 sets of 12 reps using an EZ-curl bar
2. Seated dumbell curls	3 sets of 15 to 20 reps
3. One-arm preacher curls	3 sets of 10 to 15 eps
4. Low-pulley cable curls	4 sets of 15 reps

Routine B
1. Low-pulley cable curls	1 set of 15 to 20 reps as a warm up
2. One-arm preacher curl	4 sets of 12 reps
3. Barbell curls/seated dumbell curls	3 supersets of 10 to 12 reps each

Routine C
1. Seated dumbell curls	3 sets f 15 to 20 reps
2. Barbell curls	4 sets of 20 reps
3. One-arm preacher curls	4 sets of 15 reps
4. Cable curls	3 sets of 30 reps

Jay Cutler

To say Jay Cutler is one of bodybuildings fastest rising stars is an understatement. In six years he went from winning the heavyweight class of the Teen Nationals to winning the prestigious New York Night of Champions. Together with Markus Ruhl and Nasser El Sonbaty, Jay's one of the most massive bodybuilders around, weighing over 250 pounds in contest shape and upward of 280 to 300 in the off-season.

With his 2000 Night of Champions win, Jay has established himself as one of the new forces in bodybuilding. If he keeps improving the way he has over the last couple of years, many feel the Mr. Olympia title is his.

The following is a competitive history of Jay Cutler:

1993   Teen Nationals – NPC, heavyweight, 1st
1996   Nationals – NPC, heavyweight, 1st
1998   Night of Champions – IFBB, 12th
1999   Arnold Classic – IFBB, 4th
        Ironman Pro Invitational – IFBB, 3rd
        Olympia – IFBB, 15th
2000   Night of Champions – IFBB, winner

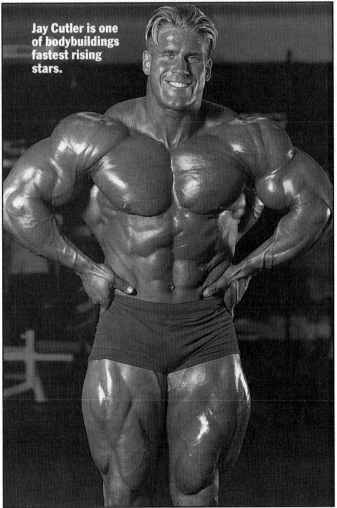

Jay Cutler is one of bodybuildings fastest rising stars.

Legs

Jay first got inspired to start serious leg training from photos of Quadzilla himself, Paul DeMayo. He was so impressed with Paul's freaky legs that he started doing just about every exercise there is for legs, especially thighs. As the opening quote shows, Jay's hard work paid off as his legs ballooned into two huge pillars of power. Jay's legs now rival his idol, Paul DeMayo's, and perhaps only the leg-king himself, Tom Platz, could claim a larger set of wheels.

"Yes, in fact I had a symmetry problem because they got so big! At 19 I stopped training quads and really haven't worked them hard since. I used to go into the gym and squat five plates every single workout. My legs got so big that I had to stop."

– Jay Cutler, 2000 Night of Champions winner, on his "problem" of having legs that responded too fast to training.

With his quads way out of proportion, Jay modified his leg training and started hitting hamstrings first. His first exercise is typically a lying leg curl, usually the Hammer Strength version. he does two medium warm up sets and then blasts out 3 to 4 sets of 8 to 10 reps, pyramiding up in weight with each set.

For his second exercise, Jay moves on to standing one-leg leg curls. He does 2 sets of 10 to 12 reps.

After standing curls, Jay moves on to seated leg curls, again utilizing Hammer Strength equipment. Once again it's 2 all-out sets of 10 to 12 reps.

To finish off his hamstrings, Jay does 3 to 4 sets of stiff-leg deadlifts. He uses a medium weight on this exercise (about 225) and goes for the maximum stretch on each rep.

With hamstrings out of the way, Jay starts his quad training. As his thighs have all the mass they'll ever need, Jay rarely does squats anymore. Instead he begins with leg presses, and even these are done with medium weight, about six plates a side. For variety Jay alternates his foot positions from toes out and in, to feet wide and narrow. In effect Jay treats the leg press as four sub-exercises. He does one warm-up set and then two working sets to failure.

Jay's first inspiration for leg training was from photos of Paul DeMayo.

For his second thigh exercise, Jay moves on to leg extensions. Again shape and cuts take precedent over size, so he limits the weight to 100 pounds or so. Jay squeezes each rep at the top, and stretches his legs between sets. He does just 2 sets of 10 to 12 reps.

To finish off two of the greatest legs in bodybuilding, Jay does 2 sets of dumbell lunges. Those who think lunges are for sissies haven't witnessed Jay's legs separating into slabs of cut muscle as he performs each rep. All four heads of his quads pulsate, and his hamstrings look like two bands of steel cables.

Back

It's not surprising that someone as massive as Jay Cutler comes from the old school of body-building; three or four exercises per muscle group and as much weight as he can handle in good style. Jay's back routine is a perfect example of this training philosophy.

Jay has divided back training into two halves, exercises for detail, and movements for mass. He usually starts his back workout with the exercise he feels is the best warmup movement there is, lat pulldowns. Besides adding width to his lats, pulldowns give his lats a good stretch and prepare his back for the heavier movements to come. Jay pyramids up in weight, and does one medium set for 10 to 15 reps, and then three working sets for 10 to 12 reps.

Jay's second exercise is the movement he feels is the core of his back routine – barbell rows. He places the exercise second in his routine as his back is by now fully warmed up from the pulldowns, but still has plenty of energy left to hit the rows heavy. Jay alternates between standing on a platform and standing on the floor. Jay uses a medium width, reverse grip on this

Monica Brant and Jay Cutler

exercise, the same one made famous by six-time Mr. Olympia, Dorian Yates, possessor of one of the greatest backs in bodybuilding history. Jay finds the reverse grip puts most of the stress on the lower lats, where they attach to the lower torso. One of Jay's peculiarities is that he doesn't bend over to the familiar 45-degree angle like most bodybuilders. Instead he only leans about 20 degrees from the vertical. He finds leaning any further not only puts extra stress on his lower back, but also doesn't give him the feel he wants. Jay does one medium set as a sort of warmup, and then two solid working sets of 6 to 8 reps.

For his third exercise, Jay moves on to one-arm dumbell rows. Rather than do the familiar version with his knee and hand on a bench, Jay lies face down on an incline bench. Doing so prevents him from swaying his body and cheating. This means using a 125 to 135 pound dumbell instead of the 200-pounder he could use on the traditional version. Jay compares this exercise to the Hammer Strength vertical row machine. As with barbell rows, Jay does one medium set and two heavy sets of 6 to 8 reps.

Jay finishes off his back workout with another of his so-called detail exercises. Most bodybuilders consider seated rows a power movement and as such pile on far too much weight. The end result is a great deal of jerking and yanking just to get the weight up. Jay on the other hand, does them in ultra strict style. This way he not only hits the lats but also the smaller contest-winning muscles like the teres, rhomboids, and rear delts. Jay does 3 sets of 10 to 12 reps.

Nasser El Sonbaty

It seemed fans were no sooner getting used to 260-pound Dorian Yates, then 275-pound Nasser El Sonbaty burst onto the scene. Nasser was one of those bodybuilders who kept showing up year after year weighing around 235 pounds and placing far down the list. But in six months he went to 275 pounds and started shaking things up.

Nasser El Sonbaty was born in Germany. His father is from Egypt and his mother from Yugoslavia. Nasser speaks many languages including Serbo-Croation, Arabian, English, French, Italian, Spanish and German. Nasser started training seriously in 1985 in Germany, with his first contest being the German Junior Nationals in May of the same year. Nasser was massive even back then and competed at 203 pounds. He came sixth in that contest at the tender age of 20. Before long he racked up three Yugoslavian Championships and became a professional bodybuilder.

Nasser had more than just a great physique and he began studies at the University of Augsburg, studying politics, psychology, sociology and history, and earned his degree in November 1992. What's even more amazing is that he was training, dieting, competing, study-ing and working at the same time! Nasser has established himself as one of the top bodybuilders in the world and this record shows why:

Nasser has established himself as one of the top bodybuilders in the world.

1990	Grand Prix Finland – IFBB, 8th
	Grand Prix France – IFBB, 7th
	Grand Prix Holland – IFBB, 8th
1991	Night of Champions – IFBB
1992	Chicago Pro Invitational – IFBB, 19th
	Night of Champions – IFBB
1993	Grand Prix France – IFBB, 3rd
	Grand Prix Germany – IFBB, 3rd
1994	Grand Prix France – IFBB, 4th
	Grand Prix Germany – IFBB, 4th
	Night of Champions – IFBB, 2nd
	Olympia – IFBB, 7th
1995	Grand Prix England – IFBB, 4th
	Grand Prix France – IFBB, 3rd
	Grand Prix Germany – IFBB, 3rd
	Grand Prix Russia – IFBB, 3rd
	Grand Prix Spain – IFBB, 3rd
	Grand Prix Ukraine – IFBB, 2nd
	Houston Pro Invitational – IFBB, winner
	Night of Champions – IFBB, winner
	Olympia – IFBB, 3rd
1996	Grand Prix Czech Republic – IFBB, winner
	Grand Prix England – IFBB, 2nd
	Grand Prix Germany – IFBB, 2nd
	Grand Prix Russia – IFBB, winner
	Grand Prix Spain – IFBB, 3rd
	Grand Prix Switzerland – IFBB, winner
	Olympia – IFBB, disqualified

1997   Arnold Classic – IFBB, 2nd
          Grand Prix Czech Republic – IFBB, 3rd
          Grand Prix England – IFBB, 3rd
          Grand Prix Finland – IFBB, 4th
          Grand Prix Germany – IFBB, 2nd
          Grand Prix Hungary – IFBB, 2nd
          Grand Prix Russia – IFBB, 3rd
          Grand Prix Spain – IFBB, 2nd
          Olympia – IFBB, 2nd
          San Jose Pro Invitational – IFBB, 2nd

1998   Arnold Classic – IFBB, 2nd
          Grand Prix Finland – IFBB, 3rd
          Grand Prix Germany – IFBB, 3rd
          Olympia – IFBB, 3rd

1999   Arnold Classic – IFBB, winner
          Grand Prix England – IFBB, 6th
          Olympia – IFBB, 6th
          Professional World Cup – IFBB, 6th

Nasser kept packing on weight until he was tipping the scales at 270 pounds of striated muscle.

Chest

Nasser is another of those mass-monsters that seemed to take over in the 1990s. Not content to stay at 230-235, Nasser kept packing on weight until he was tipping the scales at 270 pounds of striated muscle. To some such physiques were the next logical step in body-building evolution. For others such madness has turned bodybuilding into a freak show. Whatever your view, few can argue that when Nasser steps on stage, judges and audience alike, are treated to one of the greatest displays of beef that can possibly be imagined.

Nasser is one of those bodybuilders who incorporates a great deal of variety into his training. As his chest is one of his best bodyparts, we'll look at it in more detail.

Nasser realized early on that building the lower chest was fairly straightforward, while filling in the upper chest took time and creativity, and it wasn't long before he started prioritizing his upper chest training. Nasser usually starts his chest routine with a basic incline movement like barbell or Smith Machine presses. Whichever one he picks, he sticks with it for about four consecutive workouts, and then rotates. He does two light warm-up sets and then pyramids up in weight for sets of 15, 12, 8, and 6 reps respectively.

For his second exercise, Nasser moves on to either flat or decline flyes. He always keeps a slight bend in his elbows to take the stress off his shoulders. nasser also points out that the weight should be lifted with the chest muscles and not the biceps. Yet he continuously sees bodybuilders trying to lift the weight be bending at the elbows and bringing the biceps into play. Nasser uses a non-lock out style and does not let the dumbells touch at the top. As his chest is already warmed up from the inclines, Nasser jumps right to his four working sets of 15, 12, 8, and 6 reps.

Nasser's third exercise demonstrates just how committed he is to upper chest training, as he goes back to the Smith Machine and does another four sets of 15 to 6 reps. For many, eight sets of inclines (in two groups of four) would be overkill, but one look at Nasser's upper chest and you should get the picture.

Nasser concludes his chest training with two shaping and stretching exercises, dumbell pullovers and cable crossovers. He does 4 sets of both, doing his customary 15 to 6 reps in pyramid fashion.

Back

It's funny how an off-the-cuff remark can be blown way out of proportion. But his is exactly what happened to Nasser El Sonbaty in the mid 1990s when he casually said in an interview that one of his goals for the upcoming year was to improve his back.[1] No sooner had the comment escaped his lips than reporters latched on and made it sound as if Nasser actually had a sub-par back. To say Nasser was pissed is an understatement. His back was not weak, and fully complimented the rest of his massive physique. But now judges and fans alike had it ingrained that Nasser was suffering "back there."

Nasser El Sonbaty

Such scrutiny could ruin a lesser body-builder, but we all know Nasser is made of stronger stuff than that. And to show that he had nothing to be ashamed of, he turned around and promptly won the Arnold Classic!

A typical back workout for Nasser consists of four exercises performed for 4 sets each. He doesn't train back and biceps together on the same day as by the time he finishes back training, his biceps are wiped. In fact back training is such a good biceps builder, that he takes it into account when training the smaller muscle group.

Nasser starts his back routine with one-arm dumbell rows. Not only is this a great warm-up exercise, but also he likes the concentration you get from training the lats one at a time. Nasser offers this tip for beginners; keep your back straight and concentrate on using just your lats. There should be little or no shoulder movement. Try to visualize your arms as hooks and not active participants in the exercise. Nasser typically does 4 sets of 15 to 8 reps, pyramiding up in weight with each set.

Nasser's second back exercise is one of the mass-kings, barbell rows. He alternates between a straight and EZ-curl bar, and uses a reverse grip. This allows him to pull his elbows further behind his body and put the lats through a greater range of motion. This is one exercise Nasser pulls no punches on when it comes to weight. His philosophy is that heavy weight builds thickness, and on a basic power movement like barbell rows, it doesn't make sense to pussyfoot around. By trial and error, Nasser has discovered that keeping his torso at about 45 degrees to the floor is most effective. Any lower and the lower back is stressed. Too high and the traps take over.

Next up is seated cable rows. Many bodybuilders consider cable exercises "shape and detail" movements, but not Nasser. For his this is another mass exercise. As he pulls back to the vertical, Nasser arches his chest and squeezes his shoulder blades together. Again it's 4 sets of 15 to 8 reps in pyramid fashion.

Jean-Pierre Fux

To finish off his back workout, Nasser does dumbell pullovers. He finds this is an excellent movement for not only putting some beef in the upper lats and serratus, but also giving the lats a good overall stretch. The key he says is to keep the arms slightly bent and keep the butt lower than the bench.

Reference:
1) Sonbaty, Nasser El, Shot in the Back, *Flex* magazine, Volume 17, No. 7, September 1999.

Jean-Pierre Fux

Jean-Pierre (or JP as he prefers to be called) Fux was born in Naters, Switzerland, in 1968. Always athletic, at the age of 10 he became interested in bodybuilding, after deciding that he wanted to look like his swimming coach, a champion bodybuilder. At the age of 16 JP started training seriously.

His life easily could have taken him on a different direction, though we're pretty sure that with a last name like Fux, substitute teaching wasn't in the cards. He chose competition, and quickly rose through the ranks. Within a few short years he was the World Bodybuilding Champion. Here's his impressive record:

1993	World Amateur Championships – IFBB, heavyweight, 4th
1994	World Amateur Championships – IFBB, heavyweight, 1st
	Mr. Universe – 1st
1996	Arnold Classic – IFBB, 9th
	Grand Prix Czech Republic – IFBB, 5th
	Grand Prix England – IFBB, 9th
	Grand Prix Germany – IFBB, 8th
	Grand Prix Russia – IFBB, 2nd
	Grand Prix Spain – IFBB, 7th
	Grand Prix Switzerland – IFBB, 4th
	North American Championships – IFBB, heavyweight, 3rd
	Olympia – IFBB, 8th

San Jose Pro Invitational – IFBB, 5th
1997   Grand Prix England – IFBB, 8th
Grand Prix England – IFBB, 9th
Grand Prix Germany – IFBB, 8th
Grand Prix Hungary – IFBB, 5th
Grand Prix Spain – IFBB, 5th
Olympia – IFBB, 7th
1998   Arnold Classic – IFBB, 4th
Olympia – IFBB, 10th
1999   Grand Prix England – IFBB, 16th
Olympia – IFBB, 16th
Professional World Cup – IFBB, 12th
Toronto Pro Invitational – IFBB

Even though he hates leg training, JP agrees there's nothing quite as satisfying as leaving the gym after a brutal leg training session.

Behind every great man there's a woman, and JP is no exception. The last word goes to JP, and his comments about his girl-friend: "Karin does everything she can for me. During the first three years of our relationship I didn't make much money in this sport. Karin works as an elementary school teacher and she supported us both. I had maybe ten guest posings per year, but with Karin's help I was able to get the food and supplements I needed. I hope I can now give Karin back the support she gave to me."

Legs

For North Americans weaned on baseball, football and hockey, it sometimes comes as a shock to learn that the number one sport in the world is soccer. Every four years the world's best soccer players come together to play in the World Cup, next to the Olympics, the largest sporting event in the world.

For Swiss native, Jean-Pierre Fux, the call of soccer came at an early age. By the age of 16, Jean-Pierre had eight years experience under his belt. One of the "side effects" from all those years running the field was a pair of legs that made his upper body look small and weak.

Jean-Pierre was lucky in that when he first started bodybuilding, there was a former national champion training there. When he recognized the young Fux's great potential he set him up on a program that contained a wide variety of exercises. Within a year, Jean-Pierre had gained over 60 pounds of muscular bodyweight, and it wasn't long before he was the World Heavyweight Champion.

Jean-Pierre is the first to admit that he hates leg training. At least hates the actual exercises. But he'll also agree there's nothing quite as satisfying as leaving the gym after a brutal leg training session.

As soon as Jean-Pierre arrives at the gym the first thing he does is spend 10 to 15 minutes stretching. He believes far too many bodybuilders give stretching a short-shift, and fail to recognize that it not only helps prevent injuries, but actually aids in muscle recovery.

Although Jean-Pierre usually alternates between two different thigh workouts, he always does leg presses, squats, and leg extensions in his routine. But he uses different rep ranges and foot positions to keep the muscles guessing. Here are two sample routines Jean-Pierre uses to build those columns of power:

Routine A

1. Leg presses	1 set of 18 to 20 reps
	2 sets of 8 to 12 reps
2. Leg extensions	2 sets of 12 to 15 reps
3. Squats	2 sets of 6 to 12 reps

Routine B

1. Leg extensions	1 drop set of 80 to 100 reps
2. Squats	3 sets of 8 to 12 reps (different foot position)
3. Leg presses	2 sets of 8 to 12 reps (different foot position)

Paul Dillett

Hailing from Montreal, the largest French-speaking city in Canada, Paul Dillett has been competing since 1991. Paul has made his mark on the bodybuilding world by breezing past those who have been competing for a decade or more. Dillett has consistently placed in the top five in several of the Olympia show-downs, and remains a force to be reckoned with on stages from Long Beach to London.

Paul was born in Montreal, Quebec on April 12, 1965. He was very athletic as a youth, running track, playing basketball, hockey and football, and boxing. At the age of 18, Paul took up bodybuilding. For two years Paul was a professional football player in the Canadian Football League (CFL), playing middle line-backer for the Toronto Argonauts. But he wanted to dedicate himself to bodybuilding, so he retired from football to seriously build his body.

"I'd say I put on about 20 pounds the first year. I was always a quick gainer because, even though I was too thin for my height, I was always muscular and had the genetics to put on size without much effort. I was one of those people who train seven days a week. I didn't know what a day off was. I thought that eating Pepperidge Farms cakes was good and I drank milkshakes full of ice cream. Those extra calories during that initial year helped me to gain size … At first I thought that all you were supposed to do was eat. To me that meant

Paul has made his mark on the bodybuilding world by breezing past those who have been competing for a decade or more.

everything. I didn't realize there was a method to the madness."

Fortunately, he figured that part out, as his record shows:

1991   North American Championships – IFBB, heavyweight, 2nd
1992   North American Championships – IFBB, overall winner
        North American Championships – IFBB, heavyweight, 1st
1993   Arnold Classic – IFBB, 4th
        Ironman Pro Invitational – IFBB, 4th
        Olympia – IFBB, 6th
1994   Grand Prix England – IFBB, 4th
        Grand Prix France (2) – IFBB, 2nd
        Grand Prix France – IFBB, winner
        Grand Prix Germany – IFBB, winner
        Grand Prix Germany – IFBB, 3rd
        Grand Prix Italy – IFBB, 2nd
        Grand Prix Spain – IFBB, 3rd
        Olympia – IFBB, 4th
1996   Arnold Classic – IFBB, 3rd
        Grand Prix Czech Republic – IFBB, 3rd
        Grand Prix England – IFBB, 3rd
        Grand Prix Germany – IFBB, 4th
        Grand Prix Russia – IFBB, 4th
        Grand Prix Spain – IFBB, 2nd
        Grand Prix Switzerland – IFBB, 2nd
        Ironman Pro Invitational – IFBB, 2nd
        Olympia – IFBB, 5th
        San Jose Pro Invitational – IFBB, 2nd
1997   Arnold Classic – IFBB, 6th
        Grand Prix Czech Republic – IFBB, 6th
        Grand Prix England – IFBB, 4th
        Grand Prix Finland – IFBB, 5th
        Grand Prix Germany – IFBB, 4th
        Grand Prix Hungary – IFBB, 4th
        Grand Prix Russia – IFBB, 5th
        Grand Prix Spain – IFBB, 4th
        Ironman Pro Invitational – IFBB, 5th
        Olympia – IFBB, 5th
        San Jose Pro Invitational – IFBB, 5th
1998   Olympia – IFBB
1999   Night of Champions – IFBB, winner
        Olympia – IFBB, 7th
2000   Night of Champions – IFBB, 3rd

Paul Dillett has consistently placed in the top five in several of the Olympia show downs.

Besides his presence on stage, Paul has strong personal opinions: "In the past few years I think bodybuilding has been judged more on name, reputation, and last contest entered. I mean, let's judge a show based on what's happening on the day of this competition, not on the one that was decided six months ago … I don't know if it's getting out of hand or not, but the fact is athletes are extreme personalities. That's why we attain the level of excellence we do and

Paul's legs are among the best on the pro circuit.

others don't. Maybe they stay amateurs. I guess my point is this: No one says that Michael Jordan jumps too high or that skiers ski too fast, yet there seems to be this judgement from within that bodybuilding is getting too extreme … I happen to think that beauty is in the eye of the beholder, and so is the word extreme. You have to please the fans with both muscle and conditioning these days. If that is extreme, then I guess the sport is extreme … no one ever wins Mr. Olympia any more. It's a gift. I'm not trying to insult anyone or put anyone down, but the fact is, bodybuilding is a matter of opinion. On the other hand I can't say that Dorian doesn't deserve to win. What most judges should realize is that they're not making a call that is necessarily "correct." They're making a call based on their own personal preference and opinion. That's obvious every time you see some blocky guy winning the symmetry round … And I think that the sooner most bodybuilders accept that it is an opinion and not a win, the better off they'll be."

Legs

When you are 6'1" and 280 pounds, maintaining good body proportions is a chore all by itself. Early in his career, 1999 New York Night of Champions winner, Paul Dillett recognized that with his tall frame, filling in his legs would be a priority. Let's face it, most of the "great legs" in bodybuilding history belong to bodybuilders in the 5'2" to 5'9" category. From Tim Belknap and Tom Platz to Lee Priest and Paul DeMayo, shorter bodybuilders seem to have an advantage for building large wheels. Conversely few bodybuilders over 6-foot became famous for their legs. Even two of the all-time greats, Arnold and Lou Ferrigno, never quite got their lower bodies up to the standard of their gargantuan upper bodies. Paul vowed from an early age that his legs would never be referred to as sub-par. And he made good on this promise as his legs are among the best on the pro circuit.

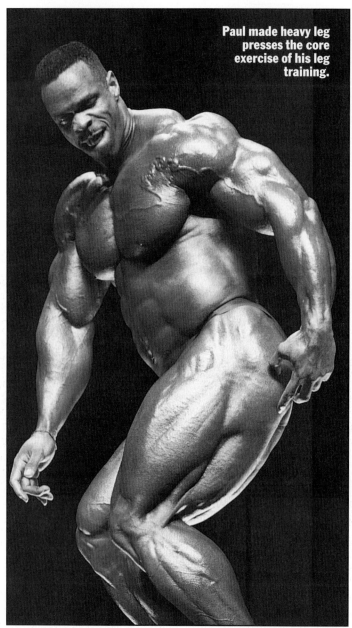

Paul made heavy leg presses the core exercise of his leg training.

You'd expect us to say that Paul spends hours at the squat rack. And it is true he's done his fair share of this universal leg builder over the years. But he found that with his height, squats never gave him the feel he wanted. They also tended to put more stress on his lower back than he desired. So Paul said to hell with the pundits, and made heavy leg presses the core exercise of his leg training.

Paul doesn't jump right into leg presses though. He first does 3 light to medium sets of leg extensions to warm up the muscle and get a good supply of blood in there. On some days he'll do straight sets with both legs, while on others he'll do the one-legged variety. Paul emphasizes both the positive and negative part of each rep. He's not one for sacrificing form just to boost his ego with a few extra pounds.

With his thighs fully warmed up, Paul starts getting serious. This means 4 to 5 sets of all-out leg presses. He alternates between wide and narrow stances to target different parts of his thighs. Although the recommended depth for leg presses is about a 90-degree angle between upper and lower leg, Paul goes for a full range of motion by lowering the weight until his knees touch his chest. But unlike some that bounce the weight off the chest just to keep it moving, Paul stops for a split second to reduce momentum. This not only keeps maximum tension on the thighs, but also reduces the stress on his knees. Paul pyramids up in weight with each set, doing 10 to 15 reps per set. Then on the last set he reduces the weight and blasts out a set of 20 reps.

Paul's third exercise is the hack squat. Paul feels this exercise offers all the advantages of barbell squats without the negative aspects. For example he can shift his legs forward and back to target different parts of his thigh. With barbell squats you are limited to moving the feet in or out. Another reason Paul prefers hacks is that they keep the involvement of the glutes to a minimum. Paul feels conventional squats place too much stress on the butt.

To finish off his quads, Paul goes back to the leg extension and does another 4 sets of 10 to 20 reps each. As his thighs are pretty much wasted by this point, he doesn't need to go that heavy.

Ernie Taylor

Ernie is another of those bodybuilders who just seems to come from nowhere and make a big impact in a hurry. A native of England, Ernie came from nowhere to place third at the 1997 New York Night of Champions. In fact he accomplished this amazing feat in just six years. he first started training in 1991 and within four years had won the heavyweight class at the British Championships.

Ernie has made a name for himself for having excellent proportions, and two of the largest, freakiest triceps ever to grace a bodybuilding stage. Here's his competitive record:

1997   Night of Champions – IFBB, 3rd
1998   Night of Champions – IFBB, 5th
        Olympia – IFBB, 8th
1999   Night of Champions – IFBB, 6th
        Olympia – IFBB, 13th

Back

Although his triceps have gotten him the most attention over the years, his back is not far behind. And wouldn't you know it, Ernie just happens to train at Temple Gym in Birmingham, England, home to one of the greatest backs in bodybuilding history, Dorian Yates. The six-time Mr. Olympia winner recognized Ernie's potential early on, and made it a point to keep an eye on the lad. Probably the most important lesson Ernie learned from Dorian was that quality always beats quantity. For this reason he adopted Dorian's brief, but intense form of training. In short you won't find Ernie doing 20 sets per bodypart, two to three times per week.

Ernie usually starts his back training with close-grip pulldowns. He does two medium weight sets for 15 to 20 reps, and then one all-out set for 10 reps. He does the first two sets medium intense as this is the first exercise in his back workout and he wants to be sure his back is fully warmed up before assaulting it further.

For his second exercise, Ernie likes to target the center back with seated cable rows. He prefers the straight bar over the narrow, cambered bar, as it gives him a better back contraction. Ernie also prefers the "stretch forward" version as opposed to the "stationary torso" version. But he never goes back past the 90 to 100 degree mark with his torso. He's doing this primarily for his lats not

Ernie has made a name for himself for having excellent proportions, and two of the largest, freakiest triceps ever to grace a body-building stage.

lower back. To give his lats maximum contraction, Ernie holds each rep in the contracted position for about two seconds. He typically does 2 sets of 12 reps.

Exercise number three is one-arm rows on the Hammer Strength machine. Ernie finds this exercise stricter than the dumbell version. As with seated rows he holds each rep for two seconds. He does just one all-out set for each arm for 12 reps.

To finish off his back, Ernie does one high intensity set of front pulldowns. He advises beginners against the behind the head version as it can be murder on the shoulder joint, particularly the rotator region.

With eight total sets completed for his lats (2 warm-up and 6 heavy), Ernie moves on to traps. Although most bodybuilders train traps with shoulders, Ernie finds most of his back exercises also stimulate the traps to a minor degree, so he figured he might as well get them out of the way.

Ernie does just two sets for his traps, one set of 6 to 10 reps each of front and rear shrugs on the Hammer Strength shrug machine. He's tried barbell and dumbell shrugs in the past, but the Hammer Strength machine works best for him.

Mike Matarazzo

Mike Matarazzo

Michael Matarazzo was born in 1966. All his life he's been a fighter, perhaps it's in his genes: "I was a boxer, my father was a boxer, and that's what got me by … I was never in the amateur ranks or nothing like that, but I sparred and used to bounce the bag around … There was this wise guy in a bar. Now, he was Irish and I'm Italian, and the two don't mix. He knew I was a fighter, and one thing led to another, and we went at it. I put him down, and walked away, but the guy comes up and puts a knife in my right side … I look back at those times and boy, I was a jerk. I had a quick temper, and I wonder how I got through it. When you're a fighter, you gotta have this attitude. You believe you can't get hurt. Pro boxers think they're inhuman – it's the only way they can do what they do. I realized I had to get out of it, that that life wasn't for me."

Mike got smart, and dedicated himself to bodybuilding:

1991 USA Championships – NPC, overall winner
USA Championships – NPC, heavyweight, 1st
1992 Arnold Classic – IFBB, 15th
Ironman Pro Invitational – IFBB, 5th
1993 Arnold Classic – IFBB, 6th
Night of Champions – IFBB, 8th
Olympia – IFBB, 18th
Pittsburgh Pro Invitational – IFBB, 2nd
1994 Arnold Classic – IFBB, 9th
San Jose Pro Invitational – IFBB, 8th
1995 Florida Pro Invitational – IFBB, 7th
South Beach Pro Invitational – IFBB, 7th
1996 Grand Prix Czech Republic – IFBB, 9th
Grand Prix Russia – IFBB, 9th
Grand Prix Switzerland – IFBB, 9th
Night of Champions – IFBB, 5th
Olympia – IFBB, 13th
1997 Canada Pro Cup – IFBB, 2nd
Grand Prix Germany – IFBB, 11th
Grand Prix Hungary – IFBB, 10th
Grand Prix Spain – IFBB, 10th
Night of Champions – IFBB, 4th
Olympia – IFBB, 13th
Toronto Pro Invitational – IFBB, 2nd
1998 Night of Champions – IFBB, 3rd
Olympia – IFBB, 9th
San Francisco Pro Invitational – IFBB, 7th
Toronto Pro Invitational – IFBB, 3rd
1999 Olympia – IFBB, 11th
2000 Night of Champions – IFBB
Toronto Pro Invitational – IFBB, 6th

Mike doesn't fool around when training. For him, the gym is serious stuff.

And what about that sour reputation that Mike has? "Yeah, a lot of people call me an asshole. I don't make small talk. I don't bullshit, not when I'm in the gym at least. The gym is serious. It's all concentration. I may come across mean and nasty, but it's just that I've got no time for anybody else when I'm training. When I'm out of the gym, I'm a different person. I'm a great guy!"

Achim Albrecht

Achim Albrecht was born in Muenster, Germany, on July 2, 1962. He left home at the age of 13 to explore the world! Achim gives the best explanation: "… Unless I take the time to explain fully, everyone assumes that I had such a terrible home life. That's why I don't tell people casually exactly how young I was when I left home. It demands an explanation that I don't always have the time for or care to give…

My father is an old soldier who saw action on the Russian front during the war. He was badly wounded. He had a very rough time. Actually, not just my mother and father, but all people of their generation who were close to the war, from every country, had it rough. First my

Achim thanks all those who supported him over his competitive career.

parents had this terrible war that stole their youth, and then all Germans had to rebuild their country up from the rubble that was left. Sure, my father was a tough man. He had to be able to survive. But he was also a very fair man. I couldn't screw with him, for sure, but there was never any loss of caring. The war had left him so disabled that his doctors strongly advised him not to overstress himself traveling to visit me last year. Even though he had to get a special medical certificate, he pushed them hard to allow him to fly over anyway. That was the act of a caring parent …

Maybe I inherited his strong will. Both my brother and sister stayed on to lead normal lives at home, and are now successful with good jobs. I was the one who couldn't wait to conquer the world … I don't usually advertise the age I left home because it leads people to make false judgements, but it was very young … 13 … I left to work with a traveling fair … I did educate myself to some extent as I traveled around from job to job. Believe me, being away from the security of home at 13 and having no one to look after you is an education in itself. Looking back, I don't know if leaving home was the smartest thing to do, but at the time I would have fought anyone tooth and nail who tried to stop me. That's the kind of boy I was, I guess. I just don't want to give the impression that I'm advising other boys to follow my example…"

Achim discovered many things, one of which was bodybuilding: "I became interested in bodybuilding when I was around 18 or 19, but it was more on-and-off training. Once I started training regularly, I found that I made good progress, so I tried to move to where I felt I could train with the best. By age 20, I entered my first contest."

And he did very well:

1990 World Amateur Championships – IFBB, heavyweight, 1st
1991 Olympia – IFBB, 9th
1992 Arnold Classic – IFBB, 4th
1993 Arnold Classic – IFBB, 10th
      Grand Prix France – IFBB, 5th
      Grand Prix Germany – IFBB, 7th
      San Jose Pro Invitational – IFBB, 4th
1994 Arnold Classic – IFBB, 8th
      Olympia – IFBB, 17th
      San Jose Pro Invitational – IFBB, 5th

1995   Houston Pro Invitational – IFBB, 3rd
        Niagara Falls Pro Invitational – IFBB, 3rd
1996   Canada Pro Cup – IFBB, 4th
        Night of Champions – IFBB, 10th

Achim retired from active competition to become "Brachus," a pro wrestler with the WWF. The last word goes to Achim: "I am not leaving bodybuilding … I told you that I will always be a bodybuilder. I am just leaving competition. I would like to thank all those who supported me over my competitive career. I intend to give my new career 100 percent effort, and I hope they will check in on me from time to time to see how I'm doing."

Shoulders

Watching Achim train shoulders is like a scene right out of the '70s. Where other bodybuilders

While other bodybuilders are using all the new high-tech training gadgets, Achim is still pounding his muscles with dumbells and barbells.

are becoming slaves to all the new high-tech training gadgets, Achim is pounding his muscles with dumbells and barbells. You won't find him subscribing to the high intensity form of training either. Eight to ten sets is considered a warmup! For a large muscle like shoulders he'll average 20 to 25 sets before he feels satisfied. By today's standards this is overtraining, but there's no denying the results.

Achim begins his shoulder training with behind the head barbell presses. His first set is for 20 reps, and then he'll add some weight and do 3 to 4 sets of 6 to 8 reps. If he's feeling particularly strong that day he may go up to a weight that limits him to two or three reps.

After barbell presses, Achim moves on to dumbell presses, dumbell laterals, and bent-over laterals. Here's a typical Achim Albrecht shoulder workout from the mid-'90s:

1. Seated barbell presses
   5 sets of 6 to 8 reps
2. Seated dumbell presses
   5 sets of 6 to 8 reps
3. Lateral raises
   5 sets of 6 to 8 reps
4. Bent-over lateral raises
   5 sets of 6 to 8 reps
5. *Front dumbell raises
   5 sets of 6 to 8 reps

*once or twice a month

Roland Cziurlok

Back

And they keep coming! Every year sees a whole new crop of bodybuilders graduating from the amateur ranks, clutching their pro cards to their massive chests. Most get a crash course in humility the first time backstage when they witness the likes of Dillett, Ruhl, and Coleman. One or two shows and you never hear from them anymore. But every once in a while, a guy comes along that has the necessary muscle artillery to compete on an equal footing with the established pros. Roland Cziurlok is one such bodybuilder.

Roland was like many bodybuilders early in their careers in that he routinely spent six days a week, three hours a day, working out. A typical workout would involve six exercises for six sets each. That adds up to 36 sets for just one muscle group. Can you say overtraining everybody?

Through a combination of trial and error, and some good advice from more experienced bodybuilders, Roland cut his workouts in half. He still employs a good deal of variety in his training, but the total number of sets has been greatly reduced. To illustrate let's look at his back workout.

With one of the widest backs on the pro scene, it's not surprising that Roland starts his back workouts with front pulldowns. He does two, light 20-rep warm-up sets, and then proceeds to do 3 heavy sets of 12 reps each. We should emphasize that heavy is a relative term. Roland uses about 70 percent of the maximum weight he can handle, but does so in ultra strict fashion. How the set feels is far more important than the number on the stack.

Amy Zych, Roland Cziurlok and Shannon Meteraud

As he's pulling the weight down, Roland squeezes his shoulder together and holds it for a second or two at the bottom.

Exercise two is the behind-the-head pulldown. Roland uses the same grip and bar as front pulldowns but keeps his torso more upright. This brings more of the teres, rhomboids, and upper lats into play. Again he does 3 heavy sets.

After his two basic width exercises, Roland moves on to his primary thickness exercises. First up is seated pulley rows. Roland does the full stretch version of this exercise, and squeezes his shoulder blades together as he pulls the bar to his lower rib cage. You guessed it, 3 sets of 8 to 12 reps.

After rows come more pulldowns, but this time he uses a narrow, reverse grip. By using a narrow reverse grip, most of the stress is placed on the lower and center lats, as opposed to the upper, outer lats targeted by wide grip pulldowns. Another slight change is that Roland uses a higher rep range, averaging 15 per set.

To finish off his back, Roland does his favorite back exercise, barbell rows. Most bodybuilders start with this exercise and go extremely heavy. But Roland prefers to leave it till last as by then his back is fully warmed up, and more important he can use less weight but get the same degree of stimulation. Even though he could row with well over 200 pounds, Roland limits it to between 120 and 160 pounds.

The previous is Roland's primary off-season back routine, but close to a contest, he'll add on a couple of sets of straight arm pushdowns and standing one-arm cable rows.

Roland Cziurlok is one guy that has the necessary muscle artillery to compete on an equal footing with the established pros.

Greg Kovacs is the quintessential new-age genetically gifted bodybuilder.

Greg Kovacs

The next step in bodybuilding evolution? Today we yawn at the sight of yet another bodybuilder who weighs just 240 pounds, whereas 20 years ago 235-pound Arnold Schwarzenegger was considered the most massive bodybuilder in the world. Even 260-pound Dorian Yates was dwarfed at one Olympia by 280-pound Nasser El Sonbaty. The inevitable evolutionary progression of bodybuilding makes yesterday's champs seem like today's shrimp. On that developmental road from Grimek and Ross to Park and Pearl; and Arnold and Sergio to Lee Haney and Dorian Yates; and from Yates to Dillett and Sonbaty, comes a new giant who weighs almost 400 pounds in off-season condition and competes at over 300 pounds. His name is Greg Kovacs. He is the quintessential new-age genetically gifted bodybuilder – bigger than once thought humanly possible and stronger than anyone dared to imagine.

Greg was born in Fonthill, Ontario, Canada, in 1968. Blessed with great genetics, at the age of 17 Greg weighed 240 pounds before he ever touched a weight! Today he weighs between 360 and 390 pounds most of the year and drops to 300 to 330 for competitions. At 345 pounds, he was measured and found to have a 65" chest, a 40" waist, 35" thighs, 23" calves and 25" arms, and a height of 6'2. Despite being a famous bodybuilder, it is only recently that Greg has been entering contests. And who can blame him? He makes so much money from guest appearances and endorsements on behalf of supplement giant, MuscleTech, he doesn't need to starve himself for contest money! But we guess the fans kept asking him, and he finally indulged all of us by competing:

1997   Night of Champions – IFBB, 16th
1998   Ironman Pro Invitational – IFBB, 16th

In person he's amazingly friendly, and a real crowd pleaser. He's a genuinely nice, charming, "let's have a beer" kind of guy. Always a hit at trade shows, Greg is a major force in the sport of bodybuilding. Not bad for a guy who's been in two contests!

Chest

It doesn't seem that long ago that *Muscle and Fitness* magazine was writing about Lou Ferrigno breaking the 60-inch chest barrier. No sooner had Arnold been listed in the Guinness Book of Records for having the largest muscular chest at 57-inches when Ferrigno upped the bar to 60 inches. Now along comes this Canadian colossus and 70 inches has gone by the wayside!

Despite not having placed at a major pro bodybuilding contest, Greg Kovacs is one of the most popular bodybuilders in the world. As the official model for MuscleTech supplements, Greg travels around the world promoting himself and the company he works for. Go to any trade show or contest, and you'll find Greg manning a MuscleTech booth surrounded by hundreds of awestruck fans.

As with Arnold and Lou Ferrigno before him, the center of Greg's gargantuan physique is his chest. It's not only the size of the bloody thing that gets attention, but its strength. As the story goes Greg walked out of the audience at a powerlifting meet when he was in his late teens, and took the 500 pounds just completed for a single, and commenced to do 8 to 10 reps with it. Nowadays the guy routinely reps with over 500 pounds and inclines 675 for reps on the Smith machine.

Here's a typical Greg Kovacs chest workout:

1. Incline Smith presses   3 to 4 warm-up sets of 15 to 20 reps
                                         2 to 3 heavy sets of 6 to 10 reps
2. Flat bench presses   1 to 2 warmup, 1 to 2 heavy sets for 6 to 10 reps
3. Seated bench press machine   1 to 2 sets of 6 to 10 reps
4. Incline dumbell flyes   1 to 2 sets of 6 to 10 reps
5. Cable crossovers   1 to 2 sets of 12 to 15 reps

Despite not having placed at a major pro bodybuilding contest, Greg Kovacs is one of the most popular bodybuilders in the world.

Porter Cottrell

For most pro bodybuilders the highlight of their career is winning their first major contest. But for Porter Cottrell, it's probably the night he was summoned to help a dying Mohammad Benaziza. Just after winning a Grand Prix event Mohammad went back to his hotel room and collapsed from a diuretic overdose. With his electrolytes all but depleted, Mohammad's heart stopped. Despite the best attempts of Porter, a trained firefighter, to revive him, Mohammad became a casualty of the "ripped at all costs" mentality of modern bodybuilding.

Porter was born in Hart County, Kentucky, in 1961. Porter admits that while he wasn't the largest teen in high school, he made up for it with his speed. After working for a number of years designing machines for a company called Louisville Bedding, Porter opted for a career change and became a firefighter: "I've been in situations that I don't want in print, but I will tell you one that totally scared the shit out of me. Very few people experience a backdraft, but I experienced one within the first two months of being in the fire department. We were at a fire in a three-story house. There was just smoke showing, and we were getting ready to ventilate. A captain and another firefighter went from the side of the house up the stairs to the second floor, and while we were ventilating, they opened a door, and that's where the fire was. When you have the potential of a backdraft, you have all the elements of a fire except one – oxygen – and when they opened that door, boom! The windows blew out of the house, the storm doors blew out of the house, and it blew about a ten-foot hole out of the roof. That was one of the worst situations I've been in."

Porter has established a reputation for always being in shape and rarely misses the top ten.

Porter's first bodybuilding contest was the 1983 Mr. Louisville, in which he placed second. By 1988 Porter had won the Junior Nationals, and just two years later had won the light heavyweight division of the Nationals. With a number of pro wins to his resumé, Porter has established a reputation for always being in shape and rarely misses the top ten. Here's his record:

1988   Junior Nationals – NPC, overall winner
        Junior Nationals – NPC, light heavyweight, 1st
1989   Nationals – NPC, light heavyweight, 3rd
1991   Nationals – NPC, light heavyweight, 1st

1992　Chicago Pro Invitational – IFBB, winner
Grand Prix England – IFBB, 5th
Grand Prix Germany – IFBB, 4th
Grand Prix Holland – IFBB, 7th
Grand Prix Italy – IFBB, 5th
Niagara Falls Pro Invitational – IFBB, winner
Night of Champions – IFBB, 2nd
Olympia – IFBB, 8th
1993　Chicago Pro Invitational – IFBB, winner
Night of Champions – IFBB, winner
Pittsburgh Pro Invitational – IFBB, winner
1994　Arnold Classic – IFBB, 3rd
Grand Prix England – IFBB, 9th
Grand Prix Germany – IFBB, 7th
Grand Prix Spain – IFBB, 5th
Olympia – IFBB, 5th
San Jose Pro Invitational – IFBB, 2nd
1996　Arnold Classic – IFBB, 8th
San Jose Pro Invitational – IFBB, 10th
1998　Night of Champions – IFBB, 6th
San Francisco Pro Invitational – IFBB, 6th
Toronto Pro Invitational – IFBB, 4th
1999　Night of Champions – IFBB, 9th
Toronto Pro Invitational – IFBB, 3rd

A typical shoulder workout for Porter starts with dumbell presses.

Shoulders

Porter Cottrell has learned two crucial lessons over the last couple of years. First, far too many young bodybuilders let their egos dictate their training. And second, most people under-estimate the value of a good warmup. The shoulders are especially unforgiving when it comes to heavy weight. Some muscle can be regularly abused without too many repercussions, but not the shoulders. Even with the best intentions, the shoulder may cause problems down the road, especially if they have been regularly subjected to the pounding of 300-pound behind-the-neck presses.

Armed with this knowledge, Porter begins every shoulder exercise with a couple of warm up sets. Many bodybuilders believe that it's only necessary to warm up on the first exercise. This may be true for some muscles but not the shoulders. Porter thinks it's essential you do a couple of light, warm-up sets every time you switch exercises.

A typical shoulder workout for Porter starts with dumbell presses. He finds a slight incline puts less stress on the shoulder joint while still targeting the front delts. he also doesn't believe in locking completely out. He does two warm-up sets of 20 to 25 reps and then pyramids up in weight and down in reps for 3 to 4 sets.

Next up it's 3 to 4 sets of side lateral raises. Again he does a couple of warm-up sets before increasing the weight. To keep things strict, Porter sits down on a bench. Standing up makes it too tempting to cheat. He uses a quick, explosive style on the way up, and lowers ultra slow, emphasizing the negative part of the rep.

Exercise number three is bent-over lateral raises. Again strict style is king on this exercise and Porter lies face down on a low incline bench. With his chest braced against a pad,

Jim Quinn goes to the gym to work, not to take up space.

it makes it very difficult to cheat. Again he does 3 to 4 sets of 8 to 10 reps.

To finish off Porter does 3 to 4 sets of shrugs. He prefers the dumbell version to the barbell version. He also holds the dumbells more to the front than the traditional side position. But he admits it's more of a personal preference thing than any biomechanical advantage. One thing he stresses is not rolling the shoulders. This doesn't add anything extra to the exercise. But it does increase the risk of impinging a nerve or stressing a disk.

Jim Quinn

Jim was born in Syossett, Long Island, on February 2, 1960, and grew up in Huntington Station, Long Island. Jim was a natural athlete, and attended college on a football scholarship, graduating with a degree in Business Administration. At the age of 18 he started weight training. And the 6' 1", 275-pound football star started competing:

1987	USA Championships – NPC, heavyweight, 4th
1988	Nationals – NPC, heavyweight, 3rd
	North American Championships – IFBB, heavyweight, 4th
	USA Championships – NPC, heavyweight, 5th
1990	North American Championships – IFBB, heavyweight, 1st
1991	WBF Grand Prix – WBF, 4th
1993	Chicago Pro Invitational – IFBB, 7th
	Niagara Falls Pro Invitational – IFBB, 4th
	Night of Champions – IFBB, 11th
1994	Arnold Classic – IFBB, 14th
	Chicago Pro Invitational – IFBB, 12th
	Ironman Pro Invitational – IFBB, 10th
	Niagara Falls Pro Invitational – IFBB, 12th
	Night of Champions – IFBB, 13th
	San Jose Pro Invitational – IFBB, 12th
1995	Houston Pro Invitational – IFBB, 11th
	Night of Champions – IFBB, 14th

Jim made the jump to the WBF in 1991, but rejoined the IFBB after Vince McMahon's federation folded. Jim was always one of the largest competitors onstage, and although since retired, would fit in quite nicely with today's emphasis on pure beef. The thought of big Jim,

Markus Ruhl, and Nasser El Sonbaty in a posedown would be worth the price of admission alone.

The last word goes to Jim. When asked what he thought his best qualities were, he answered: "Honesty, integrity, commitment, tenacity and relentlessness … also my ability to get along with different types of people, and definitely my sense of humor. I'm down-to-earth and unpretentious, a good Catholic brought up very well. All in all, I'd consider myself a good person, a good employee, and a very good friend. I can see how some people could perceive me as an SOB in the gym, but I'm there to work, not to take up space."

Back

It's funny how one person's blessing is another's curse. Most bodybuilders would kill to have Jim Quinn's shoulder width and mass. But Jim finds that his naturally wide shoulders (not to mention those enormous arms) make it difficult for him to feel his back during back workouts. Of course it didn't help matters that early in his career he flung around as much weight as he could handle without any attention to proper technique.

The defining moment in Jim's back training came after reading an article by Dorian Yates on back training. Let's face it, when the big Brit talks back training, everyone sits up and takes notice. The guy had one of the greatest backs in bodybuilding history. In the article, Dorian suggested a number of tips to help those who had trouble feeling their back muscles. One tip was to use a reverse grip on many back exercises. Another tip was to concentrate on pulling with the elbows rather than the arms. Too much focus on the arms and the forearms and biceps take over.

Besides Dorian's advice, Jim read how Mike Francois improved his back by adding deadlifts to his training.

Armed with all this, Jim redesigned his back workouts. A typical back session starts with

Jim Quinn battles it out with Gary Strydom, Mike Christian, Berry DeMey and Rich Gaspari.

front pulldowns using a medium, reverse grip. At one point he pulled all the way down to the chest, but after talking to Dorian on the phone, discovered that once the bar reaches chin-level, the back muscles are fully contracted. Jim usually does 5 sets of pulldowns, pyramiding up in weight with each set.

Jim's second exercise is deadlifts. Again Dorian set the tone. Most bodybuilders go all the way to the floor on this exercise but Dorian points out that it's difficult to do this without rounding the back. And as soon as you round the back the lower back ligaments and disks are put under great stress. So Jim only bends forward to about knee level. In fact to keep proper form Jim performs this exercise in a power cage with pin supports set at knee height. Jim's exceptionally strong on this exercise and works up to 600 pounds for 3 sets of 10 reps.

For his third exercise, Jim goes back to the front cable pulldown machine, but this time uses a wide grip. This exercise is great for adding width to the upper, outer lats. Five sets of 8 to 10 reps is the norm.

To finish off his back, Jim alternates between reverse-grip T-bar rows and one-arm Hammer Strength rows.

Dexter Jackson

With two second place finishes and one third place finish in 2000, Dexter Jackson has established himself as a force to be reckoned with in the new millennium. To many Dexter is an example of what bodybuilding should be about, proportions, symmetry, and good muscularity. Dexter places high on all three.

Dexter grew up in Florida with his first contest being the First Coast in 1993, where he competed as a 157-pound lightweight. Just two years later he won the light heavyweight class at the 1995 USA Championships, carrying 188 pounds on his frame.

Currently Dexter competes at 210 to 220 pounds, and if the pendulum were to swing away from the mass at all costs approach, back towards the classical symmetrical look, then Dexter will take his place at the top. Here's Dexter's short but impressive competitive record:

Dexter Jackson has established himself as a force to be reckoned with in the new millennium.

1995   USA Championships – NPC, light heavyweight, 1st
1996   Nationals – NPC, light heavyweight, 6th
1998   North American Championships – IFBB, overall winner
         North American Championships – IFBB, light heavyweight, 1st
1999   Arnold Classic – IFBB, 7th
         Grand Prix England – IFBB, 4th
         Night of Champions – IFBB, 3rd
         Olympia – IFBB, 9th

Professional World Cup – IFBB, 4th
2000 Arnold Classic – IFBB, 5th
Grand Prix Hungary – IFBB, 2nd
Ironman Pro Invitational – IFBB, 3rd
Night of Champions – IFBB, 8th
Toronto Pro Invitational – IFBB, 2nd

Chest

Dexter usually starts his chest workout with flat barbell bench presses. He's a firm believer in warming up, and does two or three light sets before adding weight to the bar. His first workout set is 185 pounds for 10 to 12 reps, followed by 250 for 8 to 10 reps, 405 for 6 to 8 reps, 435 for 4 to 6 reps, and 455 for 4 to 6 reps.

Dexter's second exercise is incline dumbell presses, followed by flat flyes as his third and final exercise. Here's his routine in shorthand:
1. Flat barbell presses   4 to 5 sets of 12 to 4 reps
2. Incline dumbell presses 4 sets of 12 to 4 reps
3. Flat dumbell flyes   4 sets of 8 to 12 reps

Eli Hanna

Weighing around 315 pounds in the off-season and about 290 in contest shape, Israeli newcomer, Eli Hanna, is one of the giants on the bodybuilding scene. Eli was born in Tel Aviv in 1968. By the age of seven he was taller than anyone else in his class was, and as expected basketball became his passion. Before long he was playing for one of the top junior teams in the country. But at around 15 the iron bug bit, and Eli picked up his first barbell. Despite standing 6'3" Eli began to fill in, and soon captured the junior Israeli bodybuilding championships. Like Arnold before him, Eli was drafted into the army, but his bodybuilding reputation had preceded him and he was allowed to skip many maneuvers and drills in order to train. The results paid off as he won the NABBA Mr. Israel twice during his service years.

When Samir Bannout visited Israel in 1989, the two struck up a friendship, and it wasn't long before Eli was pumping iron at Gold's in Venice Beach. From 255 pounds to 315, the Israeli giant kept adding mass, and soon

Eli Hanna, is one of the giants on the bodybuilding scene.

had second place finishes at both the NABBA Mr. Europe and Mr. World contests. Finally in 1998 he was rewarded with a first at the NABBA World Championships.

Recognizing the potential of Eli, *MuscleMag International's* Robert Kennedy signed Eli to be one of the spokespersons for Bob's new Formula One line of bodybuilding supplements. The following is Eli's short list of bodybuilding accomplishments:

1997   European Championships – NABBA, tall, 2nd
       World Championships – NABBA, tall, 2nd
1998   Universe – Pro, NABBA, 2nd
       World Championships – NABBA, tall, 1st

Training Routines

Rather than go into detail on one of Eli's bodyparts, we thought we'd give you a general sample of some of his training routines.

Chest
1. Flat barbell bench presses   2 sets of 20 reps warmup
                                  4 sets of 8 reps
2. Incline bench presses   4 sets of 8 reps
3. Incline dumbell flyes   4 sets of 8 reps
4. Flat dumbell flyes   4 sets of 8 reps

Legs
1. Leg extensions   2-4 sets of 20 reps warmup
                                  4 sets of 8 reps
2. Squats   4-5 sets of 12 to 15 reps
3. Lunges   4 sets of 8 to 10 reps
4. Leg presses   4 sets of 8 reps
5. Stiff-leg deadlifts   4 sets of 25 reps
6. Leg curls   4 sets of 25 reps

Back
1. Chins   2-4 sets to failure with bodyweight
2. T-bar rows   4 sets of 8 reps
3. One-arm dumbell rows   4 sets of 8 reps
4. Seated cable rows   4 sets of 8 reps
5. Behind-the-head pulldowns   4 sets of 8 reps

Eli is a spokesperson for Formula One.

Edgar Fletcher

Edgar Fletcher grew up in North Braddock, Pittsburgh. There was nothing about the teenage Fletcher to suggest he had great bodybuilding potential. He weighed just 110 pounds as a high school senior. But thanks to friends on his wrestling team, he gained nearly 30 pounds on a regular weight-training program. By the time he graduated he was up to a solid 140 pounds.

After high school Edgar enlisted in the army and was sent to Germany. While there he met an experienced German bodybuilder who sort of took him under his wing. Within a few short years Edgar was making a name for himself at the National level. Here's his competitive record:

1990   Nationals – NPC, heavyweight, 2nd
1992   Nationals – NPC, heavyweight, 3rd
1993   Nationals – NPC, heavyweight, 3rd

1994   North American Championships – IFBB, heavyweight, 4th
        USA Championships – NPC, heavyweight, 4th
1995   Nationals – NPC, heavyweight, 3rd
1996   North American Championships – IFBB, heavyweight, 3rd
        USA Championships – NPC, heavyweight, 3rd

Edgar regularly changes his exercises for variety.

Biceps

Despite his 5'6" height, Edgar weighs 220 pounds in contest shape, and at the center of his outstanding physique are two genuine 21-inch arms. But it's not just the size of his arms that draws gasps, it's their shape and quality as well. All three heads of his triceps are perfectly proportioned, and his biceps' peak rivals such greats as Ronnie Coleman and Robby Robinson. To quote Greg Zulak, "You can't take your eyes off them, they're mesmerizing."

Up until a few years ago, Edgar says his biceps' peak and shape wasn't up to National caliber. Edgar knew that complacency rarely wins contests, so he set to work modifying his biceps' training. The first thing he did was reduce the amount of weight he was using on each exercise. He made up for this by performing each rep in ultra strict style. He also started putting more emphasis on exercises that would target the outer head of the biceps, the part that gives the biceps most of its peak.

The following is an example of Edgar's revised biceps' training. Keep in mind he regularly changes the exercises for variety.

Edgar usually starts his biceps training with hammer curls, a favorite of such greats as Vince Taylor and Nimrod King, two guys known for their great biceps peak. Most people view hammer curls as a forearm exercise, but that's not the case. They also target the outer head of the biceps. Edgar does one or two light warmups and then does three quality sets of 6 to 8 reps, using the same weight for each set.

Exercise number two is one of his favorite mass-builders, seated alternate dumbell curls. Edgar performs these on an incline bench as he finds the angle gives his biceps a slightly better stretch. He also uses a thumbless grip to minimize forearm involvement. Again it's 3 sets of 6 to 8 reps using the same weight for each set.

To finish off his biceps Edgar will do either dumbell concentration curls or barbell preacher curls. No matter which exercise he chooses, Edgar performs his reps in a slow and controlled manner. He does 3 sets of 6 to 8 reps.

Don Long

Don Long was born in Philadelphia, in 1966, but moved to North Carolina when he was three. Like most top bodybuilders, Don was athletic in high school, being involved in football and wrestling. For those who've witnessed the 250-pound Long onstage, and assume he was always massive, he weighed but 160 pounds when he graduated high school.

Don had a unique entry into competitive bodybuilding, exotic dancing! Don was working construction when a couple of co-workers suggested he join them in their side venture of exotic dancing. It wasn't long before his athletic physique was garnering him such compliments that he was making more money from dancing than construction. Don took up weightlifting to improve his physique, and it wasn't long before he was competitive on the national level:

1992   Junior Nationals – NPC, light heavyweight, 5th
1993   Nationals – NPC, heavyweight, 4th
1994   Nationals – NPC, heavyweight, 3rd
1995   Nationals – NPC, overall winner
        Nationals – NPC, heavyweight, 1st
1996   Night of Champions – IFBB, 3rd
1997   Arnold Classic – IFBB, 12th
        Night of Champions – IFBB, 7th
        San Jose Pro Invitational – IFBB, 7th
1998   Arnold Classic – IFBB, 8th
        San Francisco Pro Invitational – IFBB, 11th
1999   Arnold Classic – IFBB, 12th
        Ironman Pro Invitational – IFBB, 8th
        Toronto Pro Invitational – IFBB, 7th

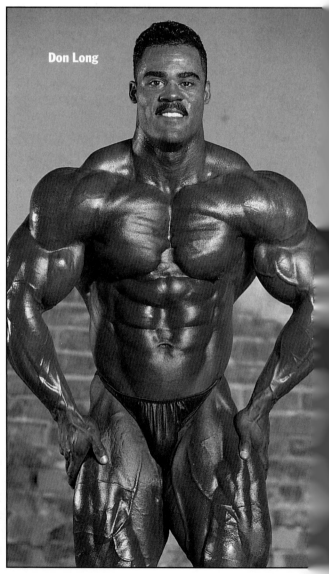

Don Long

It would be nice to end the story here and say Don is tearing up the competitive ranks, but life can be cruel at times. In August of 1999, Don was diagnosed with severe hypertension. Then just one month later he caught a severe cold that he just couldn't shake. One month later his worst fears were confirmed when it was discovered that his kidneys had suffered severe damage and his only hope for survival was a transplant. By a tragic turn of events Don had gone from the posing platform to a dialysis machine. As of this writing Don is waiting on a kidney transplant.

Biceps

When he competed in the late 1990s, Don was one of the few bodybuilders to sport true 22-inch arms. Many bodybuilders claim such measurements, but Don had the beef to actually stretch the tape to that most coveted number. As his biceps grew much easier than his triceps, we'll look at the latter to see how he built those enormous slabs of meat.

By a tragic turn of events Don had gone from the posing platform to a dialysis machine.

Don usually started his triceps routine with cable pushdowns. He did the first set with about 90 pounds for 20 reps, and then went 110 for 16, 130 for 12, 150 for 10, and 165 for 8 to 10.

Don's second exercise was lying EZ-bar extensions, also called skullcrushers. He did 4 sets starting with 115 pounds for 20 reps, and then added 50 pounds to bring the weight up to 165 pounds. He did 12 reps with this weight and then went up to 185 pounds for 2 sets of 8 to 10.

Don's third exercise was one-hand cable pushdowns using a reverse grip. Again he did 4 sets in pyramid fashion, going from 70 to 100 pounds.

To finish off his triceps Don did 4 sets of rope pushdowns. Because his triceps are tired by this point, and the strictness of the exercise, Don uses less weight than regular pushdowns. He starts with 70 pounds and works up to 100 pounds for 10 to 15 reps.

Appendix

Exercise Descriptions

Abdominals

Crunches – You will need a flat bench or chair to perform this exercise. Lie down on the floor and rest your calves on the bench. Adjust your distance from the bench so that your thighs are perpendicular with the floor. Now bend forward and try to touch your thighs.

Comments – Most bodybuilders consider crunches one of the best abdominal builders. At first you may want to perform the movement with your hands by your sides. As you get stronger, place your hands to the side of the head – doing so adds the weight of the arms to your upper body, thus making the exercise more difficult.

Muscles involved – Crunches primarily work the upper abs, but there is some lower ab stimulation as well. The exercise also brings the hip abductors into play, although to a much lesser extent than situps.

Bent-leg, leg raises – You can use the chinup bar on the Universal multistation or a freestanding version. Jump up and grab the bar with both hands. With the legs slightly bent, raise them up to the parallel position. Lower them slowly until they are once again in line with the upper body.

Comments – Some bodybuilders perform this movement with the legs straight. This is not recommended as straight-leg leg raises place unwanted stress on the lower back. While perhaps not noticeable now, it may lead to problems down the road. Don't swing the legs up and down as this only defeats the purpose of the exercise. You want to lift the lower body using abdominal power, not momentum.

Muscles worked – This exercise primarily works the lower abdominals, but there is some upper abdominal and hip abductor stimulation.

Lying leg raises – Lie down on the abdominal board, with your hands grabbing the handgrip behind your head (i.e. your head is toward the hand-grip/ foot rest, unlike situps where your feet are closest to the hand-grip/ foot rest). With your legs slightly bent, raise them to the vertical (or just short of the vertical) position. Pause a second and then slowly lower them. Try not to touch the board at the bottom. This will keep the tension on the abdominals throughout the exercise.

Comments – Once again, don't perform the movement with straight legs. Also, resist the urge to use your upper body to pull your legs up. Use only abdominal strength. Finally, start with the abdominal board placed in the lowest position. As you get stronger you can increase the board's angle, thus making the exercise more difficult.

Muscles worked – Lying leg raises primarily work the lower abdominals, but the upper abs and hip abductors also come into play.

Roman chair situps – The Roman chair looks similar to a low incline bench, but it has a pair of foot supports at one end. Anchor your feet under the supports (they are usually round padded rollers) and lean back on the bench. Pause at the bottom and then return to the starting position. Try to use only your abdominals and not your hip flexors.

Comments – Roman chair situps are very effective for working the lower abdominal region. By bending and locking the leg, it's virtually impossible to cheat. If there's a disadvantage to this exercise it's the stress placed on the lower back. Many bodybuilders find arching the back in this manner very painful. Our advice is to give them a try and see how they feel. If there's any back pain, substitute one of the other abdominal exercises.

Muscles worked – Roman chair situps primarily work the lower abdominal region, but the upper abs are also stimulated. Depending on the ratio of your leg/ upper body length, you may find the hip flexors taking much of the strain. Only you can judge how effective the exercise is for the abdominals. If you feel your abs are doing very little, switch to another exercise.

Rope crunches – Kneel down facing away from a pulldown machine and grab the attached rope. Bend forward so that the rope is straddling your neck (i.e. one side of the rope touching each ear). With the knees and feet kept firmly on the ground, bend forward until your forehead is a couple of inches from the floor. Return to the starting position by raising the torso a foot to a foot and a half from the floor.

Comments – This is one of the hardest exercises to master as the body tries to cheat by rocking the torso up and down. Even with good technique, some individuals get nothing out of this exercise. Others find they have to tire the abs out first with another exercise before they derive any benefit from rope crunches.

Muscles worked – Rope crunches work the entire abdominal region. The obliques, hip flexors, and serratus also come into play.

Chris Cormier, Ronnie Coleman, Flex Wheeler and Kevin Levrone.

Legs (thighs)

Squats – Place the barbell on the squat rack, about shoulder height. Step under the bar and rest it across your traps and shoulders. Step back, away from the rack, and place your feet slightly less than shoulder width apart. Now in a slow and controlled manner bend your knees and descend toward the floor. Stop when your thighs are approximately parallel with the floor. Pause for a second and then return to the starting upright position.

Comments – Most consider squats to be the king of the thigh builders. If done properly they will build you a phenomenal set of thighs (quadriceps). Done improperly they may put you in traction! For starters, try to use a squat rack with "catchers." These are pins, which will stop the weight if you get into trouble. If none are available, make sure you have one or two spotters watching you (besides the safety feature, spotters can tell if you are performing the exercise properly.)

Always wear a belt when performing squats. Also don't bounce at the top or bottom of the exercise. Remember you have a loaded barbell on your shoulders, which is putting a lot of stress on your spine. Keep control of the weight throughout the movement.

Make sure you rest the bar across your shoulders and traps, not on the bony protrusion at the base of your skull. Do so and you will need regular chiropractic visits!

Finally, to put most of the stress on the thighs, try resting the heels on a 2-inch block of wood. If you perform squats flat-footed, much of the lifting will be done by your glutes. In addition, keep your stance shoulder width or less. The wider the stance the more glute involvement (this is why powerlifters use a fairly wide stance, they need the tremendous power of the glutes to help in lifting such huge poundages.)

Muscles worked – While primarily a thigh builder, squats will stimulate the whole leg region. Even with a narrow stance, the glutes will come into play. Also, the calves and hamstrings are used in stabilizing the legs as you move up and down.

Finally, and much less obvious, the spinal erectors (lower back muscles) are needed to keep the body upright. In fact they are often the weak link in the chain. Most injuries obtained while doing squats center around the lower back region. This is why you must concentrate when performing this exercise.

Leg presses – You will need to use the leg press machine to perform this exercise. Sit in the seat and place your feet on the pressing board. Your stance should be about shoulder width, but this can be varied to work different parts of the thigh. Extend your legs to the locked out position, pause, and then bring them down until your knees touch the chest. Perform the movement in a slow, controlled manner.

Comments – Although leg presses don't give the degree of thigh development as squats, they are a close second. And if you have knee or back problems, the leg press will adequately work the thighs without aggravating these areas.

As with squats, the wider the stance the more glute involvement. By making a V with the feet (heels together, toes apart) you can do wonders with the inner thigh region (vastus medialis).

Perhaps the greatest advantage of leg presses is the amount of weight you can use. Unlike squats, where the lower back is a limited factor, the leg press allows you to pile on hundreds of pounds of plates. It won't be long before you have 6 to 8 (or more), 45-pound plates on each side. Provided you do the exercise in good style, you can really let the ego go wild on this exercise. The lower back is virtually eliminated, and even the knees don't have the same stress placed on them.

If there is a word of caution it concerns hyperextending the legs. If you place the feet low on the pressing board, there is the risk of locking the legs and actually forcing them into a hyperextended position at the knee joint. When performing the exercise, don't forcefully lock out the legs, as this may damage the knee's supporting connective tissues (ligaments, tendons, and cartilage.)

Muscles worked – The design of the leg press means that most of the stress is placed on the thighs. There is very little glute involvement, and the spinal erectors are all but eliminated from the exercise. The calves and hamstrings only play a small role in stabilizing the legs during the exercise.

Hack squats – You need a special machine to do this exercise. Place your feet about shoulder width apart on the machine's incline footboard. Rest the pads on your shoulders and slowly squat down until your thighs are parallel with the floor. Using thigh power alone, return to the starting position.

Comments – There are two variations of the hack machine. One version uses shoulder pads for supporting the weight. The other relies on two handles placed low on the machine. The user must grab the handles to lift the weight. Most bodybuilders find the shoulder pad version the most comfortable.

To get the exercise's full benefit, make a slight V-shape with your feet (heels together, toes apart). As with any type of squat, don't bounce at the bottom as this places tremendous strain on the knee ligaments.

Muscles worked – Hack squats will give your outer thighs that nice sweeping look. By bracing your back against the machine's backboard, the strain often associated with regular squats is greatly reduced.

Leg extensions – If you've ever had a sports-related knee injury, then this exercise should be familiar. Leg extensions are among the most popular of rehabilitation exercises. Sit down on the machine's bench and place your feet under the padded rollers. Raise the legs to a locked position and squeeze the thighs. Lower back to the starting position and repeat.

Comments – Most gyms have a machine that incorporates the leg curl and leg extension into it. In other words you perform both exercises on the same machine. The same weight stack is used, but for leg extensions you sit on the end and use the lower rollers, while for leg curls you lie face down and use the upper rollers. Your gym, however, may have the exercises on separate machines. Many bodybuilders lie on their backs when doing leg extensions. You can't use the same amount of weight, but this is made up for by working the thighs through a greater range of movement.

Resist the tendency to drop the weight into the starting position. As with other exercises, 50 percent of the movement is the negative (lowering) phase of the exercise. For variety you can perform the exercise one leg at a time.

Muscles worked – Extensions are great for building the thigh muscles around the knee area. They're also a very effective physiotherapy exercise. Following knee surgery, most athletes are limited in the amount of direct leg exercise they can perform. Leg extensions are great for strengthening, not only the lower thigh, but also the associated tendons and ligaments.

Sissy squats – Depending on your strength levels, you may need to hold on to a weight during this exercise. Place your feet in a V position, and leaning back, squat down until your thighs are at least parallel with the floor. If you have trouble holding your balance, grab a stationary

Appendix

upright for support. If you can do 15 to 20 reps with relative ease, hold a plate with your free hand against the chest.

Comments – You can do this exercise with a dumbell or weight plate held to the chest. Most bodybuilders find the plate most convenient, but it's personal preference. Don't get carried away with the amount of weight. Save the heavy poundages for your regular squats and leg presses.

Muscles worked – Sissy squats are similar to hack squats, in that they will add a great sweep to your outer thighs. Although more isolated than regular squats, sissy squats involve the glutes to some degree.

Legs (hamstrings)

Leg curls – Lie down on the leg curl machine, with your feet placed under the round foot supports (often called rollers). Pretend you are doing biceps curls (which in fact is what the hamstrings are – leg biceps) and curl the leg toward your bum. Pause at the top, and slowly lower the legs back to the starting position.

Comments – Some gyms have up to three variations of the leg curl machine. Two of them force you to lie face-down on a bench. The bench may either be straight or partly angled. The angled bench forces you to do the exercise more strictly. It keeps you from swinging the legs up. Many gyms have a third leg curl machine that allows you to stand up and work one leg at a time. It's similar to one-arm concentration curls for the biceps.

Just as you wouldn't do biceps curls in an awkward manner, so too must leg curls be performed in a slow, rhythmic style. No jerking or bouncing the weight, and try to avoid lifting your bum off the bench. If you have to raise your glutes, you're probably using too much weight.

Muscles worked – Leg curls primarily work the leg hamstrings, although there is some calf involvement. The glutes and thighs only come into play to stabilize the legs during the exercise.

Standing leg curls – Position yourself in the machine with the knee of the working leg resting on the pad. With the supporting leg locked straight, curl the other leg upward to just short of the butt. Lower back down until the leg is just short of a lockout.

Comments – Standing leg curls can be considered the concentration curls of hamstring exercises. They offer the advantage of being able to devote full attention to each leg separately. The downside is that you have to support the bodyweight on one leg. For the average bodybuilder this is no big deal. but for someone with knee or back problems it may be too stressful. The other disadvantage is that many gyms don't have this particular style of leg curl.

Muscles worked – Standing leg curls target all the muscles collectively known as the hamstrings. The glutes and calf play a secondary role.

Seated leg curls – Once again you'll need a special machine to do this exercise. As each brand is slightly different we'll describe the version manufactured by Atlantis of Laval, Quebec, Canada. Set the machine's roller so that it rest on your heel. Sit down in the chair and push forward on the upper handle. This lowers the roller arm so you can place your feet on top. With the feet positioned on top of the roller, return the adjustment handle to the starting position. Lower the knee pads down until they are snug on your thighs. Curl your legs back until they are just short of touching the main frame underneath. Raise the legs back up to just short of a lockout.

Comments – The advantage of the seated over the lying leg curl is strictness. It's very easy to cheat on the lying leg curl, by throwing the butt up into the air, or pulling with the arms. The seated leg curl, however, forces you to move the weight with just your hamstrings. As a word of caution, many seated leg curl machines allow the legs to go past the locked out position, thus hyperextending at the knee joint. Always keep control of the weight on the way up, and don't let the legs straighten completely out.

Muscles worked – Seated leg curls primarily work the hamstrings, but the glutes and calves also play a small role.

Stiff-leg deadlifts – Place an Olympic bar on the floor in front of a block of wood, or on the end of a flat bench. Stand on the block or bench and with the legs slightly bent, grab the bar with a shoulder width grip. Raise the torso up to the standing position, pause for a second and then bend forward until the plates are just short of touching the floor.

Comments – Although the name says stiff-leg, keeping the legs completely locked can put excessive stress on the lower back. Always keep a slight bend at the knee. Also never bounce for the same reason. The lower back ligaments receive enough abuse in life without you giving them another reason to act up.

Muscles worked – Although the lower legs do not bend as in a traditional leg curl, the hamstring muscles do cross the hip joint and are thus stimulated by extension at the hip. The lower spinal erectors and glutes also come into play on this exercise.

Appendix

Chest

Flat barbell bench presses – Lie on your back and take the barbell from the supports, using a grip that is 6 to 8 inches wider than shoulder width. Lower the bar slowly to the nipple region, and then press it back to the locked out position.

Comments – King of the chest exercises, bench presses are performed by virtually ever top bodybuilder. A few points to consider. Don't drop the bar and bounce it off the chest. Yes you can lift more weight this way, but you are robbing the exercise of its effectiveness. You also run the risk of breaking ribs or splitting your sternum. Then there is the pec-delt tie-in to worry about. Dropping the bar in a loose fashion increases the risk of tearing the area where your chest muscles connect to your shoulder muscles. To avoid the previous nasties, lower the weight in a slow, controlled manner,and then push it back to arms length.

Whether you lock the arms out or not is your personal preference. Some bodybuilders find stopping just short of a lock keeps the tension on the muscles throughout the movements. Others find locking out feels more comfortable. As the split is about 50/50 on the issue, try both methods and chose one (this applies to virtually all the exercises.)

Another point to mention, don't arch your back off the bench. Once again you may increase your lift by a few pounds, but at what cost? Arching decreases the amount of pectoral stimulation, and it certainly is no benefit to your lower back.

If you have trouble keeping your back on the bench, perform the movement with your legs up in the air. You will not be able to use as much weight, but there is no way you can arch your back when in this position.

Muscles worked – Flat bench presses primarily work the lower chest region, but the whole pectoral-deltoid area is stimulated. You will also find your triceps receiving a great deal of stimulation. Finally, the muscles of the back and forearm are indirectly used for stabilizing the upper body during the exercise.

Incline barbell presses – If using an adjustable bench, set the bench to an angle of about 25 to 30 degrees. Incline bench presses are performed in the same manner as flat benches, the only difference being instead of lowering the bar to the nipple region, bring it down to the center of the chest, just under the chin.

Comments – Most bodybuilders find angles above 30 degrees place too much stress on the front delts, and not the upper pectorals. Of course your bone structure may dictate the opposite. You may have to play around with the bench's angle to see what's best for you. If you don't have access to an adjustable bench, make do with the fixed version. In many cases these fixed benches are closer to 45 degrees, which is too steep for working the upper pecs. You may find that slightly arching the back can shift most of the stress from the shoulders to the chest. But be careful, as the lower back was not meant to be arched to any degree. A better solution is raise one end of a flat bench. You can use a couple of pieces of wood, another bench, or a specially constructed wooden block (most gyms have these for performing bent-over rows) to prop up the flat bench.

Muscles worked – The incline barbell press primarily works the upper chest. It also stresses the front delts and triceps. Most bodybuilders find inclines excellent for the pec-delt tie-ins. Remember, as you increase the angle, the stress shifts from the upper chest to the shoulders.

Flat dumbell presses – This exercise is similar to the barbell version, but you use two dumbells instead. Start by sitting on a flat bench, and cleaning (lifting) a pair of dumbells to your knees. Lie back on the bench and with the dumbells pointing end to end (i.e. they form a straight line across your chest like a barbell) lower them down to your sides. Pause at the bottom, and then press to arms length.

Comments – The advantage of using dumbells is the greater range of movement at the bottom. A barbell can only be lowered to the rib cage, whereas the dumbells can be dropped below the rib cage. This gives the chest muscles a greater stretch. But be careful as the lower part of the movement is the most dangerous, and if you drop the dumbells in an uncontrolled manner, you run the risk of tearing the pec-delt tie-ins. Although there is much personal preference, most bodybuilders find a dumbell spacing about 6 to 8 inches wider than the shoulders to be the most effective.

Muscles worked – Dumbell presses are great for developing the pec-delt tie-ins. If you squeeze them together at the top, the inner pecs are also worked. And no matter how much you try to eliminate them, the triceps and shoulders will be involved. This is fine, as at the beginning stage you want to work as many muscles in conjunction as possible.

Incline dumbell presses – This is the inclined version of the flat dumbell press. With the exception of the angle, the exercise is performed in the same manner.

Comments – Because you have to hoist the dumbells up higher to get them into starting position, it might be a good idea to obtain the help of a spotter. Most bodybuilders lift one of the dumbells up, and have a partner pass the other one. If the numbers are available, have both dumbells passed to you.

Without sounding too repetitious, lower the dumbells slowly, and go for a full, but controlled stretch at the bottom.

Muscles worked – Incline dumbell presses are an excellent exercise for developing the upper chest. Because of the increased angle, they also hit the front deltoids. And like most chest exercises, there is some secondary triceps involvement. If your shoulders are taking too much of the weight, drop the bench's angle a few degrees.

Dips – One of the simplest but most effective of chest exercises. Most gyms have a set of parallel bars for doing dips. If your gym doesn't, you can make do with the Universal shoulder press. Start the exercise with your arms in a locked out position. With the chin on the chest, lower your body down between the bars, pause, and push yourself back to arms length.

Comments – Dips are considered by many to be one of the best (and the best by Vince Gironda) chest exercises. To keep the stress on the chest, lean forward and flare your elbows out to the side. If you keep vertical and have your elbows in tight, the exercise is more of a triceps builder. As with other chest exercises, don't bounce at the bottom. Doing so places much stress on the pec-delt tie-ins.

Muscles worked – Dips primarily work the lower, outer chest. They produce that clean line under the pecs. They also stimulate the front delts and triceps, so for this reason dips are an excellent beginning exercise.

Flat flyes – Start this exercise in the same position as dumbell presses. Instead of having the dumbells pointing end to end, rotate your hands until the palms are facing and the dumbells are parallel with your body. With your elbows slightly bent, lower the dumbells for a full stretch. Pause at the bottom,a nd then squeeze the dumbells up and together, over the center of the chest.

Comments – Flyes are more of a stretching exercise than a mass-building movement. Still with practice, you'll eventually be using considerable weight. Always lower the dumbells in a controlled manner, no matter what the poundage. Drop them too fast and you'll rip the pec-delt tie-in. Treatment for such an injury is surgery and many months of rehabilitation.

Muscles worked – Flyes work the whole chest region. Fully stretching at the bottom works the outer chest region and squeezing together at the top develops the inner chest. This gives your chest that clean line up the middle. As there will be some pec-delt tie-in strain, be careful at the bottom of the movement.

Incline flyes – This is the same exercise as the previous, but you use an incline bench. Once again go for a full, slow stretch at the bottom.

Comments – As with incline dumbell presses, the incline bench dictates lifting the dumbells up higher. You may need a partner to hoist the dumbells into position. In fact it's probably a good idea to have the dumbells passed to you, whether you can lift them or not. Jerking heavy dumbells from the floor puts a great deal of stress on the biceps and lower back. Better to be safe than macho.

Muscles worked – Incline flyes put most of the stress on the upper pectorals. They also strongly affect your chest/ shoulder tie-ins. Once again, by squeezing the dumbells together at the top, the inner chest can be worked.

Decline barbell presses – Position a decline bench (the Roman chair is often used) so that the bar can be brought down to the lower chest. The reps are performed in the same manner as flat and incline bench presses.

Comments – Many gyms have decline benches that have the bar supports welded to the back of the bench. If the bench's angle is adjustable, vary the angle to get the maximum feel in your pectoral muscles. You can substitute dumbells in place of the barbell.

Muscles worked – Decline presses are similar to dips in that they work the lower, outer chest region. They are a good substitute if you find your front delts taking most of the strain during flat bench presses.

Cable crossovers – Stand between the two cable uprights and grab an overhead pulley handle in each hand. Adopt a runner's stance (one leg forward and bent the other back and bent just slightly) and bring the handles forward and down so that they meet about waist high. Return to the starting position with the arms stretched out to the sides about head high.

Comments – Cable crossovers are another exercise where proper technique is an absolute must. If you let the arms fly back too fast you run the risk of tearing the pec-delt tie-in. Also, to ease the stress on the shoulder joint, keep a slight bend in the elbows.

Muscles worked – Cable crossovers are great for working the center of the chest. There is some front delt involvement as well.

Pec-dek flyes – Sit down on the machine's chair and grab the handles (Apex style) or place the elbows behind the pads (Nautilus style.) Push the arms forward until the handles or pads are just about touching. Return to the starting position with the handles or pad positioned out to the sides or just behind the body.

Comments – Don't let the arms fly back too fast. This is a great way to tear the chest or shoulders. Also try to use as little arm power as possible. Think of the arms as extensions of your chest muscles. If using the Nautilus model open the hands and just push with the arms.

Muscles worked – Pec dek flyes are similar to cable crossovers in that they are great for hitting the inner chest. They also work the pec-delt tie-ins.

Back

Chinups – You will need access to an overhead bar to perform this exercise. Most Universal multistations have one attached but a wall-mounted version is just as good. Jump up and grab the bar with a grip that is about twice your shoulder width. Now pull yourself up and try to touch the chest off the bar. Lower back down to the starting position in a controlled manner.

Comments – Chins are considered by most to be the best back exercise. In fact most bodybuilders of all levels make them the mainstay of their back routines. They give the individual that great V-shape. When doing the movement, try to pull with the large back muscles (latissimus dorsi), not the biceps and forearms. Don't drop back to the starting position in such a manner that you yank your arms out of the shoulder socket! Do the exercise nice and slow.

At first you will find it easier to do the exercise to the front. As you get stronger you can pull up so the bar is behind your head. There is little difference between the two. When you reach a point that you are doing 12 to 15 easy reps, attach a weight around your waist, or hold a dumbell between your legs. This increases the resistance and keeps th e muscles growing.

Muscles worked – Chins primarily work the large latissimus (lats) muscles. They also stress the smaller back muscles like the teres. Finally, the rear delts and biceps are brought into play.

You will find that by pulling to the front, the lower parts of the lats are worked the most. Conversely, pulling behind the head stresses the upper section. Keep in mind that these divisions are not carved in stone, and at the beginning level, it is adequate to do either one. If you have the strength, you might alternate the two on the same day or alternate days.

Lat pulldowns – Although not quite as effective as chins, pulldowns enable you to adjust the amount of weight. Chins force you to use your bodyweight, whereas the lat machine allows the user to select the desired poundage. Instead of pulling yourself up to an overhead bar, the bar is brought down to you. Take a wide grip (about twice shoulder width) and sit on the attached seat, or kneel down on the floor. Now pull the bar down, either behind your head, or to the front and touch your chest. Pause at the bottom and squeeze your shoulder blades together. Return to the out-stretched arms position.

Comments – Whether you pull to the front or to the back, is a personal decision. There is little difference between the two. Either version will add tremendously to back width, giving that much coveted V-shape. Generally speaking, when you pull to the front, you hit more of the lower, upper back (i.e. the lower insertions of your lats.) Pulling behind the head works the upper regions of the lats and the rear delts. There is so much overlap between the two movements, however, that at the beginning level, either movement is sufficient. You might want to rotate both movements, either on the same day or alternate back days.

Keep your grip fairly wide as narrow grip pulldowns place much of the stress on the biceps. In fact many bodybuilders often perform narrow grip chins and pulldowns, as biceps exercises!

Finally, because you have to grip the bar, the muscles of the forearms get a good workout. In fact they may be the weak link in the chain.

Muscles worked – Lat pulldowns work the whole back region, from the large latissimus muscles, to the smaller teres, rhomboids, and rear deltoids. They also stress the biceps and forearms.

Appendix

Bent-over barbell rows – Bend over at the waist so that your upper body is just short of parallel with the floor. Grab a standard barbell, and using a wide grip, pull it up the abdomen. Lower slowly and then repeat. Concentrate on using the upper (lats) back muscles and not your spinal erectors.

Comments – You must be especially careful on this exercise. Any sudden bouncing or jerking will put great stress on your lower back. If you have to "throw your lower back into it" you are using far too much weight. Take off a few plates and do it more strictly. The only part of the body that should move is the arms. Your upper body and legs should remain stationary. To get a full stretch, stand on some sort of low platform. Most gyms have specially constructed boxes that enable you to stand on while performing bent-over rows. The extra 10 to 12 inches of stretch will add greatly to the exercise's effectiveness. As a final point, bend your knees slightly. This will help reduce the stress on your lower back.

Muscles worked – This exercise is considered by most to be one of the best back builders. It's particularly effective in producing thickness in the back. Besides the back muscles, bent-over rows stress the biceps and forearms. Finally, because of the bent-over position, the exercise stretches the hamstrings and spinal erectors.

T-bar rows – Many gyms have a long bar that has one end bolted to the floor. By placing plates on the free end and grabbing the short cross bar, a variation of the barbell row can be performed. Called T-bar rows (because of the bar's shape), they are an effective substitute for the barbell version. Grab the cross bar and pull the plates up to the chest/ abdominal region. Squeeze at the top and then lower back to the floor. Don't touch the plates off the floor, but stop a few inches from it.

Comments – Once again don't bounce or jerk the weight up. Like barbell rows, T-bar rows place a great deal of stress on the lower back. Keep your upper body stationary, and only lift the plates with your back muscles and arms. If your gym does not have a specially designed T-bar, you can do the same movements with one end of a regular Olympic bar pinned in a corner. Check with the gym's management first however. Rotating an Olympic bar on one end may damage the bar's sleeve/ball bearing mechanism. If you are allowed to do the exercise, try to use an old bar. In fact your gym may have an old bar set aside just for this purpose.

Muscles worked – T-bar rows work the same muscles as the regular barbell row. The lats, teres, rhomboids, rear delts, biceps, forearms, and lower back, all come into play. Because of the assortment of muscles worked, both types of rows are excellent mass builders.

* Note: If you have lower back problems, you might want to avoid these exercises. If you must do them, start off by using light weight. Gradually build up the poundage over time. Don't make the mistake of slapping on 45 pound plates from day one. This will come with time. Keep in mind that lower back injuries often don't heal. You may have them for life. Therefore the emphasis should be on preventing them. In a manner of speaking, rows can be a double edge sword. Done properly they will help strengthen the lower back, thus reducing the chances of future injuries. Done improperly they may be the cause of the injury! So pay strict attention to your exercise style. Don't get carried away with the weight, and don't lift with the lower back.

Seated pulley rows – You will need a cable machine to do this exercise. Grab the V-shaped pulley attachment, and sit down on the floor or associated board. With the legs slightly bent, pull the hands into the lower chest/ upper abdomen. Pause for a second and squeeze the shoulder blades together. Now bend forward and stretch the arms out fully.

Comments – You can perform this exercise with a number of different pulley attachments. The most frequently used is the V-shaped double handle bar. Some bodybuilders like to use a straight pulldown bar. Still others use two separate handgrips. Our advice is to experiment with the different attachments, and select the one that feels the most comfortable. Cable rows can also be performed on the lat pulldown machine. To get the full effect, lean back and pull the hands to the lower chest. The direction of force should be about 90 degrees to the body.

When doing the seated version, keep the legs slightly bent. Performing the exercise with straight legs won't do your lower back any good.

Muscles worked – Seated pulley rows are another exercise that works the whole back region. They are more of a thickness movement than a width builder. As with other rowing exercises, seated pulley rows work all the major muscles of the back. They also stimulate the biceps and forearms.

One-arm dumbell rows – Instead of using a barbell or cable, you can do your rows using a dumbell. Bend over and grab a bench for support. Place one leg behind the other, in a runner's stance. Grab a dumbell with the arm that is furthest from the bench (i.e. the bracing arm is closest to the bench) and stretch it down and slightly forward. Pause at the bottom and then pull the dumbell up until the arm is fully bent. The exercise is comparable to sawing wood.

Comments – One-arm rows are great because they allow you to brace your upper body. This is essential if you have a lower back injury. Even though your biceps will be involved in the exercise, try to concentrate on using just your back muscles. Once again, no bouncing or jerking the weight. If you have to contort the body to lift the weight, the dumbell is too heavy.

Straight-arm pushdowns – Stand two to three feet in front of the lat pulldown or triceps pushdown machine. Grab the attached bar with a shoulder width grip and with the arms kept in a locked out position, push the bar down to the thighs. Raise the bar back up until the moving plates are about an inch from the stationary plates.

Comments – For the taller members out there, you may find the plates touch before you get a good stretch at the top of the exercise. One suggestion is to adopt a wide stance. The wider you spread your legs the lower you'll go to the floor. Those with a gymnastics background will benefit the most from this technique. Because of the virtual elimination of the biceps and forearms, you won't be able to use nearly as much weight as a regular pulldown.

Muscles worked – This is as pure a back exercise as you'll find. It is especially useful for hitting the upper and outer lats, just under the armpits. Straight-arm pushdowns make an excellent first exercise in a pre-exhaust superset.

Dumbell pullovers – Grab a dumbell and lie face up across a flat bench. With the hips dropped below bench height, and the arms kept nearly straight, lower the dumbell behind the head to a comfortable stretch. Return to the starting position with the dumbell positioned at arms length above the chest.

Comments – Some people prefer doing this exercise while lying lengthwise on the bench. Others prefer doing the movement with an EZ-curl bar. Try all three and see which works best for you.

Muscles worked – Pullovers are one of those exercises that incorporate a large number of muscles. For some it's a great lat exercise, while others get a great chest stretch. The serratus and shoulders also play a role.

Appendix

Machine pullovers – Sit on the machine's chair and depending on the model, place the elbows behind the pad, or grab the overhead bar. Push the arms down in front of the body to the machine's maximum range of motion. Return to the overhead position.

Comments – At the risk of being hounded out of the bodybuilding hall of fame, machine pullovers are one of the few machine exercises that are actually better than the free-weight equivalent. With dumbells you only get about 90 degrees of motion before gravity starts interfering. But most pullover machines keep the tension on the lats for 150 degrees or more.

Muscles worked – Machine pullovers are another great exercise to hit the back muscles without the biceps playing a major role. The serratus and shoulders play a minor role.

Shoulders

Behind-the-head shoulder presses – With a grip that is about 6 to 8 inches wider than shoulder width, take a barbell from the rack. Lower the bar behind your head, stopping just short of your traps. Push the bar to arms length and then repeat.

Flex Wheeler

Comments – Don't bounce the bar off your neck. If you strike either of the top vertebrae (atlas and axis) you run the risk of nerve damage. Perform the exercise in a slow and controlled manner. You don't need a rack to position the bar, but cleaning a loaded bar to your shoulders, doing your reps, and then having to lower it back to the floor is very energy-consuming. After a few months it will be impossible. So either use the squat rack, or even better, the shoulder press rack. Most gyms have a special seat with a vertical back support. Two long supports enable the user to position the bar behind the head. All you have to do is reach back and lift the bar from the racks. Once your reps are finished, it's a simple matter of laying the bar behind your head.

Muscles worked – Behind-the-head presses work the entire shoulder region, particularly the front and side delts. They also stress, to a lesser degree, the rear delts and traps. Finally, as with most pressing movements, the triceps are brought into play.

Front military presses – This exercise is performed in the same manner as the previous, except instead of lowering the bar behind the head, it's lowered to the front. Bring the bar down until it just touches the upper chest. Once again, no bouncing, just smooth controlled reps.

Comments – Most bodybuilders find it more comfortable to lower the bar to the front. It also eliminates the risk of striking the head or neck. There is a tendency to arch when doing the exercise, so be careful. A slight arch to bring the bar to the upper chest is fine, but nothing excessive.

Muscles worked – Front presses put most of the stress on the front and side delts. The rear delts and traps receive some stimulation, but not to the same extent as rear presses. The upper pectorals are worked if you lean back when doing the exercise.

Dumbell presses – Instead of performing your pressing movements with a barbell, grab two dumbells and hoist them to shoulder level. You can stand or sit when pressing the dumbells, but if standing, be careful not to excessively arch the lower back.

Comments – You can press both dumbells at the same time, or in an alternating fashion. As with the barbell version, be careful of the lower back. Try not to arch excessively, and don't drop the dumbells into the starting position.

Muscles worked – This exercise stresses the whole deltoid region. Particular emphasis is placed on the front and side deltoids. There is some secondary trap and rear deltoid involvement.

Barbell shrugs – Grab a barbell using a shoulder width grip. With your arms locked, raise the bar up trying to touch the shoulders against your ears. Squeeze at the top of the movement, and then lower the bar down.

Comments – There are a number of variations to this exercise. Instead of raising and lowering the bar in a straight line, you can rotate the bar in a circular direction. Also, you're not limited to using a barbell for the exercise. Many bodybuilders find the Smith machine is more comfortable. Instead of taking the bar from the floor, you can have it set at any desired height, making it easier on your lower back. The Universal bench press can also be used for shrugs (in fact more serious bodybuilders use the machine for shrugs than bench presses!) Try to keep the arms, legs, and back straight throughout the movement. And watch the lower back!

Muscles worked – Barbell shrugs are by far the best trapezius builder. Make them a regular part of your training and you will have traps that give the Incredible Hulk pause! Besides the traps, your forearms, hamstrings, lower back, and rear delts will be indirectly stimulated.

Dumbell shrugs – This is simply a variation of the barbell version. Hold the dumbells about shoulder width apart and perform the movement like the barbell variety.

Comments – You can hold the dumbells parallel or pointed end to end. The choice is yours. If you hold them end to end, watch you don't bang them off your thighs. Try keeping them in front of the body and slide them up the front of the thighs.

Muscles worked – Dumbell shrugs work the same muscles as the barbell version. Since you will be using less weight you can generally lift more weight with one barbell than two dumbells) the lower back will not have the same strain placed on it. In fact we strongly recommend using dumbells if you have a pre-existing back problem.

Upright rows – Start the exercise by holding a barbell at arms length. Using a narrow grip (about 3 to 5 inches) lift the bar up the front of the body, keeping the elbows flared to the sides. Squeeze the traps together at the top, and then lower into the starting position.

Comments – Which muscles are worked depends on the grip used. Generally, any hand spacing, five inches or less, puts most of the stress on the traps. Widen the grip and the side deltoids come into play. In the routines presented above we are suggesting the exercise as a

Appendix

trap builder. But you can easily substitute for one of the delt exercises. Just remember to keep the grip wide when doing so.

If you have weak or injured wrists, you might want to think twice about performing this exercise. Upright rows place tremendous stress on the forearms and wrists. If you experience minor pain when doing the exercise, try wrapping the wrists with support bandages. This should enable you to complete your sets in comfort. Of course you're the only one who can determine if the pain is just a nuisance or representative of something more serious. If in doubt skip the exercise.

As with barbell curls, upright rows give you the option of adding a few cheat reps at the end of the set. Limit such cheat reps to one or two. Don't make the mistake of cheating from rep one.

Muscles worked – With a narrow grip, upright rows primarily work the traps, with some secondary deltoid stimulation. A wide grip (6 inches or more) will shift the strain to the side delts, with the traps now playing a secondary role. The forearms are worked no matter what grip you use.

Lateral raises – You can perform this exercise seated or standing. Grab two dumbells and, with the elbows slightly bent, raise them to the side of the body. As you raise the dumbells, gradually rotate the wrists so that the little finger points up. Many bodybuilding authorities, including Robert Kennedy, liken the wrist action to pouring a jug of water.

Comments – You can do the exercise with the arms completely locked, but most bodybuilders find it more effective to bend the arms slightly and use more weight. Lateral raises can be done to the front, side, or rear (explained in detail later.) Instead of using dumbells, a cable may be substituted. Either version may be performed with one or two arms at a time.

Muscles worked – You can use lateral raises to work any head of the deltoid muscle. Most intermediate bodybuilders use them for the side delts, as the front delts receive ample stimulation from various pressing movements. Side laterals will give your delts that half-melon look. There's not much you can do to widen the clavicles, but you can increase your shoulder width by adding inches to the side delts.

Bent-over laterals – This is the bent over version of regular side laterals. By bending over, the stress is shifted from the side to the rear delts. You can do the exercise free standing, seated, or with your head braced on a high bench. The latter is for those with lower back problems or individuals that have a tendency to swing the weight up.

Comments – Concentrate on lifting the dumbells with your rear delts and not your traps and lats. For variation try using a set of cables. You will have to grab the cable handles with your opposite hands, so the cables form an X in front of you. This exercise is popular with bodybuilders in the months leading up to a contest.

Muscles worked – When performed properly, bent-over laterals primarily work the rear deltoids. There is, however, secondary triceps, trap, and lat stimulation. If you're not sure what a fully developed rear deltoid looks like, take a look at a recent picture of Paul Dillett. His rear delts contain as much muscle mass as most bodybuilders whole deltoid region!

Smith machine shrugs – With a shoulder width grip, lift the bar from the support catches. Keeping your arms straight, lower the bar as far as the traps will allow. Shrug your shoulders as high as you can, trying to touch your deltoids off your ears. Pause, and then lower to the starting position.

Comments – Smith machine shrugs are great for those with lower back problems. Unlike a standard barbell, which has to be taken from the floor, the Smith machine allows you to start and finish the exercise at waist level.

Muscles worked – As with barbell and dumbell shrugs, this exercise primarily works the trapezius muscles. They also place secondary stress on the delts and forearms.

Reverse pec flyes – Sit down in the pec deck machine facing the backrest. Depending on the model, either grab the handles with the hands or place the forearms in front of the pads. Bring the arms back to a comfortable stretch, which for most people means having the elbows slightly behind the body, or the arms straight out to the sides (depending on the model.) Return to the starting position.

Comments – The advantage of this exercise over bent-over dumbells is that it puts little or no stress on the lower back. The machine also makes it a bit more difficult to swing and bounce the weight up with body momentum, something many people do on bent-over laterals.

Dorian Yates

Muscles worked – Reverse pec flyes primarily hit the rear delts, but the teres, rhomboids, and traps, also come into play.

Triceps

Triceps pushdowns – You will need to use the lat pulldown machine for this exercise. Grab the bar with a narrow grip, anywhere from two to eight inches. With your elbows tight to your side, press the bar down to a locked out position. Pause and flex the triceps at the bottom, and then return the bar to about chest high.

Comments – Take a false (thumbs above the bar) grip when performing triceps pushdowns, and resist the urge to flare the elbows out to the sides. If you have to swing to push the bar down, you probably have too much weight on the bar.

Muscles worked – Triceps pushdowns work the entire triceps region, especially the outer head.

One-arm dumbell extensions – Grasp a dumbell and extend it above your head. Keeping the upper arm stationary, lower the dumbell behind the head. Try to perform the movement in a slow rhythmic manner.

Comments – It's possible to work up to 75 plus pound dumbells, but keep in mind the elbow joint, and associated tissues (ligaments, cartilage, and tendons) were

Appendix

not designed to support huge poundages. Never bounce the dumbell at the bottom (arms in the bent position) of the exercise. Try to place the emphasis on style rather than weight.

Muscles worked – Although it works the whole triceps region, this exercise is great for the lower triceps.

Lying triceps extensions – Place an EZ-curl bar on the end of a bench. Lie down on the bench so that the bar is above your head. Now reach back and grab the bar and hoist it to arms length. Keeping your elbows by your sides, lower the bar to your forehead. Extend the bar back to arms length.

Comments – If you are wary about lowering the bar to your head, lower down behind your head and lightly touch the bench. Don't bounce the bar off the bench, but merely pause and then extend the arms. Try to keep the elbows tight against your sides.

Muscles worked – This is one of the main triceps mass builders. It stresses the whole triceps particularly the long rear head of the muscle. Lowering the bar behind your head brings the lower lats and upper chest into play. The exercise also works the intercostals, located just below the rib cage.

Upright dips – For this exercise, you use the same apparatus as when performing dips for the chest. With a few minor modifications, you can shift the strain from the chest to the triceps. For starters keep the elbows tight against the body. Flaring them to the sides will work the chest. Also, unlike dips for the chest, where you bend forward, keep your body as vertical as possible. In fact some bodybuilders lean back slightly to get that extra degree of triceps stimulation.

Comments – As with most exercises that rely on lifting your bodyweight, you will eventually reach a point where you can bang out 12 to 15 reps with ease. To increase the resistance, hold a dumbell between your legs, or attach a plate to a special dipping chain. Before you know it you will be dipping with 50 to 100 pounds!

With regards to safety, be careful at the bottom of the movement. Although dips are an excellent triceps exercise, they also place much stress on the front delts, particularly the pec-delt tie-in. Don't bounce at the bottom. Perform the exercise in a slow and controlled manner (you might want to write out the phrase "in a slow and controlled manner," in black letters and post it to your bedroom wall. It's perhaps the most important piece of advice we can give, and this is why it's emphasized so much.)

Muscles worked – Performed in an upright manner, dips place most of the strain on the long rear head of the triceps. Because of the weight used (minimum of your bodyweight) they also work the other two heads quite nicely. And even though you may attempt to eliminate other muscles form the exercise, the front delts and chest will take some of the strain. Once again this is fine at the beginning level where the goal is to add overall muscle mass.

Triceps kickbacks – With your body braced on a bench, bend over and set your upper arm parallel with the floor. Grab a dumbell and extend the lower arm back until it's in the locked position (i.e. your whole arm is now parallel with the floor.) Pause and squeeze at the top, and then lower back to the starting position.

Comments – Resist the urge to swing the dumbell up using body momentum. True, you can use more weight, but it won't give the same triceps development. Keep the upper arm locked against the side of the body. As with bent-over laterals, if you have trouble keeping stationary, or have a weak lower back, place your free hand on a bench or other such support.

Muscles worked – Triceps kickbacks are great for giving the triceps that horseshoe-look. They are especially useful for developing the long rear head of the triceps. They are a favorite exercise during the precontest months.

Reverse pushdowns – This exercise is performed in the same manner as regular pushdowns. The main difference is that you grab the bar with your palms facing up. Keep your elbows locked against the side and extend (push) the bar downward. Flex the triceps at the bottom, and then return to the starting position.

Comments – You won't be able to use as much weight in this version of pushdowns, so don't become alarmed if you have to drop the weight 20 to 30 pounds. This exercise is great for finishing the triceps off after a basic movement like lying triceps extensions or dips. Concentrate more on the feel rather than the weight used.

Muscles worked – This is another great movement for the long rear head of the triceps. A couple of sets and you will feel your triceps burning from elbow to armpit!

One-arm cable pushdowns – With your body in the standing position, grab one of the upper cable handles. Push the handle down, lock out the arm at the bottom, and then return to the starting position.

Comments – You can do this exercise either palms up or palms down. You might want to reach across with your free hand and grab your shoulder on the same side that is being exercised. Besides the bracing effect, you have your free hand in a position to spot yourself on the last couple of reps. As with the previously described reverse pushdowns, go more for the burn rather than huge poundages.

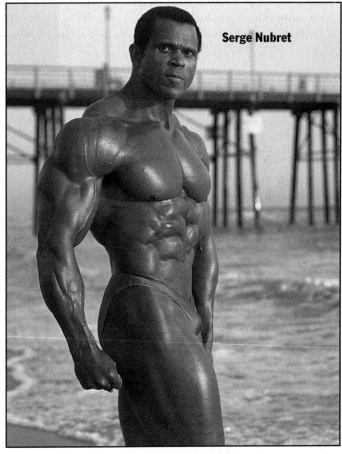

Serge Nubret

Muscles worked – This is another great finishing exercise for the triceps. A palms up grip will place most of the strain on the rear triceps, whereas a palms down grip will hit more of the side head.

Narrow presses – Lie down on a flat bench with an Olympic bar or EZ-curl bar placed on the supports above you. Grab the bar with a narrow (shoulder width or less) grip and lower it down to mid chest. Push upward as if doing a regular bench press.

Comments – You will need to experiment with different grip widths to find the one that maximizes triceps involvement and minimizes wrist stress. As with flat bench presses, don't bounce the bar off the chest or arch the lower back.

Muscles worked – Narrow presses primarily work the triceps, but the front delts and pecs also come into play.

Appendix

Biceps

Standing barbell curls – Perhaps the most used (and abused!) exercise performed by bodybuilders. You can use the standard Olympic bar, a smaller straight bar, or an EZ-curl bar. Grab the bar slightly wider than shoulder width and curl it up until the biceps are fully flexed. Try to keep your elbows close to your side, and don't swing the weight up with your lower back. Lower the weight back to the starting position in good style. Don't simply let the thing drop! Not only are you losing half the movement, but also you run the risk of tearing your biceps tendon (you can ask Dorian Yates, Lou Ferrigno, or Tom Platz, what this feels like).

Comments – Barbell curls are considered the ultimate in biceps exercises. Many bodybuilders forget that the negative (lowering) part of the movement is just as important as the positive (hoisting) section. Try to lower the bar with about the same speed as you curl it up.

Keep your back straight and no swinging. If you want to cheat, save it for the last couple of reps. For example perform 8 to 10 reps in good style and then cheat one or two more. Don't abuse a good thing, however. One or two cheat reps are fine, but cheating from the start is counterproductive. At your level of development, you'll get all the stimulation you want from strict reps.

If you have weak wrists or forearms, you might want to give the EZ-curl bar a try. The bar's bent shape allows you to rotate the forearms slightly, thus reducing the tension on the wrists and forearms. We should add that most bodybuilders use a straight bar, but play it by ear. Give both types a try and pick the one that is the most comfortable, and produces the greatest biceps stimulation.

Muscles worked – The barbell biceps curl works the entire biceps muscle. Also, because you have to forcibly grip the bar, the exercise will give you a great set of forearms. Finally, the front delts and lower back come into play for stabilizing purposes.

Standing dumbell curls – Instead of using a barbell, grab two dumbells. Although it's possible to simultaneously raise both dumbells, most bodybuilders do what are called alternate dumbell curls. As the name implies, you curl the dumbells one at a time. Start the dumbells by your sides with the ends pointing to the front and back (i.e. the dumbells are parallel to one another). As you curl, rotate your palms from the facing in position to a facing up position. This is called supination. Many bodybuilders are not aware that the biceps has two main functions. Besides the better known curling movement, the biceps also rotate the forearms. You can see this if you hold your arm by your side and rotate the hand back and forth. Notice the biceps flexing as the hand approaches the palm up position. By using dumbells, you can take advantage of this physiological trait. Now we should add that you would have to use a really heavy dumbell (more than you could curl) to get the full effect of supination. Still every bit helps, so give it a try.

Comments – Once again, limit any swinging to the last one or two reps. And even then it's probably not necessary at this stage of your development. Try to put total concentration into each and every rep.

Besides the psychological aspect of curling one dumbell at at time, there may be a physiological basis. Neurologists suggest that when two arms are used simultaneously, the brain has to split the nerve impulses. Whereas by alternating the dumbells, you get full nerve transmission to each biceps. How much is fact and how much is theory, is open to debate. And although you have no control over nerve impulses, you do have control over exercise performance. So choose the version that feels most productive. As a final comment, Arnold favored the alternating version. Need we say more?

Muscles worked – Dumbell curls are great for working the belly of the biceps. They also reduce the stress on the wrists and forearms. In fact many bodybuilders suggest starting your biceps workout (this only applies to intermediate and advanced bodybuilders who are performing more than one exercise for their muscles) with dumbells so as not to overstress the weaker areas.

Preacher curls – Also called Scott curls, this exercise is great for working the lower biceps region. Start by sitting on the stool or bench connected to the preacher board. Adjust yourself so that the padded board fits snugly under your armpits. Take the barbell (straight or EZ) from the supports and curl it until the biceps are fully flexed. Lower to the starting position and repeat.

Comments – Although biceps length is genetic, you can create the illusion of length by building the lower regions. Some Scott benches are positioned fairly high and require you to stand up when doing the movement. If your gym has both, give both a try and pick the one that suits you.

Of all the biceps exercises, this one is the most dangerous if not performed in good style. Under no circumstances should you drop the barbell to the bottom position. You can easily rip the biceps tendon from where it inserts on the forearm bone. The only option open to you then is surgery and many months of inactivity. With a little attention paid to good style you can avoid the aggravation.

Muscles worked – Although they work the whole biceps muscle, Scott curls are primarily a lower biceps exercise. Because you are braced by the padded board, it's virtually impossible to cheat and bring your lower back into the movement. Finally, you will notice a great deal of forearm stimulation. This is fine, as you will need a strong grip for many of your other exercises.

Incline curls – You will need an incline bench to perform this exercise. Unlike incline presses for your chest, use a bench with an angle of at least 45 degrees. Anything less will place too much strain on your front delts. Lie back on the bench and grab two dumbells. Curl the dumbells up until the biceps are fully flexed. All the tips suggested for standing dumbell curls apply here as well (rotate the hands from a facing in, to a facing up position, don't swing the weight up, etc.)

Comments – Once again you have the option of curling both dumbells simultaneously, or alternately. When you lower the dumbells, be careful not to hit the side of the incline bench. In fact, this is another reason for starting the dumbells in a forward pointed position. If they are in the standard end to end position, they have less clearance with the bench.

The advantage of using the incline bench is that it limits the amount of cheating you can do. Let's face it, you can't swing very much if you have your back braced against a rigid board.

Muscles worked – Incline curls work the whole biceps region. Many bodybuilders find that they are great for bringing out the biceps peak. Of course this is more genetic than anything else. The exercise does provide some forearm stimulation, but not to the extent as the various barbell curls.

Concentration curls – Sit down on the end of a bench and grab a dumbell. With your elbow resting on your inner thigh, lower the dumbell down, and then curl it back up. Perform one set, and then switch arms.

Appendix

Comments – Most bodybuilders perform concentration curls in the seated position. A few (including Arnold Schwarzenegger) like to do the movement in the standing, bent-over position. Instead of bracing the elbow against the thigh, it's held down and away from the body. Keep the shoulder on the exercising side, lower than the free side. Resist the urge to swing and use only biceps power. As with all dumbell curls, you may want to supinate the hands when performing the exercise.

Muscles worked – Most bodybuilders consider concentration curls more of a shaping and peaking exercise than a mass builder. Keep in mind that peakness and shape are primarily due to genetics. Unless you have the genetics, you will never develop biceps peaks like Robby Robinson. Still, you'll never know unless you try, and this is where concentration curls come in. The exercise cannot change your genetics, but it can maximize whatever potential you might have.

One-arm preacher curls – Instead of using a barbell, try preacher curls with a single dumbell. Remember to lower slowly and not bounce the weight at the bottom.

Comments – By using a dumbell you can adjust your upper body to take some of the stress off the biceps tendon. Many bodybuilders find preachers hard on the forearms and elbows. Using a dumbell allows you more flexibility than the rigidity of a barbell. A barbell puts the force at 90 degrees to the upper body. A dumbell allows you to vary this angle, thus placing less stress on the forearms and elbows.

Muscles worked – Dumbell preacher curls place most of the stress on the lower biceps. As discussed above, they treat your forearms and elbows with more kindness than the barbell version!

Standing cable curls – For variety try standing biceps curls with a set of cables. Whether you work one arm or both at the same time, is up to you. If doing them one arm at a time, grab the machine with your free hand for support. It's extremely difficult to stay stationary when exercising one side of the body.

Ronnie Coleman

Comments – As with most cable exercises, go for the feel rather than the amount of weight. Cable curls are an excellent way to finish off the biceps after a basic movement such as standing barbell curls. Of course you can take the opposite approach and use them as a warm up exercise. Many bodybuilders (including Franco Columbu), suggest starting your biceps workout with cables or dumbells. This warms up the area and doesn't put the same stress on the elbows and forearms that barbell curls do.

Muscles worked – Standing cable curls are another so-called peaking and shaping exercise. They work the whole biceps region, and if performed one arm at a time, allow you to really concentrate. For a great pump, try finishing your biceps workout with a couple of high rep (15 to 20) sets of cable curls.

Narrow-reverse chins – Grab an overhead chinning bar with a shoulder width, reverse grip. Pull your body up until the bar is touching your mid-chest. Lower back down until your arms are just short of a lockout.

Comments – Despite being a variation of the regular chinup, one of the best back exercises, the narrow reverse grip puts much of the stress on the biceps. As with regular chins, avoid swinging the body when performing the reps. You may need to experiment with different width grips to maximize biceps tension.

Muscles worked – Narrow chins primarily work the biceps and lats, but the forearms, teres, and rhomboids also come into play.

Calves

Standing calf raises – You will need access to the appropriate machine to do this exercise. Rest your toes on the attached block of wood, and rest the pads on your shoulders. From here the exercise is straightforward. With your legs locked, rise up and down on your toes. Stretch all the way down and flex up on your toes as far as possible. Go for that intense burn!

Comments – Even though this is primarily a stretching exercise, don't be afraid to load the machine with hundreds of pounds of weight. Keep your back and legs straight. The only movement is at the ankle joint. Although calf injuries are extremely rare (the calf muscle is composed of extremely dense muscle fiber, which makes tearing very difficult), you still shouldn't bounce at the bottom of the movement, as you might strain the Achilles tendon.

Muscles worked – Standing calf raises work the entire calf muscle, with the primary focus on the upper (gastrocnemius) calf region.

Calf flexes on leg press machine – This is another example of using a machine for an exercise it was not designed for. Instead of pressing the weight with your thighs, you flex the weight platform using only your feet. As with the standing version, go for the maximum amount of stretch at the top and bottom.

Comments – The advantage of this exercise is that you don't have the entire weight pushing down on your spine. The disadvantage is that it will take a bit of practice to get the foot positioning correct. Still, the exercise is an adequate substitute if you don't have access to a standing calf machine.

Muscles worked – Most of the stress is placed on the lower calf, but the upper calves are also worked. If you really want to get that extra burn in the lower calf, use less weight and bend your legs slightly. This will shift all the stress to the lower calf. After one set of these your calves will be burning like crazy!

Donkey calf raises – With your toes resting on a block of wood (at least four inches thick is recommended) bend over at the waist and have a willing training partner sit on your lower back. Flex up and down on your toes, going for the maximum stretch. If you find one rider too light, try to fit a second on your back.

Appendix

Comments – The bashful and shy might want to avoid this exercise! Also, many upper class gyms (health spas) advise you not to do them. You see, the general public is intimidated by people riding on top of one another, especially if they are going up and down!

Having said that, donkey calf raises are considered by many to be the best calf exercise. Such bodybuilders as Arnold, Larry Scott, Franco Columbu, and Frank Zane, made extensive use of donkey raises. The exercise is seen less frequently in gyms today. No doubt the presence of fancy new equipment and increased numbers of general fitness trainers has contributed to their decline. Still, if you check out Gold's or World gyms in California, you will see numerous bodybuilders burning their calves with donkey raises. And one look at their lower legs gives testament to the exercise's effectiveness.

Muscles worked – Donkey calf raises work the whole calf region. If you keep the legs completely locked, most of the work is done by the upper calf. Bend the legs slightly and the lower calves take most of the strain. For variety you might want to include both in your training. Remember, when doing the bent leg variety, you will need to use less weight, as the lower calf cannot handle the same weight as the upper calf.

Seated calf raises – You will need a special machine to do this exercise. Sit down on the machine's chair and place the padded knee rests on your legs. With your toes on the block of wood, stretch up and down as far as you can.

Comments – Because it works the lower calf, you will need to use less weight. Go for at least 20 reps and try to feel every one of them. No bouncing the weight on your legs. Even though the supports are padded, improper style can injure your knees.

Muscles worked – Since the legs are bent, most of the stress is placed on the lower calf (soleus), but there is some secondary, upper calf involvement.

Contributing Photographers

Josef Adlt, Jim Amentler, Arax, Alex Ardenti, John Balik, Doris Barrilleaux, Garry Bartlett, Vince Basile, Caruso, Eric Chapman, Paula Crane, Ralph DeHaan, Denie, Bill Dobbins, Richard Finnegan, Irvin Gelb, George Greenwood, Robert Kennedy, Chris Lund, Jason Mathas, Mitsuru Okabe, David Paul, Rick Schaff, Joe Valdez, Russ Warner, Art Zeller

Arnold Schwarzenegger